MINERVA'S OWL

MINERVA'S OWL

THE TRADITION OF WESTERN POLITICAL THOUGHT

Jeffrey Abramson

HARVARD UNIVERSITY PRESS

Cambridge, Massachusetts

London, England

First Harvard University Press paperback edition, 2010

Library of Congress Cataloging-in-Publication Data

Abramson, Jeffrey B.
    Minerva's owl : the traditional of western political thought / Jeffrey Abramson.
        p.   cm.
    Includes bibliographical references and index.
    ISBN 978-0-674-03265-1 (cloth : alk. paper)
    ISBN 978-0-674-05702-9 (pbk.)
    1. Political science—History.   I. Title.
    JA81.A32 2009
    320.01—dc22   2008043390

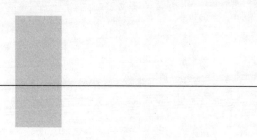

For Jackie

CONTENTS

MINERVA'S OWL

THE CANON OF POLITICAL THOUGHT

This book invites readers to join a conversation about politics, a very old conversation, going on for nearly 2,500 years now. It is not the only or the oldest conversation about politics, but it is a distinctly continuous and influential one.

The conversation begins over a particular historical event, the trial and execution of Socrates in 399 BC on charges of corrupting the young. Socrates' execution caused one such corrupted youth, his pupil Plato, to detach himself sufficiently from the politics of the moment to stand outside events and judge them according to an ideal of justice that transcended the fiats of power. Without this moment of critical detachment, the conversation could not have begun. But it is equally the case that the conversation—if it was to be a *political* conversation—required engagement as well as detachment, a sense of allegiance or loyalty or attachment to a way of life worth criticizing.

Over time the conversation has left behind a set of canonical texts, which provide a common store of learning and reference. The texts constitute a canon, in the sense that later works offer commentaries on earlier ones. No one starts anew. A cumulative learning is passed on, but as it passes, it is changed, reinterpreted, and transformed without ever being overthrown or abandoned. Socrates taught Plato, who paid his teacher the compliment of writing almost always in the name of his mentor. So thoroughly did Plato inhabit the mind of his teacher that we cannot say for certain where the historical Socrates differs from the Socrates that Plato created. Aristotle in turn came to Athens to study at Plato's school. He paid his teacher the different compliment of arguing with him. Aristotle tutored the young Alexander, but this did not stop the student from going on to conquer the Greek world.

Rome started as a republic but ended as an empire; along the way its greatest thinkers, from the slave Epictetus through the senator Cicero up to the emperor Marcus Aurelius, sought to revamp Greek ideas on justice to fit the morality of imperial ambition. Early Christians, such as Saint Augustine growing up in the provinces conquered by Rome, culled from Plato a doctrine henceforth known as Neo-Platonism that became Christianity's retort to the "earthly" justice of Rome, pallid in comparison to the heavenly justice of God's city.

Islamic scholars of the ninth and tenth centuries recovered the lost works of the canon, translating the Greek classics into Arabic and beginning the tradition of commentaries on the works of Plato and Aristotle. It was through these translations that classical political philosophy became known to medieval Jewish scholars living under Islamic rule. The canon next worked its way back to Christian Europe by way of these Hebrew and Arabic translations. In different but parallel ways, scholars working within their own religious communities grappled with the implications of Greek rationalism for the truths of divine revelation.

In secular form the canon was revived with new purpose by Machiavelli during the Italian Renaissance, as he returned to the classics and the history of Rome in search of fresh ideas for restoring to Italy the lost glory that was the Roman republic. Machiavelli's theory of republicanism became a bridge connecting the ancients and the moderns. In the tumultuous decades from the English Civil War to the Glorious Revolution, philosophers such as Hobbes and Locke used the canon to fashion new ideas about the origins and legitimacy of government. In time these ideas became the intellectual and political basis of liberalism and constitutional government; the American Declaration of Independence literally lifted its most soaring phrase about the right to revolution from the pages of Locke.

Liberalism brought in its wake both a conservative and a radical response. The radical critique began in France, where Rousseau seized on the ideas of Hobbes and Locke to push liberalism in a far more egalitarian direction—a direction that, for a time, the French Revolution followed before collapsing into terror. The fate of the Revolution in turn provoked the classic conservative response given by Edmund Burke, a critique that in some ways returns to Aristotle for core arguments about the limits of political change and about the distinctive importance of custom, tradition, and the familiar to political life.

Kant found in Rousseau's notion of the general will a basis for his own, more systematic arguments about human freedom and equality. But both intellectually and politically, liberal doctrines took a different course in Germany, as Hegel commented on Kant, and Marx commented on Hegel. In ways that proved lasting, Marx purposely sought to put a stop to the conversation I am describing, rejecting the idea that there ever is anything distinctly "political" to talk about at all, and seeking to translate political concepts into underlying material realities driving the "production" of ideas. The Marxist rejection of political theory as "ideological" gave rise to modern sociology, and it is only in the last generation or so, with the restorative work on justice by John Rawls, that political theory once again stands at the center of a liberal arts education.

This book is based on introductory lectures on political theory that I have been giving over the past twenty-five years. Until now I have never sought to write those lectures down. I do so here, persuaded that they may be of use to the continuing student in all of us. The canon of political thought presents us, as one of my teachers used to say, with political arguments as enduring and eternal as such arguments possibly can be. For someone reading the texts for the first time, they are an awakening to why politics matter, just how much is at stake. But even for the politically active, they remain a place to revisit for inspiration and instruction. The arguments, after all, do not go away with political experience; they are more likely to come home to roost.

My hope is that this book will help make the great classics of political theory accessible to the general reader, as they ought to be. Political theory is not a specialty; it confronts us with the actual dilemmas of political life. To the end of engaging the reader in the political arguments going on, I adopt an informal, almost conversational tone. In particular, I pause frequently and fondly to reflect on my own teachers and students, the better to capture the sense that we are engaged in a dialogue not unlike that which takes place in the classroom.

I do not cover the entire history of political thought in this book. The selection I make—a selection more recognizable than idiosyncratic—is meant to isolate and illumine the core contrast between ancient Greek and modern political theory. It comes as a deeply surprising and jarring realization that some of the most brilliant minds of antiquity did not share our basic convictions about human nature, equality, and democracy. Aristotle confronts us with notions of a natural aristocracy in the human condition; Plato argues that the state should censor art. Together they disdain the private and economic life and would make the domain of politics all-encompassing rather than limited, as we today are wont to do.

By laying out the alternative views housed in Greek political theory, I hope to hold our own to account. Our most settled political convictions are often the most shrouded. The temptation at first is to dismiss the ancients as relics and to approach the history of political thought as a comforting tale of progress that validates contemporary wisdom. But this will not do. The controversy between ancient and modern political ideals is a live one—to repeat, as close to an eternal and unavoidable debate as politics present. Only by engaging that controversy can we gain the ground from which to see into the philosophical foundations of contemporary politics, both the solid rock and the shifting sand. Only by risking our politics by questioning them in the light of alternatives can we possibly educate ourselves in ways that either deepen or undo our prior commitments.

What happens to my students' politics, in the partisan sense of the term, is none of my concern. I take the same attitude toward readers of this book. But I do hold all of us responsible for defending our views, whatever they are, in a consistent and coherent fashion. We cannot extol freedom of personal choice on some issues (say, abortion) and reject it on others (pornography, for instance) without explaining the difference. If we hold that persons are entitled to equal political rights but not equality of income, health care, or education, then we need a theory of equality that explains where to draw the line.

To this extent our politics are bound to change once we take political theory seriously. Out on the street, consistency is not always a political virtue: politicians broker compromises and strike deals in ways that answer to the slogan "Politics makes strange bedfellows." But if we are to know when and when not to compromise, we must first know what is at stake.

No one writing about Shakespeare or biology prefaces getting down to work by defending the importance of the topic; I treat the case for studying political philosophy as similarly without need of labored justification. The political insights one gleans by reading Plato or Hobbes or Rousseau make up an important part of any liberal education—any education that seeks to call out the human and progressive in us, and by doing so, to keep alive the hope for a better world.

Over the years I have found that my students come to political theory with a particular understanding of what politics is all about. They tend to see politics as about friends and enemies, and the political knowledge they seek consists of practical strategies for ensuring victories for friends and defeats for enemies. While this attitude is clearest in post–September

11 apocalyptic views of foreign policy, it characterizes the passions raised by domestic politics as well.

I do not think this beginning understanding of politics is wrong so much as it is limited. It assumes that the difference between friends and enemies is always obvious and that justice is always or mostly on one's own side. But what if fighting for our own is not the only or best political emotion? What if as citizens we have an obligation to criticize as well as serve our country? What if what the people want is not just? Political theory makes such questions imperative. In doing so, it does not prove immediately relevant in the way we first expect. In fact, it asks us to take a detour into issues that make any immediate course of action difficult. But the promise of that detour is that those who take it come back to politics as more fully realized human beings, committed to holding the powerful to account.

Realism and Idealism in the Young

Over the years that I have been introducing young persons to the study of politics, the real thing continues to excite and repulse them—excite them because it is the privilege of the young to believe in change, to feel the good blowing in the wind, to pin messianic hopes on this new candidate or that long-awaited movement. Their excitement is not naïve but informed about the perils of politics. It is precisely the sense that they are signing up for a cause that appeals to the young.

Some literally have signed up. Over the years I have watched them march off to fight or protest wars, join the Peace Corps, do HIV prevention in Africa, missionary work in Asia, knock on doors during the New Hampshire primary, picket or protect abortion clinics. But even those who do not literally march feel the desire to participate in politics. They are not prepared to accept the status quo as the best we can do, but prefer gambling on politics even when they know the risks of defeat are high.

But as is true of the passions of the young generally, their political hearts are easily broken. It is not defeat itself that they cannot take; it is the sense of betrayal, of finding hypocrisy where they expected to find idealism. They had not expected that their own generation would not simply witness but somehow manage to learn to live with—just as their elders had—war, tyranny, genocide, famine, terrorism, and plain old corruption. The tribalism that was supposed to have been long since removed to the dustbin of history ends up being the future, not the past, of politics.

And so cynicism replaces idealism, marching gives way to retreat, realism picks up where romance ends. As I watch these changes going on year after year, I find it harder to convince young people that there is any purpose in studying politics, especially studying it through old and canonical works that—even conceding their greatness as philosophy—certainly have not carried the day. I find my students sorting out into two categories.

For some, perhaps the majority, politics is too important to study; these are the realists who pride themselves on knowing the difference between what works in practice and what triumphs only in the pages of books. For them the only school of politics is the street, and the sooner they cease reading about it and start trying their hand, the better. They expect to have to break a few eggs to make politics work, and they resent philosophical recipes that pretend otherwise.

But there are always some who take the opposite view and conclude that study is too important to waste on politics. They know what they've learned in biology or chemistry or even social psychology, but what do they actually learn by studying something as amorphous as politics? Isn't the whole point of calling something "political" to accept that there is nothing systematic to study, that it is all relative and subjective? Even more than their realist counterparts, these otherwise studious souls are committed cynics when it comes to the very idea of political theory. They challenge me to explain how philosophy and politics can possibly go together when all around them they see the rising tide of political irrationality. Given the evident force of unreason in politics, they concede that there might be something to studying military strategy or even the tactics for running campaigns and winning elections. But they cannot fathom how philosophy might contribute to understanding a subject matter that, by its very nature, seems resistant to rational inquiry.

This is the challenge but also the privilege of introducing persons to political theory: to confront the cynicism that at times seems the only honest response to the wide chasm separating political reality from ideals of justice. The study of political theory does not deny the fault line separating political ideals from political practice; in fact it insists on it as the start of the conversation about how to hold the powerful to account. What I hope will whet my readers' curiosity and set fire to your imagination is that everyone, even the most self-interested of political operatives, has *some* political philosophy, some vision of the purposes for which power is sought and wielded.

Imagine, for a moment, what politics would be like were politicians to woo us in the naked language of self-interest, without any appeal to our moral longings for freedom, for equality, for peace, for the good of the next generation, for the state of the environment, for the well-being of the poor and the health of the sick. Such an unadorned politics, were it possible, would be quite different from our own; appeals to our moral nature are the common stuff of politics. Of course, it may be that those who make these appeals do so only for their own selfish or partisan gain—so my young cynics are quick to remind me. But the fact remains that the language of political theory—this conversation I have been describing about competing visions of the good life and the ends of society—*is* the ordinary language in which real politics is conducted.

Political philosophers do not invent the terms in which politicians make their case; they simply take notice that appeals to our better nature are among the most powerful of political forces. Justice moves us; causes arouse us; beliefs and values spark passions. The work of political philosophy is thus not so far removed from the actual course of politics after all. But whereas the rush of events rarely gives citizens time to consider what their values are, and how to practice ideals consistently, political theory carves out a place for us to ask the sorts of questions justice demands. To inhabit that space is already to take a political stance, with who knows what consequences.

Liberals and Conservatives

Throughout the history of political thought, strong disagreement has persisted between two competing political positions in particular. According to one school of thought, dating back to the Greeks, political principles are arrived at by asking the question, "How can the power of the state best be used to deliver the good and virtuous life to the people?" Philosophers of this school disagree on what the ultimate good is. Some identify it with happiness or the general welfare, others with human perfection, still others with wisdom, spiritual salvation, or moral purity. But they agree that political values should be considered but means to higher ends and goals, and that we judge political arrangements by their contribution to bringing us closer to the ultimate moral ends of the good life. In this way of thinking, there can be no "rights" belonging to individuals that trump the power of politics to make people virtuous. For what is right in politics is explicable only when we directly ask and answer the question of what is good for human beings, what fulfills or realizes or perfects our nature. Unless we first know what fulfills our nature as fully functioning human beings, we cannot possibly have a standard or ideal against which to judge political choices.

In the opposing school of thought, commonly given the name of liberalism, political practice involves us in a paradox: on moral grounds of justice and fairness, the state must refrain from enforcing morality on the people. Instead, justice requires politics to bracket or put aside substantive moral issues, such as how people should conduct themselves religiously, sexually, or artistically. The fact of the matter is that individuals give different answers to the question of what is good for them, answers that reflect first-order, ultimate commitments tied to differences in religion, tradition, family, and upbringing. It is not the mission of politics to resolve these strong moral disagreements by siding with the answers of some over others. This would be to treat persons unequally and deprive individuals of their equal capacity to "choose their own good in their own way." Thus a just state is a neutral state, devising procedures whose moral value derives precisely from the framework they provide for permitting persons to agree to disagree about their ultimate moral ideals.

Of course even those who subscribe to the liberal school of thought quarrel over how neutral the state must be, and whether it is always right for a just state to refrain from taking moral sides on a particular issue. No one quibbles, for instance, that the law can prohibit slavery, even if the result of an apparently voluntary contract, on grounds that to be a slave is inconsistent with human dignity. Nor does anyone seriously disagree that a democratic state can mandate compulsory education to a minimum age, given the importance of an informed citizenry to making democracy possible. But do tolerant societies have to tolerate the preaching of intolerant ideas, even if those preaching them would abolish tolerance if they had their way? May a state outlaw the Muslim custom of requiring women to veil themselves in public, on grounds that such a custom is not good for women? These are issues on which even liberals disagree.

Still, it is possible to outline a basic difference between liberal and conservative thought in contemporary politics. For conservatives, the state's paramount mission is to deliver the moral virtues to the people. What is good for people is not necessarily that they be left free to make choices for themselves; what is good is that the state use its resources to make those choices virtuous. Thus, to take one contemporary example, some conservatives argue that the state should prohibit same-sex marriage in order to enforce a moral conception of the sacred purposes of marriage. By contrast, liberals may hold personal moral views that same-sex marriage is wrong. But when it comes to politics, they strive to set aside those personal views and see the value of politics as permitting persons who disagree on the issue of same-sex marriage nonetheless to share the same political system on equal and fair terms. This argues for tolerating the moral choices of others even when one disagrees with them.

This debate between liberals and conservatives will be familiar to the readers of this book. It is but the latest iteration of a long-running controversy in the history of political thought that shows no signs of abating. Each school of thought illumines deficiencies in the other, and it seems unlikely that the debate could or should ever finally be won by one or the other side.

The Possibility of Democracy

There is one political value that I do endorse and that is democracy. Churchill's famous quip that democracy would be the worst form of government were it not for all the others is clever but not much of a brief for democracy's own virtues. What makes for a persuasive and positive defense of democracy? Should we emphasize the populist streak in democracy, lauding the "rule of the people" as enlightened and tolerant? Or should we emphasize the constitutional streak, suggested by the alternative notion that democracies are characterized by the rule of law and not by the rule of people? (This view of democracy was actually carved in Latin into the façade of the law school I attended, which translated as "Not under the rule of people but under the rule of law.") Should we define democracies as governments in which majorities rule or as governments in which minorities have rights against the majority?

It turns out that defending the possibility of democracy is no easy task. The Greek critique of democracy as likely to substitute public opinion for justice is a serious one. I hear echoes of it every year when I ask my students to defend the claim that democracy is the best form of government. They prove quite elegant in expressing distrust of the power of the people, and especially of majorities. Those who come from countries without constitutional protections are often able to give moving personal testimony to the impossibility of democracy when "the" people do not exist but are divided among warring tribes. But I rarely find persons who can defend popular sovereignty with the same verve they muster on behalf of individual rights against the people.

We have become used to defending democracy as if it were a received truth, a dogma. But when we do not examine our democratic commitments, we are easily shaken by the strong assault on self-government made by figures as revered as Plato and Aristotle.

It would be nice and comforting if the purpose of reading political theory were simply to validate our core political convictions. But this is not the case. Political theory is inherently subversive rather than satisfying. Each of the great philosophers I am about to discuss knew that politics requires hard choices of us. Thinking with their help does not make those choices any easier. But it does make them unavoidable. Perhaps not today or tomorrow. Finally, however, we study at our peril, knowing that politics may someday require us to act even before our studies are concluded.

The Socratic Invitation

Permit me a personal ending to this introduction. Many years have passed since I first read Plato's *Republic* as a college student in search of inspiration. I understood little of it, but I fully felt—I still feel—the force of Socrates' promise that learning can change who we are. To say "it was all Greek to me" back then is to say that the *Republic* was marvelously mysterious, suggestive of a hidden realm of higher pleasures, intellectual power, and utopian politics. From the moment I met Socrates, I yearned for initiation into the promised better life where the truth of justice replaced the lies of power. I loved the prospect that studying would set me free, that the coming life of the mind would be radical and revolutionary, dramatic and dangerous, transforming and transcending. This was how it felt, and it felt good.

I can still smell the pleasant aroma of cherry pipe tobacco that my professor was free in those days to exhale over us; for years afterwards that scent clung to the pages, and just smelling them wafted me back to him and his love of Socrates. The longer my professor dwelled on a passage, the more deeply the smell attached to the words, so for the longest time I could tell what he thought were the most important parts of the *Republic* just by putting nose to book. And so through a combination of the senses I became addicted to the *Republic*. I think I can say this accurately, having read the *Republic* every year of the several decades I have been teaching Plato on my own.

My professor was already old when I arrived at college, neither famous nor destined to be. Years later, when I went to visit him and talked about how much his course had meant to me, he deflected the praise by saying, "It was Socrates—Socrates has a way of calling out the best in all of us." That passion came through in his course, and I left enticed, enthralled, enchanted with the promise that there was knowledge out there that seeped inside your soul, that possessed you rather than your possessing it.

All in all, when I arrived at college the *Republic* appealed to my desire to be high-minded and morally grave. John F. Kennedy's assassination two years before still registered in my gut; the television news was full of images of fire hoses flattening civil rights marchers against brick walls; the reality of a war in Vietnam was just forcing itself into my life. With politics such as this, little wonder then that a shock of recognition went through me as I read Socrates' allegory of the cave. This was exactly how I felt, as if I were living underground, a prisoner of ignorance so total I had not even realized that I had been living in the dark.

Speaking these thoughts lo these many years later, I am chagrined to remember just how quickly I fell under the Socratic spell. The problem was not with the enchantment but with the desperation of it, as if there really were ivory towers ready to give sanctuary to refugees from the cave. I do not wish for a moment that others should feel the same way about themselves. Indeed, we all do well to wonder whether it is a good thing at all to read and reread the same book so many times. I have read the *Republic* when there was still a hot Vietnam War, a cold war, a Soviet Union, and a Berlin Wall; when Zimbabwe was still Rhodesia, Nelson Mandela was rotting in jail, the West Bank belonged to Jordan, and Tito ruled a united Yugoslavia; before there was a man on the moon, quarks, AIDS, personal computers, or the Internet.

One wants to participate in his or her own times, not sit them out on the sidelines with a long-dead Greek white guy. There is a danger that devotion to reading the classic texts can become a retreat into the proverbial ivory tower, a distraction from entering into the flux of events unfolding in a particular time and place. Still, I open this book with Socrates as a thinker with the uncanny ability to awaken our love and fear of politics. Socrates' genius as a teacher was to approach the young on their own terms, accepting the passions and curiosities of youth for what they are—the aliveness to experiencing the world for the first time that alone makes education and change possible. If we understand Socrates, he will understand us in turn and, I still believe, call out the best in all of us.

The privilege of introducing readers to political thought carries with it a heavy responsibility. I begin with a few disclaimers. First, however eager we are to get on with practicing our politics, the study of political theory will impose many a pause and detour on us. Politics at one level *is* about practicing the possible; at another it is about extending the bounds of the possible. The great and radical and subversive lesson of the *Republic* is that the bounds of political realism are far broader than those defending their advantages under the status quo will ever let on, that reconsidering one's politics requires reconsideration of so many subjects not thought "political"—music and art, for instance—and their effects on the young: myths and storytelling; marriage and child rearing; family life and sexual relations; the nature of human desire; the force of reason; the role of anger and honor; the truth about the gods; the fear of death; the study of mathematics and philosophy. Everything is up for grabs; nothing is to be accepted merely because it has always been that way or because it would disappoint family and friends if one were to wander. Socrates takes his students, those most eager for a political career, on a long intellectual detour whose outcome is uncertain. He characteristically warns that detours have consequences, that it is one thing to claim that we seek political power to serve just causes, but it is another to pause and examine what justice is—a pause that may dissuade us from ever actively pursuing a political career in the end.

Such a lifelong detour was the fate of Socrates' greatest student, Plato. So lasting was Plato's fondness for his teacher that, with rare exceptions, he always wrote in the name of "Socrates." I will have occasion to suggest that Plato may have disagreed with the historical Socrates on key political issues. Still, he never strayed from the lesson he had learned firsthand while attending the trial where his teacher was condemned to death for "corrupting" young students. As one of those young students, Plato recalls (in a surviving letter) that he had fully expected to launch his political career after completing his studies. But matters were unsettled in Athens, as bitter rivalries between oligarchic and democratic factions led to frequent and bloody rebellions. Plato's attitude was that one party was the equal of the other in injustice, and he tells of Socrates' fate—and his own:

Once upon a time in my youth I cherished . . . the hope of entering upon a political career. . . . It fell out, moreover, that political events took the following course. . . . [A] revolution occurred
. . . and thirty came into power. . . . Some of these happened to be
relatives and acquaintances of mine, who accordingly invited me
forthwith to join them. . . . No wonder that, young as I was, I cherished the belief that they would lead the city from an unjust life . . .
to habits of justice, . . . so that I was intensely interested to see
what would come of it.[1]

Plato saw "in a short time that these men made the former government
look in comparison like an age of gold." He minces no words of criticism
in recounting how the oligarchy of the Thirty sent "Socrates . . . [,] who
I should hardly be ashamed to say was the most just man of his time,"
to fetch an innocent person for execution. Socrates "refused and risked
any consequences rather than become their partner in wicked deeds."
Observing "all this . . . [,] I withdrew in disgust from the abuses of those
days."[2]

When the tyranny of the Thirty was overthrown, a democracy came
to power, and "once more, less hastily but surely," Plato remembers being "moved by the desire to take part in public life and politics." He kept
waiting for an opening, but matters turned out otherwise:

[S]ome of those in control brought against . . . Socrates . . . a most
sacrilegious charge, whom he least of all men deserved. They put
him on trial for impiety and the people condemned and put [him]
to death. . . . The result was that I, who had at first been full of ea-
gerness for a public career, as I gazed upon the whirlpool of public
life, . . . finally saw clearly in regard to all states now existing that
without exception their system of government is bad.[3]

To what end Plato's disappointment and detour? Who willingly seeks
out Socratic education, knowing it is likely to make one a misfit in the
real world? These are serious questions Socrates asks his students, and he
expects most of them to take the warning and return to the avenues of
ambition most likely to lead to quick success. I do not want to preach or
pontificate. There is nothing wrong with ambition, with wanting a share
of worldly success. But I do want to pose sharply the essential, beginning
Socratic questions about politics: Who ever promised that politics and
justice go hand in hand? How radical must the changes be that could ever

heal the breach? What are we prepared to abandon to pursue justice? Socrates taught a long time ago, but little in subsequent political history has bridged the chasm, closed the fault line separating the imperatives of power from the ideals of justice.

Here is another disclaimer. Socrates' students were about the same age my students typically are and that I was when I first read the *Republic*. There are, however, no women gathered around Socrates, nor poor students, even though it is true that Socrates never charged a mina for his teachings. We have only young men of privilege commanding slaves in the distance, relatively unconcerned with the need to earn money, disdainful of those who are. This is not a world to which many of us could or would want to belong. After all, it is well and good to idealize the moral dimensions of education, but what if one needs to make a living with one's education? Socrates readily thought that such economic imperatives disqualified one from the leisure necessary to pursue knowledge for its own sake. His theories on education have their own politics, an openly elitist, inegalitarian class politics whereby only the privileged few enjoy the luxury that sponsors high-minded attitudes toward learning.

The question of how welcome women are in Socrates' educational vision is difficult to answer. On the one hand, Socrates insists that the sex of a person is irrelevant to those qualities he seeks to educate. This is the Socrates who insisted against Greek custom that women were fully qualified to lead a public life, even to assume leadership roles in his ideal republic. On the other hand, Socrates spoke with great venom about women as mothers and so thoroughly despised their role in family life that he suggested abolishing families altogether for the political elite. We will have to take a sustained look at whether Socratic education can be rendered gender free without undermining its very nature.

Looking back on my own youthful enthusiasm for Socrates, I confess I should have offered more resistance. I had not expected to find that the philosopher who first awakened me to reflect on political values would be a thinker who saw little value in democracy. The problem Socrates sees with democracy is partly procedural—as if merely counting up votes provides any assurance that what is popular is also just. But Socrates' deeper problem with democracy lay with the substance of its vision of freedom. Democrats do not like to supervise choices; they identify liberty not with the virtue of choices made but with the sheer autonomy exercised in the act of choosing. For Socrates, such a view mistakes license for liberty and makes it inevitable that democratic regimes will implode from within, pulled apart by the very freedom they give persons to pursue whatever desires or interests they happen to have.

It is one matter to defend democracy against tyrants; it is quite another to defend democracy against a Socrates who criticizes democracy in the name of justice. We are committed to thinking of democracy and justice as necessarily yoked; if democracy is not a sufficient condition for just outcomes, it is at least a necessary condition. But Socrates rejects this connection.

How is it possible that the very philosopher who found his own freedom by turning his gaze inward in search of self-knowledge would oppose a form of politics that would grant all persons the same capacity to free themselves through self-government? Much later in the history of political thought, Hegel would suggest that there was an important difference between Socrates and Plato. The teacher's revolutionary contribution was to see that side of freedom which depends on *self*-determination; in Socrates there was "the tendency to look deeper into oneself and to know and determine from within oneself what is right and good."[4]

Thoughts such as these were far beyond me during that first year of infatuation with Socrates. But I do remember the disclaimer Socrates loved to issue to his own students—all that stuff about his not knowing anything except that others did not know either. It is true that Socrates did not think it fair to charge his students because, after all, his method did not provide students with marketable know-how. Some years back a friend of mine came home raving about his first year at a prestigious law school. Unabashedly he said that getting a law degree from this high-ranking school would be like hanging a "power medallion" around his neck. "Power medallion" education is worth money, in Socrates' Athens or in the United States. It is a tool, an instrument for making a living. But Socrates provides us with no such tools. In place of an instrumental view of learning—external credentials to chisel our place in the existing order—he offers a moral view of learning: internal confrontations that change who we are.

One last preliminary. With the *Republic* we begin our study of political philosophy. As I have already said, the study of politics is a detour from the practice of politics, and those most interested in politics are sometimes the first to grow tired, impatient, or even bored with the subject. I have sympathy with this impatience we are likely to feel when reading all this ancient matter. Politics *is* about action; the politically committed do not long have the luxury of sitting on the fence. They—

we—must "plunk," as one of my professors used to put it, choose a side, join up, march to a cause. Politics is not a seminar, not even one led by Socrates.

It might help to see that political philosophy is not as wide a detour as it seems. Political theory is really just a fancy term for coming to clarity about the moral values we always act on whenever we act politically. It is not as if we had a choice or the ability to act politically without some underlying moral commitments. The choice is only whether we examine those commitments and dare to consider them against alternatives.

Subjecting implicit values to explicit consideration is already a political act, and a potentially subversive one. It can confuse us, convince us of inconsistencies, move us to question what we silently assumed to be the case, what we never heard questioned. The *Republic* is Plato's ever present challenge to declare and defend our first-order political principles and see if they can survive the test of rational examination. To this examination, with Socrates' help, we now turn.

1

PLATO'S *REPUBLIC*

THE DEBATE OVER JUSTICE BEGINS

The *Republic* begins one day when a group of young men escape from the city for a holiday. They do what young people often do when they want to get out of the city: they gravitate down to the water, to the sea, in this case the Piraeus or port area of Athens. Like most ports, the Piraeus was—and still is today—a mixing ground where sailors and traders, foreign imports and peoples mingle with locals. On this particular day the Piraeus is the place to be because it is hosting a first-of-its-kind religious festival. Processions to the gods move through the public ways, the Athenians taking turns with celebrants from Thrace, who, we are assured, put on quite a show.

The *Republic* ends the same day, in the next world, about as far from the Piraeus as you can get. But like the Piraeus, the netherworld is a port of entry and exit, with new souls arriving all the time and old souls bound for earth in an endless cycle of reincarnation.

In between the port of entry into Athens and the port of rebirth, a group of young men will build a city, fight wars, dabble in sport, poetry, and music, redistribute property, and recognize women as political equals, all only to abandon political power finally for the higher pleasures of philosophy and wisdom.

It is quite a day, most of it taking place in the imagination, of course, but no one emerges unscathed from what imagination reveals. Socrates will be executed in Athens for supposedly corrupting the young on days such as this. One of the young listeners, Polemarchus, will throw himself into politics and will also be put to death. Two others in attendance are Plato's real-life brothers, and they foreshadow the fate of Plato, for whom the day's devotion to his teacher stretches into a lifetime.

Little of this could be foreseen when the drama starts. The day's festival is over, and the young men are waiting for the real fireworks to begin after sunset, when for the first time a sunset spectacular will feature a never-before-seen torchlight parade on horseback to honor the goddess.[1] As they wander about, the young men bump into Socrates and Glaucon, Plato's brother, who have come to the Piraeus to observe how the festival will go. It is typical of Socrates to be out and about, popping up in places that youth frequent. Platonic dialogues put Socrates at drinking parties, on porticos, in conversation with nervous fathers about the education of their sons.

On this particular occasion Socrates has seen enough of the festival and is preparing to leave the Piraeus with Glaucon when the other young men urge him to stay and witness the premiere of the torchlight parade. Socrates playfully responds with a kind of mock awe: "On horseback . . . that is novel. Will they hold torches and pass them to one another while racing the horses, or what do you mean?"[2]

Although Socrates is making fun of youthful enthusiasm for anything new, still he takes young persons' pleasures seriously enough to agree to stay and see what the fuss is about. It is as if the pleasures of the young have to be given their due, neither judged nor dismissed, certainly not skipped. Thus it comes about that Socrates accompanies the young men to the home of one of them, Polemarchus, whose family lives and does business down at the Piraeus. When they retire to the house to wait for nightfall and the start of the entertainment, no one has the slightest intention of talking about politics, justice, or any other such serious topic. *Not* thinking about justice seems one of the privileges of youth, since there will be time later in life to worry about such matters and make up for any mistakes committed. (During the 2000 presidential campaign, for instance, then-candidate George W. Bush made a virtue of acknowledging that, although he had committed his share of youthful indiscretions, he had long since matured.)

As the *Republic* begins, the young men are in a playful mood, toying familiarly with Socrates. And yet no one makes it to the torchlight parade that night. Somehow—exactly how is always a mystery—the young men's easy attraction to visual splendor and outdoor festivals gives way to festivals for the mind. This shift is accomplished without loss of the passion the young men first feel at the prospect of witnessing pyrotechnics. Only in the end what keeps them up all night down at the Piraeus is the discovery of the beauty of conversation.

It is certainly Socrates' mission in the *Republic* to change, elevate, and sublimate youth's natural eroticism. But the enthusiasms of eros are never repressed, never denied. Plato is always at pains to depict Socrates as lacking in physical beauty ("snub-nosed" is the favorite description). Yet in the *Symposium,* Plato shows that Socratic "seduction" needed neither physical beauty nor drink nor sex; it was a matter of how young men's passions respond to what we still today call platonic love.

Enter Cephalus and a Father's Advice

Picture, then, Socrates arriving at the home of Polemarchus in the Piraeus. There we meet up with Cephalus, Polemarchus' father. We know three pieces of Cephalus' biography: he is old, he is rich, and he is not a citizen of Athens but a merchant given resident alien status to live down in the Piraeus. Socrates right off mentions that Cephalus "seemed very old to me," and Cephalus volunteers that the pleasures of the body "wither away in me."[3] Cephalus seems old psychologically as well as chronologically. He refers to the time fast approaching when he must make preparations to die. Indeed when we first meet him, Cephalus has just propitiated the gods with a sacrifice, and he is sitting "on a sort of cushioned stool . . . crowned with a wreath."[4]

As to his wealth, we learn that Cephalus is old, not new, money. He regards money with the detachment that comes from inheriting rather than earning it. His grandfather accumulated the family fortune, his father squandered some of it, and Cephalus rates somewhere between the two in terms of his merchandising talents. Still, as opposed to Plato's own aristocratic lineage, Cephalus belongs to a rising middle class in Athens whose wealth is tied to trade rather than land.

You and I do not expect a polite dinner guest to draw attention to a host's age or income, but Socrates does both. Cunningly, he flatters Cephalus by asking him to serve as our advance scout as to what it is like to be old, reporting back what he has learned from standing on the "threshold of old age." Cephalus takes the bait and plays the role of the wise man (though, as we shall see, Socrates plays him for a fool). It is not as bad as people say, Cephalus reports. In fact old age works a great release and liberation from "the mad masters" of the body.[5] Cephalus congratulates himself on no longer chasing after women the way he did when young; at long last he has arrived at a plateau where he can enjoy the very pleasure of conversation Socrates is giving to him now.

I do not know if young people today have ever met a contemporary Cephalus. The Cephalean remark I hear repeatedly from friends is that they "would never want to be twenty again." Such a remark may provide consolation to those of us who can no longer wreak havoc the way we (claim we) did when young. But one never hears a twenty-year-old wish to be fifty unless the young person is in serious trouble. I suspect that we are supposed to see through the thin rationalization Cephalus offers for the sobriety of old age. Cephalus is a great literary creation, a precursor to Polonius in *Hamlet,* boastfully offering the benefit of his supposed wisdom but in fact spouting only hackneyed platitudes.

Socrates must have been a strange dinner guest indeed. Cephalus has just credited his own excellent moral character for cushioning the usual impact of old age. Socrates listens and—I am not making this up—decides to "stir . . . him up" by suggesting that "other people" will say it is money, not virtue, that relieves Cephalus of the burdens of old age.[6] Cephalus apparently thinks he is being congratulated and agrees that "gentlemen" like him—not the newly minted rich who actually care about money—know how to use their wealth well. When Socrates follows up by asking what, then, is the greatest good money can provide the elderly, Cephalus makes the argument that turns the night's conversation into a discussion about justice. Money makes it possible for him to be just, to settle his accounts with the gods and men alike: "[W]hen a man comes face to face with the realization that he will be making an end, fear and care enter him for things to which he gave no thought before."[7] This is a remarkably frank statement on Cephalus' part but hardly one that casts justice in an attractive light. For Cephalus, the greatest good of wealth is in "not having to depart for that other place frightened because one owes some sacrifices to a god or money to a human being."[8]

Cephalus does not know it—he does not even want to know it—but he has just offered a "theory" of justice. It turns out that as a practical man involved in the merchandising business, Cephalus has developed ideas on the subject of fairness—ideas that I call an "accountant's" concept of justice. Justice for him is not very complicated; it is a matter of honest bookkeeping. Everyone in life is a borrower and a lender (Polonius would warn against this); we each borrow from the gods and exchange goods with fellows. When the time comes, we should pay back debts and call in loans.

The notion that justice is a matter of settling accounts is one appropriate to old age and its moments of reckoning. Cephalus concedes that he was not much interested in settling accounts when he was young and had a lifetime yet to close the books. Only the fear of death has given him a belated reason to practice justice. It is expected that we run up debt when young; the important thing is to make amends before dying.

Much later in the history of political thought the French philosopher Pascal will suggest that the smart money gambles on the existence of God. If God turns out not to exist, then all you are out by living as if the divine did exist is the finite time and effort you put into believing in a fiction. But if God turns out to exist, and you gambled by not believing, then a much worse fate—eternal damnation—awaits. (Of course, Pascal's wager did not factor in the possibility that God would be most offended by, and most damning of, those who believed in divinity only as a way to hedge their bets.)

Cephalus is too traditionally pious to express his commitment to justice as a gamble, but he does talk as if he is now sitting there crowned with a wreath, sacrificing to the gods, to cover himself in the next life. For the young men listening to the exchange between the two older men in the room, the constant reference to the fear of death cannot be what they anticipated talking about while passing the hours until the start of the night's entertainments.

In the introduction to this book I suggested that we all live out some political philosophy, without the need to put it into words. Cephalus is a great example of someone who acts on the basis of views he has never had occasion to ponder. Socrates takes it upon himself to see what will happen if Cephalus is made to defend views he does not even know he holds. So Socrates poses a hypothetical. What if a friend lends you a weapon when sane but asks for it back after going mad? Is it still just to give back a weapon to a madman?[9] Cephalus admits that returning the weapon does not seem right. And so Socrates can point out that there is at least one case in which the simple equation of justice with "paying back" a loan does not work.

Exit the Father, Enter the Son

Rather than continuing the conversation, Cephalus excuses himself, "for it's already time for me to look after the sacrifices."[10] Cephalus may well have a protective sense that it is far too late in life for him to realize that a few strategic sacrifices will not turn him into a just man. At any rate, his son Polemarchus jumps in to defend his father, and Cephalus happily "bequeaths" the argument to his son. Polemarchus accepts the bequest, with the making-light-of-death remark that he will be inheriting other things from his father shortly.

In place of his father, Polemarchus reasons as follows. One cannot be overly legalistic when it comes to justice. His father's mistake was in seeking one simple rule to follow in all cases. But there are cases and there are cases. Far from being blind to who is who in the world, the just person distinguishes what is owed to friends (to do them good) from what should be done to enemies (to do them harm). Thus Socrates' hypothetical has an answer: if it is a friend who goes insane and wants his weapon back, then keep it from him for his own good.[11]

If Cephalus' views on justice seem fitting for old age, Polemarchus has the ardor of the young for the partisanship in justice. With youthful enthusiasm Polemarchus makes the virtues of friendship and the virtues of justice the same. Socrates in short order will teach him that justice is a different and higher virtue than friendship, that justice in fact operates as a moral brake on what one can do to help friends, family, and country. But it is difficult to side totally with Socrates against Polemarchus. The young man's starting ethic may be narrow and partisan, but it is intense, militant, and strong. From the moment Polemarchus jumps in to rescue his father, he is the spokesperson for loyalty to one's own. Polemarchus sees the world for what it often is: a place of competition and conflict. Justice is a fight for your side, and when you fight, you fight to win. But one can hardly win by blindly following the rules when one's enemies are only too ready to dirty their hands. Justice must be prepared to answer tit for tat, to defend, to retaliate, yes, even to use unjust means if that is necessary to achieve just results. All of this is suggested in the brusque way in which Polemarchus says that he wishes as much harm to his enemies as he wishes well for his friends.

Let me give an example of where I find Polemarchean justice tempting. Some years ago I was taking a course on justice during wartime. Yes, war is hell, my professor acknowledged, but it would be a hell of a lot worse if each side could do whatever it takes to win: bomb cities, deliberately target civilians, leave enemy sailors to drown with their torpedoed ship, release poison gas, engage in nuclear blackmail, plant bombs on commercial air flights, and so on. Of course, obedience to justice during wartime is risky business. To illustrate the risks, the professor deliberately took a hard case: England's violation of Norway's neutrality in April 1940 during Word War II. As a neutral, Norway retained the right under international law to continue commercial trade with Germany.

Germany depended on this trade for a year-round supply of much-needed iron ore. The ore was mined in Sweden, another neutral. During the winter, when Swedish ports froze, the ore was moved to a warm-water port in Norway, where German ships called for it.

Hitler could have overrun Norway at will but chose not to, since the nation's neutrality worked to Nazi advantage. Winston Churchill, then First Lord of the Admiralty, fumed at having England's hands tied by the rules of neutrality and finally persuaded his government to mine the Norwegian harbor. Once the mines were laid, Hitler no longer had any interest in respecting Norwegian neutrality. In fact the Nazis had already planned a military invasion of Norway, and they quickly occupied the country with tremendous cost to the lives and property of the Norwegians.

My professor told the story to convince us that England was wrong, and that under the circumstances England had not shown the kind of supreme emergency that might justify violation of international law. He worried in particular that England had imposed a loss of life on the Norwegians that the Norwegians themselves had not chosen. But the story had the opposite effect on me: I thought Churchill a great hero, a practitioner of Polemarchean justice in dire circumstances in which the difference between friends and enemies left no room for neutrals.

World War II was hardly the only war to call out the Polemarchus in us; the conflict with Al Qaeda speaks to the same certainty about the justice of one's cause. But does the difference between friend and enemy always line up with the difference between good and bad? Socrates begins his cross-examination of Polemarchus by asking the young man what exactly he knows about his friends and enemies. Does he always choose good people for friends and bad people for enemies? Polemarchus gives the appropriate visceral response: no, of course not, I do not know, objectively speaking, that my friends are good, I only know they *seem* good. But mistakes are possible, appearances are deceiving, people change.[12] Socrates quickly pounces on this. Since friendship is faulty, Polemarchus will sometimes place the just person in the paradoxical position of doing good to friends who are bad and harm to enemies who turn out to be good.[13]

Polemarchus might have tried to escape—I wish he had—by arguing that just people remain loyal to their friends even when, or especially when, they go bad; that the bonds of friendship create special obligations of solidarity. Later on in the history of political thought, Aristotle will wrestle with this precise issue of our remaining obligations when friendship sours. But Polemarchus does not pursue such arguments. Instead he asks permission to take back his original subjective assumption that friends only *appear* to be good. Ideally speaking, he now argues, true friends are always good and real enemies are always bad. When these ideal conditions are met, it will work out that devotion to my side, my family, and my friends *is* justice.

Polemarchus' amended position permits him to maintain the vengeance in justice, the one-sidedness of the ethic, the self-righteous crusade of the just, out to eliminate the evil barbarians at the gate. But now Socrates asks a perplexing question: even if your enemies are bad persons, "is it the part of a just man to injure" them, indeed to injure "any human being whatsoever?" Polemarchus says, "Certainly, . . . bad men and enemies ought to be injured."[14] After all, crime, theft, conflict, war exist: how else is justice to win the fight if it does not wield the sword, erect gallows, build prisons, and in general punish its enemies? Socrates never answers these questions. Instead, by focusing Polemarchus' attention on what one owes to the *other* side, he wants to wean the young man away from his "mine versus thine" ethic.

For Polemarchus, the paradigmatic cases requiring justice are in fact not so much international disputes as domestic disputes of the kind Cephalus brought up: material conflicts over debts, loans, money, and property. Disputes over "goods" of this sort do seem to trigger possessive, competitive zero-sum logic where the goods are either mine or yours. As Socrates gently puts it to Polemarchus, it must have been "some . . . rich man" who first coined the saying that "it is just to help friends and injure enemies."[15] Since the wealthy already have theirs, a code of justice that identifies the good with protection of what belongs to me and my friends is comforting. But Polemarchus must see that the "high opinion" he has of himself as defender of friends against enemies may amount to nothing more than a self-serving identification of the "good" with what is "mine." If he is to pursue justice, he must be prepared to transcend the insular ethic of friendship and follow justice when it conflicts with the interests of family and friends.

The particulars of Socrates' final refutation of Polemarchus are as follows. To injure any man, even an enemy, is to make that person worse as a human being—worse in respect to the traits of character that make for a good person. Now justice is one of those human traits that we diminish in others when we injure them. Polemarchean justice therefore creates an odd paradox in which justice breeds its opposite.

To highlight the oddity, Socrates compares the practice of justice with the practice of other human skills, say, of music or horsemanship. Do musicians use their music to make other persons less musical?[16] Do those knowledgeable in riding horses use that skill to make others less able to ride? Polemarchus admits the opposite is likely to be the case. How, then, can he explain the alleged antagonisms of justice?

I suppose that musicians in the real world compete with one another often enough. As I am writing this, I am reading of a brewing dispute among scientists at MIT. One laboratory at the university made an offer of an assistant professorship to a young woman. A senior professor and Nobel laureate at another MIT laboratory wrote to discourage her from accepting the offer, since the two labs were in "competition," and he could therefore in no way cooperate with or mentor her if she took the post. I do not know what model of scientific inquiry the Nobel laureate had in mind when he sharply differentiated between "his" lab and "their" lab, but his behavior seems insufferable for the very reasons Socrates puts forward. Scientists, as scientists, do not try to impede the work of other scientists, however much, as seekers after grant money, they are in financial competition. Socrates makes the parallel point about musicians. As lovers of music, they owe their loyalty to the good of music; that loyalty trumps the more parochial and competitive logic of friends versus enemies.

Socrates prods Polemarchus to understand that justice is equally transcendent of loyalty to friends. This is a huge jump for Polemarchus; he resists the "moral conversion" to a new set of values that essentially devalues what he hitherto has believed in most strongly. Perhaps "belonging" has a special appeal to the son of a resident alien of Athens denied political citizenship. Perhaps as the son of a merchant, Polemarchus assumes that disputes over material goods are the paradigmatic cases of justice. But what Socrates argues is that true knowledge of justice requires a kind of "paradigm shift." Polemarchus should understand that justice ultimately distributes goods of the soul and that these "goods" are good not because they are mine but because they have value in and of themselves.

Enter Thrasymachus

Polemarchus rolls over and plays dead far too quickly. Neither he nor we have any idea yet what these "higher goods" are that justice delivers. What a breath of fresh air Thrasymachus is, as he bursts into the conversation unable to control his anger at the "nonsense" and "inanities"

Socrates has been spouting.[17] Thrasymachus is a recurring figure in political history—rude, violent in temper, disdainful of conventional wisdom, the realist, the cynic, the skeptic, the unmasker of hypocrisy, the new thinker, the paid political consultant, the amoralist, the immoralist, the speechwriter, the adviser to princes, the power behind the throne. He is Creon in *Antigone* saying the state is mine or Louis XIV echoing "L'état c'est moi." He is Machiavelli teaching a new political science to masterless men, or he is Nietzsche wanting to stand the world of morality on its head.

When we first meet Thrasymachus, he is comfortably ensconced at Cephalus' home. From other dialogues we know that Thrasymachus is a professional teacher, a member of the school of Sophists, who concentrated their teachings on the art of rhetoric and public speaking. As a course taught to political hopefuls, rhetoric seemed to Socrates nothing but the skill to make the weaker argument the stronger. And he and Thrasymachus clash straight off on the rules for talking justly about justice. Thrasymachus astutely skewers the one-sidedness of the famed Socratic method: the great master never risks an answer himself as to what justice is; he contents himself with exposing the fallacies in other's views. Let Socrates for once answer the questions he asks about justice and then we can attack him for a change, Thrasymachus challenges.[18]

Thrasymachus lacks the patience to pull off this role reversal. He is itching to show off his smarts and certain that he will not wither as others have done under cross-examination. So Socrates has to offer little encouragement to Thrasymachus before that man proudly announces that yes, he does know the right answer to the meaning of justice, and only a teacher such as him is daring enough to reveal the unadorned and unadulterated truth: justice "is nothing other than the advantage of the stronger."[19] Period. Done. That is all there is in the world—one code, the code of self-interest. Justice is not the name for some other moral code controlling self-interest. It is merely dress-up clothing, camouflage, cosmetics designed to make pursuit of self-interest more palatable. Perhaps the strong could rule by force alone, but somewhere in the development of civilization, strength went to those who realized they could best cow others into obeying them by convincing the masses that they were obeying "justice."

Ever since, the strong have used their power to translate whatever was to their advantage into laws and rules and codes, and they call all that "justice." But it is essentially a con game, an efficient way of getting others to accede to the self-interest of the rulers. Near the end of our study of political theory we will see Marx revive this argument that justice is simply what serves the interests of the ruling class (until class itself is abolished). The idea, however, is present already in the debates swirling around fifth-century Athens.

Here is Thrasymachus' evidence. Justice is relative; it varies from city to city, constitution to constitution. The very diversity of legal systems shows us that justice is not natural but a product manufactured by politics. The only constant is that in each city, rulers manufacture the rules to fit their interests.

But do rulers always *know* what is in their best interests? Are they infallible, or do they sometimes make mistakes about what will be to their advantage? In asking these questions, Socrates sets the same trap for Thrasymachus that he had set for Polemarchus when he asked about friendship and good judgment. Thrasymachus first gives the sensible answer that real-world leaders are not as perfectly savvy as always to recognize their own interests. But then Socrates declares "check." Since mistakes are inevitable, rulers end up making rules of justice that sometimes work to their disadvantage—exactly the opposite of Thrasymachus' definition.[20]

This is a beautiful move on the chessboard. Thrasymachus is persuasive at first because he speaks the language of realism to justice. But Socrates steals his realist's thunder by playing off the real-life ways in which rulers obviously make mistakes and hence cannot perfectly rig the game of justice in the manner Thrasymachus assumes.

Thrasymachus needs a way out of this trap, and one of the young bystanders, Cleitophon, offers him an elegant escape. All Thrasymachus need claim is that rulers have the raw power to enact laws that *seem* to be in their self-interest. Whether or not justice so declared works out *objectively* to be to the rulers' advantage is beside the point. The point is merely that rulers everywhere *try* to translate self-interest into law. From Cleitophon's vantage point there is ironically nothing "real" about justice. It is merely a matter of whatever *appears* to be in the interests of the ruling class.[21]

Cleitophon is a more thoroughgoing cynic about justice than even Thrasymachus. Thrasymachus at least claims that justice exists, that it *is* to the advantage of the stronger. Cleitophon claims that justice is entirely flimsy and arbitrary: sometimes the rules work to the advantage of the stronger, sometimes they do not. What is not flimsy, however, is the brute power to make the rules. Only rulers have that advantage.

In a show of conversational hospitality Socrates offers to let Thrasymachus out of check. Does his opponent wish to accept Cleitophon's strategic move? Surprisingly, Thrasymachus rejects this option. As if, Thrasymachus stridently announces, "I call a man who makes mistakes 'stronger' at the moment when he is making mistakes."[22] Treating Socrates and the others as slow on the uptake, Thrasymachus promises he will take more care in the future to talk "precisely." The strong, he now clarifies, are only really strong, and rulers are only really rulers, when they *correctly* pursue their self-interests. Now it so happens that rulers can arrive at the knowledge they need to be genuine rulers once they have my advice. I, Thrasymachus, know how to teach the precise skills, the political craft it takes to assert one's own advantage. This knowledge is eminently teachable and available to anyone, whatever his bloodline.

Thrasymachus is shrewd enough to see that he has to reject Cleitophon's advice. What use is Thrasymachus to future rulers unless there is a difference between what appears to be in their self-interest and what truly is? Thrasymachus, perhaps the first professional political consultant, hires himself out to teach the difference.

Socrates seizes on an apparent point of agreement between Thrasymachus and him. Both are teachers who view justice as a form of knowledge, a set of skills that can be taught just as the skills of any craft can be taught. Whether we think of medicine or shepherding or horse training, all would agree that practitioners of these crafts have been trained in some appropriate way. Socrates focuses on the knowledge it takes to be a good doctor. When a doctor is practicing the art of medicine, does he use his knowledge to assert his own advantage or the welfare of his patient? If the patient comes to the doctor in a weakened condition, does the doctor, as a doctor, rule over the weaker person, or does he try to make the weaker person stronger? The questions answer themselves if we truly understand what we mean by a good doctor. Similarly, shepherds are masters of their flock, and trainers rule over horses. But as skilled practitioners, shepherds and trainers use their power to take care of the weaker beings put in their care. Unless shepherds tend the sheep, they simply are not good shepherds.[23]

Since justice is a form of knowledge like these other crafts, it should resemble them in being a skill that we value precisely because it enables the just person to help others. No one would go to a doctor who simply asserted the doctor's advantage over the patient. The same is true about justice.

These Socraticisms drive Thrasymachus into a fury. As if, he testily responds, doctors *really* care about their patients. We all know doctors are in it for themselves; they bother with patients only insofar as they get paid. Who would learn medicine in the first place unless the material rewards were there? Come off it, Socrates, you can almost hear Thrasymachus say. Would you have us believes that shepherds fatten their flocks for the benefit of the sheep? It is only because the flock will be fleeced in the end that anyone hires a shepherd to keep an eye on them. The shepherd example in particular infuriates Thrasymachus to the point where he rudely asks Socrates whether his nurse knows he is out without a handkerchief, spewing this kind of stuff out of his nose.[24]

As an analyst of human motivations to learn, Thrasymachus seems spot on here. How many of us today would still want to be lawyers or doctors—would put the years into law school or medical school—if the rewards of money, high repute, and status were not there? This is the question that exercises Holden Caulfield in *The Catcher in the Rye*. He disdains his father's corporate law practice but finds that lawyers who serve the poor are the bigger phonies and hypocrites, doing it only for show and tell.

Suspicions about the hypocrisy of those who claim to be motivated by justice and public service run deep in the young listeners surrounding Socrates. Tapping into that skepticism, Thrasymachus ups the ante. Whenever we abide by (what the rulers say is) justice, we are being played for fools and suckered into serving the interests of others rather than our own. We should free ourselves to imitate the behavior of the rulers and assert our own advantage. Of course in doing so, we will behave in ways the rulers will insist are "unjust." But so be it. We need the daring to turn conventional definitions of justice versus injustice upside down. What the world calls injustice is in fact what we *ought* to be doing, since it serves our interests and permits us to liberate the most natural desires within us. Injustice, in other words, is natural to our psyche and will make us happy. Justice, by contrast, is a fiction that represses our innermost drives, makes us unhappy, and frees only the rulers to have it their way. In making this argument, Thrasymachus anticipates by centuries Nietzsche's call for a "transvaluation of values."[25]

The conversation between Thrasymachus and Socrates now stands at a crossroad. Thrasymachus has made a *psychological* argument on behalf of a new morality. For him, injustice proves its value by making us happier than justice does. Socrates could respond to this challenge in one of two ways. He could argue that Thrasymachus' morality is wrong because his psychology is wrong. Taking this path would require Socrates to show that the pleasures gained through acts of injustice are short-lived and spurious and that more lasting happiness accompanies justice. Alternatively, Socrates could respond to Thrasymachus by insisting that issues of happiness are irrelevant to issues of morality and that it simply is our duty to be just whether or not we are made happy by doing the right thing. This is the argument that, later in the history of moral thought, Immanuel Kant will make. Kant taught that moral behavior must be strictly motivated by an obligatory sense of duty and not by a desire to achieve the reward of happiness from doing one's duty.

Socrates is no Kant. He accepts Thrasymachus' premise that moral life has ultimately to be defended in psychological terms, and with a demonstration that the virtues of justice are in tune with expressing human nature rather than repressing it. In other words, if it is "wrong" to behave unjustly and assert one's self-interest at the expense of others, then Socrates must persuade us that such behavior is "bad" in a psychological sense, that it sponsors a self-defeating strategy of hedonism that will leave the pleasure seeker in pain and poverty. Much of the burden of the *Republic* is in getting young persons, attracted to the intuitive connection between self-assertion and happiness, to reflect on the psychological characteristics that come in the wake of self-interest and on whether they want to end up with such qualities.

Doctors and Patients, Pilots and Passengers

With all this in mind, let me return to the doctor-patient relationship. Thrasymachus has scored points by arguing that doctors really are in it for themselves. True, they treat patients, but only to gain money, status, and reputation. So the patient is merely being "used" to satisfy the doctor's self-interest after all. But that is precisely it, responds Socrates shrewdly. We, the patients, willingly pay doctors to treat us because otherwise there is little in it for doctors. Strictly speaking, when the doctor is exercising his skill and learning *as a doctor,* the patient is the primary beneficiary. In recognition of this, we pay doctors in order to motivate them to serve us. So, Socrates concludes, Thrasymachus actually proves too much. It is true that no one treats patients without some gain in mind, and that we commonly pay doctors to provide the necessary incentive for them to help us. But this only proves that doctors gain few personal benefits *from the actual art of doctoring.* Far from exposing the doctor as entirely consumed by self-interest, the fact that the doctor is also a moneymaker (he wears two hats, as it were) shows that when he is wearing his doctor hat, the interests of the patient rule. In modern philosophical terms, Socrates distinguishes the *motives* of the doctor from the *grounds* that oblige us to reward the doctor.[26]

What is true of doctors is true of pilots who sail ships. They rule over the passengers, but they use their knowledge of navigation to get the passengers where they want to go. The same is true of the way shepherds and horse trainers use their knowledge as rulers of sheep or horses—for the benefit of those in their charge. Indeed, "there isn't ever anyone who holds any position of rule, insofar as he is a ruler, who considers or commands his own advantage rather than that of what is ruled."[27]

This is Socrates' initial attempt to refute Thrasymachus' description of the self-interested behavior of rulers. Everyone listening to the dialogue, or in our case reading it, knows that there is something fantastically wrong about Socrates' conclusion. Whatever logical steps got Socrates to this point, it seems off-base to offer such an apologetic view of rulers as always acting on behalf of the people. Let's agree with Socrates' premise that the doctor qua doctor does not profit from the actual gaining or practicing of medical knowledge. Still, Socrates concedes that doctoring becomes a rational choice for persons only when it is a means to self-interested ends. This is a conclusion that Thrasymachus could and should have accepted. After all, Socrates has not shown that doctors will voluntarily treat a patient knowing beforehand that the patient cannot pay, or has a contagious fatal disease, or is likely to die in some way damaging to the doctor's reputation. Actually, Socrates' logic could convince one more than ever that the happiness of doctors depends on what is in it finally for them. The very fact that doctors have to wear two hats is evidence that no one is made happy by the altruistic aspects of the profession alone.

Clearly Socrates has to do better, and Plato knows it. Socrates promised to show that acting justly is its own reward and brings happiness in its wake. But he certainly has not shown that serving patients is in and of itself a sufficient reward to make doctors happy, poor and unpaid though they might be. And in regard to political rulers, he is far from showing that they are made so happy by serving the interests of others as to want nothing for themselves. The intuitive appeal of Thrasymachus' contrary position—that rulers are in it entirely for themselves and will do to us whatever it takes to serve their own interests—remains intact.

In search of a more convincing psychological account of how justice and service to the interests of others could possibly make doctors, pilots, and politicians happy persons, Socrates tries out three arguments at the end of Book One. First, justice is stronger and mightier than injustice; as the saying goes, there must be honor among thieves. Perfectly unjust persons do not even make a good gang. By contrast, justice makes it possible for persons to cooperate, be loyal, have friends, and enjoy peace.[28]

Second, justice is wiser than injustice. People wise in mathematics or music do not try to get the better of other mathematicians or musicians but work together to produce proofs on the one hand, harmony on the other. Unjust persons, by virtue of always putting themselves first, do not demonstrate any comparable wisdom.[29]

If we are keeping a ledger, many of the character traits that we commonly think make persons happy—strength, loyalty, friendship, peace, harmony, wisdom—are in the justice rather than the injustice column. Socrates' final argument places pleasure as well on the side of justice. Thrasymachus has played off the seemingly obvious senses in which the life of justice is all about sacrificing pleasures, but now Socrates defends justice as simply the best way to achieve lasting pleasure. This argument is at the moral core of the entire *Republic,* and yet it is the least persuasive one when Socrates first offers it.

What Socrates sketches at the conclusion of Book One—and it is no more than a sketch—is more fully expressed in Plato's dialogue, the *Gorgias.* There Socrates asks us to picture the soul of the wicked as a sieve or perforated jar.[30] Unjust persons are engaged in a self-defeating attempt to keep the pleasures they seek from sifting right through them. At first it may seem as if the unjust have a leg up on the just when it comes to pursuing pleasure, since they free themselves to pursue desire without restraint. But the kinds of pleasures they race after have a way of sifting straight through their souls, leaving them as far from achieving satisfaction as they were before the race began. We know this because the unjust consume pleasure after pleasure, constantly feeling a need to replenish the momentary satisfaction each act of consumption delivers. Nothing lasts. Unjust persons may visualize themselves as great and free masters, but psychologically they are enslaved to desires that control them more than they control their desires.

Consider this example. When Philippine dictator Ferdinand Marcos was overthrown after a long and violent rule, crowds entering the former palace found over five hundred pairs of shoes in the closet of Imelda

Marcos, his wife and companion in corruption. I suppose Imelda Marcos must have gotten *some* pleasure from buying pair after pair, but apparently each purchase brought such a fleeting pleasure as to leave her obsessively purchasing ever more shoes. At some point it seems improbable that she bought shoes to wear them.

Is there a solution to the soul as sieve, to the evaporation of pleasure? Perhaps this is just the nature of pleasure, to be fleeting. Socrates suggests that, while the pleasures of the body and its senses are necessarily short-lived, the pleasures of the mind are permanent. Our body depends on external objects to arouse its sensations—water to drink, food to eat, and the like. By contrast, the pleasures of contemplative activity are under our own control. Once the mind experiences delight from knowledge, that joy does not sift through us but attaches to our very identity, changing who we are in irreversible ways. The pleasure is internalized in the form of character. By moving the sources of pleasure inside us, the mind gives us the "higher" pleasure of experiencing freedom. By depending on external objects for its arousal, the body enslaves us to "lower" pleasures.

The distinction between "higher" and "lower" pleasures becomes one of the great motifs of the *Republic*. In a moment we will see that Socrates' own students resist the distinction; the last thing they want to hear is that justice requires achieving some disembodied existence. Before reading of their resistance, we might pause to consider what to make of this basic Socratic notion that it is possible to rank the way people find pleasure in life. Should we, in a more generous, egalitarian, and democratic spirit, reject the entire endeavor to sort out whose happiness is better than whose, accepting instead that there is simply a diversity of ways of being happy, no one necessarily better than any other? Much later in the history of political thought the English philosopher Jeremy Bentham will reject Socrates' urge to *judge* the worth of other persons' happiness with the retort that "pushpin [a trivial child's game] is as good as poetry" so far as producing pleasure is concerned.[31]

When I think back on two of my greatest teachers, I see now that they took different sides on this weighty issue. My college Shakespeare professor was a firm believer in the life of the mind. He made us memorize passages from the sonnets and plays—not a little bit but a whole lot. We suffered through the memorizing, the braver among us finally challenging the old man as to why it was so necessary to commit sonnets to memory. "You will thank me one day," he growled. "You will thank me one day when you are waiting for a bus, or in a long line at the post office, or hiking through the mountains, or lying on the beach. You will thank me because, wherever you are, you will have Shakespeare with you, Shakespeare *in* you; you will hear him when you fall in love, when you go to war, when you betray a friend, when you go to sleep. What greater gift could I give you?" My professor was a crusty old man, king of the hill at a very small liberal arts college. I doubt he knew much about any way to live other than to adore books and language. He probably never made a choice to prefer the life of the mind over the pleasures of the body; it just happened to be what made *him* happy. But does this prove that his pleasure in reading Shakespeare was really better or "higher" than the pleasures other persons achieve in more material ways?

I thought of such questions years later while listening to a staggeringly eloquent lecture by Michael Walzer in his class on the history of political thought. He was lecturing on John Stuart Mill's famous line "It is better to be Socrates dissatisfied than a fool satisfied." Walzer asked how Mill could possibly know *that*. How was it even possible to compare one person's happiness to another's? This led him to consider one of Plato's key arguments. In order to compare the pleasures of the mind with the pleasures of the body, we need a qualified referee, judge, or umpire. The only qualified person would be someone who had personally experienced pleasure in both realms. Socrates treats it as obvious that people who achieve mental pleasure also experience bodily pleasure, but the same is not true in reverse. Thus the only competent judge is the person leading the life of the mind. And in all instances, Socrates reports, such a person will prefer the happiness achieved through mental activity to the happiness of satisfying bodily appetites.

Walzer offered a simple refutation of Socrates that I pass on now. Referring to Walt Frazier, a then famous professional basketball player for the New York Knicks, he humorously asked whether his own pleasure in teaching philosophy was better than Frazier's pleasure playing basketball. "*I* have played basketball," Walzer noted. "I know what it feels like to play basketball the way *I* play basketball. But I do not know, I could not possibly know, what it feels like to play basketball as well as Walt Frazier does, experiencing the joys of playing before a cheering crowd at Madison Square Garden, displaying consummate talent, winning fame and wealth alike. To experience *that* pleasure in playing basketball, I would have to *be* Walt Frazier."

Walzer used his homespun example to point out the obvious ways in which lives are not comparable. There never was a time when Walzer "chose" the life of the mind over the life of being Walt Frazier, made happy by being a great basketball player. The democratic implications of this example have long stayed with me. Years ago the Boston Celtics used the gym at the university where I taught as a training facility. I would imagine inviting an aging Larry Bird to class and asking him what it was like, now that he had to face up to the time fast approaching when he would no longer be able to play professional basketball. Fortunately I never acted on this fantasy.

Socrates cannot win his argument over Thrasymachus—at least not yet—because he has not offered us any vantage point from which we could see how the life of the mind, and the just behavior that comes from freeing the mind to control the body, cut the better path to happiness. Perhaps it is true that the happiness of the philosopher endures through a lifetime while that of the basketball player burns out quickly. But Book One ends with a dud, no one at all certain what Socrates even means by happiness, let alone by justice.

2

THE STUDENTS REVOLT AGAINST UTOPIA

Plato apparently wrote what now forms Book One of the *Republic* as a stand-alone piece. Only years later did he return to the drama and have Socrates accept Thrasymachus' challenge to come out of hiding and reveal his own thoughts on justice.

The Socrates of Book One seems much as Plato must have experienced him in real life—taking on rivals, outfoxing them, impressing listeners with the power of the "Socratic method." But if all we learn from the Socratic method is the art of out-arguing people, then we have not learned much at all. Socrates warned against misuse of his teachings. The point was not to score debating points (making the weaker argument seem the stronger, Socrates liked to say). The point was to reason out the truth.

When Plato sat down in his mature years to pick up the thread of the story about that day down in the Piraeus, he abandoned the Socratic method. He did not abandon Socrates; with rare exceptions, he continued to write in Socrates' name. But this Socrates is different. He has given up the self-effacing response to the Delphic oracle's declaration that no man is wiser than Socrates. He used to understand the Delphic wisdom only negatively: not that he was smart but that the supposed wise men were even dumber. But now Socrates acknowledges that exposing others as frauds and fakes is not enough; a wise person must prove able to build as well as to tear down.

Much that Plato has Socrates say about justice comes as a surprise. The Socrates of the *Apology* made self-knowledge the key to genuine freedom, even if individuals came to question the justice of the laws as they became aware of their own independent sense of right and wrong. The Socrates of Plato's *Republic* places the emphasis on what is objective, not subjective, about freedom and justice. Whether this difference represents a shift from the historical Socrates to Plato speaking as Socrates is not a question I will pursue. But the *Republic* does try to imagine a state whose institutions are so perfectly just that the tensions Socrates faced in Athens between his obligations to his inner sense of morality and to the external laws no longer exist.

At any rate, the book we now know as the *Republic* starts over, despite the apparent victory Socrates scores over Thrasymachus in Book One. The action picks up on the same day with the conversation still going on inside Cephalus' house. Plato appoints his own real-life brother, Glaucon, to be the prime mover of the conversation. Bold enough to criticize his teacher, Glaucon ("undaunted" as ever) chides Socrates for silencing Thrasymachus without persuading anyone that justice is the true human good. Glaucon is a self-reflective person, in the Socratic sense; he has turned his gaze inward and recognized his own attractions to pleasure-seeking. Glaucon would *like* to be convinced that justice is its own reward, that doing well is conducive to well-being. But "I've yet to hear from anyone" a satisfactory defense of justice.[1]

What would satisfy Glaucon? I do not wish to locate Glaucon philosophically so much as to recognize him as a particular kind of student. Socrates refers to him as having an "erotic" personality.[2] When Socrates makes this remark, he is alluding to Glaucon as a "lover of boys," in the approved Greek tradition. Glaucon, we are told, is not especially discriminating in his loves; he is passionate about all kind of boys, able to find qualities to love in all. While Socrates will set out to teach Glaucon to love virtuously, he counts on the undisciplined daring and indiscriminate curiosity of Glaucon to move the discussion along. Glaucon is curious about all kinds of ideas; he can appreciate what Thrasymachus had to say about nature and self-assertion, even while being open to Socrates' contrary position. But Glaucon faults Socrates for presenting arguments that are technically solid but morally empty—apparently a common criticism of Socrates at the time. In particular, Glaucon harps on the ambiguity in Socrates' refrain that justice is "good" for persons. Such an equation of justice with "the good" makes no sense unless Socrates specifies what exactly the good is for human beings. Everyone agrees that the human good has something to do with happiness, but this hardly helps, since we disagree about what happiness is.

In many Platonic dialogues the youths surrounding Socrates are little more than stick figures or yes-men. Plato characterizes his brother as a more worthy and charming student. Glaucon begins by dissecting the ambiguity in the seemingly straightforward claim that "justice is good." One possibility is that justice is "good" in the trivial sense that, say, eating ice cream (in moderation) is good: a "silly delight" or "harmless pleasure" that we enjoy but from which we derive no particularly good results or consequences.

The second possibility is the opposite: we could mean that behaving justly is drudge work, onerous and burdensome, not enjoyable but good only for its consequences. We all know examples in this category: exercise ("no pain, no gain"); foul-tasting medicine or painful surgery. Working for a wage is "tiresome and disagreeable," but we do it for the money.[3]

The third category is behavior we do for *both* the joy and the benefits it brings. We experience pleasure in the activity *and* we have the additional satisfaction of achieving results that are good for us.[4]

Glaucon now lays down his first challenge. Most teachers praise justice only as necessary drudgery. Glaucon pleads with Socrates to offer a different, more psychologically appealing defense of justice. If justice truly is "good in and of itself," then it must be good in the third category sense—good not merely as a way station on the road to a desired destination but as a pleasurable activity in its own right.

Glaucon illustrates his dissatisfaction with the traditional defenses of justice by floating an idea that would have a profound future in the history of political thought. Imagine a time before there ever was an Athens, before there was any government at all, a time we today call the "state of nature."[5] Glaucon does not suggest any such place ever existed, but he uses the image to separate what is "natural" about us from what is socialized into us. Glaucon's initial thought is that justice is hardly a natural instinct. Left to nature, human beings must have behaved much like Thrasymachus said, each aggressively asserting self-interest and doing whatever it took to survive. Nature is jungle warfare in which not only instinct but also reason tells me to take from you before you take from me. The best that can be said for justice is that it was invented out of necessity, as a necessary evil to cure the greater evils of war in the state of nature.

Who came up with the idea of justice? In whose interests would it have been to declare a truce? Anticipating Nietzsche by centuries, Glaucon speculates that the weak became the first proselytizers for justice, law, and government. They banded together and agreed to restrain their natural lusts in exchange for peace and security. Thrasymachus, of course, had pegged justice as in the interests of the stronger; Glaucon suggests its origin may have been the opposite.[6]

However necessary justice may be, Glaucon's point is that it is still a sacrifice of our natural pleasure seeking. The trouble with thinking of justice as "deterrence" is that it opens up a tension between nature and society, between happiness and justice. Conventional morality teaches Glaucon to experience himself as a house divided.

Glaucon is not done. As yet another way to illustrate the tension between nature and justice, he retells the marvelous story of the ring of Gyges.[7] Gyges was a poor shepherd to the king. The immense inequality between shepherd and king was not due to nature, nor was it just. But the law certainly said that the flock belonged to the king, and Gyges was merely to tend the sheep faithfully. One day the shepherd discovers a magic ring. Twisting the collar of the ring one way makes him invisible; twisting it back safely returns his visibility. Gyges does not hesitate to exploit the complete liberty of action that invisibility gives him. With absolute assurance that he will not be caught, Gyges carries out perfect crimes and, in short order, seduces the queen, kills the king, and rises from the lowest to the highest position in the realm.

Glaucon uses the Gyges tale to pose for Socrates the core question of whether justice is truly its own reward. Socrates' ethic leads to the absurd conclusion that Gyges would have been not only a better person but also a happier man had he remained a poor shepherd. No one believes this to be the case. With Gyges' ring, "no one . . . would be so adamant as to stick by justice and bring himself to keep away from what belongs to others and not lay hold of it, although he had license to take what he wanted."[8]

The story is structured to block any easy rebuttal. Gyges' happiness is *not* compromised by sleepless nights, guilt, or fear of being caught. The invisibility factor gives him the fruits of crime without the anxiety. Who would be foolish enough to think any person should turn away from all he is *free* to have? (I remind you, in this context, of Bill Clinton's answer—"Because I could"—to the question of why he had an affair with White House intern Monica Lewinsky. Apparently he relied on the mystique of the presidency to make his doings inside the White House invisible.)

Glaucon has other arguments to offer, but we can leave them aside, since they essentially restate the thesis that justice is not good for us in any way that seems to fulfill our natural human desires and tendencies.[9]

What is interesting is the way Adeimantus, another of Plato's brothers, joins in to support Glaucon. Glaucon presented arguments that were largely of his own making; Adeimantus quotes the established authority of others to illustrate problems with justice. But as Adeimantus reviews the descriptions of the gods offered in Homer and Hesiod, we get a glimpse of how skeptical young persons have become of received wisdom. Adeimantus has read all kinds of pious defenses of justice, but he cannot help noticing that even the gods practice injustice; they are up there constantly warring among themselves. And all they seem to expect from us is a few strategic sacrifices to atone for any offenses, just as Cephalus surmised.[10]

Socrates Responds: The Call to Utopia

To meet the brothers' challenge, Socrates has to address the fundamental issue raised about the individual's good. The looming question is personal and not yet political: why should anyone believe that the seemingly unnatural, onerous, and repressive demands of justice bring about a person's own happiness?

Socrates' response is distinctive, especially for modern readers accustomed to procedural rather than substantive theories of justice. From a procedural point of view, justice is the virtue that permits persons to live together on fair terms, even when they do not agree on the content or substance of their ultimate moral values—on what constitutes the good for human beings. What persons *can* agree on is a framework or set of procedures for fairly resolving disputes *without* appeal to the correctness of their own substantive or religious views on the good life. Only by bracketing or putting aside our irresolvable differences on ultimate moral values do we become capable of agreeing on fair or just terms for social cooperation.

Socrates rejects this procedural approach to justice. For him, it is impossible to know *how* to treat persons fairly—to know what is owed to them—without first knowing *what* is good for them. Justice is a virtue precisely because it delivers to people the goods they would wish to have if they correctly understood what it was that fulfilled their natures and made them happy in the best way that human beings can achieve happiness. This explains why Socrates will argue that knowledge of justice waits upon knowledge of the good. Knowledge of the good is "prior" to justice, in the sense that we must first know what is good for persons

40

before we can fashion just procedures and institutions that deliver the good life.

The *Republic* arrives at its substantial theory of justice through an elaborate construction of a utopian state where rulers with philosophical knowledge of the good use their knowledge for the benefit of persons who lack the capacity to know for themselves what is good for them. Socrates may have famously taught his listeners to "know thyself," but Plato's politics rest on the notion that most people cannot achieve appropriate self-knowledge. Each of us is a person of a definite character type or mental disposition. Some, actually most, of us are dominated by appetitive passions that make us good at, and fulfilled by, a life of producing and consuming material goods. Others are marked by a spirited or high-strung disposition that responds to a love of honor and a disdain for the disreputable. These persons are good at, and made happy by, the life of soldiering and guarding the city. Finally, a few have self-governing souls dominated by a love of reason and knowledge; these and only these persons have the wisdom to discover the good on their own and to govern the city according to that knowledge.

Socrates woos his young listeners into discussing justice in these terms by granting them the power to build their own perfect state from scratch. Nothing is to be accepted because of its age or authority, an approach likely to resonate with young freethinkers suddenly elevated to the status of "founders." Nothing is to be rejected merely because it seems impossible. Socrates demands only that the young follow up on their concern for the place of justice in their own lives with a parallel concern for the place of justice in the life of the city. He suggests that a detour into political thought will help clarify the psychological question at hand by giving us a glimpse of justice "writ large." By looking at a blown-up model of justice as it might exist in the ideal or utopian state, we should be in a better position to detect justice in the miniature, justice in the life of the individual.[11]

This is an odd suggestion, for at least two reasons. First, it assumes that what makes cities and individuals just is the same feature, with political justice being but a larger version of psychological justice. But it is far from clear that any such parallel between how to make a city just and how to make an individual just exists. It might be, for instance, that there is great tension between the good of the city and the good of individuals. Second, the sudden proposal to construct a city is an odd, backdoor sort of way to introduce politics into the day's conversation. Up to this point, when the various young men take turns speculating about justice, they are thinking about themselves and their own individual happiness. They have literally escaped the confines of the city to take their holiday down at the sea, and the last thing on their minds as they await nightfall and the promised light show is to think about politics. There is something of a ruse in Socrates' offhanded suggestion that they build a city in order to find what justice and happiness mean in their own lives. Right away he has *sub silentio* reoriented his students' thinking by premising the entire ensuing conversation on the assumption that there is some connection between politics and psychology, between the qualities that make a city and an individual just.

Aside on Utopian Thought

Plato specifically describes his speculations as utopian, not a blueprint for actual political reform. He did offer more practicable political advice in two other dialogues, specifying in one particular codes and laws and in the other specific qualities to look for in a statesman. Interestingly, in those two dialogues Plato departed from his custom of writing in Socrates' name, perhaps to flag the difference between the practically achievable and the ideal in politics.[12]

Many persons are stymied by the *Republic*'s utopianism and resist it. This is quite understandable; after all, what purpose is served by a theory of politics that can never be practiced? In my own classes, I find that an intriguing debate breaks out each year between the realists and the idealists. For the realists, it is a cause for celebration that politics is the art of the practical. Much like Socrates' students, they give voice to a certain world-weariness with moralizing and are attracted to politics precisely because it promises to get things done. Politics takes place in what, later in the *Republic,* Plato will call the "cave." What the realists want to obtain are the skills to be effective in the cave.

Others also reject Socrates' invitation to construct a utopian city, but ironically only because they are too idealistic. They want politics always to be just and for this very reason cannot abide the unscrupulous methods it takes to change the world. In the Old Testament, Moses condemns the slave generation of Hebrews to die wandering through the desert for forty years, so that only a purer generation born in freedom can enter the promised land. During the French Revolution the Jacobins imposed terror on their own people in the name of fraternity. In more recent times,

China under Mao during the Cultural Revolution sent whole segments of its population to "reeducation" camps where they were to be reprogrammed into the new ways.

It is the idealist, more than the realist, who comes away from the *Republic* fearful of the ruthlessness of those who attempt to make politics perfect. Immanuel Kant once referred to humanity as "crooked timber" that resists certain sorts of straightening. Utopians tend to forget this truth.

Does Socrates? I had one teacher in graduate school who taught, along with many other scholars, that Socrates is satirizing and poking fun at those who have faith in radical political change. A more persuasive interpretation of Plato's utopianism was offered by Judith Shklar in brilliant lectures she offered in ancient political theory to generations of undergraduates before her untimely death at the age of sixty-three. She read the utopian elements of the *Republic* as a lament rather than satire. The lament was for the distance between ideals and reality in political life. According to Shklar, Socrates believed in his ideals but used them mostly as a foil to expose the pervasive injustice of the status quo. Most political theorists teach that one first has to know what justice is before knowing injustice. Mindful of the horrors of Nazism, Shklar inverted the curve of political learning: only when the vice is known can the virtues take root. And for her, few if any works surpassed the *Republic* when it came to awakening our disgust at the pervasiveness of injustice. Here, in its sweeping condemnation of existing states as corrupt, lay the *Republic's* enduring practical significance.

Building the First City:
The Difference between Humans and Pigs

Strangely, Socrates' first attempt at constructing utopia is rejected by the young listeners as their idea of an anti-utopia. Socrates proposes what he calls a healthy and moderate city of need; Glaucon and the others ridicule it as a city fit only for pigs.[13] Here is the difference between student and teacher. Socrates begins by stripping the goods that human beings absolutely need down to the basic material provisions of food, clothing, and shelter. These needs generate economic activity, as human beings strive to produce the necessary provisions. But they do not generate culture or the civilized tastes for art and the like, since art is not a similarly natural need.

But even uncivilized peoples would have been rational enough to devise cooperative schemes for producing material goods. They would have noticed that persons vary in what they are good at producing.[14] By cooperating, the person good at cobbling shoes can exchange goods with the person good at chopping firewood. Both achieve their individual good by agreeing to limit themselves to one task and by exchanging one product for the other. The limits are just because each person does what he or she is talented at by nature, and each receives from the other necessary and equivalent goods that he or she was not able to make as well.

Socrates' vision of the sociability of exchange in this first city is similar to what the economist Adam Smith would make famous as the "invisible hand" by which market societies achieve collective goods through the self-interested motivations of individuals. No one aims at producing for the general welfare, and yet a collective good emerges from the logic of the market.

Over the years I have noticed that my students join with Socrates' students in finding the market city's apparent health and harmony rather unattractive. Glaucon's objection is to the absence of specifically *human* desires from the city of need. Pigs eat, but human beings *dine,* he teases his mentor. Where are the tables, the relishes, the extras in this city?[15] Once more described as "erotic," Glaucon is typically frank in stressing that the only city he would recognize as human is one that is awash in luxuries. What it means to be human is to have a fevered imagination that creates desires which transcend satisfaction of physical need. Nature dictates needs, but humans choose their own wants, their own tastes. (A famous line from a Bob Dylan song captures the erotic point: "Your debutante knows what you *need* but I know what you *want.*")

Here is a sample of the "extras" which Glaucon wants in his city: couches, tables, and other furniture; incense; courtesans; relishes, perfume, cake; paintings, embroidery, gold, ivory.[16] Unless we are building a luxurious city of this sort, Glaucon intimates, he'd rather go off to watch the torchlight parade on horseback.

My students' objections to the city of need tend to be different, more democratically phrased. They are stymied by the starting assumption that each of us is good at one and only one task. Each year, in varying ways, they ask questions along the following lines: Why can't I be a jack of all trades, or why can't I at least want to get better at cobbling shoes, even though right now I am more useful to others splitting firewood? Maybe I'm just tired of chopping wood. Perhaps I've just become lazy and prefer not to work at all. Or maybe it is that I am good at collecting butterflies, though this is of no use to others. Moreover, even if we assume Socrates is right that each of us is good at one and only one task, who decides what that task is? What if there is a surplus of persons good at cobbling? Is there some hidden political authority that shifts assignments around? Or does Socrates mean simply that the logic of supply and demand would cause people to migrate to wherever they are needed?

I tend to think it good that today's students ask questions about economic justice that Socrates' students did not. Remember that Glaucon and the others do not anticipate having to work to make a living; that is why they can quickly dispense with questions about work and justice, and move the discussion to allegedly "higher" planes. But for students who do envision "making a living," Socrates' starting assumptions about justice and talents are troubling. By insisting that persons "specialize" in the one function for which nature makes them most competent, a society according to Socrates achieves justice along the lines of "from each according to talent and to each according to talent."

Even if we accept that nature distributes talents and aptitudes unequally, Socrates' views on justice do not follow. As the contemporary philosopher John Rawls persuasively argued, the distribution of natural talents is arbitrary from a moral point of view—a matter of brute luck in the natural lottery of birth. Luck also governs whether a person happens to be born at a time and place which value his or her particular skills; some societies equate the good with athletic talent, others with money-making ability. From the modern point of view, Socrates never satisfactorily explains why a society is just simply because it reflects the luck of birth and the accident of social values.

As the *Republic* proceeds, Socrates will defend his starting assumptions about justice and equality, but this is a long while in coming. What happens immediately is that the privileged youth gathered down at the Piraeus lose interest in questions about economic justice. They want to discuss luxury, not labor. With a show of reluctance Socrates agrees to expand economic activity to produce unnecessary luxury items, even as he warns that the politics it takes to reconcile justice and luxury will be difficult to maintain.

In any city that caters to the full range of human desires, life inevitably evolves in a military direction. First, desire produces domestic conflicts, as new businesses and production compete for increasingly scare land and resources. Socrates playfully describes the vats and fires of per-

45

fume makers as emblematic of the new and expanding economy, taking up land at the same time that land is more seriously needed to build hospitals for persons made sick by the immoderation of their new desires. At some point these domestic conflicts over land spill over into foreign conflict, as the city seeks to annex land in neighboring states.[17] Enter the existence of war and the need for the city to become a military and not just an economic association.

The Rise of the Military City

No one down at the Piraeus that night seems surprised to find that war is a feature of life even in the ideal republic being founded. No one even asks Socrates to justify going to war with a neighbor for the sake of annexing land. Did that land lie fallow? Was the neighboring state so little populated that no one is displaced by the republic's expansion? Instead the perspective on justice is entirely domestic; no sustained analysis is given as to the effects on neighbors of the republic's pursuit of its own welfare. We shall see that Socrates does address issues of *jus in bello,* or restrictions on the *means* of warfare. He offers a code of military ethics that would keep Greeks from enslaving fellow Greeks, plundering corpses, or scorching the countryside.[18] But absent is a discussion of the just *ends* of war.

In the city of need, the people at large are full participants in the activity of the city. But as a new military city rises, Socrates leaves them behind. They have neither the talent nor the desire to make the transition from economic life to military and political life. To an Athenian audience, Socrates' dismissal of the people at large from the public life of the city must have seemed strange. Aristotle was no more sympathetic than Plato to democracy, but he did reflect the prevailing Greek notion that the polis was a "shared association" between rulers and ruled, sometimes even taking the form of ruling and being ruled in turn. But Plato's ideal republic is not an association between the rulers and ruled at all; his ideal arrangement is one in which a knowledgeable elite class of guardians is raised almost from birth in isolation from the people. By dint of their natures and their training, they come to protect the people, as all good guardians do; and they come to rule benevolently for the people's own good. But it is their *superiority* in knowing what is good for the people, and not their *sharing* similar conceptions of the good with the people, that qualify them for holding power.

At this point the discussion in the *Republic* becomes almost exclusively a discussion about the qualities that distinguish persons for careers as guardians of the city. Socrates refers to both soldiers and rulers as "guardians," and ultimately he will sharply distinguish between those qualified to lead and those qualified only to guard the city in the military sense. But it is with the military that he begins.

Military Psychology: The Spirited Type

Many profiles of the good soldier focus on the physical rather than the psychological. Socrates is certainly aware—how could he not be—that soldiers need certain bodily characteristics, such as sharp senses, strength, and speed.[19] But what distinguishes the person who is fit for combat is not so much the body as it is a mental toughness that makes a person capable of courage. Not all persons—in fact very few—are psychologically disposed to respond to danger in courageous ways. What we are looking for is that rare character type who is "fearless and invincible in the face of everything."[20]

And yet, at the same time, we are looking for soldiers who are not *so* fearless as to be reckless and bloodthirsty. With soldiers, the enduring mystery is how we can arm persons without having them turn their weapons against us.[21] Socrates immediately rules out two possibilities, both of which have a long hold on military history. The first is to motivate soldiers by paying them; mercenaries are hardly likely to make good guardians, since they are only after money and personal gain. A second possibility is to recruit soldiers from the citizenry at large, requiring citizens in turn to put down their plows and take up arms. But there is no reason, Socrates insists, reverting to the principle of "one person, one job," to credit ordinary individuals with the potential for courage. Their appetitive passions attract them to a consumer lifestyle, not to asceticism, self-sacrifice, and a willingness to die for others.

For Socrates, the only persons fit for, and attracted to, the life of a soldier are those rare characters whose souls are dominated by *thumos,* commonly translated into English as "spirit."[22] The translation is problematic because contemporary psychologists do not have any equivalent in their mapping of mental geography. We still refer to a conflict between reason and desire, but Socrates complicates this dualism by suggesting that each of us contains three mental zones: reason, desire, and this middle or mediating ground called "spirit." Although every person experiences all three mental states, we differ in which one predominates. The key to the person who will make a good soldier is a mental disposition dominated by spirit.[23]

Spirit is neither rational nor irrational, neither appetitive nor cerebral. It is the emotional or excitable current in us that functions as a swing vote in the soul, sometimes the ally of reason, oftentimes the handmaiden of desire. But standing alone, spirit is a volatile and disordered source of energy or enthusiasm. We still speak of horses today, for instance, as being "high-spirited." If that spirit can be harnessed and trained, the horse is capable of great racing feats. Unbroken, the horse is unruly and unreliable.

So it is with human beings. There are high-strung, temperamental, or angry types among us. Spirit makes them ferocious, hotheaded, easily aroused to anger, vengeance, and revenge. They are especially sensitive to questions of honor and shame. We need such a disposition in soldiers, but only if trainable. Somehow spirit, which is so naturally volatile, has to be disciplined so that soldiers become "public-spirited." Soldiers have to feel that esprit de corps that makes them willing to die for country.

What makes an individual's mental spirit capable of being put to military and civic uses? Consider the story of Leontius, who was walking near the Piraeus when he came upon fresh corpses piled at the side of the road by the public executioner. Leontius' reaction will be familiar to anyone who has driven slowly by a car wreck and found it impossible to resist straining for a good hard look at the injured, possibly dead occupants. Leontius "desired to look, but at the same time he was disgusted and made himself turn away; and for a while he struggled and covered his face. But finally, overpowered by the desire, he opened his eyes wide, ran toward the corpses and said: Look, you damned wretches, take your fill of the fair sight."[24] Leontius gets *angry* at himself for having the desires he in fact has. Or more exactly, he gets angry at his eyes, almost as if they were in someone else's head. In the end, Leontius' anger is not strong enough to overcome the desire to look, and he gives in to an appetite for gawking. But for a while the anger makes Leontius resist and struggle against the desires he considers shameful. This struggle, and the fury that fuels it, is the sign of spirit at work. Leontius' spirit responds to a sense of shame, a sense of the difference between what it is disgraceful to desire and what it might be honorable to enjoy. In Leontius' case the sense of shame apparently was not quite strong enough to permit his spirit to control desire. But an alternative ending was possible, given the sensitivity of persons of spirit to issues of shame and honor.

What we want in a solider-guardian, then, is a spirited type whose highest passion in life is to do what is honorable. For the sake of honor some persons forgo all kinds of creature comforts; they eschew the normal appetites of life in favor of attaining public honor and esteem. They love medals and badges, ribbons and citations, prizes and parades, fame and reputation. They have an aversion to being thought to have done anything vile.

Precisely because spirit and not reason is in charge of their emotions, these persons are incapable of figuring out on their own *what* behavior ought to be honored. Their psychology is such that they need to be directed toward ends assigned to them by others. But this is good, since the motivation to please others is what moves spirit toward public-spirited uses. We—the city—need to raise, train, and educate persons from early on in life so that the idea of serving the city is bred into them as the highest life of honor. When the soldier's spirit is wed to attaining public honors, then he or she can be a reliable guardian, ferocious on our behalf but protective of one's own.

Several years ago the *New York Times* reported on studies which confirm that the psychology of those craving fame and honor is indeed different from that of persons motivated, say, by a desire for wealth. Fame seeking "appears rooted in a desire for social acceptance, a longing for the existential reassurance promised by wide renown."[25] Socrates' point about spirited types is similar: they take their cue as to what the honorable course of action is from what their society in fact honors.

Spirit is not the exclusive province of either sex and is rare in male and female alike. But the fact remains that some women are capable of serving as soldiers, just as many men are not.[26] This point confuses Socrates' students, since it seems to contradict Socrates' overall insistence that persons of different natures are good at different tasks. Men and women differ by nature, so how can both be good at soldering? Socrates' answer is that the sex difference is irrelevant to the search for spirited types. Bald-headed and hairy men naturally differ when it comes to hair, but no one would think *this* natural difference had any relevance for recruiting soldiers.[27] The sex difference is similarly irrelevant.

Later in the *Republic*, when discussing the corruption of various regimes, Socrates will lambaste women with great venom. I will consider this critique in due order, but it is worth noting now that Socrates' keeping a lookout for the exceptional spirited woman is not an endorsement of sexual equality across the board. Within each sex there are the exceptional individuals who transcend their sex. But outside the guardian class the average person remains very identifiable as either a man or a woman. Even within the guardian class Socrates contradicts himself by having it both ways: while women can be guardians, they can never be quite as perfect a guardian as a man. Female sex does not disqualify, but male sex superiorly qualifies.[28]

Military Education and Training

Socrates discusses education twice in the *Republic*. In a manner of speaking, the division is between early childhood education and higher education. But the two kinds of education ultimately reflect two different careers for guardians. Those dominated by spirit rise no higher than the life of the solider; for them, education is to be conceived entirely in political and utilitarian terms. Soldiers need not, and in some instances must not, know the truth. But they must always know what is honorable. Higher education in the truths about justice and the good life is reserved to those whose souls are dominated by reason and who are marked by their natural superiority in wisdom to rule the city.

Both courses of Socratic education have been criticized. The curriculum for political guardians seems overly theoretical, as if philosophical wisdom is both necessary and sufficient to make leaders capable of good practical judgment. The curriculum for soldiers seems too manipulated, as if soldiers need never learn to think for themselves.

Before pursuing the specifics of Socrates' curriculum for soldiers, I want to broach the general question about when, if ever, soldiers should think for themselves. On the one hand, order in the ranks seems to demand that soldiers must generally follow commands. But the Nuremberg trials made clear that "following orders" is no defense for having carried out a command to commit a war crime or crime against humanity. But how do we devise courses that teach soldiers the difference between lawful and unlawful orders? How do we encourage soldiers to think upon the *legality* of their orders without encouraging them to think upon the *wisdom* of their superiors?[29] The least one could say on behalf of Socrates' "utopian" speculations is that they shine a bright light on real problems of how to educate soldiers who even today are hardly expected to think for themselves.

In the *Iliad* a famous incident occurs in which a common foot soldier dares to question the authority of the general, Agamemnon. For stepping out of line, Odysseus gives the soldier a physical beating. Socrates seems to be approving Odysseus' punishment when, near the end of the *Republic,* he alludes by name to this soldier as a foolish person.[30]

I mention this story from the *Iliad* because Socrates is firm in believing that the education of future soldiers begins, if it is ever to begin, in the nursery with the first stories we read to children. Education for better or worse is taking place all the time, and Socrates discusses three areas where moral character is being formed unawares. The first is in storytelling, poems, plays, and the like. The second is through music. And the third is in dealing with sex. In all three of these areas Socrates places surprising emphasis on *nurture* rather than *nature.* Persons may be born with a natural potential to become soldiers, but that nature is easily corruptible and needs to be trained from early childhood in state-controlled schools and barracks if the potential is to be realized. Socrates takes "the dispositions of human beings as though they were a tablet [to] wipe clean."[31]

Censorship of the Poets

The first order of business is to nurture the traits of character that make for courage. But take a look at the stories and myths we tell young children.[32] What should we do with passages in which Homer has Odysseus meeting up with Achilles in the underworld and asking the greatest of warrior heroes what it is like to be dead? Achilles mournfully responds that he would rather be a slave on earth than king of the underworld, so terrible is it to be dead. Such poetry is fine as poetry, Socrates appreciates, but it is bad politically since it makes children fear death. This fear is the last emotion we should be instilling in the soldierly soul.[33]

Or what should we make of the stock religious stories about the gods on Mount Olympus and about one god overthrowing another, fathers devouring sons, sons killing their fathers, rivals making war on one another, scheming to ensnare and trick humans in their various conspiracies? Such stories, *even if they are true,* should not be told to impressionable youngsters, who might well wonder about the extremes of injustice in the heavens.[34]

The irony is considerable when Plato has Socrates criticize the poets for corrupting the young, since this was the charge Athens leveled against Socrates. We might have expected Plato to bear witness to the evils of censorship and to have been a strong advocate of freedom in education and art for art's sake. But the theory of early education in his *Republic* is quite otherwise. Plato has Socrates turn the table on his accusers, as it were, and make the case that it is not Socrates' new ideas about the gods that pollute the minds of the young but some of the most revered and traditional teachings about the gods. How are we to make decent people of our children if we teach them that the gods are responsible for evil? How are we to raise soldiers to behave honorably if the great Achilles himself was not ashamed to fall apart after the death of his friend Patroclus and then take bloodthirsty revenge by burning captives alive and by dragging the corpse of Hector (who killed Patroclus) around his dead friend's tomb?[35] Do we want soldiers inspired by such bloodthirsty atrocities?

Here is one place where Socrates sets out to reform the heroic ethic as Athenians traditionally understood it, replacing it with a military ethic that would have required Achilles to behave decently even to his enemies. Ultimately Plato will propose a new paradigm for heroism entirely, demoting the warrior king in favor of the philosopher king. But even as a model for warrior heroism, Achilles is unreliable. Homer has Achilles withdraw from combat on account of a quarrel over a love interest in an enslaved woman; he comes back to fight not for the sake of country but to avenge the death of his lover, Patroclus. Socrates finds in such stories the wrong morals for soldiers.

Censorship and Music

An ideal republic controls music even more tightly than it controls poetry and plays. Musical rhythms, Socrates remarks, have great capacity to "insinuate themselves into the inmost part of the soul."[36] Sometimes this is for the good, as when music softens the disposition of a guardian made too rough by time in the gymnasium. But at other times, taste in music threatens the moderation we seek in spirit and sets ferocity on fire. Aesthetics must defer to politics if the city is to train its guardians well.

The details of Socrates' analysis of musical modes then prevalent in Greek life need not detain us, but perhaps we can understand his point by considering contemporary examples. One rhythm—think of John Philip Sousa and marching band music—paints harmonious pictures of orderly patriotic processions. Another kind of music—think of a slow movement from a Brahms piano sonata—is fit for moments of contemplation and introspection. Yet another—the beat of a hard rock song—may be great for dances, concerts, and parties but hardly for study. We do not want soldiers to be contemplative in their barracks listening to piano sonatas. Nor do we want them routinely aroused by the beat of rock music. (During the Vietnam War, a favorite among American troops was a rock and roll anthem, "Born to Be Wild.") This leaves what we do want, the harmonious rhythms of a military march. Socrates' analysis of music in his own time reaches parallel conclusions about the good versus bad influence of music on the young.

Concern for the influence of music on morals has a long history from Socrates to the present. The Third Reich considered Wagner, Beethoven, and Bruckner to be authentic German music; anything composed by Jews was degenerate. In both the Soviet Union under Stalin and China under Mao the doctrine of "socialist realism" made classical compositions suspiciously counterrevolutionary, to be replaced by folk music as more authentic to a proletarian society. In the United States the birth of jazz prompted groups to object to the spread of "negro" rhythms. A later age gave (temporary) voice against Elvis and his hips and the way he too spread black music into the mainstream. Today most young people are familiar with a litany of complaints against rap music for combining lyrics and beat in ways that are said to promote violence.

There are two ways to approach Socratic-like attacks on music. One is to consider the empirical evidence for the allegation that music corrupts the young. But it is notoriously difficult to separate out music as a *cause* of antisocial behavior from cases in which music merely *accompanies* the conduct. The other is to address the moral, not factual, basis for the musical criticism. Socrates was particularly concerned about self-control in soldiers, but many have used his arguments to censor music in civilian life generally. Some years ago Allan Bloom, the scholar and translator of an acclaimed edition of the *Republic,* updated the Socratic criticism of Athenian music into a vast attack on "the closing of the American mind" by the influence of rock and roll, among other forces. Bloom saw his students as becoming less educable, as they arrived at college experienced in sexual matters and distracted by the pervasive playing of rock and roll in cars, dormitory rooms, and college quads. But the book provided no persuasive argument for why students' private sexual lives or musical tastes had anything to do with their education. Students are always students, as Socrates certainly knew, properly swimming in the passions of youth. For Socrates, this opened their minds; for Bloom, it closed them.[37]

Sex Education

This is not to deny that Socrates was concerned with the sexual educa-tion of future soldiers and guardians. He sees military and sexual life in rough competition for the soldier's spirit. The city needs soldiers to be lovers of a certain sort, but ones that express love in patriotic devotion, not in personal trysts. Things being what they are among the young liv-ing in close military quarters, spirited emotions might easily seek satisfac-tion in sexual rather than civic ways. As we just saw, even the great Achil-les permitted his sexual passions to interfere with military duty—once over the enslaved woman taken away from him by Agamemnon, and again over the death of Patroclus. To avoid such distractions, the soldier's spirit must be desexualized without destroying its erotic potential to make soldiers love one another in proper patriotic ways.

Recall that Socrates has argued for recruiting women as well as men into the military. But this proves confusing to the young men around Soc-rates. They are used to exercising naked in the gym and wonder whether it would not be shameful to appear unclothed before women recruits— and equally if not more immodest for women to dare to exercise naked in front of men.[38] Socrates does not hesitate to accept the propriety of men and women exercising together in the nude. The traditional sense of sex-ual privacy has to be revised in favor of the honor the sexes do each other by seeing only the spirit, not the body, next to them.

Aside: Sex in the Military

Consider two contemporary policies of the American military that argu-ably rest on a Socratic basis. The policy on fraternization applies to all military personnel, whether male or female. It regulates conduct and prohibits sexual relations between a commissioned officer and an en-listed member. The military defends the ban on fraternization as neces-sary to maintain the special bonds of esprit de corps. A cohesive fighting unit is one in which love of country is no distant abstraction but an im-mediate experience of camaraderie with persons for whom one is willing to die.

Maintaining the special intensity of esprit de corps is difficult. Soldiers might well be confused about *what* they are feeling for a fellow soldier if actual sex and love are in the air. Moreover, pairings can threaten morale in the troops, as Greeks raised on the tales I have already mentioned about Achilles' quarrel with Agamemnon would have recognized. Soldiers cannot fight one another over sex and still fight well together.

In the story of Achilles and Patroclus, Socrates' students were familiar with the gay variant of the fraternization problem. Recall that Achilles sat "sulking" in his tent over the incident of the enslaved woman and refused to fight. His spirit is finally aroused to combat only when his lover Patroclus is killed; Achilles then responds with an atrocious display of ferocity, as I have mentioned—not only killing Hector for killing his friend but also dragging Hector's corpse until its skin is flayed off.[39] Socrates regards Achilles as letting personal love get in the way of duty and decorum.

But the current American policy on gays in the military goes beyond the fraternization problem. Under the "don't ask, don't tell" policy, the U.S. military accepts gays and lesbians in the service, as long as they keep mum about their orientation. Merely *telling* other soldiers of one's sexual preference is considered grounds for discharge, if that preference is same-sex.

What is so threatening to military life about merely knowing that a fellow soldier is gay or lesbian? It may be that the policy is based on rank prejudice and there is no good argument to support it. But at times the military makes a Socratic-like argument. Spokespersons draw a crucial distinction between civilian employment, where gays and lesbians should be protected against discrimination, and the special conditions of military service. In ways that are uncommon in civilian workplaces, the armed forces train persons to bond emotionally. Precisely because military life asks soldiers to see one another as comrades, same-sex orientation is said to create problems even when there is no actual fraternization. It is one thing for two straight soldiers to say to each other, in the slogan of the Marines, "Semper fi" (always faithful). It is supposed to be a more confusing matter to feel those ties to a soldier who has just confessed to being gay. Confusion, or even revulsion, may tear asunder the ties the military depends on. I do not find these arguments persuasive, but it is interesting how they make use of certain Socratic themes.

The Material and Economic Surroundings of the Soldier-Guardian

Plato completes his account of the rearing of young persons for guardianship by considering the influence of environment and property on human psychology. Nowhere is his obliteration of the line between the political and the personal more apparent than when he turns to issues of housing, meals, property, and finally family life. The modern distinction between "civil society" and the "state" disappears, as the state politicizes all social and family relationships among guardians.

Speaking through Socrates, Plato springs two surprises on his brothers. The first is that they will not be allowed to possess any personal property or to grow wealthy the way rulers customarily do. Instead they must lead an ascetic existence, appropriate to military life. They will be paid no salary but will be supported by the state, housed in common barracks, and fed at common tables.[40] Shorn of private possessions, the guardians can now be trusted not to shear us, their flock. The private incentives that tend to corrupt soldiers and leaders have simply been removed from the environs.

At this point Adeimantus interrupts to ask how such a spartan lifestyle can possibly make the guardians happy.[41] I suppose Plato must have had something in mind when he left it to Adeimantus to raise questions about *individual* happiness in the overall scheme. Remember that, like Plato, his brothers had realistic expectations that they could go into politics and be among the next generation of Athenian leaders. But Adeimantus is not interested in being guardian of the utopian republic, if it is going to cost him pleasures and happiness of the ordinary sort. He has certainly understood the choice of lives Socrates has placed before him—either the private life of economic activity (in which appetites for material goods and a consumer lifestyle can be satisfied) or the public life of the guardian (in which the rewards are honor and public esteem in lieu of money and property).

Adeimantus is surprised a second time when he notices that something else he values is missing from the guardians' lives: the enjoyments of family life. Socrates had slipped in some remark about how men and women must "live together" in the barracks.[42] Adeimantus asks for clarification: why don't the guardians train together but go back to their families and homes to eat and to sleep?[43] Almost reluctantly Socrates announces that they have no families or homesteads waiting for their return. A proper esprit de corps requires the remarkable psychological transformation whereby these young persons regard the country as their family.

Such a transformation would be impossible if guardians had private families. It would be inevitable, in such circumstances, to prefer the welfare of one's own children to the public welfare. The half guardian/half family member would be perpetually subject to conflicting obligations. Think, for example, of the lifeguard's duty toward two drowning children, one of them hers. Assume that (1) only one can be rescued, (2) the chances that the rescue will succeed are equal for both, and (3) there is no reason to value one child's life more than the other's. Which one should she save? To avoid such conflicts of interest, Socrates isolates guardians from the temptations of family loyalty.

The practical arrangements start with immediately removing newborns from birth parents and placing them in a communal nursery. There children will be reared to regard as brothers and sisters all those with whom they grow up in the common nursery.[44] How large a contingent of siblings a future guardian might have Socrates never says. Aristotle, we shall soon see, makes fun of the "weak and watery" bond such fictional siblings could share en masse. (Aristotle wonders as well what happens to the incest taboo in utopia, if no one knows his or her blood relations.) Once their birth children are taken to the nursery, the birth parents no longer know who is who in the nursery and will regard as their children all who were born at approximately the same time.

Abolition of private families for guardians is among Socrates' more utopian proposals. Some of the greatest Greek tragedies deal with tensions between loyalty to family and loyalty to the state; the Orestes cycle, for example, portrays the fate of the House of Agamemnon from the time the general sacrifices his daughter, Iphigenia, to placate the gods and permit the Greeks to embark for Troy on favorable winds. That sacrifice of family for the sake of country sets in motion a series of fated tragedies, whereby his wife, Clytemnestra, kills Agamemnon on his victorious return from Troy to avenge the death of her daughter. Vowing revenge in turn for the death of his father, Orestes eventually kills his mother and her lover, and is then hounded by the Furies for his matricide. But a resolution is finally arrived at, when Orestes demands judgment for his crime and is absolved.

As Hegel famously pointed out, it takes until Sophocles' *Antigone,* performed around 441 BC, before a Greek tragedy portrays the tension between family loyalty and duty to the state as absolutely irreconcilable. Antigone's loyalty to her family demands that she bury her dead brother even though he was a traitor to the state. King Creon's loyalty to the state prompts him to refuse Antigone permission to honor a traitor with proper burial. Plato's proposal to abolish family life for the sake of the state seems a cure for the fractured ethic that Sophocles portrays as having come to disturb Athens.

Politics and Eugenics: An Aside

Turning to marriage, Socrates remarks that the choice of mate is far too important to be left to the vagaries of love. Here again he makes intimate private matters the subject of political regulation. Like many before and after him, Socrates was a believer in the science of eugenics and suggests that the state needs to arrange marriages to control for the quality of their offspring.[45] Socrates' science is of limited interest to us, since it predates knowledge of genetics. He surmises that procreation works best when women and men are in their prime reproductive years, and he wants to be on the lookout for birth defects, secretly hiding away the defective "in an unspeakable and unseen place" in order to protect the purity of the line.[46]

Although there is little to learn from the science of eugenics in the *Republic,* there is much to glean from its ethics. I take it that we now possess the scientific knowledge to engage in the "quality control" Socrates proposed. Fertility clinics can test artificially fertilized eggs for genetic defects before implanting them in a woman. Should they? Clinics typically fertilize more than one egg in order to increase the chance of success. Beyond doing genetic screening on the eggs, should they permit parents to select the sex of the embryo(s) they wish implanted? (In India a sharp rise in abortions of female fetuses occurred once ultrasound testing was common enough for parents to know the sex of the fetus.). Finally, advertisements in college newspapers sometimes seek an egg donor for a woman who wishes to have a child with her partner but cannot produce fertilizable eggs herself. These advertisements sometimes specify genetically linked characteristics the couple is "shopping for": race, eye color, height, intelligence as measured in IQ and SAT scores. Is there anything unethical about this kind of buying (and selling)?

Socrates, of course, would have had no trouble dismissing eugenic selection of features such as eye color, since such a feature has no relevance to the qualities of spiritedness he wished to inbreed. But the race-based eugenics practiced in Nazi Germany did put a premium on purifying the "superior" physical features of the Aryan race and in exterminating the Jews to avoid pollution of the master race. It is one thing to defend Socrates against ridiculous charges that he was some proto-fascist out to practice eugenics in the same horrible ways. But it is quite another to recognize that putting the state in charge of "quality control" of offspring is an inherently dangerous business. In our own country, for instance, laws against miscegenation prohibited nonwhites and whites from marrying, precisely to protect the white race from being "mongrelized."

I am not suggesting that today's fertility scientists are Nazis. To the contrary, there is something profoundly liberating and democratic in using science to treat infertility as a curable disease rather than a moral curse. As opposed to the state-controlled eugenics in the *Republic,* the current new biogenetics empowers individuals and couples to make their own procreative decisions. Still, one of the many things we get from reading Socrates is an occasion to pause and reflect on what goes wrong, as well as right, when we seek to extend human mastery over birth itself.

Privacy and Publicity in the Ideal Republic

In her great work *The Human Condition,* the philosopher Hannah Arendt quotes these memorable lines from a William Blake poem: "Never seek to tell thy Love / Love that never told, can be." Reflecting on this couplet, Arendt suggests a basic distinction between love and politics. Love eschews publicity; it withers in the light and flourishes in the dark. Love is about keeping secrets and hiding places. By contrast, politics welcomes the light, seeks publicity, and revels in public debate. Publicity renders politicians accountable for their behavior. They owe us a public defense of their reasoning, whereas lovers never do. Thus when politics is practiced in the dark, it is bound to go badly. It substitutes emotions proper to love for the reasoning proper to politics. Conversely, when love is "told," it is diminished.

Arendt sees the *Republic* as collapsing the wall between politics and love, between public space and private hideout. Plato's scheme destroys love by making marriage and mating a public business. Whatever else such publicity does for the guardians, it can hardly make them lovers of any intimate sort. Where would they go?

It is not just love that is threatened in the *Republic.* Arendt gives us grounds to lament that Socrates drags politics out of the light and into the "unspeakable and unseen places" where defective offspring are hidden. But politics has to speak; otherwise there is no way to hold guardians to account.

There is much to recommend Arendt's critique. As an analysis of fascism, her book captures the threat of placing politics in total control of private as well as public life. But it will not do, in the manner of many cold war scholars but never Arendt, to read fascism back into history and accuse Plato of being its intellectual forebear. The *Republic*'s regulation of the guardians' private lives is meant to assure that they serve *us*.

Admittedly Plato permitted his distrust of self-interest to carry his political corrective to extremes. His solution to the threat of Thrasymachus and the ethic of self-assertion was to banish the very existence of private interests among those who would be our guardians. This may well be a solution worse than the disease. As Hegel would point out, it led Plato to construct so substantial a state as to eliminate the personal freedoms that Socrates stood for when he taught us to "know thyself."

3

OUT OF THE CAVE AND INTO THE LIGHT—

AND BACK AGAIN?

Equality is not a value in Plato's *Republic*. In another dialogue Plato has Socrates debate a leading democratic teacher of his day, Protagoras. To express faith in the equality of all persons, Protagoras constructed a myth in which Zeus sends his messenger Hermes to give mankind the two gifts that make political community possible—a sense of justice and a sense of honor or shame. Hermes asks how he should distribute these gifts. Should they be given only to some persons, as is the case with other skills such as medical art or sculpting talent, or should they be given equally to all? Zeus instructs that all must share in the civic arts if communal life is to be possible.[1]

This is not a faith Plato shared. His *Republic* is founded on an alternative myth (a "noble lie") which sees human beings as similar in that all are born from the same earth but different in that they are formed from different metals. Crucially, only some persons—in fact very few—possess the mettle it takes to know what justice is. In the Socratic formulation, knowledge *is* virtue. Thus to know justice is do justice; the knowledge carries with it an imperative to conform conduct to reason. But this is not a knowledge that is democratically teachable. Far from Protagoras' extolling the capacity of every person to have a "sense" of justice, Plato makes the requisite knowledge deeply theoretical and philosophical in ways that are beyond the mental capacity of the average person. The average person can follow justice, if prompted by suitable myths that are comprehensible, but only the elite few can actively discover and define justice for the rest of us. Thus political community can never be "self-governing" in the way democracy requires; a rational state is one which draws a bright line between rulers and ruled.

Plato's views on natural hierarchy were already apparent from his search for the few with the spirit it takes to be good guardians. But even within the guardian class, inequality is the norm. Those whose souls are dominated by spirit can climb no higher than the life of the soldier. Only those with the rational capacity to govern themselves can be trusted to govern others. Thus Plato proposes a split among guardians, with a few of the few serving as rulers or political leaders.[2] The soldier-guardian learns the difference between honor and disgrace by following orders. By contrast, the ruler-guardian uses reason to give the orders that are good for others to follow.

Let me reset the scene for a moment. The conversation has been going on for some while now down at the Piraeus. The day must be waning, and night approaching with its headline act, the premiere of a torchlight parade on horseback to honor the goddess. No one has mentioned the nighttime schedule for a while, although perhaps the young men are watching the clock. I like to think they might have been watching the clock, and not simply because teachers have to make allowance for students being students. It is just that there must have been something odd and off-putting about Socrates' entire approach to politics, first stripping guardians of wealth and family, and now culminating in the notion that philosophers should rule.

Socrates' own students go along with this bit of historical reversal (Socrates made king rather than condemned to death, as it were). But don't we do better to express frustration at this point? The very idea that philosophers should rule strikes us as ridiculous, some kind of bad joke, and the kind of remark that gives utopian speculation a bad name. It is a bad joke partly because it is not going to happen. But it is a bad idea for the more important reason that thinkers make terrible leaders. In whatever removed ways they may be wise, intellectuals are hardly in touch with what the people want. In a democracy this is precisely the relevant political knowledge, and it seems far better to ask the people directly about their interests than to deputize the wise to know what people "truly" want.

Of course, this is precisely Socrates' point. The trouble with democracy is that it is ruled by whatever the people happen to want, whether or not the popular desires are just, or even good for the people. Knowledge of the good and the just is no easy matter of introspection. It requires deep philosophical reflection on the human condition that only a few care to, and are capable of, undertaking.

First Sightings of the Future Rulers: Curiosity

How, then, do we find the few who know better than we do what is good for us? As we begin to sort out rulers from soldiers, Socrates suggests that we keep a lookout for persons whose psyches are as dominated by reason as others' are dominated by spirit or by appetite. Only we should not expect to find Reason with a capital *R* stirring in the young; there would be something odd about that. Instead Socrates makes a stunning suggestion. The characteristic we are searching for in students is curiosity pure and simple—curiosity without bounds, curiosity about everything and anything.[3] The more naïve, innocent, and incessant the inquisitiveness, the better. The curious student is a pure dilettante who will read anything, flit from one subject to another, wonder and awe never flagging. Above all, the curious student does not have an "instrumental" attitude toward education, narrowly focused on those skills that will be of use in a chosen career.

What is so good about raw curiosity? To be naturally inquisitive is to have a love for knowing how things work in the world. Just the prospect of knowing excites the imagination. The word "philosophy" in Greek literally meant love of wisdom, and this is what Socrates spies in the curious student: a passion for knowledge for knowledge's sake. It is as if the student gets an erotic charge out of learning, in the same way that others get an erotic charge out of sex or wearing the uniform.

Socrates specifically describes the ideal student's relation to learning as an "erotic" one.[4] Many accounts of learning oppose the discipline of reason to the disorder of desire and would have students accept that knowledge is necessarily a dry and dusty affair. I have said as much to my own students, and will repeat the same warning now: we can hardly expect to *like* every page of the *Republic*. But Socrates was a different and, no doubt, better teacher for seeking to arouse his students' eroticism, enthusiasm, passions, and energy. Unless they were so engaged, they would never find their happiness in the strange journey into philosophy Socrates wishes them to take.

Curiosity and Beauty

How do we educate a student's natural curiosity without destroying its passionate nature? Socrates begins with a topic he believes will arouse everyone's curiosity. We all *see* beautiful things around us, and yet we do not *know* what makes them beautiful.[5] Red and yellow roses appear different, but they both can look beautiful: What is the quality they share that we "see" when we see beauty in both of them? Is the beauty a substance in them, or is it merely a notion in me, the beholder? And then again, tomorrow or the next day the roses wither, their beauty, if it ever was substantial, fades: where did it go?

So it is with people. I am attracted to someone for his beauty, and yet seen in a certain light, at a certain time of day, the person does not *seem* beautiful, or he ages, or I change and the judgment about beauty changes. Socrates uses this common experience to show how, as a visual perception, something as important to us as beauty has no permanent reality; at the level of sensation it is mere gossamer, fragile and fleeting in time. Now Socrates asks us this question: wouldn't you be curious, wouldn't you want to know what beauty *is* rather than merely how it *appears?*[6] What if I could teach you a way of possessing beauty permanently, its timeless, unchanging essence?

It is striking, in a book about justice, for Socrates to start with the example of beauty. The eros of the young is strongly tied to the world of the senses and to matters of appearance. In this dialogue they start with curiosity about seeing that torchlight parade on horseback. Socrates recognizes and even welcomes this visual eroticism. He will, however, try to show, even with something as clearly visual as beauty, that the eyes are bound to disappoint us, leaving us feeling a lack. In the manner of Keats's "Ode on a Grecian Urn," we would prefer that beauty have some permanence, some staying reality beyond the inevitable comings and goings of time and appearance.

Normally we make do by accepting that beauty is merely subjective and relative. But such an admission undercuts the pleasure of erotic life. It is difficult, at one and the same time, to be terribly attracted to another person's beauty and yet be thinking that this thing "beauty" is not in him at all but is merely in my eyes. Worse, if beauty is merely a matter of appearance, then it gives no promise that our most embodied reactions to a person will last.

Socrates seizes on the frustration to woo us toward thinking about beauty in new ways. Consider the common experience that X can appear beautiful at times, but not at others. This teaches us that X itself cannot *be* the beautiful, otherwise it could not sometimes become the not-beautiful. It must be the case that X *appears* beautiful because it "participates" or "shares" in something *immutable* outside itself that we recognize as beauty. This beauty does not change when X changes; it remains always what it is, beauty in and of itself, and we recognize objects and persons as beautiful only insofar as they share in this unchanging essence. In this sense, then, there is an "Idea" or a "Form" of Beauty, and individual objects can embody that form or participate in the ideal for a while.

But if we are really to know what beauty is, then we should be curious to apprehend with our mind, and not our eyes, what the permanent, eternal, objective, unchanging Idea or Form of Beauty is.[7]

The Theory of the Forms or Ideas

Take the case of chairs. In the lecture room where I teach Plato there are various kinds of chairs. Some have four legs; some swivel on one leg; some have one leg broken off and are sitting three-legged off in the corner. They look different, but no one ordinarily has trouble recognizing all of them as chairs. Why? It must be because we have some Idea or Form of Chairness in our minds, and it is against this standard or template that we recognize objects as participating in Chairness. Indeed, unless we had such a mental concept of Chairness, our eyes would simply be bombarded by a mass of atoms and would have no ability to recognize various atoms as constituting a chair.

Of course, no one has ever seen Chairness. There are only particular chairs in the world, just as there are only particular trees and particular persons, all distinct and yet similar in some regard. But although Chairness is not in the visual world, it exists in what Socrates calls the intelligible world. Indeed, it is only the embodiment of Chairness in sensory objects that makes it possible for chairs to be seen as chairs.

At times in the *Republic* Socrates expresses his doctrine of the Forms in a vocabulary about a "higher reality" in ways that may strike readers as mystical or religious—as if the Forms are ontologically laid up in heaven. But the way in which this "higher" or "truer" reality exists is not the same as the way in which the world as we see it exists. The world of the Forms exists only as mental constructs, and is "in" our mind, not out there.

Socrates' talk of a higher reality has to be understood allegorically, as a metaphor to prompt a yearning in us to make the effort it takes to grasp difficult concepts. The theory of the Forms is meant to inspire a sense of imprisonment in us, a sense that what passes for reality is not all there is to the world.

Parable of the Cave

Socrates offers a parable about our imprisonment, a story famous to this day.[8] Teaching this story is always one of the highlights of the semester, and students frequently come up after class to tell me about a cartoon or movie they are sure was inspired by Plato's fable.[9] The story goes as follows. Imagine persons living in an underground cave, open to the light at one end only. They are chained in the cave so they can look only in the direction away from which light is seeping into their world. Higher up is the light of an artificial fire. Between the chained persons and the fire runs a curtain or wall of the kind used in puppet shows. Behind the wall other unseen persons carry puppets, artificial objects, dolls, idols, and wood figures.

The result is that inhabitants of the cave see only the shadows of artificial objects projected onto the wall they face. For these prisoners, *this* is their reality; they have nothing else with which to compare it and hence will treat the mere shadows of puppet figures as if they were real.

It is difficult to see how anyone living in such a cave could possibly learn that it was a cave. But imagine that some persons manage to unchain themselves, to turn around and stare into the sunlight. The immediate experience would be confusing, even painful to the eyes, and most persons would give up at this point, convinced that whatever was behind them was harmful. Still, it is possible that some would persevere and be so attracted by the light that they scramble out of the cave. What would their experience be?

At first they would be blinded by the light; everything would appear fuzzy, out of focus, and less real than what they are used to, and most persons would happily return to the cave. But some may have what it takes to persevere long enough for their eyes to adjust to the light and to appreciate that there is indeed a higher reality out there, that they have been living underground in a cave. What would these few "enlightened" souls do with their enlightenment?

The last thing most of them would want to do is return to the cave; they would leave their home, their neighborhood, their country behind, and make a life for themselves in the new world. So to this extent their knowledge has no political significance: they free themselves but leave others enslaved in the cave.

Still, there could be some rare soul who, having received truth and enlightenment, feels obliged to bring her learning back down to the cave. How will this "enlightened" person fare back down in the cave? When she starts the descent, her eyes are no longer used to the dark, and she stumbles about. Far from seeming wise, she seems dysfunctional to the cave dwellers. Her knowledge and claims to higher wisdom are of no use to them; all they can see is that this supposed learning has made the returning native a misfit in their world.

The parable of the cave is a sobering story. Socrates tells it to give his students a tragic sense about politics. Even if, on a day like today, they succeed in constructing an ideal republic, knowledge of the ideal will always remain politically impotent. Most persons live in a cave and simply would not recognize the truth even if it were presented to them. They would treat the sudden arrival of philosophers as if they were, well, as if they were Socrates, and they would execute them.

The Philosopher Guardian, Justice, and Democracy

Where does this leave us? Socrates wants to hold together two different psychologies in his students that will always be in tension with each other. On the one hand, he wishes them to become philosophers whose highest passions are for knowledge, regardless of its political utility. He seeks to ignite this passion by orienting his students toward unlocking the secrets of the Forms or Ideas. As philosophers, they will achieve the higher pleasure that a life devoted to learning truth can bring.

What makes the pleasure "higher" is that, once we know what the Idea of Beauty is, we can "possess" that form of beauty permanently, in ourselves, and escape from the ups and downs of chasing fleeting and temporary pleasures. To go back to the "sieve" metaphor of the *Gorgias,* certain pleasures sift right through our souls, leaving nothing behind, and requiring us to reap tomorrow a new supply of the same temporary pleasure. This is what happens to most of us who chase the appearance of beauty. But if I approach beauty less as a matter of accidental appearance and more as a mental apprehension of some pure standard or Ideal, then knowledge of that Ideal stays with me, indeed, changes who I am. To repeat, knowledge *is* virtue for Socrates, and this is why to know beauty is already to seek beauty in virtuous ways. Once I respond to the beauty of Plato's words and thoughts, that experience does not fade. It attaches itself to my own being. When Socrates defends the life of the philosopher as the life offering the highest happiness, it is the permanence of its pleasures he has in mind.

On the other hand, Socrates also wishes his students to become guardians and rulers of the city, postponing their own happiness as philosophers in order to go back down into the cave and serve the happiness of the whole. In his famous term "philosopher king" (and queen) he offers a life that holds these two aspects together. The reason why philosophers should rule is that their long detour into the study of the Forms will at long last give them knowledge of the Idea of Justice—indeed, knowledge of the Good and why justice is a good.

No one who avoids this detour can possibly know what Justice is, as opposed to what appears to be justice in this or that city, according to these or those persons. This is Plato's ultimate challenge to democracy. Ordinary people can certainly know their own interests. And democracy can certainly register and retrieve what the people *think,* or *believe,* justice is. But this is the cave talking. Democracy reduces to empowering public opinion, not knowledge. And unless one endorses public opinion as a good way to find justice, then democracy is a flawed form of government. By contrast, rule by philosopher guardians is rule according to disinterested knowledge of what justice truly requires. When we are sick, we go to experts (doctors) who know what health is; when we want to train horses, we seek persons who know how to train horses; we want the pilot of the ship to sail according to knowledge, not the navigational opinions of the passengers. It should be similar with politics, and thus the ideal republic would be one where philosophers rule.

But there are at least two problems here. First, it is difficult to understand how philosophers are fulfilled or made happy by going back into the cave and practicing politics. Socrates has just enticed us with images of the pleasure of contemplating the perfection of the Forms and Ideas, only to tell us now that the happiness of the city depends on our forgoing philosophy for a while in order to practice politics. This might make sense if Socrates allowed that philosopher guardians could use their knowledge of the Form or Idea of Justice to fashion a practical politics; but his parable of the cave tells us that any such effort will end in tragedy for them without doing the city-cave any good. Far from governing according to the truth, the guardians are authorized to employ myths, lies, and deceptions in the cave. They might know the truth, but politics works by noble lies.

It is difficult to see how Socrates staves off the tension between philosophy and politics which his own musings open up. For the individual, the tension is a psychological one: I would be happier avoiding public life and pursuing the more contemplative pleasures of study. For the city, the tension is a political one: actual cities will forever fail not merely to live up to the ideals of justice; they will not even know what it is they are striving for.

The second problem with presenting the philosopher kingdom as the utopian ideal has to do with the whole notion of "Justice in and of itself." Socrates repeatedly discusses justice as if it were something universal and objective, the kind of item it takes a trained expert truly to know. His relentless criticism of democracy depends on persuading us that justice has this objective status and that we should turn to experts, not the people, to discover what it is. But is Socrates right about the objective status of our political ideals? Consider one of his favorite and enduring similes, comparing the state to a ship on a journey ("the ship of state").[10] Many people have different interests in the ship and its voyage: there is the owner and the profits he seeks; there are the merchants who have placed cargo aboard; there is a crew sailing for wages; and there are passengers seeking to arrive safely at their destination.

Aboard real ships, quarrels and conflicts no doubt break out, and sometimes owners, merchants, crews, and passengers vie for control. But the ship is in trouble if the untrained crew is at the helm, or worse, if the merchants aboard decide that their talents for making money somehow qualify them to sail the ship. We recognize that piloting a ship requires expert knowledge and that all are better off if the pilot with knowledge of navigation is left to "rule" the ship. For Socrates, knowledge of justice is to the ship of state what knowledge of navigation is to the literal ship.

As far as it goes, the analogy is persuasive and seems to expose the fundamental weakness of democracy, as if the passengers should rule aboard ship. But we should ask Socrates a question no one does in the *Republic:* who decides where the ship is sailing, what its destination is, and what the purpose of the voyage is? Once this question is posed, the example is no longer damning of democracy. For the pilot's expert knowledge of navigation does not equip him to decide where the ship sails, only how to sail where the others want to go. The decision as to the ship's destination is inescapably a *political* decision, one that is determined not by expert knowledge but by accommodation of the various interests that owners, merchants, and passengers have in the ship's voyage. There is no one, and certainly no "right," answer as to where the ship should sail. It is the same with the ship of state. No wisdom is "higher" or more "true" than the wisdom ordinary people are capable of when they consider charting a course for the state, whether they should stay the course or change direction. Such decisions are not like the decisions we leave to experts on matters such as tuning an orchestra or treating pneumonia. Socrates' search for "justice in and of itself" tends to take the politics out of politics.

Truth, Politics, and Democracy

What light does the parable of the cave shed on contemporary politics? Recall that the parable illustrates the political impotency of truth. In recognition of this, Socrates permits guardians to govern through myths, noble lies, omission, and deception.

An interesting question is whether democratic leaders have similar reasons to lie. Sometimes it is thought that lying is always unethical in a democracy, since the people cannot make informed decisions unless they have truthful information. But some moral philosophers accept that even democracies have need of state secrets, quiet diplomacy, and deceptions necessitated by national security. Democratic leaders should never deceive the people for personal or partisan gain, but there may be occasions when the public good is best served by keeping people in the dark.

The difficulty in actual cases is in determining whether our leaders are indeed lying or deceiving for the public rather than their private good. Consider four cases in modern American history when presidents have attempted to justify some act of deception.

The Cuban Missile Crisis. In 1962 the United States discovered that the Soviet Union had placed missiles in Cuba. Considering the missiles to have offensive capabilities, the U.S. government demanded their removal. After negotiations failed—the Soviet Union at one point offered to remove the missiles if the United States would remove its missiles from Turkey, but President Kennedy publicly rejected this—U.S. forces established a naval blockade of Cuba, and the world teetered on the brink of nuclear war as Soviet ships approached the blockade. The Soviet Union apparently backed down and removed the missiles.

That was the public version. But it turns out that the United States secretly let the Soviets know that, although it could not publicly link removal of U.S. missiles from Turkey to the Soviets' removal of their missiles from Cuba, it would remove some missiles from Turkey in due course once the Cuban crisis was resolved. This is what happened, but President Kennedy never acknowledged such a tacit deal. The public portrait showed a tough-minded president forcing the Soviets to back down. Did the president put out the deceptive version to serve his own political fortunes, or did he believe that publicizing the deal would have jeopardized it? It is difficult to judge either the motives of President Kennedy—no doubt they must have been mixed—or the necessity of the deception.

The Monica Lewinsky Affair. During his second term in office, President Clinton lied to a grand jury investigating his sexual relations with White House intern Monica Lewinsky. He also lied in a deposition in a civil case when asked about sexual relations with another woman. These lies, allegedly constituting perjury, became one of the bases on which the House of Representatives voted to impeach the president. Although Clinton for many months denied that he had lied ("it all depends on what you mean by 'sexual relations'"), he has since conceded that he deliberately set out to deceive the American public. No doubt he did this to protect his own term in office. But he also sincerely believed that no president should ever have been asked under oath about intimate sexual matters. Many ethicists conclude that the public's need to know about the private sexual life of a president is too slight to support impeachment charges, even when a president lies to cover up his behavior.

Weapons of Mass Destruction and the Iraq War. As grounds for declaring war on Iraq, the Bush administration presented to the American people and to the world evidence that Saddam Hussein possessed weapons of mass destruction, including material necessary to build a nuclear weapon. No weapons of mass destruction were found, but it remains unclear whether administration officials sincerely believed that Saddam had them, or whether they knew that much of the evidence was bad but presented it anyway as a pretext for going to war. Suppose, for argument's sake, that the Bush administration knowingly deceived the American public (and the world) about the existence of weapons of mass destruction. Can that deception be justified? Some argue that concerns for human rights justified the overthrow of the brutal Iraqi dictator, regardless of whether the regime possessed weapons of mass destruction. The problem was in marshaling popular support at home and abroad for going to war for humanitarian reasons. On this view the Bush administration did the right thing in seizing on the weapons issue as a way of selling a just war to the people. It may be that the war was not just in any event, but I leave that question aside.

Terrorism and Eavesdropping. After September 11 the Bush administration authorized intelligence agencies to eavesdrop on various international telephone conversations. Some of the eavesdropping was unlawful. When news reports revealed the program, President Bush scolded the press for informing the enemy about secret intelligence gathering in time of war, thereby arguably destroying the program's worth. By contrast, the president defended his "noble lie" to Congress and the American people.

I mention these issues to show that we cannot entirely escape the lessons of the parable of the cave. In a democracy, no one should make the Socratic argument that the people are too ignorant to be told the truth. But in a post–September 11 world, even democracies sometimes act as if it is best that the people not know what their government is doing. In the case of Al Qaeda, their leaders may well be hiding in literal caves as we discuss these matters. The question facing democracies is whether we also have to practice politics in dark and secret ways if we are to win.

Anti-Utopia and the Democracy of Tyranny

In the concluding books of the *Republic,* Plato departs from utopia to explore actual forms of government.[11] By comparing his ideal philosopher kingdom to familiar but flawed forms of government, Socrates hopes to persuade us that his ideal city is indeed supreme in political justice. More than that, Socrates offers a comparison of the predominant personality types in various regimes—from the philosopher king to the warrior to the oligarch to the democrat and finally to the tyrant—until he can oppose two "ideal types" against each other: the perfectly just life of the philosopher ruler to the perfectly unjust life of the tyrant. Such a comparison at long last yields an answer to the question that keeps his students awake through the night and away from the torchlight parade: does happiness come to the just or the unjust?

Plato's cycle of change or revolution from the best regime to the worst could stand as a treatise on its own. As in all his writings on politics, Plato offers a tragic view of change, tracing a constant downward spiral of decay and corruption. The stages through which politics regresses are presented as if they occur in chronological order. But Socrates is mostly interested in ranking various cities in order of their descending moral value. I stress this because it must give us pause that democracy is the next-to-last state to make its appearance.

Within each regime Socrates locates the cause of change in dissent among elites.[12] Unlike theorists of revolution who talk of revolt from below, rising expectations, or uprisings of the oppressed, Socrates focuses exclusively on the inevitable ways in which cracks, fissures, and factions will divide elites and lead one power group to overthrow or replace another. Moreover, elites divide not so much over material issues as over status and honor. Plato's theory of revolution is a theory of respect and resentment.

In the cycle of change, politics and psychology change in corresponding ways. On the one hand, it takes individuals with a certain psychology to construct a certain kind of city. But on the other, the nature of the city rubs off on its inhabitants, reared and educated according to the city's values.

The Crumbling of Utopia

It is with some surprise that we learn that not even utopia is immune to decay. One criticism of utopia is that its very permanence would bore us with perfection; recall the lament that there is nothing as boring as an endless succession of sunny days. But Socrates' vision of utopia is curious in seeing its inevitable demise. Sooner or later even wise philosopher kings make mistakes. They will match the wrong persons in marriage; matings will beget children who enter the guardian class without the right qualities.[13] Factions then splinter the guardian class, as older members hew to the ancient ways, while the misbegotten new ones display taboo passions for property.[14]

Once guardians have a taste for property, they turn on their own population, seizing land and reducing farmers to serfs. The wisdom that once ruled their souls is replaced by the dominance of spirit and war-making. Naming this regime a "timocracy," Socrates considers the way regime change plays out in the psychology of individuals.

Timocracy and the Warrior Personality

He imagines the process going like this. With the introduction of property, the guardians live in private homes and private families. But some philosophical fathers cling to the old way and eschew the new tastes for property and the pursuit of war. The son will watch as others leapfrog over his father by adjusting to the new ways. His mother will complain that the family is being left behind and will blame the father's old-fashioned commitment to reason instead of to honor, war, and property. Her complaints will take root in the son's psyche, instilling in him resentments and a desire to avenge the family's honor. In this way the son's character becomes dominated by spirit, and we witness the arrival of "timocratic" man corresponding to the values of a warrior regime.[15]

Note how much blame Socrates heaps on family life, and especially on mothers. This harsh tone about women's corrupting influence may seem surprising, given Socrates' recruitment of women into the guardian class. In the ideal republic the state has absorbed and annihilated the private family, at least for members of the guardian class. Likewise, the state abstracts political office from gender. Men and women, qua guardians, are judged in terms of relevant features such as spirit that are not biologically determined. But once private families reemerge, Socrates' tone turns especially harsh toward women as mothers. It is they who put the sting of resentment into their sons. As to the daughters who once were also guardians, the account falls silent.

Birthed by women as mothers, timocratic politics and timocratic psychology come into being. But timocracies will not prove stable. The defect in the regime is that love of honor is undermined by the growing love of money.[16] The first timocrats seized property but were not yet seized by it. Sooner or later the desire for money will outstrip the desire for honor; timocracy decays into oligarchy, or the rule of the propertied few.[17]

Oligarchic Personality: Tightfisted Wealth

Oligarchy in turn produces the corresponding oligarchic man, in whom the desire for money is the chief passion of life. Here is how oligarchic man arrives. Once again, the mother puts the sting of resentment into her son. The father remains an honorable man in a dishonorable world. But instead of being honored, he is widely regarded as a fool for refusing to use power to enrich the family. At first the child emulates the father, but he learns that old values hamstring the old man and hasten the family's fall into poverty.

No child "humbled by poverty" can afford a sense of honor. Instead the son gives his soul over to greed and the making and accumulating of money. The possession of money for its own sake is now the ruling passion of his life.[18]

No politics that combines political power and private property in the same hands can prove stable. Oligarchy is really two cities, the rich in their enclaves and the poor in their hovels.[19] Instead of a unity, the city is more like an armed camp where the wealthy few stand guard over the many poor. Such a situation cannot last; the poor want what the rich have, and they seize power in the name of equality and freedom for all. The cycle of change has now arrived at democracy—for us the highest form of politics, for Socrates the next to worst.

The Democratic City and the Passion for Liberty

Democracy is defective in both its political ideals and its psychological moorings. Politically, the democratic ideal of freedom is so tilted toward letting individuals do what they please that there is no unity to the city at all. Walking through a democratic city, remarks Socrates, is like walking through a bazaar or general store: all possible lifestyles are on display.[20] No rulers exist anymore to help persons choose wisely; the whole point of politics has become the freedom to choose for oneself.

To a modern ear, such freedom of choice seems commendable; to Socrates, democracy mistakenly treats freedom of choice as if it were the highest political value, to the neglect of teaching persons to make good choices. In fact the whole problem with democracy is that it dispenses with the idea of there being any such thing as the "good" or "right" choice for individuals to make. All democracy values is the *freedom* of a choice.[21]

Likewise the democratic understanding of equality is flawed in dispensing with necessary distinctions between rulers and ruled. Worse, democracy does not actually deliver equality but empowers the many who are poor to plunder the few who were rich. The hidden rapaciousness with which the many seek equality means that class tensions are constantly being exacerbated in a democracy. As we shall see shortly, class warfare prepares the way for democracy to morph into tyranny.[22]

Psychologically, the insides of democratic man resemble the city in enshrining love of liberty as the dominant desire in life. In retrospect, we can see that the oligarch had a restrained love of money: he loved *making* rather than *spending* it. His psychology therefore was tightfisted, and he kept his family on a short leash, permitting them to spend on necessities but not luxuries.[23]

Such moderation is difficult to maintain. Once some families start being conspicuous consumers of luxury goods, then the mother complains once more to the son about the father's stinginess. She implants in the next generation the desire to spend rather than save, to consume rather than work. In place of the father's miserly love of money, the next generation grows up to love the things—all the things—that money can buy. In this way desire is unleashed in the son's soul. The ruling passion in a democracy may be the yearning to be free. But freedom is understood as a license to pursue desire pure and simple, whatever one happens to desire.[24]

For Socrates, the very love of liberty is what is psychologically corrupting about democracy. The license politics now gives to the individual to pursue the full range of desires inevitably unleashes licentious behavior. There are no standards, judgments, or distinctions between what it is good and bad to desire. All the democrat knows is that we should be free to pursue the desires we happen to have. So democratic man is not a particular man; he is every sort of man imaginable. Political democracy obliterates the distinction between rulers and ruled; in parallel ways psychological democracy obliterates the self-government that comes when reason rules over desire. We feel free, but it is an anarchic kind of freedom, as we flit aimlessly from satisfying one desire to another.

No democratic city can prove stable. The ethic of consumption defeats the work ethic and turns the many poor into idle drones.[25] Increasingly dependent on plundering the rich, the poor become fearful of resistance or counterattack. They are ripe for the arrival of the demagogue, who sparks their suspicion of looming conspiracies. With politics teetering on anarchy, the poor yearn for some strong authority figure to restore order and to quell their anxiety about the counterrevolution of the rich.

Like sheep being led to the slaughter, the poor willingly invite in the populist demagogue.[26] Since they were never interested in political power for its own sake, they surrender it to the supposed savior, who at first does their bidding and completes the destruction of the rich. But with no opposition left standing, the demagogue turns on the people themselves and establishes a tyranny.

Tyrannical Politics and the Psychology of Love

Politically, tyranny enshrines the desires of one person into law. Ironically, the democratic politics of freedom promotes its own opposite. "Too much freedom seems to change into nothing but too much slavery."[27] What is true of the politics of the city becomes true as well for the psychology of private persons. The democratic personality, by liberating desire to rule the soul, prepares the way for a vast psychological tyranny. It used to be that children respected their parents and students their teachers; now everyone is Thrasymachean man, approaching other human beings as mere objects to use for one's own purposes. Every beastly, savage, mad, drunken desire is out in the open and out of control. Eros is unfettered from any sense of shame or prudence, and men now do what they used to dare only to dream.[28]

In Freudian psychology these are the Oedipal desires (the son's de-

OUT OF THE CAVE AND INTO THE LIGHT

sire to have the mother and murder the father), but for Freud their force remains largely unconscious and in the land of dreams. For Socrates, the desires are actually awake and acted upon, and the tyrannical personality "doesn't shrink from attempting intercourse, as it supposes, with a mother or with anyone else at all—human beings, gods, and beasts; or attempting any foul murder at all."[29]

If love of wisdom is the guardian's chief passion, and love of honor is the soldier's, and love of freedom is the democrat's, what moves the tyrant? Once more Plato's tragic vision of life comes to the fore when he names "love" as the guiding force in a tyrant's life.[30] Plato knew and quotes the saying we still use today, that love can be a great tyrant.[31] Love is up for grabs; with the erotic curiosity of the young, the hope is to guide it toward higher loves of learning. But the danger is that love will overwhelm reason and drive a person mad. Nothing has to be tutored more carefully than the great reservoir of eros the young have. But democracy destroyed the possibility of supervision and thus paved the way for love to take its twisted and tyrannical turn.

Whose Life Is Happier: The Unhappy Tyrant

By now, night surely has fallen over the Piraeus. I imagine that the torchlight parade on horseback is under way, but no one gets up to leave. Socrates finally is going to address the central discomfort that young persons feel toward "high-minded" talk about morality and justice. They know they *should* be just, but they want to *want* to be just. Can Socrates in the end motivate them psychologically to choose justice for its own sake? Can Socrates persuade them—you and me—that such a choice would make us happy?

For Socrates, the key realization for young people is that giving in to the tyranny of desire is inherently self-defeating. Instead of controlling desires, a hedonist is controlled by them.

This is so for several crucial reasons.

First, the tyrant can neither love nor be loved. That the tyrant cannot be loved is obvious from the way he never leaves home without a (reliable) bodyguard.[32] The tyrant does not even know what it is like to have a friend, surrounded as he is only by flatterers, sycophants, and pretenders.[33] But the tyrant can no more give love and friendship than receive them. The only way he knows how to love people is to possess them, to treat them as objects whose purpose in life is to give him pleasure. Such possessiveness reduces love to a property relationship that destroys what makes love special in the first place. Far from feeling genuine affection for another human being, the tyrant is so trapped by narcissism as to love no one but himself.

Second, the tyrant cannot even enjoy freedom. We commonly think of the tyrant as the only free person left standing. But psychologically speaking, this is backwards. The tyrant is constantly needy, always lacking some object of pleasure, repeatedly in need of going outside himself to secure or replenish fleeting sources of pleasure. In this way he becomes dependent on or enslaved to these objects. He may think he owns them, but they own him psychologically. His very will to master the world has boomeranged, and he will forever feel some lack, some poverty that he seeks to cure by running after pleasure upon pleasure.[34]

Third, the tyrant can never be satisfied. Not even the most ordinary form of happiness—the simple state of feeling satisfied—is available to the tyrant. There is no end to his desires, no purpose to them, never enough. If you remember the image of the soul as a sieve in the *Gorgias*, the pleasures of the tyrant (conquests, power, money, sex, and so forth) are all fleeting and temporary. Nothing attaches to who he is. There is the need to do today what one did yesterday and will do tomorrow, tasting victory again, having another sexual encounter, getting more gold, and so on.

Fourth, the tyrant cannot escape fear. No one trusts him, and he trusts nobody. Ordinary sleep is impossible; freedom of movement is out of the question; the simple feelings of peace and recreation are beyond him. All the relentless pursuit of pleasure brings in the end is the pain of perpetual anxiety.

With these arguments Socrates has kept his promise to provide a more persuasive refutation of Thrasymachus than he was able to mount in Book One. By interesting his students in politics and focusing their attention on the common good of the city, Socrates has transformed their understanding of their selves in ways that make the former appeal of the self-interested life seem meager indeed. Socrates defeats Thrasymachus by being the better psychologist as well as the better moralist. Simply in terms of the ordinary meanings of happiness—satisfaction, absence of fear, peaceful sleep, friends, love, experiencing freedom—the life of injustice is the most unhappy.[35]

It is one thing to show that the unjust life is an unhappy one; it is quite another to show that the just life is happy, and that the most just person is the most happy. Perhaps neither life is a happy choice; perhaps misery is our fate no matter what path we take; or perhaps some mixed or hybrid combination of just and unjust behavior is the recipe for happiness. How, then, does Socrates prove the positive and forge the connection between justice and happiness, between what is morally right and what is psychologically pleasant?

Whose Life Is Happier: The Higher Pleasures of the Mind

The test case for marrying justice to happiness is the life of the philosopher, devoted to the "higher" pleasures of the mind. The philosopher is the ideally just person because he or she alone knows what justice is. And for Socrates, as we have seen so often, *knowledge* of justice carries with it the moral imperative to *behave* justly. This is a peculiar, and peculiarly Socratic, concept which assumes that ignorance is the source of vice and knowledge its cure. I am not certain we should follow Socrates' lead here; surely there are people who perversely choose to do wrong even when they know the right thing to do. But it is crucial to the Socratic vision that genuine knowledge carries with it the motive force to act in conformity with that knowledge. This is why he can offer us the life of wisdom as already the life of justice.

Wise and just, is the philosopher *happy?* There are many writers who have portrayed great thinkers as suffering greatly. I think of standard accounts of Beethoven as a tortured genius or Michelangelo suffering on the scaffolds as he composed the beauty we see today on the dome of the Sistine Chapel. These accounts portray pain as the midwife of genius and suggest that great thoughts and great unhappiness often march together. What is true of genius seems even more true of the mental frustrations the rest of us experience in trying to make our brains work.

Later in the history of political thought John Stuart Mill will reflect on Socrates' defense of the happiness achieved by living the life of the mind and agree, but only with the telling remark I quoted earlier: "It is better to be Socrates dissatisfied than a fool satisfied."[36] I am not certain that Socrates would accept this rarefied understanding of happiness. However much he challenges conventional definitions of happiness, he stays within shouting range of the common person's expectation that to be happy *is* to be satisfied. Socrates sets out to persuade us that the pleasures of the mind are *experienced* by anyone who can experience them as more satisfying than the pleasures of the body.

Part of what makes pleasures of the mind preferable is that they are under our control. They are "here" anytime I want to enjoy them because they are inside me; they are in fact who I have become by virtue of appreciating the pleasures of the mind. This is why the life of the mind frees, while the life of physical appetite enslaves.

Another reason why the life of the mind is happier is that the pleasures are lasting. Consider the way New Englanders talk about the seasons: what makes summer so pleasant is that it is so fleeting. Socrates generalizes this point to cover all sensory experience. In some fundamental way, sensing pleasure is dependent on sensing pain: the thirstier we are, the more intense the pleasure of drinking; the more tired, the more pleasant it is to sleep. But pleasures of the mind are not locked into this dialectic with pain; they do not ebb and flow but take up residence inside us and form our character.

Who Judges Whose Happiness Is "Higher"?

Finally Socrates reaches for his last argument, one I previewed in an earlier chapter on Book One. If the question is which pleasures are higher, those of the mind or of the body, then we need a judge, an umpire, a referee. But who is qualified to judge? Socrates takes it as a given that persons who experience the pleasures of the mind still experience the pleasures of the body; their love of learning does not somehow disembody them. But the reverse is not true of those who remain addicted to bodily appetites; they simply have never experienced the pleasures of the mind.[37] To use John Stuart Mill's phrasing, we might say that fools do not know what it is like to be wise but that wise men have had the experience of being foolish.

What choices, then, are made by those who have experienced the pleasures of both the mind and the body? For Socrates, it is self-evident that no one who has climbed the ladder and appreciated the joy of wisdom ever willingly kicks the ladder down or climbs back into the cave. No person who has arrived at knowledge says, "No thanks, I prefer ignorance."

This, then, is Socrates' defense of the life of the mind as offering the highest pleasure human beings can know. Has he persuaded us? Speaking for myself, when I was young I found it difficult to resist the invitation to journey upward and onward, from the cave into the light, from the lower to the higher. But it is one thing to judge oneself and to aspire to change for the better. It is another to sit in judgment of other persons and to limit their aspirations. Socrates asks us to do both. He wants some individuals, but only some, to journey with him, while leaving others behind with the "lower" or "lesser" happiness that fits them. Such a use of the "higher/ lower" comparison pushes Socratic politics in an antidemocratic direction. He could have—I think he should have—praised the diversity of ways in which human beings experience pleasure and urged all of us to enrich the reach of our own erotic lives by feeling the passions for learning that we typically feel for the urges of the body. But his views on human equality preclude such an open invitation to the life of the mind. As great as its pleasures are, they are not for everyone.

Socrates does not wield this inequality to justify rulers in simply abandoning the lower classes to their fate. To the contrary, rulers use their knowledge of what is objectively good for different sorts of persons— what happiness fits what kind of human nature—to deliver the good life to everyone. Indeed, in his utopia the only persons who sacrifice their happiness, at least temporarily, are the philosophers, who must postpone the life of the mind while taking up the duties of politics.

But the altruism of the guardians is of a peculiar sort. Even if we accept that they serve our happiness, they still judge us and find us wanting. No political democracy can be built on such a tendency to judge and to rate whose happiness is better. For Socrates, that was the point. For us, I hope it is a point of resistance.

Socrates overestimated the ability of anyone to stand inside anyone else's shoes and judge the internal happiness of that person. And there is a reason he did this which I will try to capture with one personal story. Some years ago I gave a talk at a university on juries and justice. Two of my former teachers, George Kateb and Michael Walzer, were in attendance, and you can imagine I was a bit nervous—well, more than a bit. I argued that the reason why we need to represent different demographic groups on the jury is that there is no such thing as impartial justice, there are only the different views on justice influenced by a juror's race, religion, sex, age, education, and the like.

Afterwards I was aware from questioning that Walzer was sympathetic to my views but Kateb was not. I remember Walzer saying to me, in so many but not these exact words, "The difference between George and me is that I'm all demographics and George is all mind." This remark has stayed with me because it was such a respectful way of locating the difference between two great teachers. Walzer accepted that he was a particular sort of person reflecting in part the particular views and values that come from having been born into a certain community at a certain historical time. Kateb aspired to a more universal sense of self, using the rational powers of his considerable mind to reason not as the particular person he happened to be by birth but as an abstract and disembodied Everyman appealing only to ideas whose truth transcended cultural or biographical influence.

Socrates sees the life of the mind as bestowing on us—or rather on some of us—this demographics-transcending, universal status. Mind ultimately has the capacity to reason itself free and pure of the influences of one's own time and place and to apprehend the objective truths housed in the Forms or Ideas. This is why, strange to say, Socrates' writings on politics and justice are so profoundly antipolitical in the end. Justice floats free of the laws, customs, or traditions of any political city; justice exists as an ideal, but one that can never be embodied in actual political institutions. That justice *escapes* and *transcends* politics was all for the good, as far as Socrates was concerned. It empowered philosophy to stand outside of politics and to offer it judgment.

It was Socrates' great accomplishment to offer a transcendental theory of justice, to teach us that justice is something different from whatever the city says it is. I do not think it an exaggeration to say that political philosophy was born at the moment when Socrates distinguished between power and justice. But its very transcendent status left Socratic justice without practical possibility. It remained to Socrates' successors, beginning with Aristotle, to bring justice a bit more down to earth.

4

At the conclusion of her lectures on Plato, my teacher Judith Shklar would remark that the *Republic* remains the most radical book ever written on politics. Lest we mistake Plato for some contemporary firebrand, Shklar clarified that she used the word "radical" in the dictionary sense of "getting to the root of matters." For Shklar, what Plato got to the bottom of was not so much justice as injustice. The merit of his utopian speculations on what it would take to bring about radical political change was to shine the brightest light ever shone into the cave and on the injustices that fester there. Shklar identified with Plato's tragic and pessimistic sense of the impossibility of reform. For her Plato's exposé of injustice was far more important than any plans he left behind for building Utopia.[1]

In part I pass on to you this tragic reading of the *Republic*. If the book inspires us, it is not as a call to action. Although Socrates was executed as if he were in fact calling his students to arms, no teacher has ever been less guilty of such a charge. The *Republic* is a vast meditation on the unbridgeable chasm, the fault line that separates the task of the teacher from the task of the political actor. The teacher, the philosopher, stands apart from politics and judges it according to ideals. This act of judgment, this criticism, *is* the contribution that philosophy can make. But philosophers mistake both the nature of politics and the nature of philosophy if they permit some burst of idealistic enthusiasm to sweep them over the chasm in a vain and ultimately tragic effort to impose ideals on a recalcitrant reality. To refer again to Kant's great metaphor of humanity as so much "crooked timber," there are some "straightening outs" that just go against the grain. Plato understood but regretted this, leaving us with a tragic sense, both about the limits of politics and about the limits of philosophy.

I hope it does not escape notice that the interpretation of the *Republic* I offer is not wholly pessimistic about change. During that conversation down at the Piraeus, as day turns to night and our attention turns from torchlight parades to the pleasures of thought as we have never experienced thought before, our sense of self shifts. Along with Socrates' own students, we stand back and reflect on the meaning of happiness. This very act of self-reflection, this very seeking of self-knowledge, changes who we are. No one who learns to observe his or her own behavior in some detached and analytic way goes back to being the same person observed. Some of the person always remains in the posture of the observer and critic. This is why Socrates counted on the transforming effects of self-knowledge. There is a kind of moral perspective that attaches to seeking self-knowledge.

In the *Republic* the transformative effects of self-knowledge center on examining the meaning of happiness. Socrates could have tried to elevate his students morally by lecturing them that the concern for happiness is egotism and selfishness, which they must forgo. Certainly we all have heard such lectures. But this is not Socrates' approach. He seeks to work within the proper desire to be happy and to persuade us that happiness, properly understood, already has its own moral compass.

To find this moral compass requires some change in our understanding of happiness. Everyone lives in a body, but youth most of all. It is natural that we seek pleasures in embodied ways; the very intensity of pleasure seems to depend on its having physical expression. I have often thought that it is the great merit of Plato, in contrast to the Neo-Platonists who came after him and claimed his legacy, to accept as quite natural and moral the physical dimensions of pleasure and happiness.

The trouble is that all of us get confused by our own eroticism, but most especially when we are young. There is a Thrasymachean voice in all of us that urges us toward immediate forms of gratification. The voice comes through so loud and clear that we find it difficult to hear any other voice from within. But there are other voices just as natural to us. There are the calls of spirit to a life of honor and the pleasures of reputation and public duty. We are capable of rational reflection and the choice of which appetites we wish to affirm and which we wish to deny. We are moral creatures for whom freedom from being controlled by desire is as important an ingredient in happiness as the freedom to express desire without shame.

At his best, Socrates urges a harmonious psychology in which the physical and mental pleasures are each given their due. The change he works on his young companions that day down at the Piraeus is not that they should think of themselves as if they were disembodied agents of pure reason. The change is only to redirect some of their erotic curiosity from body to mind. Of course there are many passages where Socrates insists on a rigid hierarchy in our personalities, with reason controlling desire. In the subsequent history of political thought, some Christian writers turned these passages into a Platonism that justified a repressive understanding of the need for the soul virtually to escape the body as from a prison. But a Christianized Plato is a far cry from the Socrates who kept the light on for the erotically curious. Unless a young person is alive erotically to the world and to persons in it, there is no motive force to *attract* him or her to others. And without attraction, there is no morality. Far from repressing eros, Socrates seeks to tap into it.

In my mind's imagination, Socrates' students left the Piraeus that day as changed persons, better persons for having reflected on the nature of love, eros, and happiness. But where did they go when they left the Piraeus? In theory their new psychology had a new home in an ideal republic that would provide the social and political environment in which their revamped selves could flourish. But that republic does not exist, and these young persons on the way back to Athens may well be like the philosophers trying to return to the cave—misfits who can never really return home.

Perhaps in somber recognition that he has made it difficult for his students to find their way back, Socrates sends them instead on a final flight of imagination to a mythic and "demonic" place where souls who have lived before wait to be reincarnated.[2] A soldier named Er was once mistakenly pronounced dead, and his soul was taken up to this place. When the mistake was discovered, Er was permitted to observe and to take his report back to us about what to expect after death. Er observed that souls are immortal and that the choices we make in this life do not end there but have eternal consequences. For a thousand years those who lived justly and wisely enjoy a perfect bliss. For a thousand years the unjust pay back tenfold in suffering what they made others suffer. After these years of reward and punishment, souls line up to choose their next life. The choice is free and democratic; lots are drawn, and souls choose for themselves in the order of the lots. Since there is no shortage of good lives, even those choosing last have as much and as good to choose from as the first.

Yet even under conditions of free choice and abundant supply, many persons lack the wisdom to choose a good life. They get seduced by glitter and greedily rush to snatch up a life whose future gives raw meaning to the expression "All that glitters is not gold." By contrast, the wise are patient and rationally weigh the kinds of pleasures being offered. Their knowledge renders them, but only them, capable of making a genuinely free choice. And thus wisdom makes us happy not just once, not just in one passing life, but in all the lives our immortal souls have led and will yet live.

From the republic visited for a day down at the Piraeus to a land visited by Er is a long way. Both places are equally mythic, and in myth at least justice is its own reward. I suppose, as they walked back to Athens from the Piraeus, the young men might have taken inspiration from the myths. Still, the closer they got to Athens, the more they must have realized that the central questions about justice remained to be answered. And these were whether they would find justice at home, and if not, what they should do about it.

5

ARISTOTLE'S *ETHICS*

THE HABITS OF VIRTUE

Aristotle is not for the young. Socrates was fond of students precisely for their openness to change, experimentation, and novelty. After all, it is the privilege of the young to prefer the drift and mystery of what awaits them in life to the firm and familiar anchors of the past. True, Socrates mocks the naïveté with which the young restlessly re-create themselves in their recreations. But it is gentle mockery, lovingly accepting that infatuation with new ideas is what makes the young teachable, as well as corruptible.

By contrast, Aristotle speaks to those of us who are old before our time—sober and mature from an early age, appreciative of, and allegiant to, home, family, and friends. Most young people, Aristotle writes, do not make suitable students. "They do not find it pleasant to live in a temperate and resistant way." Just as old people who suffer from incontinence cannot control their bodies, so immaturity causes young people to lose control of their emotions and to "get no benefit from . . . knowledge."[1] Most young persons make especially bad students of politics because they "lack experience of the actions of life" and "tend to be guided by feelings."[2]

The political theorist Nancy Rosenblum once reminded me that when we were students together, we were old before our time and already knew we would become professors. And now that we are, we tend to think that we can spot those who are now what we were then. There is always a handful, but no more than a handful, of students who think of the classroom as their destination, not some rite of passage to be endured in transit to careers elsewhere. To those students, the future teachers, I suppose Aristotle might be accessible without much prodding. For the rest—the restless—I am disappointed if they do not assert the privilege of youth and resist Aristotle the first time around. I tell students to come back and visit me when they have lived more of their lives, enough to know what it means to be wary of change and protective of familiar ways simply because they are familiar. Then we can study Aristotle. But until then, I expect young persons to scoff at a philosopher who could say (around 335 BC!) that "almost everything has been discovered already" or that respect for "the long past" and "the passage of the years" should make us suspicious of new ideas entirely.[3]

In Aristotle's own time a political thinker known as Phaleas of Chalcedon thought that the crime problem could be solved by a revolutionary redistribution of property so that each had an equal share. With more experience of the world Phaleas would learn, Aristotle wryly noted, that human nature is not so malleable, that some people will still take pleasure in stealing even when they no longer feel the pain of hunger and cold.[4]

Aristotle's attitude toward Phaleas is his attitude toward Plato as well, and indeed to all manner of political enthusiasts, utopian thinkers, and would-be revolutionaries. In the end, they all make the same mistake and exaggerate what politics can do to transform human nature. Limiting our political ambitions and desire for radical change is a good, not a bad, thing in Aristotle's judgment. There is much to preserve and polish in the present. But preservation is hard work for the young, who find it difficult to curb their enthusiasm for novelty in politics as in all things.

Before we turn to Aristotle's political thought in depth, let me pause to illustrate what is at stake in the different attitudes Aristotle and Plato have toward the young. Aristotle was keenly interested in the psychology of moral development—in how we bring up children to be decent persons. For Plato, the key was knowledge—and not just any sort of knowledge but wisdom of a highly theoretical and philosophical sort. Recall Plato's belief that understanding the right thing to do compelled one to do the right thing. Aristotle did not see intellectual sophistication as carrying a moral guarantee. For him the key to good character was *habit,* the instilling of a disposition in children from an early age to take pleasure in *practicing* virtues such as generosity or courage or friendship. What makes a person courageous may be partly a matter of knowing the difference between bravery and recklessness. But it is a far more practical kind of wisdom than Socrates taught, a matter of being raised to exercise good practical judgment about when to be fearless versus what to fear.

Ultimately, Aristotle taught, the morally trustworthy person acts from inclination and without having to puzzle choices out afresh in particular cases. If lifeguards, upon seeing a drowning person a certain distance from shore, had to ruminate in each case whether they could and should save the person, rescues would be few and far between. Moreover, if lifeguards jumped into the water only to gain the fame of a glorious rescue, then they would be doing the right thing but for the wrong motives, and thus even their proper acts would not make them good persons.

Of course, Aristotle seems overly demanding here. Surely someone can be a good lifeguard without being a good person. If I am the drowning swimmer, why should I care why the lifeguard rescues me, as long as he does? Aristotle concedes as much. Still, a person's goodness should be dependable throughout a lifetime, regardless of situation, fortune, or reward, and this requires hardwiring into aspiring lifeguards a connection between desire and virtue. They must learn not only to perform the right acts but to perform them from the right motives and for the right purposes.[5] Or, as Maria Merritt puts it, virtue is secure for Aristotle only when it is in the character of a person to respond emotionally in the right way.[6] W. F. R. Hardie adds that while a good person's choices in life often seem "effortless," they are not "mindless" in the way that, say, brushing your teeth before bedtime is.[7] Virtuous behavior has to be attentive behavior, the product of deliberate choice. Yet the goal of moral education is to make choosing the good over the bad, the noble over the base, second nature to a person.

Precisely because moral life needs to be grounded at the level of habit and character, Aristotle worried that Socratic tolerance for young people's curiosity would leave some, perhaps many, of them free to corrupt themselves in irreversible ways. "[I]t is impossible, or not easy," he mused, "to alter by argument what has long been absorbed by habit."[8] Far from being a carefree time of life, or at least a time safe for trial and error, our younger years are times of great moral gravity, when we get our one and only one chance to develop proper moral character. In a sobering passage Aristotle writes that "from infancy on" our responses to pleasure and pain "dye" character into us, and once set, the dye "is hard to rub out."[9] Hence "[i]t is not unimportant . . . to acquire one sort of habit or another right from our youth; rather, it is very important, indeed all-important."[10]

In an earlier chapter I mentioned President George W. Bush's defense of his youthful indiscretions; he made light of press reports of his wayward ways while young by appealing to the widely accepted view that "kids will be kids" and that he, like most of us, grew up and out of bad habits. Parents frequently say similar things about the allowance they grant their children to sow "wild oats," even claiming that the best way to prevent misbehavior in adults is to let kids "get it out of their system." This is a common argument, for instance, for winking at underage drinking. Aristotle takes aim at arguments of this sort by offering a theory of developmental psychology that insists on the lingering effects of first habits.

It is no accident that some of Socrates' greatest teachings come during young people's parties and entertainments. In the *Symposium,* a drinking party—I mean a serious drinking party—leads to reflections on love. In the *Republic,* the hours before the nighttime entertainment featuring a torchlight parade on horseback are time enough for Socrates to woo the young into conversation about justice. There are no parallel scenes in Aristotle. It is impossible to imagine him engaged with young persons at all, except within the confines of a fairly stiff and formal teaching arrangement. The reason for the stiffness is that Aristotle asks us to feel the gravity, not the normal lightness, of youth.

I present Aristotle's theories in two parts, beginning with the account of the morally good person in the *Nicomachean Ethics.* I then turn to Aristotle's political views and his account of the good citizen. Although I separate out Aristotle's moral and political theories, he will push us to reconnect them.

The *Nicomachean Ethics* and the Virtues of Life

Aristotle's *Nicomachean Ethics* is a great rumination on the moral virtues which make some human beings happy and the moral vices that ruin others. From the beginning of his lectures on ethics—lectures that survive for us apparently only in the form of notes or summaries—Aristotle treats it as obvious and uncontroversial that the good life is a happy life. Although everyone agrees that happiness is the goal of living well, we disagree about what kinds of "goods" we need to be happy.

Some moralists who came after Aristotle did *not* agree that moral conduct aims at human happiness; it is often our duty to be self-sacrificing. For some early Christian thinkers, only Aristotle's paganism permitted him to invest happiness with moral content. In their reading of Aristotle they were only partly right. They were right that Aristotle justified human beings in *asserting* the moral worth of happiness in this world as the highest good human beings could know. They were wrong that self-assertion has to make a person selfish or hedonistic.

Aristotle saw it as his mission, as a philosopher, to listen closely to what ordinary human beings want by way of happiness and to help clarify their ideas and detect errors in their approach. The most common error was to confuse happiness with gratification of desire, whatever the desire happens to be. On reflection, many persons can be taught that the life they are pursuing "is a life for grazing animals" and "completely slavish."[11] One hears echoes of Glaucon's attack on the city of pigs.

Other human beings single out money as the good whose possession will make them happy. Still others praise study and contemplation.[12] In the face of this diversity of common opinions about happiness and human goods, what is the philosopher to do? Aristotle emphatically rejected the notion that the philosopher should simply ignore what ordinary human beings meant by happiness. It seemed to him a nonstarter that philosophers should construct some pure, otherworldly ideal of happiness that had nothing to do with what living human beings actually thought it was. The fact of the matter is, Aristotle taught, ethics is not an exact science.[13] The appropriate methods for studying morals are more akin to those in the political rather than the natural sciences.

Take, for instance, the mistake Aristotle thought philosophers of his day made when they theorized on whether we do better to choose likes or opposites as friends and lovers. Apparently some thought that scientific theorems about elements attracting opposites could be adapted to the human case. But in operating on this "higher level more proper to natural science," these philosophers simply missed everything about feeling and character that makes friendship possible among humans but not between earth and rain or sky and land.[14]

Far from resembling natural science in coming up with proofs and demonstrations, ethics will always be "political" in its methods—reaching conclusions not through some experiment but through correctly understanding the standards of behavior a given city finds honorable. And yet to regard ethics as a political subject seems counterintuitive to what we want from moral inquiry, which is some standard for holding politics to account. What can Aristotle say to the charge that he is guilty of moral relativism, reducing what is ethical to whatever the conventions and laws of a city happen to be?

Aristotle readily concedes that morality is partly relative and conventional and varies from city to city. But it would be wrong to see him as the sort of relativist who denies any natural standard by which to judge the laws and customs of a city. Here is the key. Political life is itself natural and indispensable to the human condition, and it is universally the nature of human beings to live in cities and to associate with one another around a shared or common good. Gods do not need to live in political communities because what it means to be a god is to be complete in oneself. But human beings can perfect their happiness only in association with others; a clear example is friendship, which brings into our lives a good that we cannot possibly achieve alone.

Citizenship in a political community is like friendship in bringing into our lives the virtue and the happiness that come from experiencing pleasures such as loyalty, solidarity, allegiance to a way of life that has become indispensable to a person's own sense of self. Human beings who do not experience the virtues of belonging are, to that extent, less complete as human beings, unable to achieve or realize those pleasures that come only from political attachments. In other words, human nature itself gives justification to the connection between happiness and certain virtues available only to members of a community. To learn the complete set of virtues, then, the student of ethics must not model the inquiry after the methods of natural science but should study human beings as they actually live, in cities—and different cities at that.

Why different cities? After all, shouldn't the ethical ideal be the realization of one global community that has the perfect marriage of law and morality? Here we come to what is distinctive about Aristotle's way of connecting morality and politics. What we gain from living together with others in a political community is the happiness and virtue that come from sharing a common good and allegiance to a common project. But politics cannot deliver these virtues and the happiness that comes with them, unless the community is small enough for members actually to share a common good. Past a certain number of persons or beyond a certain geographical distance, political citizenship loses any grip on friendship and ceases to deliver the moral virtues of belonging. For this reason the highest moral condition human beings can attain is within small and local communities, not in some theoretical world order. Different cities uniting persons around differing conceptions of a life worth sharing is characteristic of the human condition.

Aristotle's description of the polis as a shared association seems closer to actual Greek experience than Plato's description of the republic as sharply separating guardians from the people they guard. Although hardly a democrat, Aristotle locates the ethical content of politics by reference to the ideal of a community of equals in which citizens "rule and are ruled by turns."[15] Later on we will struggle with the severe restrictions Aristotle places on who can belong to a community of equals, but for now it is enough to see how the political ideal of shared association underwrites his approach to the ethical virtues of life.

The heart of the *Ethics* is a typology or classification of the virtues we need to navigate through various common experiences in life. Thus courage is the virtue that governs fear; temperance or self-control is the virtue that regulates bodily appetites; generosity is about money and material goods; pride is necessary to achieve the proper estimation of one's own abilities and confidence in them; mildness is germane to anger management; friendship is concerned with social intercourse; and justice is concerned with all. For all the differences among communities, every community that answers to the ideal of a shared association must practice these virtues. Without them, tensions open up between the morally good person and the good citizen that destroy the very possibility of associating with others around a common good.

Aristotle does not think that ethical teachings are reducible to rule following or law-abidingness. Instead of offering a formula, he presents his teachings one at a time, naming a virtue and describing the upbringing it would take to instill the proper character in persons so as to make them capable of courage, generosity, and the like. Aristotle replaces *rules* with *habit* as the key to moral life. Persons have to be habituated from an early age, through trial and error and the force of example, to learn the difference between right and wrong—and to take pleasure in doing right.

If persons are so habituated, two things will be true of them. First, they will not follow rules blindly but will rely on good practical judgment to know what to do in concrete circumstances. Second, they will do the right thing because it is their character to do the right thing. They will do it without compulsion and in ways that bring pleasure rather than pain. In sum, for Aristotle the moral person not only does the right thing but also does it for the right reason. His morality is to be judged not merely by his acts but by the disposition and character that motivate the act.

Persons with practical wisdom do not necessarily have the philosophical wisdom Plato made the key to virtue. They simply have learned good judgment and are adept at locating the virtuous act in between two vices. Some persons are prone to excess in life: they value money more than it is worth; they get angry more often than is decent; their appetites for food, drink, and sex seem insatiable. Other persons go to the opposite extreme and seem deficient in their ability to express anger, to enjoy physical pleasure, or even to value money appropriately. Good practical judgment characterizes those who spy the virtue in between the bookend vices of excess and deficiency.

In other words, virtuous behavior is the mean between two vices; it is the moderate midpoint. Here is a great quotation from Aristotle illustrating what he dubs "the hard work" it takes to be a morally excellent person. The quotation has to do with moderation in managing money and anger, but it could be true of virtue as moderation throughout life: "[G]etting angry, or giving and spending money, is easy and anyone can do it; but doing it to the right person, in the right amount, at the right time, for the right end, and in the right way is no longer easy, nor can everyone do it."[16] The string of qualifiers rules out any general answer about whether anger or money is good or bad: there are good reasons, good times, good purposes for spending money and expressing anger, and there are bad reasons, times, and purposes. Moral upbringing seeks to implant in the young permanent traits of character that make them capable of navigating the Scylla and Charybdis of life.

Courage

Courage is the first virtue Aristotle broaches in the *Nicomachean Ethics*. It is the virtue that governs fear and disposes persons to be brave without being either reckless or cowardly. Cowards are excessively fearful; rash persons are excessively fearless. Only the courageous person knows what dangers are worth standing firm against, and why.

The principal fear that courage regulates is the fear of death, and specifically the danger of dying in war. This makes courage a quintessentially political virtue, the character trait that makes soldiers capable of choosing a noble death over shameful flight. But merely dying is not the point; Aristotle cites the example of cowards who commit suicide rather than bear the burdens of money troubles or love's woes. The courageous person stands out in knowing what is worth dying for.[17]

Consider this example offered by Aristotle. Two soldiers fight equally well in the same battle, but one does so because he is compelled to by his commander; the other is motivated by the desire to do what is honorable. Aristotle balks at calling the first person brave, since "his behavior is caused by fear, not by shame."[18] Similarly, Aristotle chides soldiers who fight only because commanders dig trenches to the rear.[19]

In acts of courage, the motive is the pleasure derived from seeking honor and avoiding disgrace. Such a motive is far more reliable than, say, the money that motivates mercenaries to fight. Mercenaries are the first to flee when the money no longer makes the risk worthwhile.

But now Aristotle to his credit faces up to a glitch in his account. Any persuasive analysis of courage should lead us to think that brave persons make the best soldiers. But brave persons are likely to be persons who have achieved other virtues and goods in their lives and hence to have every reason to go on living. By contrast, "[p]erhaps the best [soldiers] will be those who are less brave, but possess no other good; for they are ready to face dangers, and they sell their lives for small gains."[20] Aristotle leaves the matter unresolved, but his musings are a chilling reminder of what it must take for the good person to die willingly for country.

Let me take up one final issue about bravery. What if a person does not know the risk at hand? Aristotle insists that moral behavior has to be voluntary; but is an act voluntary if done in ignorance of the risks?[21] Consider, as a study of risk taking, the case of the astronauts aboard the space shuttle *Challenger*, which blew apart shortly after launch in 1986. Sadly, we must add to this tragedy the subsequent explosion that doomed the shuttle *Columbia* when it burned up and broke apart on reentry in 2003. In the case of *Challenger*, a design defect in a shuttle part known as the O-rings made it especially dangerous to launch the shuttle on cold days. In the *Columbia* disaster, insulating foam broke off from a fuel tank shortly after liftoff, damaging protective tiles necessary to enable the shuttle to survive the searing heat of reentry.

In both instances the astronauts did not know the specific risks attached to the O-rings or insulating foam problems. They *did* know and accept the risks inherent in space travel and in human error. But would they have thought their missions worth risking their lives had they known the specific dangers attached to defective O-rings or shedding foam? Probably not: risking life for the glory of country and science is one thing; risking life to see how bad the design flaws are is quite another. Therefore the doomed fate of *Columbia* and *Challenger* is a testament to the recklessness and bad judgment of those who ordered the launches, and not to any heroism or courage in the unsuspecting crew.

Consider another example where Aristotle helps us understand the difference between bravery and recklessness. In the summer of 2006 pro football quarterback Ben Roethlisberger was seriously injured while riding his motorcycle without a helmet. Let's assume that Roethlisberger experienced some pleasure precisely from doing what was risky. Let's assume that there was one pleasure to riding a motorcycle and an additional pleasure to riding a motorcycle without a helmet. The Aristotelian account still pushes us to see Roethlisberger's behavior as that of an impetuous person who could not possibly, on reflection, have thought it worthwhile to risk death or career-ending injury merely for the transient sensation of the wind blowing through his exposed hair. Of course, it may be that morally reckless persons make for great football quarterbacks, but that is another matter.

Generosity

Good people are habituated to be generous, to find more pleasure in giving than receiving. They have the right attitude toward money, as opposed to the miserly (who care more for money than it is worth) or the wasteful profligates (who are careless with money and bring about the ruin of themselves and their families).[22]

It is a refreshing feature of Aristotle's ethics that he does not hector students with some piety against the desire for material goods. In moderation, concern for money is a good thing, and one of the good things is that people with money can exercise generosity. Only the rich can be truly magnanimous with their gifts, endowing universities, hospitals, foundations, and the like. (Of course they usually mess up the moral opportunity wealth presents by being vulgar in flaunting their money and insisting on naming buildings after themselves and so on.) But even poor persons can be generous, since the moral significance of a gift is relative to how much money a person has.[23] This insight leads Aristotle to criticize Plato for depriving his guardians of the pleasure of generosity, since they own nothing with which to be generous.[24]

Spendthrifts certainly give away money, but the trouble is that they do so indiscriminately and foolishly. The spending is so excessive that no one being treated feels as if the gift is personal or expressive of debt, gratitude, or even fondness. While never vicious, the spendthrift's happy-go-lucky attitude threatens self-destruction.

Aristotle is far more critical of the miser than the spendthrift. He calls miserliness a vice that is "incurable" and that only deepens with age.[25] People can lack generosity in one of two ways. Tightfisted people or skinflints are deficient in giving but do not take from others; they limit their love of money to keeping it.[26] Others are prone to what Aristotle calls "acquisitive ungenerosity." They are so wed to money that they gamble for it, they pimp for it, they commit usury and robbery. It is odd to think of robbery or gambling as a failure of generosity, but Aristotle's point is that both reflect a moral character that is devoid of any sense of shame in the gain of money.[27]

Children learn generosity by example from their elders. To see the pleasure in another that comes from giving gifts is to grow up wanting to experience that pleasure. Here Aristotle seems characteristically distant from Plato's equation of knowledge with virtue. It is not so much *knowing* what generosity is that activates it; it is the *practice* of it that teaches virtue by example.

Proper Pride

Courage and generosity are familiar as moral virtues. More controversially, Aristotle lists "pride" in the column of virtues rather than vices.[28] In Christian ethics, humility is the virtue and pride one of the seven deadly sins ("pride goeth before a fall"). But for Aristotle, pride properly exercised is a mean between an excess and a deficiency in ambition. Excessively ambitious persons—we call them vain and arrogant—overestimate their own worth.[29] They think they deserve more than is actually the case. By contrast, some people seem petty, pusillanimous, or small-minded. Their vice is that they lack ambition; they underestimate or rate themselves less worthy than is the case. Lack of self-confidence causes such persons to settle for less than they should.[30]

In between the vices of arrogance and pettiness, Aristotle locates the virtue of "proper pride" or high-mindedness (in Greek, *megalopsychia,* or greatness of soul). The high-minded or magnanimous person "thinks himself worthy of great things and is really worth them."[31] There is no boast here, just an accurate sense of self. Since the properly proud person is merely telling the truth about his superiority, his behavior can be magnanimous. Expecting to be honored, he accepts the accolades that come his way without lording it over us.

Special care needs to be taken to understand Aristotle's rather anti-democratic sense of proper pride. True to our egalitarian leanings, schools today have "self-esteem" curricula that aim to instill in every child an equal sense of worth. Our view is that self-esteem is a basic good in life that each child must possess to maximize his or her potential—whatever that potential is. But Aristotle's approach to pride is relentlessly aristocratic. While he is interested in elevating the self-confidence of "small-minded" persons who in fact are capable of more, he is insistent that most persons should accept their ordinariness and that only the few properly take pride in their capacity for greatness.

I do not think Aristotle has an answer as to how we know for certain what the potential of children is. If we raise children to be humble about their own abilities, then presumably those abilities will never unfurl to their full potential. Take, for instance, giving music lessons to the young. It may become apparent, at some early age, that Jenny is not destined to become the next Yo-Yo Ma on the cello. But does this mean that Jenny should not take proper pride in being the best cellist she can be? To be sure, we do Jenny wrong if we mislead her and tell her that she is great. This indeed would be the pride that goeth before a fall. But telling the truth to Jenny—raising her to know the truth about her own cello playing—does not mean that she should cease practicing the cello or deriving pleasure from *her* playing. It just means taking proper pride, within limits, in her abilities.

When I was a graduate student, one of my teachers related this story about Winston Churchill to show the political significance of proper pride. In *The Gathering Storm,* Churchill narrates his frustration as he waited in the wings, watching lesser men such as then–Prime Minister Neville Chamberlain embark on a policy of appeasing Hitler. Churchill was certain that he was the man for the job. When finally he did become prime minister, Churchill remembers that he "slept soundly" that night for the first time in a long while, "sure [that] I would not fail."[32] A proud but accurate assessment.

I suppose that some of my students over the years, while reading Aristotle on proper pride, have conceived of themselves as future Churchills; I have taught long enough to have taken pride when a former student did indeed go on to high office. But these cases are few. More typical—what makes Aristotle's *Ethics* so indispensable—are those students who underestimate themselves in ways Aristotle diagnosed, students who are convinced that everyone else in the class is smarter than they, that they were admitted by some mistake, that any day now the truth will come out. It is through teaching *these* students, I think, that I have come to understand what Aristotle is driving at with proper pride.

Temperance

Temperance or self-control is concerned with moderation of bodily pleasures and appetites.[33] Like Plato, Aristotle condemns the self-indulgent who seek pleasure indiscriminately and hence self-destructively. They are so enslaved to the objects of their desires that they become gluttons, drunkards, addicts, or they become sexually promiscuous.[34] But unlike so many moralists who came after him, Aristotle condemns those who confuse self-control with self-denial and asceticism. Although the character type is rare, some persons are dead to the pleasures of the body, sexless, insensitive to differences and nuances in taste and touch.[35] To practice self-control as if it demanded repression of the body is "not human," and once again Aristotle points to the barricaded lives of Plato's guardians as robbing these leaders of the preconditions for living a moral life at all.[36]

Anger

People need to learn to control their anger as well as their appetites. Some persons are more controlled by anger than they control it. We describe them as quick-tempered, hot-blooded, irascible, bitter, and even resentful. Other persons suffer from the vice of meekness; they seem deficient in anger, too pardoning, too mild, and too quick to turn the other cheek.[37]

Aristotle confesses that it seems especially hard to find the mean between too much and too little anger. Here Aristotle's concerns seem quite similar to those Plato expressed about modulating the hot-bloodedness of spirit in the guardians. On the one hand, there is something manly about anger that connects it to the capacity for political rule. On the other hand, we need to find a way to teach persons the virtue of mildness without repressing their capacity to get "angry at the right things and toward the right people, and also in the right way, at the right time and for the right length of time."[38] Once again, Aristotle bequeaths no rule for measuring right from wrong anger. There are times to be ashamed at flashes of anger, and there are times to be ashamed for *not* getting angry. Getting angry at children in public for minor infractions is almost always bad form. Not getting angry at someone who insults a friend is a failure of courage as well as anger.

Friendship

Gods do not need friends to be happy because they achieve happiness and perfection alone. But for human beings, friendship is the greatest of all external goods. We know this since "[n]o one would choose to live without friends even if he had all the other goods."[39] The importance of friendship to happiness is evidence that human beings are political animals and that there are certain goods in life that no one person can achieve alone, as the political theorist Michael Sandel puts it.

For Aristotle, friendship is the ideal-type association revolving around a common good. Each friend sees the other as indispensable to her own happiness and counts good fortune befalling her friend as a good happening to herself. Friendship is remarkable in the way it yokes the happiness of one to another. I go to the Grand Canyon, for instance. I take great pleasure in the views, and I write to you, my good friend, a postcard with the simple message "Wish you were here." What do I mean by this familiar saying? Partly I wish you were here so that you too could have the same pleasure in seeing the Grand Canyon that I am having. But I mean more than this if we are friends. I mean that *my* pleasure in seeing the Grand Canyon would be greater if I could share it with you. I sense that, as good as it is to be at the Grand Canyon even by myself, it would be that much better if I could share the experience with my friend. In other words, my postcard is saying that friends share a common good in the special sense that *our* pleasure in seeing the Grand Canyon together is more than the sum of *my* pleasure and *your* pleasure in seeing the canyon on separate days. Anyone who has ever had a friend knows what I am describing, even without ever having seen the Grand Canyon.

What makes us capable of the virtue it takes to befriend? How do we distinguish the true friend from the flatterer, the sycophant, or the person using us for reputation, connections, money, sex—you name it? The world is populated with people who have been disappointed in friendship. Aristotle diagnoses two ills that destroy seeming friendships. One problem occurs when we make friends not because of who the person is but only because of what use the friendship might be. It could be as simple as wanting to impress others with the importance of my friends.[40] It might be more vulgar calculation that I can move up in the world by being introduced to my friend's friends. These seeming friendships end when the person is of no more use to us. The relationship was always just expedient.

An even more common defect in friendship is that we stay friends only so long as it gives us pleasure. In one sense, every friendship is based on the desire to experience pleasure within the relationship. We go wrong only if what pleases us about a friend is some accidental quality about the person—say, his physical appearance—rather than who the person is *as* a person. Aristotle remarks that young persons make and lose friends quickly because they so often choose friendship on the basis of physical passion.[41] When the person's appearance changes or I change or grow up or get bored, the friendship is at an end. In one of his great jabs at youthful immaturity, Aristotle remarks that the young are always falling in and out of love, "often changing in a single day."[42]

Ideally I choose a friend not because she is useful to me, not merely because he pleases me, but because I find myself made better by associating with the friend's goodness. Appreciation of the virtue in the other person moves me to wish good things for that good person. This feeling of wishing the good for another in turn becomes a good thing in my own life. But this ideal friendship is possible only between equals, who can reciprocally appreciate the good in one another. Lack of equality, according to Aristotle, means that husbands and wives can be only sort of friends. Their relationship is geared to sharing the good of children rather than to sharing a good as a couple.

Of course we do not always choose friends wisely, and Aristotle explores the sobering issue of what obligations remain when one friend disappoints the other. If a good person turns bad, then the basis of the friendship is destroyed. Still, since we once were friends, we owe something and should not lightly walk away. We should try to "rescue" the friend's character if possible and abandon him only when the vices are incurable.[43] Even then, we owe some loyalty to the "memory of the familiarity" we once had, though Aristotle does not specify what form this loyalty should take.[44]

Another possibility is that our friend's character remains the same but we grow up and out of the friendship. This is a common ending for childhood friends, and Aristotle accepts that former pals inevitably drift apart as they become interested in different things. Still, what it means to be a friend is to maintain some grip on what once was.

I once heard this story that illustrated the beauty of friends remaining friends. A group of neighborhood kids grew up playing pickup games of basketball. One person outgrew the others—literally outgrew them in height but also in skill. He went on to play varsity basketball at college. Still, during vacations he came home to join in the pickup games, and he did so without making his friends feel he was going through the motions or playing down to their level. Somehow he found a way to enjoy the games, and this permitted him to adjust his game accordingly. The pleasure of playing varsity basketball was one thing, the pleasure of playing a familiar game with friends was another, and he managed to preserve the latter while doing the former.

I have often thought that this loyalty to his neighborhood friends made the guy a better person, even if it did not make him a better basketball player in the end. Life is full of opposite stories of people leaving home, achieving success only by outgrowing friends and family and never coming back. In *Chronicles,* Bob Dylan matter-of-factly concludes that he was simply born into the wrong family, as he packs up and leaves the Midwest for Greenwich Village. In her autobiography, aptly titled *The Road from Coorain,* former Smith College president Jill Ker Conway relates how her sense of personal destiny propelled her to strike out on her own for the academic centers of the United States, even though this meant leaving behind a troubled mother.

Independent Ethical Judgment and the Quest for Public Honor

Aristotle envisions proper moral development as leaving the virtuous person with a "firm and unchangeable character" and with deeply ingrained motives to take pride in doing the right thing even when circumstances makes it expedient to do wrong. Unless morality leads to the formation of good character, a person may lack the ethical fortitude to choose the good over the popular or socially acceptable.

But how do we implant in children the character traits on which virtuous behavior depends? Aristotle emphasizes that even before the age of reason, moral development takes root by habituating children to love what is "noble" and to avoid what is "base" or "disgraceful" or "shameful." Here we reach a conundrum. Who decides what choices are noble and which are disgraceful? Aristotle is fully aware that the sense of honor is a socially assigned or constructed value.[45] Children "import" their sense of honorable choices by reference to what the surrounding society honors. In this sense, children seem not to be on the road to ethical independence so much as they seem to be motivated to do whatever is socially acceptable.

Aristotle never fully faced up to the tension between the role honor plays in his theory of moral development and the ideal of habituating children to have firm moral character *not* dependent on prevailing social customs. He avoided the issue largely because, as Merritt points out, he held to an idealized portrait of Athens as practicing the right moral norms that children would then learn by hewing to the example set by men of practical wisdom duly honored in that culture. But would not something go seriously wrong if children, moved to do the socially "honorable," did whatever was socially "acceptable?"

In this regard, consider, as many moral philosophers have, one of the most famous contemporary experiments by a social psychologist. Stanley Milgram devised a series of experiments in which volunteers were directed by the leader of the experiment, a seeming scientist, to administer electric shocks to a person in the next room whom the volunteer could not see but whose responses to the shocks he could hear. The shocks were not real, and the person supposedly being shocked was "in" on the experiment, but the volunteer knew nothing about this. Milgram found that large numbers of persons overcame their initial moral doubts and continued to increase the level of electricity being administered, despite hearing screams of pain and demands to stop from the next room. Placed in a social situation in which they were assured by an authority figure that electrical shocking was the right thing to do, ordinary persons seemed to lack the independence to act on their own scruples.[46]

Of course, administering electric shocks to a screaming person is not a noble choice, nor does it show good practical judgment about how to choose whether to obey a leader or respond to the apparent pain of others. But that was the whole point of the experiment: to show how persons who appear to be decent in most circumstances can nonetheless obey monstrous commands in certain social situations.

Why were persons not secure enough in their moral character to withstand the instructions of men in white coats to administer electric shocks? Aristotelians place emphasis on the need to instill "firm and unchangeable" character precisely to avoid the danger that our moral commitments last only so long as they are reinforced by the norms of the social group to which we belong, or of the social leaders who claim to embody those norms. And yet if we ask how we fix moral character in children, Aristotle says the key is to instill in them a desire to win honor—in other words, a desire to do what the surrounding society prizes as honorable. It is difficult to see how children, who start seeking honor as defined by society, nonetheless become ethically independent and arrive at their own fixed sense of what is honorable and what is disgraceful. To be sure, Aristotle does remark that the well-reared person *expects* to be honored but does not *hanker* after honor for its own sake. He certainly "does not . . . regard honor as the greatest good." Instead, proper moral development gives the good person a certain equanimity toward social fate. While he typically meets with good fortune in life and attains the normal goods of riches, power, and honor, he "will be neither excessively pleased by good fortune nor excessively distressed by ill fortune."[47] Around him he sees people who are thought worthy of honor simply because they are well-born, powerful, or rich. The morally decent person enjoys a certain magnanimous detachment from all this, never resentful of what others get, confident in his own worth regardless of social fortune, and disdainful of seeking honor from "just anyone."

This is the mystery of moral development in Aristotle's account. We may start by pleasing ourselves by pleasing others and seeking to be honored by them. But we end by understanding that "it is only the good person who is honorable."[48] At this point, having a sense of honor is no longer a shallow drive to win social acceptance for its own sake. It is an internal disposition, a fixed character trait that commits a person to do the good even when it is no longer expedient or socially acceptable to do so. In other words, the moral person has so internalized the sense that virtuous acts are honorable that he acts out of fixed character whenever he is brave, generous, magnanimous, self-controlled, and a good friend. He performs these acts because he chooses to. But he chooses to because this is the person he is.

This, then, is Aristotle's account of the morally good person. Are the character traits of the good citizen the same as those of the morally good person, or are there political duties and legal obligations that override an individual's morality? Is it possible to be a good citizen of a bad city? These are some of the transition questions from ethics to politics that I take up in the next chapter.

Aristotle's views on the "common good" friends share already suggest a link between ethics and politics. My own teacher Judith Shklar, however, wrote me a note dated November 25, 1983, warning me against placing much weight on friendship in politics. The note was vintage Shklar; no sooner has she praised my recently published first book than she hastened to make clear her disagreement with the book's argument. I particularly cherish the following remark: "I don't agree with you about Aristotle, which cannot come as a surprise to you. . . . I remain unpersuaded of the advantages of communal cohesion or 'civic' friendship. I think it is either a fantasy to think of 'community' as very rewarding or simply lack of experience with the restricted scope—not to mention the sheer meanness—of village life." Coming across this letter twenty-five years later reminded me of what is at stake in reading Aristotle, and how it takes a great teacher to point out the stakes.

6

SEVERED HANDS AND POLITICAL ANIMALS

Aristotle's *Politics* begins with that most un-Platonic of questions: what can observation of actual governments teach us about politics? It was James Joyce who had Stephen Dedalus muse that "history is a nightmare from which I am trying to awake." Plato's Socrates has a similar disdain for the political past: the only thing we learn from the study of history is that all regimes are corrupt.

Aristotle is typically more modest in his study of politics. Actual politicians, he notes, have to make do with less than ideal conditions. They must adjust their sights to what is practicable, given existing conditions.[1] They must understand how the institutions in place arose and how they can be made "to enjoy the longest possible life."[2] Even if there is in theory one best or ideal constitution of the sort Plato imagines, it may not be feasible for most cities to practice that ideal. Circumstances necessitate tradeoffs between stability and justice. Thus, since politics is nothing if not a practical art, Aristotle begins by collecting and classifying as many existing or past constitutions as he can find.

From his constitutional studies, Aristotle "observed" two fundamental features of politics. The first was the sheer variety of governments on display: kingships, aristocracies, oligarchies, democracies, and tyrannies. Even as basic a political question as "What is the definition of citizenship" defies definite answer, and requires us to settle for describing how the definition varies from place to place—indeed can shift overnight with the occurrence of revolution or civil war.[3] The same pluralism characterizes the answers we need to give at first blush to questions about law, equality, justice, and the common good: descriptively, every city has laws and a code of justice, but they are not necessarily the same. Presumably the ethics of the good *person* do not vary with politics, but apparently the qualities of the good *citizen* do.

105

Aristotle's second "observation" was of the similarity among all political regimes despite their differences. Every city is a "species of association"; whatever else it may be, a city is a particular way of bringing people together to accomplish purposes each of us could not accomplish on our own.[4] The city is not the only form of human association; human beings congregate in a host of different ways to achieve many different purposes. Men and women join to procreate. Families bring in slaves to meet and manage the daily necessities of households. (I turn later on to the troubling question of how an association based on slavery can be called an association at all.) Households form a village and associate with one another in various divisions of labor to produce economic goods and material well-being.[5]

Like these other forms of human association, the city is a testament to a brute fact about human nature: that we stand in need of one another. But the city for Aristotle is a different, unique, and higher form of human association. Unlike other associations which come into existence "for the sake of mere life," the city exists for the sake of a good life.[6] Uniquely, human beings have purposes beyond taking care of material necessities; we are capable of associating in freedom and leisure around a moral good, in search of an answer to what fulfills or completes or perfects our potential as human beings once material circumstances permit us not just to live but to live well. This distinction between economic associations, devoted to material goods, and political associations, devoted to moral goods, is at the heart of Aristotle's writings on politics. It is also what makes him insist that one cannot study ethics without studying the politics that make it possible for human beings to practice the virtues.

Politics and Nature

To drive home his point about the moral importance of politics, Aristotle coined his famous phrase that man is a *zoon politikon*—a political animal—by nature.[7] To a modern ear the Aristotelian insistence that human beings by nature are political seems odd. We are more apt to approach political life as all about how culture and society, law and government change, transform, elevate, degrade, corrupt, or deter human nature. It was natural for Odysseus to be tempted by the song of the Sirens; it was unnatural for him to be lashed to the mast so that he could not act on his natural impulses. We tend to think of government as so much lashing. But Aristotle's entire conception of the relationship of nature and politics is different; his core claim is that political life liberates persons to practice and to perfect the faculties that make us fully human.

Aristotle makes three arguments for why politics is natural. The first is the "all natural ingredients" argument. Since the city grows up from natural building blocks—men and women having children, raising them in families, their households forming a village, villages forming a city—the whole is natural in the sense that all of its parts are natural.[8] This is not an especially strong argument. Alfred Nobel may have invented dynamite by combining elements found in nature, but the resulting combination is nowhere found in nature and is qualitatively different from its parts.

The second argument is more distinctly Aristotelian. We can truly know what is natural to human beings only by studying persons in whom all the capacities and faculties of which human beings are capable are in fact realized, completed, actualized, or perfected. Take the case of the acorn and the oak tree. It is the nature of an acorn to grow into an oak tree. Nature designs it for this one purpose, and hence we come to know what the essence of an acorn is only when it fulfills its purpose or function of becoming an oak tree. The oak tree is immanent in the acorn, but we know this only by studying the case of the acorn which perfects its potential to become an actual oak tree. In Aristotle's distinct vocabulary, the oak tree is "the final cause" of the acorn's development and unfurling of its own potential.[9]

So it is with human beings. To equate the study of human nature with the study of beginnings and origins—as Freud did by turning to children to explore what is natural as opposed to cultural in human sexuality, or as anthropologists do by turning to primitive tribes as closer to nature than advanced civilizations—is for Aristotle a logical error. Infants neither talk nor walk. Does this mean that language and locomotion are "unnatural" to the human condition?

Aristotle's second argument implies a third way of defending the naturalness of political community. From the chronological point of view, the parts of the city—individual men and women, families, villages—come first and provide the building blocks to construct the city. But from the logical point of view, the city is "prior" to its own parts.[10] Consider the relation of the body part we call a "hand" to the whole body. It may be that the body grows in pieces and that the hands exist before the body is completed. Still, we can know that a given thing is a "hand" only if it is attached to something we first recognize as a body. Cut off from the body, lying as a bloody stump on the ground, the thing is no longer a hand. This is because the function of the hand is definitional of what a hand is, and obviously a severed hand ceases to function—and hence to be—a hand at all. In this sense, concludes Aristotle, the body is logically prior to the parts that compose it.[11]

The relation of individual human beings to the political whole is similar. Cut off from political life and from the moral goods the city makes possible, we can no longer function as fully realized and complete human beings. Take friendship, for instance. As I discussed in studying the *Ethics,* friendship is one of the greatest goods in life, a pleasure that makes us human, but no one self can achieve friendship on his or her own. Friendship completes or perfects certain human potentials and virtues that were always there but can be put into action only in the company of others. Thus Aristotle might say that "friendship" is logically prior to the friends who make the friendship. Friendship transforms, elevates, and enriches the identity of each individual friend so profoundly that we can say the individuals did not come into (full) existence until they were friends.

Aristotle thinks of citizenship and political belonging as similarly natural. There are aspects of my personality that I cannot put into action no matter how adept I become at managing a household, making a living, bringing home the bacon, lying with a man or woman. These aspects are "higher" and "political" in the sense that they speak to the perfection of my humanity that awaits my joining with others to deliberate about what goods we should pursue once the economic and biological necessities of life have been met.

The term "political naturalism" is commonly used to describe Aristotle's insistence that politics rests on natural foundations rather than, say, on the imposition of legal restraints on unruly and antisocial human instincts. For us, accustomed as we are to tracing the origins of government to some definite historical occurrence such as a Declaration of Independence or a French Revolution, the whole notion that politics comes from nature rather than human invention seems rather curious and old-fashioned. Aristotle challenges the basic conceptual apparatus that leads us to think of politics as more about deterrence than fulfillment of human nature.

Critique of Plato

In Book Two of the *Politics* Aristotle turns his political naturalism against his own teacher, Plato. While tradition has it that Aristotle arrived in Athens around 367 to study at Plato's Academy, it seems that Plato may have been away in Sicily at this time. But even if Plato was not physically present, he was still Aristotle's teacher in the profoundest sense of that term, an influence Aristotle felt all around him and against which he came to shape his own politics. In the case of Socrates, surely the teacher had some sense of his impact on the young disciple; we know their relation was close enough for Socrates, moments before the jury sentenced him to death, to mention Plato by name as someone working to avoid that outcome. Aristotle's testament to the importance of his teacher is different; it comes in the form of criticism rather than praise. But it is criticism that shows how deeply Aristotle steeped himself in Plato's doctrines. Aristotle concluded that Plato's approach to politics was fundamentally wrong, and yet it was only by grasping the significance of Plato that Aristotle was able to frame an alternative politics.

Aristotle's core complaint about the *Republic* was that it sketched a politics at war with human nature. Take, for instance, Plato's plans to abolish private property and family life for the guardians. "People pay most attention to what is their own," Aristotle reminded his teacher. "They care less for what is common," and hence "[w]hat is common . . . gets the least amount of care."[12] In Plato's republic, guardians would not know who their own biological children were; all children would be raised collectively and regarded as equally the child of any guardian couple who had conceived a child at roughly the same time. But this means that every guardian would have a thousand (fictional) children and every child would have a thousand (fictional) parents. "The result will be that all will equally neglect" the children.[13]

Plato's mistake, according to Aristotle, was to take a natural bond such as the parent-child relationship and extend it artificially into a tie among all guardians. While the tie between parent and child is a sharp and intense one, the "family" ties among guardians can only be weak and watery. "Just as a little sweet wine, mixed with a great deal of water, produces a tasteless mixture, so family feeling is diluted and tasteless when family names have as little meaning as they have in a constitution of [Plato's] sort."[14] This is not even to mention the incest threat hanging over a city where parents do not know who their own children are and siblings are ignorant of blood ties.

Aristotle launches a similar attack on Plato's proposals for abolishing private property for the guardians. "[T]o think of a thing as your own makes an inexpressible difference, so far as pleasure is concerned."[15] Plato's guardians cannot experience the common pleasures that come from cultivating what is one's own. They cannot even be kind and generous with their friends in ordinary ways, since they have no money to spend. Of course, love of money and property is rightly censured when it goes to extremes. But within bounds, caring for one's own land and family is "a feeling implanted by nature."[16] Plato's politics trade one vice (an indulgent city where self-interest and private property consume all) for another (an ascetic city where citizens cannot express their natures at all).

As is typical of Aristotle, his defense of private property is more moral than economic. Key character traits, such as generosity, friendship, and proper pride, depend on having at one's disposal the raw material to express these virtues, and to derive pleasure by doing so.

I am always reminded when I read Aristotle on private property of the great care my neighbors and I bestow on our lawns and gardens, and the obvious joy we get from the greenness of every blade of grass, while the town common stands unloved and uncared for by all. It would seem that private property gives each of us an incentive to work on our own lawns, but that collective ownership does not carry with it any collective motivation to work on the town common. While we all might benefit from not littering the town green, my not littering is not going to do much good if everyone else continues to litter. Conversely, as long as everyone else is not littering, my lapse back into littering probably doesn't make much of a difference. In modern political science, problems such as these are addressed by those who study the logic of collective action and the problem of the free rider. Aristotle concluded that Plato's guardians had no personal motive to take care of families and property that may belong to the guardians collectively but to no one guardian in particular.

An even deeper problem Aristotle sees with Plato's guardians is the static and bloodless lives they lead. Drained of individuality, they are just so many fungible commodities. Aristotle agrees with Plato that political life should inspire individuals to associate as parts of a larger whole. But Plato overemphasizes unity at the expense of individuality altogether. Aristotle accuses Plato's republic of cannibalizing its own parts, devouring the individuals and households it was supposed to serve. By its very nature a city, says Aristotle, is some sort of plurality as well as a unity.[17] Plato stresses sameness so much that the very achievement of political life—its bringing together of *different* kinds of persons to share a common good—is made impossible.

The argument between Plato and Aristotle echoes throughout the history of political thought. In modern terms, the issue concerns the proper

relation between the state and civil society. In civil society we live as particular individuals pursuing diverse and sometimes antagonistic interests.
In the state we associate around a common good that is not reducible to
overlapping self-interests. Plato thought that a state could embody such a
common good only by divorcing itself from ties to family or economic interests. Aristotle partly agreed but thought that the common good must
be one that harmonizes with rather than abolishes our differences.

One can see from Aristotle's relentless criticisms of Plato that he wields
political naturalism to support "conservative" political conclusions. By
referring to Aristotle as a conservative, I mean only that he favors a politics that seeks to conserve, or preserve, the status quo—to work within
what already exists, building on the good of the present, rather than wip-
ing the slate clean. Since institutions such as the private family or private
property have been around for a long time, that longevity is worthy of respect and gives considerable evidence that human beings were meant to
find good in these ways.[18]

But why? What is the connection between the natural and the good,
what is and what ought to be? Not everything in nature is good or to be
valued. Floods and diseases occur naturally, but this does not mean that
engineers should not build dams or that doctors should not invent vac-
cines. Philosophers have a name—the "ought/is" fallacy—for those who
deduce what should be the case from whatever happens now to be the
case. Aristotle is not guilty of the fallacy, but to see why, we must deepen
our understanding of his views on nature.

Teleological View of Nature and Politics

Aristotle is what we today call a "teleologist." In Charles Darwin's theory of evolution, nature evolves through chance genetic mutations that
happen to provide some competitive survival advantage and hence spread
over time through inheritance to a wider population. At least as far as the
theory of evolution goes, there is no "intent" or "purpose" in mutation
as an engine of evolution, and there is no apparent end state or goal toward which evolution tends—some final evolved species after which evolution will end, having achieved its purpose.

For Aristotle there is immanent logic in natural development, almost
as if nature is pregnant with its own future. Think again of the acorn and
the oak tree. Nature intends the acorn to be part of an orderly developmental process, a functional part of a whole in which the nature of the

111

acorn is to realize its natural potential to become an oak tree. What is true of acorns and oaks is true of nature as a whole. Everything that exists comes into existence designed or created purposively for a particular function. Moreover, the separately functional parts of nature are designed to work together, in coherent and organized ways, to realize the purpose nature assigns to various parts. Thus Aristotle speaks of nature "intending" something by and for everything that exists.

Political life is similarly functional. Nature designs men and women, masters and slaves, to fulfill different functions, and the good city puts these parts together into a coherent functional whole. For Aristotle this meant that there were natural limits to what we can tinker with politically. The whole can hardly function harmoniously if it is not in tune with what nature designs for individual members of the community. Aristotle's teleology regards political development, like natural development, as an orderly process, in which progress comes from realizing the potential in what already exists in inherited traditions and institutions. Of course we do not always see clearly what nature intends for us, and so mistakes are made. But reform is a process of working within existing political arrangements, seeking to understand what constitutes the good life they already make possible and how to hold our way of life to account for fulfilling its own norms and values.

An Aside on Evolution and Aristotle

There is no good way to teach Aristotle without confronting what students must be thinking: that his views on nature are so outdated, so conclusively refuted by modern evolutionary science, as to raise questions about the political views that Aristotle derives from his science. I would be disappointed if my students did not voice this objection, but they rarely disappoint. Aristotle says that nature is intentional and designed; Darwin says it is what it is by accident. What should we make of this conflict?

For some years now I have asked a colleague of mine, an evolutionary biologist, to debate these issues. I begin by reading a quote from Darwin expressing surprising doubt that nature is wholly without "design." Darwin wrote: "I cannot think that the world as we see it is the result of chance, and yet I cannot look at each separated thing as the result of Design. I am, and shall ever remain, in a hopeless muddle."[19] My colleague takes the ear as his example of the way in which nature is, and is not, "designed." If all Aristotle is arguing is that the ear has a design that makes it functional as a hearing organ, then evolutionary biologists agree that nature is designed. But if Aristotle means that the purpose came first and caused the design to be what it is, then Darwinism rejects the view that nature is "intentional" in this sense.

Since our interest is in Aristotle's politics and not science, we typically do not pursue the matter further. But the discussion does frame the precise issue that bothers, as it should, any modern reader. Aristotle applies his teleology to assign discrete purposes and functions not merely to ears, eyes, hands, and the like but to whole human beings. Just as nature had a purpose in mind when it designed a difference between ears and eyes, so nature had a purpose in mind when it designed a difference between male and female, between master and slave. Aristotle's politics makes natural *differences* crucial to making the city a functional whole.

The Difference between Women and Men

As we have already seen, Aristotle singles out the male-female relationship as the most basic form of human association. But it is a limited partnership, aiming only to fulfill the procreative purposes nature intends to accomplish by designing a difference between male and female bodies.[20] In Aristotle's biology the female is essentially an infertile male; she is meant to function passively as a vessel in which the male seed grows. When male and female play their intended parts in procreation, they can enjoy the pleasures not only of sexuality but also of a certain kind of sustained relationship to each other as a couple. But it is never quite a friendship; what they share is at best the common good of having and rearing children. The impulses of nature do not move them to be especially interested in each other's minds. Moreover, the woman finds her own happiness not in asserting some idle equality but in accepting the rule of the male, as nature intends it. The male, in turn, understands that he rules over the female not for purposes of domination but for the common benefit of the family.

Politics should build on these natural foundations to establish laws and regulations for marriage and child rearing. Since the purpose of marriage is procreation, not friendship, Aristotle can make the otherwise odd suggestion that men should typically be close to twenty years older than their spouses, so that women of eighteen, for instance, should marry men of thirty-seven.[21] Aristotle derives his marital math from the fact that men typically remain potent until the age of seventy, whereas women on average reach menopause at fifty. To make their periods of sexual potency overlap, Aristotle therefore suggests the thirty-seven/eighteen starting point (he justifies having girls wait until eighteen to marry and bear children, on the theory that the female body takes that long to mature into a form that can produce strong offspring). Of course Aristotle never quite gets around to discussing what the unmarried male is doing with his potency prior to the age of thirty-seven.

When it comes to prenatal care, Aristotle justifies a wide-ranging set of regulations in the name of what is natural. On the one hand, we should pass laws mandating exercise regimens for pregnant women, since the fetus takes its nourishment from the female body.[22] This natural fact means that how a woman treats her body during pregnancy is not just a private matter affecting her but a public health matter affecting the next generation. On the other hand, Aristotle oddly held to the notion that the mental development of the fetus is wholly unrelated to the mind of the woman; the fetus was thought to derive its mental inheritance strictly from the male. So politics has no interest in having a pregnant woman exercise her mind. It is not at all relevant to her fulfilling her natural function.

As the political theorist Susan Moller Okin pointed out in her groundbreaking book *Women in Western Political Thought,* Aristotle permits the woman's sexual function to negate the rest of her being, as if a woman's doing anything other than childbearing and child rearing would undermine reproduction of the species.[23] Okin persuasively took Aristotle to task for his biological reductionism, as if the mere physical difference in sexual organs determined a woman's destiny. In a famous passage Aristotle questions whether women are capable of subordinating their emotions to the commands of justice, but here Okin shows that Aristotle was not having politics *follow* some natural imperative so much as having his politics socially construct different gender roles for women and men in public and then legislatively enforce them through the likes of the marriage age laws and educational policies I have just reviewed.

Finally, there was the proverbial double standard in Aristotle's writings. When it came to women, he insisted that the reproductive design of their bodies signaled nature's intent that women function as reproductive vessels and *nothing else.* When it came to men, also designed by nature to play a functional role in reproduction, Aristotle saw no conflict in their having multiple functions in life, some reproductive, some political. He never made clear why the smooth functioning of nature was *not* inter-fered with when males discharged multiple functions but would be if women aspired to do anything else in life other than to bear and raise children. It might be—it certainly was and mostly still is the case—that men count on women to do the domestic work so as to free themselves for other occupations. But the mere fact that men have enforced inequal-ity on women does not make it right, and Okin relentlessly came after Aristotle for the weakness of his arguments that nature justified the tradi-tional arrangements when, in her view, the better explanation had only to do with the unjust use of male physical and economic power to domi-nate women.

Susan Okin was my friend and colleague for many years until she died suddenly in 2003, at the age of fifty-seven. I cannot teach Aristotle, or for that matter any political theorist, without conjuring up her presence or thinking back over the many years when we taught together the material from which this book derives. I will turn to Okin's lasting scholarly con-tributions in a subsequent chapter, but I pause to note here the way in which she changed the teaching of political theory.[24] For her, the flaw in Western political thought when it came to women was not some isolated defect relevant only to the case of women but one which exposed system-atic problems with prevailing theories of justice. These theories divided life into public and private spheres and then concluded that affairs of the family were somehow affairs of the heart, not matters of justice, and hence should be left for family members themselves to sort out, free from governmental interference. For Okin, the treatment of women *in* the family was no mere side issue but a fundamental indictment of justice both in the developed nations and in the developing world.

Even those who sympathized with Okin's criticisms often felt that she went too far. For instance, few persons today defend Aristotle's views on women, but they think they can be lopped off, without any damage to the rest of his philosophical system. Okin's critique was far more radical; her point was that Aristotle's entire system depended on the subordina-tion of women, and hence his politics cannot be made gender neutral. To take one example, Aristotle's views on the realm of freedom (for some men) assume the leisure time that comes only from the possession of slaves and women to do the economic and domestic work. By focusing on the reduction of women to functional supporters of male freedom, Okin meant to force a broad reanalysis of the hidden and not so hidden exploitations that support the freedom of the few. In this regard, there is an intimate connection between what Aristotle says about women and what he says about slaves. I turn now to that topic.

Master-Slave Distinction

Aristotle defends slavery, in theory and sometimes in practice, as a natural and just institution.[25] It will not do to excuse Aristotle by trotting out the familiar saw that he was the product of his times or merely echoed prevailing cultural values. Contemporaries of Aristotle argued strongly for the abolition of slavery, and Aristotle was familiar with their position. As he summarizes it, there are those "who regard control of slaves by a master as contrary to nature." They "view the distinction of master and slave [as] due to law [and] based on force," and hence as an institution that "has no warrant in justice."[26] It would be difficult to state the antislavery position more succinctly, and yet having summarized the abolitionist's argument, Aristotle proceeds to reject it.

Aristotle has enough respect for the antislavery position to acknowledge that *some* of the ways Greeks enslave persons are wrong.[27] The solution, however, is not to abolish slavery but to bring it more perfectly in tune with the intent of nature, which, as in all things, is to differentiate the ruling element from the ruled.

He begins the defense with a hypothetical. *If* nature created some persons who were but "animate articles of property," whose function was precisely to be an instrument of labor, then it would be just for a master to enslave such persons. It would be just because the institution would be benign and based on delivering to both slave and master the best lives possible and the lives that fulfill their natural telos.[28]

But are there actually natural inequalities of this extreme sort? Are some persons really but tools of labor? In the case of male and female, nature erects, for the most part, an unambiguous physical distinction to mark its intent. In the case of master and slave, nature for Aristotle likewise intends to design different bodies for different functions, though here he acknowledges that the telltale signs of natural difference are harder to detect. Indeed the "contrary of nature's intentions . . . often happens," and bodies capable of great physical labor are given to persons who nonetheless are not meant to labor.[29]

One possibility that Aristotle considers but rejects is that the female is also meant to be the slave, and so we can rely on the clear difference between female and male to distinguish slave from master. Aristotle rejects this possibility by saying that "[n]ature makes nothing in a miserly spirit."[30] The female body is specifically designed for purposes of procreation, the slave body is specifically designed for the purposes of labor, and the two must be kept separate.

At this point Aristotle is quite aware that his argument is strictly hypothetical. *If* we assume for argument's sake that some people are so devoid of reason that they function only as an instrument of labor in the hands of another, then slavery might befit and fulfill such persons' natures. But now, to his credit, Aristotle acknowledges that "actual" or "legal" slavery does not quite rest on this imagined basis. In real life, slaves are taken by force and conquest: as the saying goes, "to the victors in war go the spoils."[31]

Shifting grounds, Aristotle now turns into a critic of those who would justify slavery and the existing conventions. What is just about enslaving an enemy? Are we saying that might makes right? Do we believe that military superiority is the right sort of superiority to justify holding slaves? By asking such questions, Aristotle means to prod his own culture to bring its practices more in line with the norms of that culture, properly understood upon reflection. When fair-minded persons stop to think about it, they will come to understand that force cannot possibly provide a moral basis for slavery.

The key piece of evidence here is that Greeks do not enslave fellow Greeks, even when they defeat a rival city in war.[32] In these circumstances Greeks already understand that might does not make right, and Aristotle pushes his culture to extend this insight by reforming prevailing laws on slavery to bring the institution ever closer to the ideal of natural slavery. The guidepost for reform is that there is implicit in existing traditions a consensus that superiority in moral goodness, rather than in use of physical force, is what we expect from a master in relation to a slave.

By shifting the basis of slavery from superiority in war to superiority in moral goodness, Aristotle can then argue that slavery is a benign institution. From the slave's point of view, the association with a master brings reason and direction into a life that is without it and permits the slave to fulfill his natural function. From the master's point of view, leaving work and labor to the slave frees him to fulfill the higher functions for which he was designed.[33]

At this point Aristotle's defense of slavery stops. He has defended the institution in theory but acknowledged its abuses in practice. Reforms, but not outright abolition, are the way forward. But so many questions are pending. What does a master do to enforce slavery on an unwilling person, and what happens to the supposedly benign nature of the institution if force is necessary to maintain it? Does it matter to Aristotle whether a slave understands and accepts the enslavement as good for him? But if a slave is capable of self-understanding, then the slave must possess reason after all, and how is this consistent with Aristotle's definition of the slave as property, not person? Likewise, Aristotle says that the slave lacks reason and is dependent on the reason of the master to direct the labor of his body. But Aristotle also says that the slave, in association with a master, is capable of apprehending and understanding reason and absorbing knowledge from the master. This does not seem consistent—to define the slave as without reason but then to make the slave rational enough to be goal-oriented once the master lays out the goals of labor.

There are other questions Aristotle does not answer. Is the condition of slavery inherited, or can slaves give birth to freeborn children, just as masters can give birth to slaves? Plato at least addressed such questions in the case of the guardian class and how status as a guardian passes to the next generation. Aristotle has no similar account of whether in practice slavery is necessarily a caste system.

Aristotle goes wrong in conceiving of slavery as a benign institution, since slavery of any sort is by definition never a matter of choice but a coerced condition that strips persons in perpetuity of making free choices. But what about the masters? Is Aristotle right that slavery is at least good for *them?* In the history of political thought, some of the most astute criticisms of Aristotle on slavery take aim at the harm slavery does to the master as well as the slave. Here there are two major points. The first and more obvious one is that exercising mastery over another human being makes the master morally worse rather than morally better and reduces him to monstrous forms of behavior to maintain a person in captivity against his will.

The second and more obscure point was powerfully argued by Hegel and then by Karl Marx. Aristotle assumes that freedom from labor is the key to developing the "higher" and "moral" and "creative" faculties that elevate our humanity and fuel progress. But Marx argued that Aristotle had it backwards, that human progress comes from physical labor—that it is physical labor that is the dynamic and transformative force in life, creating economic value, new products, and discoveries in life. Cut off from the creativity of labor, the master class withers on the vine, retired into a way of life that leaves it dead and antiquated before the march of history. Hegel puts the point in terms of the master's ironic dependency on his slaves. What Aristotle supposed would make the master free and independent actually has the opposite effect, perpetuating a dependency on slaves that the master cannot control.

Justice and Nature

What do we mean by justice? In Plato's *Republic,* justice is a kind of unity or harmony that the city achieves when the principle of "one person, one job" is practiced in ways that leave everyone satisfied with the fairness of the overall arrangements. But whatever else Plato was talking about, Aristotle astutely observed, he was not talking about political justice. A republic such as Plato imagined, where there are no disputes to resolve, is a city that needs no institutions of justice in the ordinary sense.

For Aristotle the goal of political life is not the eradication of disputes but rather fair play in settling the quarrels that inevitably occur. Departing from Plato, Aristotle taught that the existence of disputes is not a sign that something is rotten so much as it is an occasion for healthy deliberation about what ways of life different persons can share. Aristotle was no democrat in our sense. He stressed that deliberation requires practical wisdom and right upbringing that few persons have. Slaves are "entirely without the faculty of deliberation"; women possess reason but "in a form which lacks authority" over their emotions.[34] Still, among men capable of reasoned deliberation about the common good, Aristotle thought they could reasonably entertain different concepts of justice.

For instance, although men agree that justice is about equality, they notoriously disagree as to who is equal. Oligarchs object to the injustice in democracies of treating equally persons who are not equal and of giving the same to all when some persons deserve more. Democrats object to the injustice in oligarchies of treating the rich better than the poor, as if it were somehow fair to give more power to persons simply because they have more property. Both sides have a point, and Aristotle set out to find the practicable middle ground between competing camps.[35]

Aristotle approaches justice as a distinctly *political* virtue. In *private,* friends and families do not need justice to get along; they are supposed to count on the power of love. No doubt Aristotle idealized the family, ignoring its harsher realities. But his point is that citizens distinctly need to get along with persons they may neither know nor especially like. Therefore politics needs to supplement the virtues of love with the virtue of justice.

One of Aristotle's breakthroughs was to appreciate that any practical theory of justice has to stay within hailing distance of what members of a community already think justice is. Everyone, not just the philosopher, has some concept of justice, however inchoate. To ignore people's sense of justice and to propose abstract ideals that have little resonance with prevailing opinions is to misunderstand the nature of politics and its relation to justice. After all, what we want from principles of justice are terms of fair play that can provide a basis for associating around a shared common good. It seems unlikely that we can find principles which speak to people's sense of fairness if we propose theories so abstract or revolutionary that ordinary persons cannot understand much less practice them. Even in regard to women and slaves, Aristotle held that the just association will be one that such persons can feel included in, despite their inequality.

This insight about the "political" rather than "philosophical" nature of justice leads Aristotle to another breakthrough. While ordinary people have a sense of justice, there is a limit to its reach. Practically speaking, large numbers of persons separated by great geographical distances cannot maintain the sense of belonging to a community that is necessary to motivate persons to treat one another justly. Thus, as we saw in the *Ethics,* political justice even at its most ideal will always remain local rather than global. I cannot emphasize this point enough. For Aristotle, the pluralism of political arrangements—the traditional ways in which we live in different communities—is not some steppingstone to a future utopia where global citizens feel the same obligations of justice to every inhabitant of the planet, no matter where they live. Such cosmopolitanism is not in our nature as human beings. It would reduce the common goods we could share to some lowest common denominator that was bloodless and unable to deliver genuine attachments to a shared enterprise.

An Aside on International Justice

Before going on with Aristotle's own account of justice, I pause to consider his rejection of cosmopolitanism and what we today call global justice. Consider this argument made by the moral philosopher Peter Singer.[36] Most of us spend some amount of money to purchase items and entertainments we do not strictly need: we have several pairs of blue jeans, and designer ones at that; we buy lattes at Starbucks, order in pizza, go to movies, buy computers, iPods, Internet services, cable television: the list of "extra consumption" is large indeed. All the while, we know that children around the globe are dying of malnourishment and disease.

Aristotle may not have known about the plight of children thousands of miles away, but we do know today. Singer argues that justice requires us to send at least some of that Starbucks money—actually a lot of it—to alleviate hunger and preventable disease *anywhere* it is occurring. His argument is straightforward: if justice means anything, it means that saving a child from starvation or disease counts for more than treating ourselves to an extra cup of coffee or item of clothing. Singer himself is quite severe with us; he would have us strip ourselves of all luxury purchases, as long as the saved money could go to bringing other persons up to a bare minimum subsistence level. And for him it does not matter, and it is certainly no excuse, that we live in the United States and the starving children live in Sudan. Justice requires treating each child's life as equally worthy anywhere on the planet.

Does the experience of reading Singer move us to change our ways? Posing this question to my own students elicits a mixed response. On the one hand, they find little *intellectual* reason to dispute Singer on the impartiality with which we should regard all suffering children. On the other hand, they find such impartiality too demanding to be emotionally plausible. Stuck in these thoughts, they become more interested in debating Aristotle's core notion that justice is a distinctly *political* virtue and that human beings cannot practice it outside the bounds of communal preference which make the politics of justice possible in the first place. Aristotle taught that justice can *sustain* itself only within the bounds of a self-governing community that engenders a shared sense of responsibility for its members' welfare. It is this sustainability that Singer's ethic of justice from afar does not seem to provide.

Justice and Equality

Since justice makes its home in different cities, Aristotle concedes that justice appears to be relative to the laws and traditions of a given city, rather than timelessly yoked to natural law and the same everywhere.[37] As in all matters, Aristotle seeks to find common ground between those who see justice as merely "conventional" and those who think of justice as rooted in nature. He allows that different cities house different ways of living, and yet each can be just on its own terms, provided the members understand themselves as included in the common way of life. Thus, from Aristotle's perspective, women could feel included rather than ex-cluded from the Athenian community, despite their inferior position, as long as they understood the existing arrangements as essential to the way of life they themselves value. Of course, not all cities that pretend to have a common good really have one. Tyrants rule only for themselves; oligarchs treat the city as the personal property of the rich. In these cases Aristotle is no moral relativist teaching that justice is whatever passes for justice in tyrannies and oligarchies. He teaches the opposite, stressing that the only just regimes are those that govern according to the common good. He differs from us in rejecting the democratic argument that equal-ity is the only form the common good can take.

But then what is the connection between justice and equality? Aris-totle set out to clarify matters by distinguishing two competing concep-tions of equality—"arithmetic equality" and "proportionate equality."[38] Each notion of equality is appropriate for some questions of justice and not for others. Some questions—the kinds that fill law courts with dis-putes over property and theft—are what Aristotle calls "rectificatory" questions. Here, courts seek to resolve disputes by taking the stolen cow from the wrongdoer and returning it to the rightful owner. In these dis-putes, justice rightly requires us to reason in strictly arithmetic terms, counting each person as absolutely equal to any other person. In other words, justice does not care who is the morally better or richer person when deciding who owns the cow. Courts strictly treat each person as equal and restore the equality disturbed by the theft by subtracting one cow from the thief and adding it back to the account of the previous owner, no matter how bad a person the owner might morally be, no mat-ter how many cows he does or does not own. Whatever the politics of the city we live in, Aristotle argues, rectificatory justice rightly understood follows the logic of arithmetic equality.[39]

But justice has to resolve other sorts of disputes as well. We debate how best to distribute honors and rewards, office holding, military rank, and the like. Here we need a theory of "distributive justice" and an ac-companying theory of who deserves what from the city. When it comes to distributing honor and power, as opposed to resolving theft, we emphati-cally care about the moral worth of persons, their fitness for office, their courage, their prior service. It would therefore be a mistake—the demo-crat's mistake, according to Aristotle—to use arithmetic equality as a measure for determining who deserves what from the city. Applied to dis-tributive justice, arithmetic equality would produce the injustice of giving the same rewards and honors to persons who made vastly different contributions to the city. Instead we should now switch to the alternative concept of "proportionate equality." The idea here is that we treat people fairly in the distribution of power and honor only if we give to them in proportion to their merits. In a mathematical equation where $X = 2y$, it would be wrong to treat X as equal to Y; likewise the "math" of distributive justice requires us to think geometrically rather than arithmetically.[40]

To this extent, oligarchs are right to reject the flat arithmetic or absolute equality theories of democrats. But democrats are right that oligarchs go wrong in singling out mere inequality in property holding as a measure of what one deserves politically. The oligarchic notions on distributive justice would be correct if the city were nothing more than a vast management company for maximizing property values.[41] But the city exists to associate persons around moral goods, not property, and so the oligarchs are as mistaken about distributive justice as are the democrats.

In the end Aristotle believes he can provide a solution to the long-running dispute about justice that has led to so many civil wars between oligarchs and democrats. Both sides mistake the proper standard for distributing political rank. Since the city aspires to associate persons around a moral conception of the good life, the distribution should favor those who can make the greatest contribution to the city as a moral project.[42] These will be persons distinguished by their moral character. In Plato power went to the philosopher kings and queens who demonstrated their superior intellect. But the city is not an association of philosophers, and its purpose is not to turn citizens into philosophers. For Aristotle power should go to the practically wise, the best exemplars of the perfection of human nature that comes to those who most fully practice the moral virtues of life.

Here is where Aristotle's writings on ethics and politics meet. Ethics is a political science, insofar as it takes a city to make persons morally complete. To be cut off from the city is to be like the hand severed from the body. But politics is an ethical science, insofar as it takes morally good persons to define and to maintain a common good.

The good person and the good citizen may not be exactly the same—it remains possible to be a good person in a corrupt city—but ideally they come together. When ethics and politics merge, then the city fulfills its purpose. That purpose extends beyond delivering material goods to the people. It reaches upward to create and to maintain a common way of living that is indispensable to the meaning community members find in their individual lives.

The Good Citizen and the Good Person

Over the years I have had occasion to reflect on the difficulty of interesting the young in Aristotle. Part of the problem is that Aristotle rarely reaches definite conclusions that young people can take away with them. He is more likely to ruminate over matters, to consider what can be said on each side of a debate, and to mull over the considerable truth in seemingly opposing positions.

Consider the marvelous but infuriating passages where Aristotle debates whether the one, the few, or the many should be the sovereign power.[43] He begins by defending the proposition that political selections should work much like medical selections: just as we leave it to doctors to judge who is qualified to be a doctor, we should leave it to experts to elect those best qualified to rule.[44] But then Aristotle turns around and acknowledges the persuasive reasons for thinking that the people achieve a collective wisdom which outstrips the wisdom that even the best experts have to offer.[45] Consider, for instance, who makes the best judge of the quality of a meal or a house: in the end it is the person eating the meal or living in the house, not the expert cook or builder, who gets to say whether the meal or the house is good.[46]

Having said all this, Aristotle draws back and notes that arguments in favor of popular sovereignty hardly apply in cities where the people are debased in their moral character.[47] At any rate, the choice between placing power in the hands of the one, the few, or the many leaves out perhaps the even better option of making "rightly constituted laws . . . sovereign."[48] No sooner has Aristotle announced this mediating position than he qualifies it as well, since general laws cannot tell us what to do in concrete circumstances.[49] All of this careful study of the pros and cons of various political positions gives Aristotle his famous sobriety, but it is not the stuff that permits the teacher of Aristotle to satisfy beginning students' understandable desire to know exactly what Aristotle thought.

In medieval times the great philosophers working within the Islamic, Jewish, and Christian traditions came to write learned commentaries on Aristotle's *Ethics* and *Politics*. The lack of a precise Aristotelian doctrine played into the writing of commentaries, as scholars committed to the truths of divine revelation nevertheless were able to adopt Aristotle's rational and logical mode of discourse and use it to craft arguments in support of the revealed truths. By the ninth and tenth centuries, in the Islamic world the emergence of "Aristotelianism" as a way to argue for the harmony between reason and revelation was well under way, spreading to Judaism and then into Christianity. By the thirteenth century, the use of Aristotle as a template was so well established that Thomas Aquinas simply referred to Aristotle as "The Philosopher."

For us, Aristotle rarely emerges as "the" philosopher. Little in our political experience answers to Aristotle's proud assertion that to study politics is to study the best that human beings can do. The horrors of the last century make Plato's cave seem very near, Aristotle's polis far away.

Even as to his own time, Aristotle could idealize the Greek polis only by discounting the bad politics does when it practices slavery. But there must have been something in Greek culture that permitted an otherwise sober thinker to proclaim the superiority of the political life over all others. Still, who among us can gaze out from the cave and find support for Aristotle's notion that politics over time works pure of its own imperfections?

7

AUGUSTINE AND THE PROBLEM OF EVIL

With Saint Augustine, the tradition of political theory enters a new phase. Questions about the proper relation of church and state, of reason to revelation, come to the fore, where they have remained ever since. These sorts of issues did not perplex Plato or Aristotle, since they conceived of politics as having its own moral compass. But with the advent of Christianity, political theory for the first time becomes embedded in the study of theology. Justice is reconceived as a divine, not human, construction.

Augustine was a prolific writer, but I will concentrate on arguably his two greatest works: the autobiographical *Confessions* and his magnum opus, the *City of God*.

The *Confessions*

Augustine's *Confessions* is the work of an older man re-membering his youth. Frequently the autobiography is described as Augustine's account of his odyssey from sinner to saint. But this blurb is misleading about both periods of Augustine's life. Although he certainly confesses to his share of sins as a young man, Augustine was always more of a tortured than a contented sinner. His confessions are not just those of a mature man coming to see in hindsight the waywardness of his youth—in the manner of Cephalus fondly recalling his former indiscretions and expressing regret only after the fact. Augustine's memory is more haunted in recalling adolescence as already a time when he wrestled with his own impulses, both wanting to enjoy life in the flesh and yet feeling uncomfortable in his skin.

As Augustine describes his tormented self-consciousness at a particularly low point in his life, "I had become to myself a place of unhappiness in which I could not bear to be; but I could not escape from myself."[1] Augustine repeatedly invokes the metaphor of an interior "civil war" to describe the anxiety that his own attractions to physical pleasure gave him. To use the Latin term for seriousness, this was a young man uncommonly weighted down from an early age with *gravitas*—with gravity.

At times Augustine can make light of his interior struggles. In a moment of comic relief he recounts the prayer in which he earnestly beseeched God to give him chastity—only "not yet."[2] But moments of levity and allowance for the passions of youth are few and far between in the *Confessions*. In this sense the *Confessions* is one of the great literary examples of what Hegel would later call the "unhappy consciousness." Although Augustine gives Christian testimony to the way in which he finally comes to joy in the love of God, the great "ought" of God's love loomed before him as a young man but escaped his grasp. He knew what he ought to will, but he still willed otherwise.

I said a moment ago that the stock description of the *Confessions* as a sinner-to-saint story is misleading about both the younger and elder Augustine. Augustine did leave his youthful attractions behind, accept conversion to his mother's Catholic faith, become celibate, and serve for many years as bishop of Hippo in North Africa. But throughout his life and in his writings a tension between two visions of Christian life remained unresolved. On the one hand, God commands us to "love thy neighbor as thyself."[3] On the other hand, Christ has risen and left this earthly abode, and by the grace of God we are saved and redeemed through Him in the Kingdom to Come. Augustine struggled with how the good Christian lives by the otherworldly orientation that is basic to the religion and yet also immerses the self in "loving thy neighbor." The brilliance of the *Confessions* is the way in which Augustine connects this theological tension to the remembrance of his own youthful civil wars.

When Augustine asked for chastity but "not yet," the postponement he asked for lasted a long time, until he was thirty-three in fact; by then he had rebuffed his mother's wish for his baptism into the faith (Augustine's father was not a Catholic), had some early sexual experiences, taken a mistress, lived with her for fifteen years (apparently faithfully) out of marriage, fathered a child, agreed to be betrothed to a ten-year-old, unceremoniously sent his mistress away, and conducted another affair while waiting for his bride-to-be to come of age (twelve was the custom).

As he narrates these years, Augustine remembers tasting the "vinegar with [the] sweetness."[4] Even as he moved like "an elegant man about

town," finding enjoyment in "the body of the beloved," Augustine recounts the flipside of giving license to carnal desire, the inevitable tor-
tures "of jealousy, suspicion, fear, anger, and contention."[5] But the special torment came from Augustine's anxiety about his own attraction to
wrongdoing. Time and again he expresses the fear he had about his capacity to choose willfully what he knew to be evil.

For Socrates, to know virtue is to be virtuous. But Augustine is a philosopher of the will's resistance to rational knowledge. What he lacked as
a young man was not knowledge of the True God but the willingness to
accept Him. In pagan thought generally, the human mind has the capacity to apprehend the Good and to raise oneself up to it by one's own efforts. In the Christian thought that Augustine largely shaped, the gap between human mind and divine being is unbridgeable by human effort,
and salvation comes only through God's gift of love and grace to us.

It is possible to trace out two competing explanations Augustine gives
for his youthful sinning. Both accounts came to have profound influence
on early Christianity. The less psychologically astute account comes out
as a kind of flat body-mind narrative. In this story Augustine takes over
Plato's dualisms—reason versus desire, the higher pleasures of the mind
versus the lower pleasures of the body, eternal truths versus mere appearances—and converts them into a theory of repression. Human love is forever prone to the corruptions of *cupiditas,* of carnal desire that must be
transcended if the person is to be capable of *caritas,* of Christian love.
Human love is embodied love; Christian love is selfless.

Plato counted on eros to climb a ladder out of its own spontaneous
and creativity energy, moving us from initial attractions to visible and
embodied forms of beauty to more abstract, intellectual, and disembodied love. But the higher loves emerge out of, and in harmony with, the
strivings of lower loves. However disorderly the strivings of embodied
love are, they are the awakening of curiosity from which all higher love
flows.

The *Confessions* can be legitimately read as shattering this Platonic
harmony between reason and desire, and replacing it with a repressive
doctrine that makes persons experience their body as "other" than their
selves and as the source of evil that must be denied or repressed rather
than fulfilled. As we shall see in a moment, Augustine once followed the
sect of Manichaeans in their belief that sexual procreation was a principle of evil and that the divine soul is imprisoned in an evil body. Augustine abandoned that doctrine in favor of an eventual accommodation of

sexuality in God's plan. But he retained a sense of body-mind dualism bound to fuel a distrust of the body: "I intend to remind myself of my past foulness and carnal corruptions. . . . [N]o restraint was imposed by the exchange of mind with mind, which marks the brightly lit pathway of friendship. Clouds of muddy carnal concupiscence filled the air. The bubbling impulses of puberty befogged and obscured my heart so that it could not see the difference between love's serenity and lust's darkness."[6] Here, even within earthly love, Augustine divides matters between the good in friendship and the lust in bodily desire. On top of this split he imposes a divide between the limits of all earthly love and the true love we find only through Christ.

When Augustine writes in these dualisms, he paints a portrait of a youth deeply concerned that evil is inside him, that he is actually attracted to evil for evil's sake, that he is capable of willingly and knowingly choosing wrong over right. If that is so, then evil exists as a choosable substance, and Augustine is locked into his Manichaean phase.

At its best, the *Confessions* offers a dramatically different and far more psychologically astute account of one youth's struggle to understand his waywardness. Consider, for instance, one of the central confessions Augustine makes—a confession that almost every reader today sees as making too much out of a slight wrong. Augustine recalls an episode of petty thievery in which as a young boy he joined with a band of friends to steal some pears from a tree belonging to a neighbor.[7]

Why did he and his friends steal pears one afternoon? Augustine runs through the obvious explanations. They might have been hungry, but this wasn't the case; in fact they threw the fruit away to some pigs, after eating at most a few. They might have wanted money, but they did not bother to sell their stolen goods. Perhaps the beauty of the pears beguiled and seduced them, in the manner of the snake beguiling Eve to steal the apple in the Garden of Eden. Augustine considers this possibility but concludes that the pears were attractive "neither in color or taste."[8]

At this point Augustine must face up to the frightening possibility that he stole the pears gratuitously, for no reason other than taking pleasure in "doing what was wrong."[9] This possibility frightens the young Augustine because it would mean that he—we—actually will to do wrong for wrong's sake.

But as he remembers the event, Augustine latches on to one detail: he is certain that he would not have stolen the pears on his own, that it somehow mattered that he was with friends: "Yet had I been alone I would not have done it—I remember my state of mind to be thus at the time—alone I would never have done it. Therefore my love in that act was to be associated with the gang in whose company I did it. . . . It was all done for a giggle, as if our hearts were tickled to think we were deceiving those who would not think us capable of such behavior and would have profoundly disapproved."[10] As wrong as it was to steal pears, at least Augustine did it with some good in mind—pleasing his friends—rather than doing it for the sake of evil itself. In his biography of Augustine, the scholar Gary Wills puts Augustine's insight eloquently. A desire for "companionship" was the "good hidden in the bad" act of theft. Of course this good, this "persistent love of fellowship," is "falsely conceived" when one steals to keep up with friends. Still, "Augustine has solved his own psychological mystery"—the commission of a seemingly motiveless theft—by tracing it to good gone awry rather than attraction to evil in and of itself.[11]

In his account of the pear theft, Wills points out the theological significance of Augustine's psychological story. According to the Manichaeans, two rival kingdoms contend eternally, the kingdom of light and the kingdom of darkness. In one kingdom the substance or matter is all good; in the other the substance is evil. Such a cosmology explains the occurrence of evil without having to attribute bad things to God but only at the cost of denying God's oneness, omnipotence, and omniscience. It explains evil only by postulating for it an objective reality, a substantial existence not created by God. For these reasons the church regarded Manichaeanism as a dangerous heresy. Yet for a time Augustine accepted its cosmology as providing a rational explanation for how evil exists.

That cosmological dualism implied a psychological dualism as well. The Manichees reviled procreation as responsible for imprisoning the divine soul in a degenerate body that seduces us to choose evil for its own sake. It is this conclusion that Augustine seeks to avoid in the pear theft story by recasting his will not as *effected* by evil per se but as *defective* in succumbing to the good, albeit the lesser good, of friendship rather than staying true to fellowship with God. Augustine comes to see how a human good such as friendship is mutable and corruptible in ways that the good that is God is not. The central drama in the *Confessions* is whether the good that friendship embodies—an ordering of love to purify it of *cupiditas*—can prepare a soul not only to receive fellowship in Christ but also to be at home in the world where the society of friendship leads us to "love thy neighbor."

As Wills points out, Augustine's story about pears and a tree is either consciously or unconsciously a reference to the story of Adam and Eve's taking of the apple in the Garden of Eden—the original sin. Eve may have been deceived by the snake into wanting the power that fruit from the Tree of Knowledge would give her. But for Augustine, it is crucial that Adam was not deceived, that he knew it was wrong to partake of the fruit and yet he did it anyway. Why? Augustine has Adam will the wrong, not for the sake of the apple but "gallantly" for Eve's sake—that she not act alone and that he not be left alone:

> After Eve had eaten from the forbidden tree and offered him its fruit to eat along with her, Adam did not want to disappoint her, when he thought she might be blighted without his comforting support, banished from his heart to die sundered from him. He was not overcome by disordered desire of the flesh, . . . but by a kind of amicable desire for another's good . . . , which often happens, making us sin against God so as not to turn a friend against us.[12]

This is a strikingly beautiful passage, for its thought as much as for its words. It parallels the central narrative of the *Confessions,* as we follow Augustine mulling over his own knowing wrongdoing, first seeking comfort in Manichaean doctrines, and then finally coming to understand the theological mystery of original sin and how it is possible for God's creatures to freely will the wrong. Even in our sin, we express a human good.

To be sure, pursuit of human goods can mislead us into choosing the lesser over the greater good that God offers. And the human goods themselves can be more or less good; Augustine's remarks about Adam and Eve suggest that it was one thing for Adam to find a companion in Eve, another to find a sexual partner. There is lurking a growing discomfort in the body that will make the Platonism of early Christianity remote from Plato's own doctrines. But Augustine staves off a wholly repressive view of mind-body relations by seeing the good we aim at, even when the body leads us astray.

Augustine keeps on coming back to the question of friendship throughout his *Confessions.* His views are complex and difficult to put together into a coherent whole. At its best, human friendship is a "nest of love and gentleness" that can bring about "unity . . . between many souls."[13] And yet in the pear story, friendship proved a "dangerous enemy" leading him into sin.[14] The problem here is one that haunts Augustine theologically as well as psychologically. On the one hand, God's graced are to relate to this world in a fundamentally detached fashion, pilgrims sojourning here with no great investment in mortal relationships. On the other hand, the command to "love thy neighbor" suggests that we ought to be invested in this world while we live here. In friendship, Augustine recalls, he *did* love his neighbor, and yet he remembers as well the failures and foibles of friendship. Some failures seem possible to overcome, as in Augustine's delightful memory of the "kiss and tell" imperative between friends during their adolescent years, familiar even to modern readers: "I was ashamed not to be equally guilty of shameful behavior when I heard them boasting of their sexual exploits. . . . I went deeper into vice to avoid being despised, and when there was no act by admitting to which I could rival my depraved companions, I used to pretend I had done things I had not done at all."[15]

But even seemingly genuine friendship is problematic for Augustine, since it is bound to end, as all attachments to mortals must. In a particularly poignant story, he recounts his slide into inconsolable grief after the death of a friend during the time he was teaching back in his home town.[16] Describing the friendship as the closeness of "one soul in two bodies," Augustine could not endure being without him, and everything that had previously been a source of pleasure when shared now "was without him transformed into a cruel torment."[17] He found "no rest in pleasant groves, nor in games or songs, nor in sweet-scented places. . . . Everything was an object of horror, even light itself; all that was not he made me feel sick and was repulsive."[18] The sole exception was the relief Augustine found in tears. In one of his most eloquent lines about losing a friend to death, Augustine notes that the "lost life of those who die becomes the death of those still living."[19]

Even so, Augustine cannot quite count his relationship as a "true" friendship, since it lacked fellowship in Christ (to the contrary, Augustine misled his friend into Manichaean heresies and even scoffed at the death-bed baptism his friend received when thought to be near the end). Moreover, Augustine sees his grief as expressing his folly in "loving a person sure to die as if he would never die."[20] He lacked the ability to love human beings "with awareness of the [mortal] human condition," and this led him to seek in friendship the permanence that can be found only in relation to "the one who cannot be lost."[21]

Theologically, Augustine's position forces him to distinguish sharply between true friendship, which we can have only when, through God's love for us, we escape the embodied self into the eternal unity of Christ, and the overinvestment in mortality that limits even the best of human friendships. Interestingly, however, it is not the transcendence but the renewal of ordinary friendship that ends Augustine's grief. When he first begins to derive solace from other friends, Augustine is acutely aware that they are a mere substitute for the departed. Hence, finding solace is just a "vast myth" that Augustine should abandon in favor of fellowship through Christ. And yet

> this fable did not die for me when one of my friends died. There were other things which occupied my mind in the company of friends: to make conversation, to share a joke, to share mutual acts of kindness, to read together well-written books, to share in trifling and in serious matters. . . . These and other signs come from the heart of those who love and are loved and . . . out of many . . . forge unity.[22]

That Augustine had a great gift for friendship is clear from the *Confessions*. But one person he could not bring himself to love was his father, Patrick. He describes his family as possessing modest resources—a few acres of farmland. Patrick, who remained a pagan until his deathbed conversion, served as a minor functionary in Thagaste for the Roman province of Numidia (in what is now Algeria). But "my father had more enthusiasm than cash," and he sent his son off for a Latin education, first to a neighboring town, and then to more distant Carthage. Augustine's response is clipped and rather ungrateful—"[E]veryone was full of praise for my father because he spent money on his son beyond the means of his estate"—but Augustine marvels that his father could care so much for helping him get ahead in a worldly way while paying little attention to his lapse into sexual immorality. His father's concern was only that his son should develop a "cultured tongue" and earn distinction as an advocate in the law courts. By contrast, Augustine portrays the tender care of his Catholic mother, Monica, her fears for his soul, and the advice he long ignored.[23]

While a student at Carthage, Augustine fell in love with the theater. What intrigued him was the paradox of the spectator's finding pleasure in witnessing the pains and sufferings enacted on stage. The young student wryly notes the way the theatergoer leaves disappointed if a play does not cause pain, whereas so long as he suffers, "he stays riveted in his seat enjoying himself."[24] All the while, the audience is aware that, were the depicted calamities to befall them in real life, they would suffer misery. But somehow watching the fictional depiction of misery makes us feel pleasure in our pain, a pleasure we call the feeling of compassion, or pity, or mercy. Augustine marvels at this oddity in human emotion. It seems to make one person's mercy dependent on the misery of another, suggesting a dark side to our compassion. As to theater, Augustine expresses distrust of the catharsis it provides. Even in real life, it would seem that "[m]ercy cannot exist apart from suffering," and Augustine ponders whether "this mean[s] mercy is to be rejected." He concludes that at times "sufferings can be the proper object of love," but he remains wary of the way charity can mask a malicious disposition: "Even if we approve of a person who, from a sense of duty in charity, is sorry for a wretch, yet he who manifests fraternal compassion would prefer that there be no cause for sorrow. It is only if there could be a malicious good will . . . that someone who truly and sincerely felt compassion would wish wretches to exist so as to be objects of compassion."[25] The German term *Schadenfreude* captures the drift of Augustine's thought regarding the joy some take in the misfortunes of others. As is his wont, Augustine compares the malice in some person's pity with the good in friendship. Tears for the agonies of another "flow from the stream of friendship." It is just, once again, that the stream can be readily diverted to serve "black desires."[26]

Politics is not a subject that Augustine broaches in his *Confessions*. But his explorations of friendship, its promise and peril, already suggest what in fallen human nature makes politics both necessary and possible. Politics is *possible* because human beings are capable of uniting in the good of friendship and community. Politics is *necessary* because that very love of things human leads us astray and needs to be disciplined. Ultimately Augustine sees an unbridgeable gulf between our higher and lower loves—a gulf that can be bridged not by human reason, as in Plato, but only through the gift of God's grace and love for us. But to see how Augustine attempts to fashion a Christian political theory, we must turn now to his political writings proper and especially to his greatest work, the *City of God*.

Augustine's Political Philosophy: *City of God*

In 410 Alaric and the Visigoths sacked the "eternal" city of Rome, the first foreign troops to invade the city in over a thousand years. Survivors fled to the Roman provinces in North Africa, bringing word to Augustine, by then bishop of Hippo, both of the carnage and of the accusation that Rome's fall was due to its conversion to Christianity less than a century before this catastrophe.

Augustine's magnum opus, the *City of God*, begins with a polemical defense of the church against these charges of responsibility for Rome's fall. To those making the accusation, Augustine points out that they owe their very lives to the sanctuary they received in the Catholic basilicas, sanctuary that the Christian Goths respected. Under pagan rules of war—witness the slaughter the Greeks carried out after their conquest of Troy—those bemoaning Rome's loss of its pagan protectors would not even be alive to complain. To those who suffered terrible injury at the hands of the Goths—Augustine's sermons tell us of his pastoral concern for women raped, trapped between the sin of attempting suicide and the shame of living—Augustine offers the pastoral advice that these injuries are not final, compared to the life everlasting and redemption that awaits those graced by God.

Although Augustine's reflections may have been occasioned by the sack of Rome, he moves beyond that historical event to place both Rome and the church in a vast world history of two Loves giving rise to two Cities, the earthly and the heavenly. Only by understanding these two paradigms can we know what significance, or insignificance, to attach to an event even as startling as the fall of Rome.

By way of preview, let me point out two themes that percolate throughout the *City of God*. The first is a strongly antipolitical stance, as Augustine sets out to devalue all matters political from the high and central place they occupied in the Greek and Roman understanding of the good life. Where Aristotle finds individuals perfecting themselves through political belonging, Augustine finds only the tragedy of human beings alienated from Christ. This debunking side of Augustine rejects the notion that any state could ever be based on true justice, that there ever could be a "Christian" political philosophy or a Christian state, since the Christian is only a sojourner here awaiting salvation in the Kingdom to Come. But although this otherworldly theme is decidedly dominant in the *City of God*, Augustine surprises us by finding considerable value in politics after all. States may not bring us justice, but they can bring us peace. In addition, although only the church can teach the true moral virtues, belonging to a political community can make a certain sort of friendship possible which, among the human goods, is to be highly prized.

The Heavenly City and the Earthly City

For Augustine, "two cities were created by two kinds of love." To the earthly city belong all those individuals ruled "by self love reaching the point of contempt for God." To the heavenly city come those guided "by the love of God carried as far as contempt of self." The earthly city is driven by the lust for domination; it is "ruled by the love of ruling." The heavenly city "looks for its reward in the fellowship of the saints . . . that God may be in all."[27]

The two cities have their origins in our expulsion from the Garden of Eden. Adam and Eve's original sin justified God's punishment on us all, his condemnation of the great wickedness in our choice to alienate ourselves from his goodness. But God by grace redeems some of his own, predestining them to belong to the City of God. The City of God abides everlasting in the next world; while its members live on earth, they live by faith and adopt the attitude of pilgrims or sojourners, "a stranger among the ungodly."[28] Blessed with the love of God and God's love for them, they assign to things merely human only what is due to passing and temporal matters. The church is not identical with the City of God, but it is Christ's representative on earth.

To the earthly city belong those destined for damnation. Augustine finds it illuminating that the Bible refers to Cain as the builder of the first city. Greed, violence, and the desire for power led Cain to kill his own brother, and in that crime lay the origin of the earthly city.[29] Ever since, cities have been founded on crime, not justice. Sometimes Cain's fratricide is repeated exactly, as when Romulus slew his brother Remus to found Rome.[30] At other times the founding crime is different, but the pattern holds true: in earthly cities, love seeks power and domination and the glory of men. In the heavenly city, residents seek the glory of God.

In comparison to the true justice that abides only in the City of God, Augustine is prepared to dismiss the possibility that any earthly city could ever be just. Augustine develops his argument by taking on Cicero's definition of a republic. From the *Confessions* we know that Augustine received a classical education and that Cicero was a central part of the curriculum. Augustine especially admired Cicero's style and was familiar with Cicero's *Republic,* only portions of which survive today.

For Cicero, it was crucial that the good city was not just any collection of human beings; it was an assembly of different social classes made possible by an agreement with respect to justice—an agreement about a common good that persons from different strata could share.[31] By Cicero's definition, Augustine argues, Rome was never a republic, "because there never was real justice in the community."[32] Justice, Augustine argues, harking back to Plato's beginning arguments in the *Republic,* is a matter of giving everyone his due. And this Rome could not do; it could not give God what is his due, but instead pridefully sought to imitate God's dominion in its own imperial glory.

Cicero worried in his own time that Rome was ceasing to be a republic; he saw the agreement that permitted various classes to harmonize their interests as falling apart. But Augustine's response to Cicero's concern is his response in his own time to those who find great loss and tragedy in Rome's fall. For Augustine, there never was any golden age of Rome, and we have reason to doubt "whether real justice [ever] flourished in that city, or whether it . . . was even then [not] a living reality . . . but merely a fancy picture."[33]

Significantly, what Augustine is doing here is denying that justice—or "true" justice—is a political concept at all, a politically realizable end. To those who might envision a "Christian" state which overcomes the split between the earthly and heavenly cities, Augustine seems to deny the very possibility. As he puts it, "True justice is found only in that commonwealth whose founder and ruler is Christ, if we agree to call this a commonwealth."[34] Here we confront Augustine's essentially antipolitical attitude. He does not set out to develop a Christian political philosophy, since the very idea that Christianity and true justice could be institutionalized in a state is false. Rather he urges "Christ's servants . . . to endure the wickedness of an utterly corrupt state," preserving their passivity and resignation *here* while awaiting their place among "the assembly of angels" in the "Heavenly Commonwealth," whose "law is the will of God."[35] Or, as he writes elsewhere, "What does it matter under whose rule a man lives, being so soon to die?"[36] Augustine adds the proviso that this resigned attitude to the ways of the earthly city assumes that "the rulers do not force [one] to impious and wicked acts."[37] But so long as this holds true, then the Christian's attitude toward the state is to render unto Caesar what is Caesar's and unto God what is God's.

Kingdoms and Republics

The antipolitical tone of the *City of God* is so dominant that it is easy to miss the positive Augustine does find in political life. Among earthly cities Augustine distinguishes between kingdoms and republics, decidedly preferring the latter. In kingdoms there is no semblance of an agreement on ruling, only a lust for power. Augustine compares such earthly cities to "robber bands," for "what are kingdoms but gangs of criminals on a large scale?"[38] By contrast, even though republics do not embody true justice, they can embody a kind of agreement between rulers and ruled. In place of Cicero's definition that the agreement is based on justice, Augustine famously offers this redefinition of what is valuable in republican life: "A people is the association of a multitude of rational beings united by a common agreement on the objects of their love[;] then it follows that to observe the character of a particular people we must examine the objects of its love."[39]

What was it that Romans loved, when the republic still held persons together by a common love? Here the classically educated Augustine agrees with the Ciceronian description of a people who displayed a striking capacity to replace love of self with love of country.[40] This love of country did not make Romans just; in fact it inspired them to seek the earthly glories of empire, wealth, war, and conquest. But Rome made it possible for persons to elevate their human love from its abject forms of self-interest into a bond of community and friendship. Even without knowing the objective truths about justice that are knowable only through Christ, the Romans knew and experienced the possibilities of political friendship through citizenship. So exemplary was Rome as a city loved by its inhabitants that God "assisted the Romans, who [were] good according to the standards of the earthly city."[41] That is to say, Augustine proves capable of distinguishing a political republic *both* from the true commonwealth we can find only in love of Christ *and* from the kingdoms that are no better than robber gangs. This explains why God was pleased for Rome "to conquer the world [and] to unite the world into the single community of the Roman commonwealth and the Roman laws."[42]

Does the work of an earthly city such as Rome prepare the way for the second coming of Christ? This is not a claim that Augustine is tempted to make. Ultimately there is but discontinuity between the earthly and heavenly cities: great imperial powers such as Rome inevitably rise and fall; their work even at best is limited to working within the realm of fallen human nature. The love and friendship Rome made possible is to be valued highly among the human goods; it makes peace, order, and a kind of fellowship possible that would not be possible apart from the state. But politics even at its best does not, and cannot, save us.

Peace

The one great end that the heavenly and earthly cities share is peace. Peace, Augustine writes, "is so great a good that even in relation to the affairs of earth and of our mortal state no word ever falls more gratefully upon the ear."[43]

Even members of the heavenly city, while they sojourn here, have need of the state's peace. They therefore willingly obey the law, as long as God's peace and earthly peace do not clash, as they would were the state to order the faithful to commit acts of impiety or iniquity.[44] Thus, for the sake of peace, the church renders obedience to the state in earthly matters but preserves care of the soul as the province of the church. This is not equivalent to modern notions of separation of church and state, since Augustine assumes a Christian ruler honoring the church. But it does mark a development of Christianity as a religion that realized its ends not through the state but beyond it.

Persecution of Heretics

Augustine's position on the persecution of heretics is an exception to the notion that Christianity eschews the sword. His principal writings have to do with his struggle as bishop of Hippo to preserve the unity of the church against the spread of the Donatists, a popular Christian sect bent on "purifying" the sacraments against allegedly immoral priests. At first Augustine's position was that coercion is powerless to bring persons into unity with the true faith and that only persuasion is proper. But the Donatists, in Augustine's view, did not reciprocate this Christian love but recruited through force. For this reason the church could call on the might of the state to prevent Donatists from harming others, even while leaving the Donatists alone in their heresy.[45] Augustine considered such use of state coercion a form of punishment, not persecution: while the Donatists could not be forced to believe, they could be punished and deterred from spreading their beliefs by force. All states, even pagan ones, have the power to wield the sword for punishments of this sort.

Finally, however, Augustine moved from advocating punishment to justifying persecution proper. Persecution goes beyond punishment in seeking to compel the heretic to accept church doctrine.[46] Augustine never quite changed his mind about the relative ineffectiveness of force in bringing persons to faith. But while faith has to be freely chosen, fear can give doubters the incentive to study hard on the truth.[47] The threat of persecution serves as a warning to examine one's errors; if the warning or its carrying out on a few heretics works to bring others to their senses, then it is justified in the way that placing some in the "short-lived fires of the furnace" is preferable to "abandoning all to the eternal fires of Hell."[48]

Unlike punishment, persecution can be carried out only by Christian rulers wielding the sword on behalf of the church. This is because persecution is justifiable only as an act of Christian love.[49] The intent to save the person's soul is crucial to the rightness of the coercion. Thus Augustine's theory of persecution carries with it limits. The church is not interested in taking the lives or property of heretics, and Augustine continually opposed execution of heretics as inconsistent with its purposes.[50] But, taken reluctantly and out of love, acts of persecution are an obligation of the Christian ruler.

Augustine draws an analogy to the wrong committed by refusing to rescue people in a house about to collapse simply because the occupants refuse to leave.[51] It is morally just to save those occupants *against their will;* likewise, it is right to save heretics when they choose even more certain and greater destruction. Another Augustinian analogy is between physical drowning and spiritual drowning: for the same reasons we do not ask the drowning victim's permission to rescue him, we do not need the heretic's permission to rescue him from spiritually drowning.

Augustine's arguments are not persuasive, since they assume exactly what is in dispute—that we could know when someone is "spiritually" drowning in the same way that we recognize when someone is physically drowning; that the Donatist house is about to collapse and bring ruin on its congregants in the same way that ruin is certain for those who stay put inside a falling house. But his arguments came to have great influence on the later church and were cited with approval during the medieval Inquisition.

In suggesting that the church could enlist the power of the state to suppress heretics, Augustine opened up, without resolving, one of the great issues that was to concern his successors. On the one hand, Augustine wrote as if the heavenly city could cede merely temporal affairs to Caesar, saving souls spiritually as only the church could. On the other hand, the very superiority of the spiritual over the temporal meant for Augustine that the proper use of things political could never be understood independently of theology and that the church ultimately could make sacred use of the sword. These issues of the proper relation of church to state were foreign to the classical canon of political thought. For the Greeks, and especially for Aristotle, political life was to be studied and appreciated on its own terms, valued for the distinctly human goods that life in the city makes possible. For the Christian, there is no such thing as independent inquiry into political values; only theology and knowledge of the divine can keep the proper hierarchical order of the spiritual over the temporal, divine justice over human justice. The unresolved institutional question was what the dominance of theology over political philosophy meant for the power of the church vis-à-vis the state. Augustine bequeathed this unresolved question to his successors.

Survival of the Classical Canon

For a thousand years after Augustine, political philosophy remained embedded in the study of religion. This was true not only for Christian thinkers but for scholars working within the Islamic and Jewish traditions as well. In fact, the recovery of Greek texts, especially Plato's *Republic* and *Laws* and Aristotle's *Ethics* and *Politics,* was the work in the first instance of Arab philosophers. By the ninth and tenth centuries Arab scholars in the great Islamic schools of learning in Cordoba, in Baghdad, and in Damascus had translated into Arabic most of the known Greek philosophical sources—sources that by then had largely been lost to the Latin West. It was through these Arabic translations that knowledge of the Greek texts passed first to Jews living under Islamic rule and then to Christians in the Latin West. Without doubt, the survival of the Greek and Roman canon depended on the work of Islamic and Jewish scholars; they bequeathed the tradition, dominant in all three religious communities throughout medieval times, of writing commentaries on Plato and Aristotle by way of exploring possible ways to reconcile the wisdom found in pagan sources with the given and unquestioned truths of divine revelation and divine law.

An early and great example of such exploration was the work of the Arab philosopher al-Fārābī in the tenth-century school he headed in Damascus. Al-Fārābī turned particularly to Plato for inspiration and wrote a text titled *The Political Regime* that clearly draws on the *Republic* for its names and classifications of various constitutions. Al-Fārābī's works on logic and politics were translated into Hebrew and were known to and praised by the Jewish scholar Maimonides, living under Islamic rule in twelfth-century Cordoba and Cairo and writing in Arabic.

We can trace a similar intellectual transmission of commentary on Aristotle from the work of Averroës in twelfth-century Córdoba, through its translation into Hebrew and eventually into Latin, leading to the rise within Christianity of the so-called Latin Averroists; it was through confronting the Christian Averroists that Thomas Aquinas came to offer his own commentaries on Aristotle and on the proper reconciliation of reason and revelation.

Like most persons of my generation, I learned this part of the canon of political theory primarily through the study of Christian philosophers, to the exclusion of Islamic and Jewish sources. This is a deficiency that needs to be corrected as we pass the canon on to future generations. But I must leave it to others to accomplish this overdue broadening, since my own education does not equip me to do justice to these underappreciated masterpieces.[52]

I limit my thoughts to one overall remark. Although there was considerable similarity in the way Christian, Jewish, and Muslim philosophers set about reconciling divine revelation with the work of reason as learned from the ancients, there was also a pronounced difference. Both Islam and Judaism originated as political religions in the way Christianity did not. By this I mean that the law of Shari'a for Muslims or of Torah for Jews was comprehensive in scope, laying down rules to govern not only the relation of person to God but also of person to person in daily social and political life. Since the prophetic lawgivers in these two religious communities already announced the true civil law as well as canon law, the confrontation with pagan sources had to find ways to reconcile the interpretation of religious law on civil matters with, say, those pagan arguments that were found persuasive. Within Islamic and Jewish communities this gave to political philosophy a certain jurisprudential tone, as thinkers concentrated on the question of how best to interpret the meaning of the received law. In his *Enumeration of the Sciences,* Al-Fārābī singled out jurisprudence as "the art that enables man to infer the determination of whatever was not explicitly specified by the Lawgiver, on the basis of such things as were explicitly specified and determined by him; and to strive to infer correctly by taking into account the Lawgiver's purpose with the religion he had legislated for the nation to which he gave that religion."[53] Judaism early on developed a similar emphasis on legal interpretation, with scholars producing the commentaries known as the Talmud, in which rabbis started with the commanded law but turned to legal analysis to draw inferences from the explicit to the implied in the commandments.

The medieval Christian commentaries sparked by the recovery of Greek sources were similar, insofar as thinkers started with the givens of their tradition in considering what wisdom to find in the pagans. But Christian canon law typically lacked the all-inclusive character of Islamic Shari'a or the Hebrew Torah when it came to governing human relations in the detail that defines civil law. In the two cities of Augustine, one already sees the influence of an otherworldly orientation that made it possible for Christian thinkers to relegate "things unto Caesar that are Caesar's" and to put aside confrontation with the merely political or temporal as relatively unimportant to a Christian's proper pilgrimage on earth. Thus, as the editors of one sourcebook on medieval political philosophy put it, medieval Christian political philosophy was theological whereas Islamic and Jewish political thought was jurisprudential.[54] The difference is that theological inquiry into sacred doctrine—a task that can be authoritatively done only by the successors to Christ—is central to Christian political philosophy, whereas inquiry into law and its proper interpretation is central to Islam and Judaism, a task that can be done by jurists.

The differences in the way persons working within these three religious traditions confronted ancient sources are suggestive. It is sometimes argued that Christian nations found it easier than Muslim nations to arrive at notions of separation of church and state, given the otherworldly orientation of their religion.[55] The reverse has also been argued: that the Christian hierarchy of the spiritual over the temporal provided theological justification for the church to command the temporal in the interest of the sacred.

Arcane on many levels, the texts of medieval political philosophy nonetheless record the momentous struggle of scholars to straddle two different intellectual worlds—the world of divine revelation to which they were committed and the pagan world of ethical and political inquiry in which they found great wisdom. The Jewish philosopher Maimonides named his most important book *The Guide for the Perplexed,* by way of validating the intellectual confusion that recovery of the classical canon brought with it to many persons living within religious communities. It was a mark of the seriousness with which Islamic, Jewish, and Christian scholars read the classical texts that they struggled to reconcile the competing claims that divine revelation and philosophy placed on them. In *The Decisive Treatise, Determining What the Connection Is between Religion and Philosophy,* the Islamic scholar Averroës took up the question "whether the study of philosophy and logic is allowed by the Law, or prohibited, or commanded." On the basis of the authority of Islamic law, he staved off objections that the study of ancient texts was heretical and argued for the contrary conclusion that Muslim law "rendered obligatory the study of beings by the intellect, and reflection on them" and that intellectual reasoning is "the most perfect kind of study" to draw out inferences from what the Law states to what it implies.[56] In his detailed commentaries on Aristotle's *Ethics* and *Politics,* Aquinas worked out a synthesis of reason and revelation that was to remain central to Christian theology for centuries, until shaken by the new physics of Newton and Galileo.

It is hardly an exaggeration to say that politics and religion today remain locked in a struggle that began in the confrontation of medieval thinkers steeped in their faiths with the rationalism of the Greek classical tradition.

8

History has been unkind to Machiavelli. His very name has entered our language as synonymous with evil. To be a Machiavellian is to be unscrupulous and duplicitous, an intriguer and schemer, a person who "practices expediency in preference to morality."[1] The equation of Machiavelli with ruthless cunning was sufficiently established by Shakespeare's time to permit the playwright's great villain, Richard of Gloucester, soon to become Richard III, to boast:

> I can add colors to the chameleon
> Change shapes with Proteus for advantages,
> And set the murtherous Machevil to school.[2]

Ever since, the label "Machiavellian" has stuck to any leader who combines cruelty with connivance in extraordinary ways. It was once even rumored that Hitler kept a copy of Machiavelli's *Prince* on his nightstand.[3] Such is the reputation history has assigned to Niccolò Machiavelli.

If only it were so simple. T. S. Eliot probably went too easy on Machiavelli when he said that no one was ever less Machiavellian than Machiavelli. I am more inclined to agree with Voltaire's famous quip, "If Machiavelli had had a prince for a disciple, the first thing he would have recommended him to do would have been to write a book against Machiavellianism."[4] Voltaire's remark captures the deviousness of the thinker; those of us who wish to offer a spirited defense of Machiavelli have to be wary lest we fall for one of the many ways wrong can wear the disguise of right. So let me begin by listing some among the numerous troubling pieces of advice Machiavelli offered rulers, as we begin to ask with due resistance what it is about politics that could possibly necessitate these strategies:

- Seizing power violently and illegally is what rulers do; to pretend otherwise is simply not to understand the nature of political ambition.
- Success brings its own justification.
- Morally conscientious persons finish last in politics, bringing ruin on themselves and their country.
- He who seizes power by arms must make sure to exterminate every last living relative of the deposed ruler, as they will never forgive him.
- Men should either be caressed or annihilated but never appeased.
- He who conquers a free city must destroy it or it will destroy him.
- War should never be avoided and can be deferred only to the advantage of the other side.
- It is better to fake religion than actually to have it.
- It is necessary to betray one's friends when the situation calls for it.
- Men sooner forget the death of their father than the loss of their patrimony.
- While it is well to *appear* merciful, faithful, truthful, humane, and religious, it is dangerous actually to be so.
- Consolidate all power in one's own hands, even if this means killing one's own brother.
- The important thing about cruelty is that it be done with dispatch, all at once, and with sufficient range to get the job done. Those whose conscience keeps them from using violence will end up spilling blood, drop by drop, wasting power while perpetuating war.

This is frightening stuff, and it would be bad enough if Machiavelli were the person he is reputed to be—a minor political functionary who, once he was out of power, tried to insinuate himself into the good graces of the reigning Medici rulers in his home city of Florence by offering the "wisdom" of his long study of political strategy. Unfortunately we cannot so readily distance ourselves from the dire implications of Machiavelli's self-consciously "new" political science. Machiavelli cer-

146

tainly was willing to advise would-be rulers on how to seize and maintain power, putting aside any judgment about the morality of their usurpations. And in his most famous book, *The Prince,* he offers "the ends justifies the means" arguments in which the sole necessity dictating violent means is the prince's own grip on power. But elsewhere Machiavelli makes a more expansive argument, aimed at showing that even, or perhaps especially, republics need leaders willing to get their hands dirty. That *princes* do Machiavellian things for their own benefit is no news at all; that leaders who aim at the common good must similarly lie, cheat, betray, and murder is the more shocking and original of Machiavelli's teachings.

The Problem of Dirty Hands

Think of it this way. Bad persons do not need Machiavelli's prompting to commit atrocities; they know all too well how to commit evil on their own. But benevolent leaders need to learn that the *common* good is not always the same as the *moral* good, and that we count on them to serve the former even if it means violating the latter. *This* teaching—that there come moments in politics when good ends necessitate evil means—is both what gives and what saves Machiavelli from his reputation for evil.

Let me offer an overview of the argument I make here about the problem of dirty hands in politics. Midway through *The Prince,* Machiavelli pauses to emphasize the freshness of his approach to politics and morality. Since so many have written on the subject, Machiavelli fears it may seem "presumptuous" of him to set a different course. But, in a sly allusion to Plato, he continues:

> [M]y intention being to write something of use to those who understand, it appears to me more proper to go to the real truth of the matter than to its imagination; and many have imagined republics and principalities which have never been seen or known to exist in reality; *for how we live is so far removed from how we ought to live, that he who abandons what is done for what ought to be done, will rather learn to bring about his own ruin than his preservation.*[5]

Passages such as this are teeming with moral distinctions—odd in someone who for centuries has enjoyed a reputation for immorality or amorality. Machiavelli does not ignore or abolish the distinction in politics, or anywhere else, between "what ought to be done" and "what is done"; in fact he insists on it. The dilemma is that pure goodness is politically impotent, and a "man who wishes to make a profession of goodness in everything must necessarily come to grief *among so many who are not good.*"[6] And then, in a final flourish which makes abundantly clear that Machiavelli addresses his Machiavellianism to those whose character is disposed to avoid evil, "Therefore, it is necessary for a prince, who wishes to maintain himself, to learn *how not to be good,* and to use this knowledge, *and not use it,* according to the necessity of the case."[7] Obviously, those who already are not good do not need to "learn" how not to be good. That is what makes the image of Hitler needing tutorship from Machiavelli so absurd. Nor can the Hitlers and lesser Hitlers be Machiavellian in the sense of *refraining* from evil when they can, resorting to it only when they must.

Perhaps, though, I am wrong about this. A student pointed out to me that a tyrant could be both ruthless and Machiavellian by making a *show* of reluctance to use violence. Her example was the alleged mastermind of the September 11 attacks, Khalid Shaikh Mohammed, who said by way of justification: "I'm not happy that 3,000 have been killed in America. I feel sorry even. I don't like to kill children [but] the language of war is victims." My student was not tempted to think the mind that conceived of flying planes into office buildings was actually reluctant to kill, but she thought the show of sincerity was all that Machiavellianism requires. If so, then there may be no way to save Machiavelli from his reputation for evil; but I will mount a defense—a defense premised on the frightening possibility that the evil that comes naturally to the wicked must be learned by those whom we want to sin on our behalf.

Machiavelli's Paganism

The customary claim that Machiavelli divorces politics from morality is correct in one regard. Machiavelli *did* reject one set of moral values— the virtues taught by Christianity—as the proper compass by which to direct the state. But as the intellectual historian Isaiah Berlin puts it, he did so only

> in favor of another system, another moral universe—the world of Pericles. . . , a society geared to ends just as ultimate as the Christian faith, a society in which men fight and are ready to die for

(public) ends which they pursue for their own sakes. They are choosing not a realm of means (called politics) as opposed to a realm of ends (called morals), but opt for a rival (Roman or classical) morality, an alternative realm of ends.[8]

More than a thousand years after the triumph of Christian ethics in his beloved Italy, Machiavelli set out to reverse course. He looked upon the dismembered state of his own Christian Florence and the Italy beyond, compared it to the glory that was pagan Rome, and took his stand—without hesitation, Berlin notes. Machiavelli did not think one could have both a personal life judged moral according to Christian standards and a public life ennobled by pagan ethics. One had to choose, and for many readers, including me, this triggers anguish—at the notion that one might very well have to sell one's soul to serve and to save one's country. The striking thing about Machiavelli is that he rarely betrayed such anguish. This lack of pause is, Berlin suggests, what gives Machiavelli his reputation for evil. We tortured souls want him to lament the tragic consequences of the sacrifices of individual moral purity necessitated by the welfare of the state, but Machiavelli felt no such tragedy. He writes within the classical ethical tradition in which sacrifices for the good of the community, rather than causing us to lose our moral way, give us the highest ethical life that human beings can achieve. This is why Machiavelli displays near relish for the moments when citizens and rulers alike have to dirty their hands and, by so doing, claim the higher ethical life that comes only from sacrificing for one's country.

Machiavelli's pagan ethics explain both his preference for republican government and yet his willingness to advise princes. He prefers republics as the system of government best suited to harmonize the interests of rulers and ruled. But he is willing to abide princes who at least, in serving themselves, bring peace, stability, and independence to Florence and, beyond that, unity to Italy. His ethical aspiration is always the same—greatness of country—and Machiavelli is willing to advise princes as well as republicans how to accomplish the national renaissance.

In introducing Machiavelli, I begin with his disquieting defense of the terrible demands of republican morality. Only since the September 11 attacks has the problem of dirty hands again absorbed our attention. The ancient Romans had a saying which formed the basis of Machiavelli's teachings on war and violence: "in bello silentio leges" (in time of war the laws are silent). Isn't it the case today that we fear that the Romans and Machiavelli may have been right, that the war on terror requires us to use methods we would rather not acknowledge? But we are reluctant with our own Machiavellianism. If war truly requires suspension of the usual moral judgments, then how can we accuse terrorists of war crimes? A question such as this makes our confrontation with Machiavelli's teachings on violence more intense and personal than our engagement with any other political thinker.

In what follows I turn first to Machiavelli's most seemingly diabolical book, *The Prince,* then to his defense of republican politics in the *Discourses.* But it is important to keep in mind that the two books are united in their teaching that fear and violence are the prime movers of politics everywhere.

The Prince: Whose Ends Justify What Violence?

The story of how Machiavelli came to write a book of advice to princes is often told as already an example of Machiavellianism. In the last years of the fifteenth century and the first decade of the sixteenth, Machiavelli enjoyed a career as a minor diplomat for the Florentine city-state. Complicated rivalries between France and the papacy controlled Florence's fate; when the pope drove French forces from Italy, Florence found it had bet on the losing side.

The papal victory led to the restoration of the Medici family to power in Florence. Though opposed to the Medici while he was in diplomatic service, Machiavelli did an about-face and wrote letters to the new powers, beseeching them to make use of his services. *The Prince,* dedicated to Lorenzo de' Medici in 1512, is part of Machiavelli's campaign to work his way back into power. Such an apparent willingness to switch sides and advise whoever happened to be in charge makes Machiavelli his own first Machiavellian, craftily responding as fortune dictates. Rousseau thought the portrait of Machiavelli selling out to the Medici so unattractive that he preferred to read *The Prince* as a satire on would-be Machiavellians rather than as an example of blatant guile on Machiavelli's part.

But the manual seems neither satirical nor insincere. Before he wrote *The Prince,* Machiavelli had written in favor of republican government, but in a way that emphasized the need for strong, armed, and ruthless leaders even in republics. In advising princes on the intricacies of violence, Machiavelli simply carried through on his overarching theme that all politics is war. He preferred republican rule where it was possible, since it stood the best chance of generating power and freedom by uniting the interests of rulers and ruled. But he was willing to get into bed with princes, as it were, without any illusion about them: they are after their own good. Still, in a time when Florence had been failed by a ruler whom he thought of as too good in Christian terms, Machiavelli entertained the thought that the very earthiness of princely ambition might, by comparison to Christian virtue, be in a country's interest.

Princes come to power in many different ways. Some inherit power, others claim it from God; in cases such as these, princes need no personal skill but can rely on the obedience given to their blood or to ancient religious customs. Other princes are installed through the arms of others and remain precariously beholden as client to patron. Still others rise and fall with the tides of fortune.

By contrast, some persons seize and maintain power through the force of their own arms and abilities. These new monarchs, these "masterless men," are the ones Machiavelli sets out to advise. They need his advice because "[i]t must be considered that there is nothing more difficult to carry out, nor more doubtful of success, nor more dangerous to handle, than to initiate a new order of things."[9] Kings and queens of England can sleepwalk through their time on the throne and yet count on the traditional obedience of their subjects; the new prince is the more to be admired for the skill and talent it takes to pull off a coup. Machiavelli combines this unabashed admiration for the daring of the usurper with an acceptance of the ambition that fuels the daring. Princes are "political" in the way most of us are not—they hanker after *their* own power and glory—and there is no use hectoring them to change their stripes.

The Prince's Ends

As to the prince's ends—for what reasons or purposes princes desire power—Machiavelli has precious little to say. *The Prince* is full of advice about the *means* of politics. But Machiavelli is not in the business of advising princes about the ends they should serve. He treats it as obvious that they seek power for their own glory. In the days before scanners and computer search engines, I used to challenge my students to keep track while they were reading *The Prince* and to let me know whether they came across a single reference to a prince serving ends beyond his own interests—any reference to a prince aiming at power in order to serve the common good or general welfare. Now, of course, such searches can be done with a click of the mouse, but even so, students confirm that the only arguable reference to princes seeking power for anything other than its own sake comes in the concluding chapter of *The Prince,* where Machiavelli urges some new leader to liberate Italy from the barbarians, thereby doing "honor to himself and good to the mass of the people."[10] But even here Machiavelli does not propose that princes have the good of the people in mind or aim at it; it is merely that a prince craving personal honor should be Machiavellian enough to see how liberating Italy will immortalize his name in history.

The Prince's Means

Although Machiavelli has little to say about the prince's ends, he has much to offer about the means necessary to achieve those ends. Machiavelli's advice, however, does not cohere into a system that anyone could learn and follow; great leadership is a matter of personal charisma, and the best Machiavelli can offer is the benefit of his study of historical examples, both ancient and contemporary, of those who achieved greatness.

What these examples show, first and foremost, is that violence is the predominant means of politics; all politics is war, and a prince who wishes to maintain himself in power "should have no other aim or thought . . . but war . . . , for that is the only art that is necessary to one who commands."[11] Even Moses, who purportedly ruled by the grace of God, is testament to the reality that "armed prophets have conquered and unarmed ones failed."[12] Well and good it was to rely on belief rather than force, so long as the Israelites believed; but Moses arranged matters so that "when they no longer believe[d], they [could] be made to believe by force."[13] Thus Machiavelli writes, "[W]hoever reads the Bible attentively will find that Moses . . . was obliged to have a great many persons put to death who opposed his designs."[14]

Much of what Machiavelli has to say about the necessity of violence is not pretty. The sheer fact that the new prince dares to overthrow an existing order means that he is bound to make "enemies in all those who profit by the old order."[15] If he is to succeed, then the usurper "will have to deal with [those he overthrows] severely." Machiavelli offers Hiero of Syracuse as a case study.[16] By force of personal skill Hiero rose from a private position to become head of the army of Syracuse. Surveying the mercenaries in his army, he astutely realized that it was not safe either to retain them or to dismiss them. So "he had them cut in pieces."[17] Likewise, Hannibal kept discipline over a mass army through many campaigns by an "inhuman" level of cruelty that nonetheless displayed considerable political acumen as to what it takes to keep one's own army from revolting in harsh times. Cesare Borgia, whom Machiavelli returns to time and time again as his ideal new prince, understood that those who profited from the old order will always remain enemies of the new ruler; he therefore acted wisely "by destroying all who were of the blood of those ruling families which he had despoiled."[18]

In the *Discourses,* Machiavelli's previously written book on republics, he reverted on occasion to the question of princes and their tactics. He makes a particular study of Philip of Macedon, father of Alexander the Great, who rose from being a "petty king" to "master of all Greece." What can we learn from his example? When Philip conquered a province, he "always organized [the government] entirely anew." To gain control, he would transfer inhabitants from one province to another, "as shepherds move their flocks from place to place."[19] In the midst of approving these tactics, Machiavelli pauses to acknowledge that "[d]oubtless these means are cruel and destructive of all civilized life, and neither Christian nor even human."[20] And in a rare moment that approaches something like anguish, Machiavelli notes that "the life of a private citizen would be preferable to that of a king at the expense of the ruin of so many human beings."[21] But these are the choices: a private person can honor the humane virtues, but a prince who dares to conquer should take Philip as a model.

The Philip story is among the most disturbing of all the endorsements Machiavelli hands out, and it is telling that he recounts the glory of this pagan prince in the *Discourses,* not *The Prince.* Machiavelli looks at the inhumanity of Philip's relocation policies and does not blink. He does not promise that all will come out well in the end; one cannot emulate both the pagan paradigm, with its splendid ferocity and pursuit of earthly glory, and the humane paradigm to love thy neighbor as thyself. There is only an ultimate and irresoluble clash of values, pagan versus Christian.

It is tempting to follow many commentators and view Machiavelli as a man of the Renaissance, whose appreciation of pagan ferocity was more aesthetic than moral. In this view, Machiavelli the artist feels a rather distant and detached attraction for what is splendid, powerful, and energetic about princes. He has all this, but he offers more—an impassioned plea to embrace the example of the ancients as offering us a moral renaissance, a way of fulfilling the highest nobility humans can express in loving their country more than their soul. Machiavelli took this message about republican virtue from his study of the ancient Greeks and Romans. He refurbished the message, emboldened it, and passed it along with great influence on the subsequent history of politics.

The Economy of Violence

Are there any limits to a prince's use of violent means? Machiavelli does distinguish between violence "well committed" and "cruelties ill committed."[22] But his distinction is not exactly a moral one. Princes use violence well when they use it massively, all at once, to secure themselves; once the job is done and enemies are annihilated, the prince can then exchange violent rule for "measures as useful to the subjects as possible." Ill-committed violence is violence that increases rather than diminishes in time, doled out in dribs and drabs that are never quite enough to get the job done. Violence is committed poorly by those who, by nature or moral conviction, are reluctant to shed blood. Their hesitancy ironically perpetuates a cycle of violence, as enemies live to fight another day and civil wars prevent peace from breaking out. As Machiavelli puts it, the ruler who commits violence poorly is "always obliged to stand with knife in hand."[23]

Well-committed violence therefore is more economical in the end. But what is being economized is not necessarily the number of persons killed; the quick dispatch of *all* of one's enemies at once may claim more victims than the slow parceling out of violence over time can ever match. What is "economized" is more a matter of the prince's power. By getting the job done and restoring peace and stability, he can then save his arms for launching attacks abroad or for repelling invasions.

Contemporary instances of ill-committed violence are not difficult to come by. In the Middle East, a seemingly endless cycle of border incidents between Israel and Lebanon followed by reprisal raids serves to enforce something akin to permanent war on the region but without war's usual promise of eventual victory for one side. Given this stalemate of small violences, many regret the waste of lives lost for no apparent purpose; some on each side yearn for a Machiavellian solution whereby their side would use violence "well" enough to get the task done, the task being to destroy one's enemies. In Iraq, critics of U.S. military policy from both left and right strangely agreed that the United States should either have committed far more troops to the field or else stayed out all together.

What is harder to come by is an example of well-committed violence. But consider the defense President Harry Truman gave of his decision to drop atomic bombs on Japan, namely, to save American lives. Dropping bombs on Nagasaki and Hiroshima was sufficient violence at once to get the job done, even while economizing on American losses. By contrast, conventional warfare—continuation of aerial bombing, along with an eventual invasion—was violence that would have unfolded in waves over time, certainly costing more American lives and possibly killing more Japanese than in a nuclear attack, siphoning off American military might from being deployed elsewhere in the world, permitting the Soviet Union perhaps to share in the eventual occupation of Japan.

But the trouble with Machiavelli's distinction between well-committed and ill-committed violence is that it privileges saving power over saving lives, and hence almost always recommends *disproportionate* uses of violence as the best course of action. The doctrine of proportionality in warfare, part of agreed-upon international law today, would have struck Machiavelli as a recipe for quagmire and stalemate, a refusal to understand the immanent logic of warfare, which is to win while minimizing costs to one's own troops. Moreover, in the case of the atom bombing of Japanese cities, the most difficult aspect to justify is the toll on civilians that the attack predictably caused. Machiavelli's economic calculus seems indifferent to whether victims are soldiers or civilians.

Atrocities and Violence

Some uses of violence struck even Machiavelli as too horrible to praise, even when they work. He had in mind *domestic* massacres—atrocities committed against one's own people. In a crucial chapter of *The Prince* strikingly titled "Of Those Who Have Attained the Position of Prince by Villainy," Machiavelli takes up the forgotten case of Agathocles the Sicilian.[24] Measured strictly on the success versus failure axis, Agathocles' meteoric rise to power would seem to deserve great praise. He "rose not only from private life but from the lowest and most abject position to be King of Syracuse."[25] And his extraordinary success was due entirely to his own arms and ability; he owed nothing to luck or to the assistance of others.

Nonetheless, Machiavelli persists in pointing out that Agathocles' "wickedness" and his "atrocities" were so glaring that they cannot be condoned. The son of a potter, Agathocles seized every opportunity to rise through the ranks until by constitutional means he became the head executive in Syracuse. But he aspired to hold power absolutely. So he "called together one morning the people and senate of Syracuse, as if he had to deliberate on matters of importance to the republic, and at a given signal had all the senators and the richest men of the people killed by his soldiers."[26]

On Agathocles' atrocity against his own people Machiavelli passes a mixed judgment. On the one hand, the massacre worked and permitted Agathocles to rule over the city without any internal strife and to defend the city against invaders. Agathocles has to be credited with "braving and overcoming perils," and his "greatness of soul" was such that "one sees no reason for holding him inferior to any of the most renowned captains."[27] On the other hand, Machiavelli balks at the prospect that Agathocles could be held out as a model. What he did demonstrated "barbarous cruelty and inhumanity."[28] In a telling passage strange for a writer reputed to think that moral judgments have no place in politics, Machiavelli writes, "It cannot be called virtue to kill one's fellow citizens, betray one's friends, be without faith, without pity, and be without religion; by these methods one may indeed gain power, but not glory."[29]

This distinction between power and glory is Machiavelli at his Machiavellian best. He sets out to manipulate the behavior of rulers such as Agathocles—not by hectoring them in conventional Christian moral terms but by appealing to the value they place on glory. For Machiavelli, it is a good not a bad thing that rulers strive for an end as pagan as glory. God controls the glory of the next world, but historians control reputation on earth. This provides a mechanism for controlling rulers' behavior, if historians can get it right, assigning and withholding glory according to the prince's service to the welfare of the state. Machiavelli sets out to keep the historical record clear about Agathocles, creating a precedent to sway future tyrants from committing atrocities by warning them that some methods of winning power forfeit the greater goal of glory. In short, Machiavelli passes a *moral* judgment on Agathocles, but it is not a Christian judgment; it is a judgment within a pagan worldview which connects personal glory to the glory of the country.

Machiavelli passes a similar moral judgment on Oliverotto da Fermo.[30] A fatherless boy, Oliverotto was raised by his uncle Giovanni, who sent him to be trained as a soldier. Oliverotto's natural talents allowed him to emerge as a leader of the troops, and he resolved to make

156

himself prince of Fermo. Entering Fermo with his troops, ostensibly to do honor to fellow citizens, Oliverotto invited his uncle and the other principal nobles of Fermo to a grand banquet. At a given signal, Oliverotto's soldiers slaughtered the gathered guests, and after what Machiavelli himself labels a "massacre," Oliverotto ruled securely for a term over the city. But he can no more be praised than Agathocles.

The Lion and the Fox

Violence may be a necessary means of politics but it is rarely sufficient. The Machiavellian ruler must be a fox as well as a lion, knowing when cunning, trickery, and deception are better suited than outright violence.[31] In sections of *The Prince* that frontally challenge the portrait of the Christian ruler, embodying the great moral virtues of life, Machiavelli writes that politics requires the successful ruler to be a master of disguise, a quick-change artist. He must certainly arrange things so that he *appears* to be "merciful, faithful, humane, sincere, and religious."[32] But while these appearances are useful, it would be dangerous always to behave according to the moral virtues. And therefore a leader "must have the mind so disposed that when it is needful to be otherwise, [he] may be able to change to the opposite qualities [and] act against faith, against charity, against humanity and against religion."[33] Machiavelli freely admits that "[i]f men were all good, this precept would not be a good one; but as they are bad, and would not observe their faith with you, so you are not bound to keep faith with them."[34]

Take, for instance, the cunning of Cesare Borgia. After taking over the Romagna, he arranged matters so that he could rule with an iron fist and yet seem merciful. Borgia deputized an assistant to put down every kind of disorder with swift and certain severity. But knowing that harshness breeds hatred, Borgia then "resolved to show that if any cruelty had taken place it was not by his orders," and he thereupon "had [his minister] cut in half and placed one morning in the public square with a piece of wood and blood-stained knife by his side."[35]

Borgia learned the lessons of deceit well from his father, Pope Alexander VI. A consummate feigner and dissembler, the pope "did nothing else but deceive men, he thought of nothing else." No man "was ever more able to give assurances, or affirmed things with stronger oaths, and no man observed them less; however, he always succeeded in his deceptions."[36] As to Moses, Machiavelli stops short of claiming outright that Moses feigned conversation with God, but the lesson for other princes is to imitate his great example, even if God does not deign actually to visit.

The Ends Justify the Means?

What is the "necessity" that justifies a prince's resort to violence and deception? At one point Machiavelli formulates his doctrine in "ends/ means" fashion. The crucial passage is this: "[I]n the actions of men, and especially of princes, from which there is no appeal, the end justifies the means. Let a prince therefore aim at conquering and maintaining the state, and the means will always be judged honorable."[37] In this formulation, the prince's own ends (conquering and maintaining the state) justify or excuse the means (violence and deception). Now I can well understand why the *prince* would be receptive to this way of formulating the "ends justify the means" argument. But why should the rest of us? What do the people get out of obeying a prince who resorts to lying and killing to achieve his own ends?

For the most part Machiavelli does not answer this question in *The Prince*. But at times he suggests an alternative formulation of the "ends justify the means" argument. The prince's ends never vary; we cannot expect the politically ambitious to be directly motivated by the public good. Still, most of us care less who is prince than that someone simply be prince, conquer his opponents, end civil war, and return the nation to peace. Peace, not power, is what ordinary citizens desire, and we can get it best when some prince is ruthless enough to use violence well. In this sense the people are indirectly served when princes are skilled and ruthless enough—pagan enough—to serve their own ends. Thus Machiavelli's argument can be reformulated: the ends of the prince (power and glory) *and* the means of the prince (violence and deceit) are both justified by the foreseeable consequences of the means (peace and domestic order). In other words, a kind of indirect hand forges a bond between prince and people after all.

Or at least the bond is forged if power is in the hands of a prince whose ethics are sufficiently pagan to do what it takes to make himself powerful and glorious by making the country powerful and glorious. This is the essence of Machiavelli's realism and explains why a committed republican could find common ground with princely ambition. At least the prince lives and dies for the political life as the highest life, and it is the revival of this ethic that promises the revival of the glory that was Rome.

The *Discourses* and the Republican Version of Dirty Hands

I turn now to Machiavelli's case for both the superiority of republican government and yet the necessity for republican leaders to emulate princes in the ways of fear and violence. Machiavelli's great work on republics took the form—common at the time—of commentaries or discourses on some ancient work. The text sparking Machiavelli's discourses was Titus Livy's *History of the Roman Republic*. Only parts of that ancient history had survived into Machiavelli's time, and he used the fragments as a starting point for reflections about what made Rome great and in what ways republics of his own day might learn from Rome's example.

The *Discourses* begins with the phrase that nowhere appears in *The Prince*. Machiavelli claims that he writes "for the common benefit of all."[38] In *The Prince*, Machiavelli wrote for the benefit of the ruler, though I have argued that there may be indirect benefit to the people from a prince ruthless enough to make his dominions great. But in the *Discourses*, actually written before *The Prince*, Machiavelli makes clear that he prefers republics to monarchies. How are we to understand Machiavelli's republican commitments if they left him room to advise princes?

I argue that the tension between the *Discourses* and *The Prince* is not as great as Machiavelli's reputation for being two-faced implies. Machiavelli's ultimate political values are always the same: freedom and aggrandizement of country. Republics are superior to principalities precisely because they promise more splendid politics, more conquests, bigger armies, more devotion, and longer life. And in the quest to achieve these sacred political ends, "that which princes are obliged to do . . . , republics are equally obliged to practice."[39]

In introducing his discourses, Machiavelli sounds two themes that resound through the ensuing work. First, in going back to the wisdom of the ancients, Machiavelli nevertheless sees himself as "open[ing] a new route."[40] Persons in his day already paid hefty sums to collect some ancient statue; Renaissance artists strove to imitate the ancients in theme and approach. Yet when it came to the study of politics, the ancient texts lay neglected. The obstacle, according to Machiavelli, is the "proud indolence" of Christian states that keeps them from appreciating the "prodigies of virtue" that pagan Rome offered in abundance.[41] When one reads in Livy of citizens and captains "sacrific[ing] themselves for their country," one begins to recover a beautiful form of politics that is in danger of being lost among Christians who dismiss such patriotic devotion as idol worship.[42] Second, it is the Roman republic, not the empire, that Machiavelli finds teeming with exemplars of civic and political virtue. Rome became great because it was a republic, and Machiavelli sets out to reforge the connection between republican government and national greatness.

Machiavelli's Republicanism

From his study of ancient Rome, Machiavelli culls several reasons why regimes that serve the common good are the best form of government. To begin with, republics have the advantage when it comes to raising armies and motivating persons to fight and to die for country. In republics, ordinary citizens experience themselves as stakeholders in the success of the regime and thus rally to defend independence at home and expansion abroad. By comparison, princes are at a military disadvantage twice over. Not only can they not rival republics in the quantity and quality of their soldiers, but also they sometimes have to leave garrisons at home "to assure their government to which the mass of the people is hostile."[43]

It is tempting to conclude that Machiavelli located the superiority of republics in military rather than moral terms. But it would be more accurate to say that their moral superiority in inspiring civic virtue, self-sacrifice, and devotion to country is what grounds the military success of republics. Whenever the spirit of liberty is at large in the land, people act on the connection between national and personal freedom. A people who value freedom highly, and see the country's independence as a precondition for maintaining their way of life, are a virtuous people willing to sacrifice for their country.

Under conditions of freedom, citizens "of various character and dispositions" emerge.[44] This diversity turns out to be one of the republic's greatest assets. Republics may not produce individual geniuses, but they make up in breadth of talents what they lack in depth. The sheer range of popular talents permits the country to adjust to changing circumstances, by drawing on whatever talents happen to be needed at the moment.

Still, Machiavelli sees republican and princely politics as operating on a continuum. The common run of humanity is not much interested in political freedom per se—in holding office or sharing power or sailing the ship of state. The popular desire for liberty consists mostly in being "able to live in greater security."[45] By ruling well, a prince can satisfy the people's desires for peace and security. But monarchies can never match republics in capitalizing on popular love of liberty. This explains why "only those cities and countries that are free can achieve greatness."[46]

Republican greatness is measurable in material as well as military terms. Population is greater in republics "because marriages are more free and offer more advantages to the citizen."[47] The fact of the matter is that "people will gladly have children when they know that they can support them." And they know they can support them when they do not fear the sudden loss of their property from rapacious rulers. In republics "we also see wealth increase more rapidly . . . [,] for everybody gladly multiplies those things, and seeks to acquire those goods the possession of which he can tranquilly enjoy."[48]

Machiavelli repeatedly stresses this deep connection between political freedom and economic prosperity, between the civic virtues a republic inspires and the work ethic that produces wealth. While he is not especially original in seeing economic activity in moral terms, Machiavelli distinctively argues that pagan virtue—devotion to good of country—is best at reaping material rewards for both individuals and country.

Although republican politics produce wealth, too much wealth—or rather too much inequality in its distribution—can threaten the civic virtues necessary to sustain prosperity. The problem is that the wealthy are corrupted by their own riches. They become "gentlemen" living off "the proceeds of their extensive possessions" without making any useful contribution to creating new wealth.[49] Their inequality of circumstances leads them to distinguish their interests from their neighbors' and to live in castles and the like, in a country of their own. When wealth turns into power of this sort, then monarchies are the only solution, since it takes absolute power to curb the ambitions of the idle and corrupt rich. By contrast, republics require a rough equality of economic circumstance, enough so that the propertied can still serve country rather than their own purse.

Dirty Hands in the Republic

Even in republics, civic virtue is not enough. In times of crisis and corruption, republics, like monarchies, require great leaders willing to employ wicked means. The *Discourses* rivals *The Prince* in the frequency of its endorsements of the necessity for force and fraud in politics.

We could have hoped that political history was a progressive story, coming ever closer to a time when the common good and the moral good come together. But, as Berlin puts it, Machiavelli dashes any such hopes. Fear and cruelty are mainstays of politics, and there is no coming age of love and reason. As I have said before, the most disquieting thing about Machiavelli is that he seems to celebrate the occasions when politics turns ferocious.

In the *Discourses,* Machiavelli dwells on two major periods when republics need the sinning leader: the founding era and the era for reforming a republic teetering on corruption.

Foundings

As to Rome's founding, Machiavelli took two stock stories familiar to his audience and stood them on their heads. The first was the story of how Romulus slew his brother Remus and seized power for himself.[50] The second was the tale of Numa laying down the first legal code by claiming that the laws had been revealed to him by divine nymphs.[51] One story is about murder and fratricide; the other is about deceit and feigning divine inspiration. In the traditional telling of these tales for a Christian people, they highlighted the immoral foundations of a pagan nation—Saint Augustine's quintessential "earthly city." Augustine saw the Romulus story as archetypal of the criminal origins of all earthly cities—just another version of the biblical story of Cain slaying Abel or Jacob deceiving his father, Isaac, into bestowing on him the birthright belonging to the firstborn, Esau. No nation conceived in fratricide, populated by rape of the Sabine women, and fobbing off laws on the people as if they were God's commands could teach us anything about justice.

In Machiavelli's retelling, Romulus and Numa emerge as exemplary founding figures. Consider Romulus first. If Romulus had murdered his brother merely for his own princely ambitions, then there would be no moral justification for the act.[52] The ends most definitely do *not* justify the means when brothers slay brothers in private life. But political life, even in republics, marches to its own moral imperatives. There are moments—foundings are among them—when the common good excuses violence. Rome was blessed with a founder who took on the gravest of personal sins for the public's welfare.

Machiavelli does not provide empirical evidence for the "necessity" of Romulus' fratricide. We certainly should pause and ask questions about alternatives that Machiavelli never broached. Did Romulus try to negotiate political arrangements with his brother? Had he exhausted diplomacy, negotiation, and every avenue for avoiding murder? It almost seems as if Machiavelli's point is that rulers of a diplomatic and compromising sort are disasters as founders. He takes it as evident that well-designed institutions cannot be the result of compromise but must embody the coherent vision of one mind. Sometimes I have the impression that Machiavelli wastes little time considering diplomatic alternatives to violence because his ethic prizes opportunities for militant heroes to arise. Romulus sets a good, not a bad, example when he acts with ferocity and dispatch to realize his republican vision.

Machiavelli structures his defense of Romulus around both the intent of the actor and also the consequences of the fratricide. It matters that Romulus was *motivated* by the common rather than personal good. By this I mean that it is not enough that Romulus did the right thing, judged by some impartial spectator. It is crucial that he was a certain kind of moral character when doing his deeds, a person acting in the spirit of civic virtue and allegiance to country above even his own brother. But how do we know this about Romulus? What is the evidence that his psychology was public-spirited rather than self-interested? Here the best we can do is to judge his motives from his behavior. Upon ridding himself of his brother, Romulus immediately used his total authority to create power-sharing institutions such as a Senate.[53] A person who killed his own brother for self-interested purposes would never have acted in this way.

Of course, consequences also matter; Machiavelli wants the ferocity of leaders to achieve good and lasting results. In Romulus' case, if we are keeping accounts accurately, the service of the Senate to the good of successive generations of Romans outweighed the harm of one never repeated fratricide. This is why Machiavelli can say of Romulus that "it is well that when the act accuses him, the result should excuse him."[54]

Machiavelli couples his praise of Romulus as founder of the Roman republic with condemnation of Julius Caesar as its destroyer.[55] In doing so, Machiavelli is aware that he is defying conventional historical wisdom. One might have expected the author of *The Prince* to share in praising Caesar. After all, Caesar enjoyed long and successful leadership as a great general. Then, when the moment came for Caesar to enter Rome and to disband his army at the city's gates, as was customary, he was daring enough to defy custom, to remain armed, and to use his army to install himself in power. And although Caesar was assassinated, still he started an empire that ruled in his name for five hundred years. So great and famous became the name of Caesar that we still know it today. But this is all wrong, according to Machiavelli. Julius Caesar deserves infamy and condemnation for overturning the Roman republic. Romulus seized power to share it; Caesar seized power for himself. There is little to praise in that, not even had Caesar succeeded.

Given the psychology of the politically ambitious, how do we keep the powerful from turning on us, from turning into Caesar? Machiavelli is clear that we cannot and should not rid politics of leaders who yearn for immortality of name. The best we can do is work within their ambitions, turning them to our advantage. That is why the historical mistake in glorifying Caesar is so important to Machiavelli. We need to correct it to motivate future leaders to avoid emulating Caesar's wicked example.

The Romulus story illustrates the centrality of violence in giving birth to free nations. Numa's case illustrates the equal political importance of lying, deceit, deception, and fraud. If anything, Machiavelli remarks, fledging republics are more dependent on deceit than on force, and no one outdid Numa in lying well and big.[56] Numa saw the need for Romans to live by law but doubted they would obey laws backed only by his authority. He therefore tricked the people into believing that divine nymphs had revealed the sacred law to him. The ruse worked, the results were extraordinarily good, and the laws based on spurious authority lasted for hundreds of years.

Numa is one of many lawgivers Machiavelli praises for creating a "civil religion" useful to politics. As I mentioned previously, Machiavelli hesitates to accuse Moses of faking receipt of the Ten Commandments from the hand of God, but his message is clear. Sometimes gingerly, sometimes openly, Machiavelli suggests that the people prosper when they are fortunate enough to find lawgivers willing to make political hay out of religion. Indeed the greatest lesson to be drawn from the civilizations of antiquity lay in "the difference of their religion and ours."[57]

Christianity is the true religion, Machiavelli begins (a testament that did not save his works from making the dread Index during the Inquisition). But precisely because it "teaches us the truth and the true way of life, it causes us to attach less value to the honors and possessions of this world."[58] By contrast, pagan religion is more politically useful because it teaches attachment to the honors and possessions of this world as if they were the highest possessions men can enjoy. Such a pagan attitude may be theologically false, but it energized men to defend with great ferocity the territory and freedom of their homelands. Quite different is the true Christian who, "for the sake of gaining Paradise," is prepared to endure injuries here on earth rather than sinning to avenge them.[59] The result is that the pagans glorified the talents of great soldiers and citizens, while Christianity glorifies the more humble and contemplative of men. In this way "the world has become effeminate and Heaven disarmed."[60]

As a way of illustrating the difference between republican and Christian virtue, Machiavelli contrasts the behavior of the man under whom he had served in Florentine politics—Pietro Soderini—with the ancient example of Lucius Brutus. This Brutus is not the one who assassinated Caesar but an earlier Brutus, who put to death his own sons when service to the state required it. Brutus had taken the lead in expelling the Tarquin kings from Rome and restoring liberty and republican government. His sons then plotted to restore the kings, and Brutus had them put to death, condemning them himself and even attending their execution. Such a terrible punishment was severe for a father to mete out to his own sons, but the spectacle of such terror is what it takes to maintain liberty against those who would conspire to take it away.

In Machiavelli's own day, Pietro Soderini was head of the republican government in Florence at a time when "new sons of Brutus" arose to threaten the republic. Soderini recognized the danger but thought that virtues such as "patience and gentleness" would suffice to put down his adversaries. Taking this course of action, Soderini proved himself a good Christian but a bad leader. He should have emulated the severity of Brutus and struck down his enemies at one blow. He should have emulated the example of Romulus and consolidated all power in himself in order to meet the challenge to the state. Instead, Soderini counseled respect for the law. In this he "was the dupe of his opinions," and his considerable personal virtue ended up costing him "his country, his state, and his reputation."[61]

Soderini also compares unfavorably to Moses. The Hebrew lawgiver "was obliged to have a great many persons put to death" for "the purpose of insuring the observance of his laws and institutions."[62] Soderini was similarly surrounded by malignant and jealous rivals. But he wished to placate their envy "without any violence or public disturbance." Soderini chose instead to appease his enemies by "bestowing benefits" on them. This proved a fatal mistake, as neither generosity nor goodness suffices to triumph over "envious malignity." The trouble with Soderini, Machiavelli writes, is that he "was in all his actions governed by humanity and patience." And while "he and his country prospered so long as the times favored this mode of proceeding," he could not change to less humane means when circumstances called for them, "and his own and his country's ruin were the consequence."[63]

Refoundings

The history of Rome echoed the history of Machiavelli's own times in showing the tendency for corruption to destroy republics. Alone among forms of government, republics are dependent on maintaining the civic virtues and the ethos of public service that make popular government possible. Institutions and structural arrangements can do only so much to guard against abuses of power. Machiavelli certainly gave study to the importance of institutions, and he provided an early case for the contribution mixed government, divided power, and checks and balances made to preventing the dominance of any one faction in Rome. Ultimately, however, the people must defend its own liberty.

As a republican, Machiavelli saw no reason to doubt the moral fiber of the people; popular rule was if anything more stable, consistent, and respectful of the law than was princely rule. Of his Roman forebears, Machiavelli noted that "for four hundred years they have been haters of royalty and lovers of the glory and common good of their country."[64] They neither "obey[ed] with servility nor command[ed] with insolence."[65] That strong base of popular virtue meant that the Roman republic survived even corrupt leaders. Where "the mass of the people is sound, disturbances and tumults do no serious harm."[66] What was insurmountable was corruption in the people. Once this settles in, reforming a republic through the ordinary procedures of self-government is no longer possible: by definition a corrupt people cannot wield power to reform itself.

At such moments republics must revert to princely politics and rule by one great and often ruthless leader. In a crucial passage, Machiavelli writes of the violent means of republican reform. Once the people are corrupt,

> ordinary means [of reform] will not suffice; they may even be injurious . . . [,] and therefore it becomes necessary to resort to extraordinary measures, such as violence and arms, and above all things to make one's self absolute master of the state, so as to be able to dispose of it at will. And as the reformation of the political

condition of a state presupposes a good man, whilst the making of himself prince of a republic by violence naturally presupposes a bad one, it will consequently be exceedingly rare that a good man should be found willing to employ wicked means to become prince, even though his final object be good.[67]

This is an extraordinary passage that encapsulates the full gravity of Machiavelli's willingness to accommodate evil in politics. Just as in Chapter 15 of *The Prince,* where Machiavelli sets out to teach princes "how not to be good," so here Machiavelli searches for the "good man" willing to employ "wicked means" for the common good. He acknowledges that the problem is akin to trying to square a circle: it is difficult to conceive how the good person can emulate the wicked in the ruthlessness of violence. But if the good are to triumph in a world of so many who are not good, if republics are to protect their freedom, the good must become Machiavellians all.

Machiavelli may not have anguished over his doctrines, but I learned my Machiavelli from a professor who brooded over the problem of dirty hands. Michael Walzer accepted that occasions do arise when the just cannot prosecute their causes without getting their hands dirty. But he accepted this only reluctantly, insisting that violence be resorted to only after all reasonable alternatives had been exhausted—if not literally as a last resort, at least something close to it. He tended to think it was in the nature of politicians to see supreme emergencies and necessities of state where there were none, but he conceded that sometimes the good can defeat the bad only by means that good people should never wish to use. As I recall, Walzer was drawn to examples from the French Resistance to Nazi occupation. This was a paradigmatic case of a just cause meeting an unjust enemy, but even here he struggled with arguments that the Resistance's cause justified the use of assassination or the fraud of pretending to be unarmed farmers as a way of attacking occupying German forces. Even when he did accept that there could be such a thing as a "just assassin" (in the words of Jean-Paul Sartre's play by that title), he tended to forbid celebration. He preferred that the assassin be regarded as a person with dirty hands, owing some sort of apology and defense, and probably forfeiting the right to advance higher in the Resistance. The assassin may have done what we wanted him to do, and yet he must pay the price for having blood on his hands.

I remember one particular example about the Resistance that Walzer used, although I do not recall whether it was a hypothetical or a historical case. Suppose a high-value military target is located inside a French village where family members of Resistance fighters live. Walzer pondered whether a Resistance member with family in the village could be asked to join in an attack from the air, when there was no time to warn the villagers and the risk of collateral damage to innocent civilians was high. If the military target was important enough, Walzer thought the Resistance might be justified in countenancing the attack. But he could not fathom a decent resistance movement that would prod the particular Resistance fighters from the village to join in the attack or punish them for standing aside. This would be carrying civic virtue and dirty hands too far.

I tend to think that the only acceptable Machiavellianism would be the reluctant sort Walzer sketched. But this is not the sort that history has given us. Machiavelli is not about hesitancy or fine-tuned calculations about the necessity for violence. He does not first seek alternatives to violence but celebrates the greatness that occasions for war give those daring enough to march large across history's stage. This might not quite make him the "Mache*vil*" that Shakespeare reviled, but it does explain why so many who are not good have found their justifications in Machiavelli's writings.

9

HOBBES AND THE KINGDOM OF MEANS

The world keeps on giving us reasons to read Hobbes. Thomas Hobbes's political vision stems from one fundamental observation: nothing is worse than war, and we should readily trade liberty for security when we must.

Like Machiavelli, Hobbes singles out fear as the fulcrum of politics. But Machiavellian man is attracted to the fearful visage of war, the ferocity of it all. The Hobbist citizen is a decidedly more modest soul, seeking contentment in peace.

Hobbes learned his political lessons during the English Civil War of the mid-seventeenth century. He lived through the beheading of a king and the religious warfare that made a ritual of impaling the heads of heretics on the posts of London bridges. Little in his surroundings gave Hobbes hope that human beings on their own would ever turn peaceful. He set out to devise a political system that would do for us what we could not do for ourselves. In Hobbes's vision we are radically dependent on the sheer power of the state to protect us from the perils of our own nature. We will always remain more subjects than citizens of the state. So great is the end of peace that people will put aside even religious fervor to obtain it, according to Hobbes's revolutionary claim.

Sadly, it does not seem to matter what year I am discussing Hobbes. The headlines continue to make the case for his tradeoffs between liberty and security. These days we are likely to hear arguments that at least Saddam Hussein managed to keep the peace between Sunnis and Shiites in Iraq; as brutal as his regime was, are not the atrocities of civil war worse? Others point out to me that the life expectancy for a Russian male has taken a nosedive since the collapse of communism. Long after Hobbes thought he had taken religion out of politics, people still kill in the name of God.

Nor is religion the only cause of political violence. The last time I taught Hobbes, we began the day before the massacre of thirty-two students and faculty on the campus of Virginia Tech. It was one of the first spring days in New England, long in coming. Life on campus was carefree, and fear of violent death was nowhere on the radar screen of my students' minds. Their interest in Hobbes was, shall I say, merely academic. When we met again two days after the shootings, they were Hobbists, at least for a time. They now "got it," saw what he was driving at, related to the tradeoffs between liberty and security, thought about their sudden desire to see more police, better armed, milling about the campus. Thankfully, it is in the nature of the young to heal and to return to play. But political violence continues to make Hobbes indispensable.

Hobbes is indispensable in other ways as well. I used to think Hobbes's ship had arrived, when Dr. Robert Jarvik invented the artificial heart in the 1970s, proving Hobbes's quip in the year 1651 that the heart is "but a [replaceable] spring."[1] But science quickly progressed beyond such mechanistic spare parts solutions to illness. With the advent of stem cell research, scientists showed they could grow tissues, organs, whole life forms themselves. Sheep and dogs have already been cloned; in principle, human beings could now design and grow their own cloned descendants. If and when the human species evolves into taking charge of its own further evolution, the central and bold claim of Thomas Hobbes—that human beings can rival and even outstrip God in creative power—will have come to pass.

Before I begin my discussion of the *Leviathan,* I offer an overview of what makes Hobbes such a tremendously important figure in the history of political thought. Think of Hobbes as holding together, through sheer force of intellect, two rival visions of human nature. On the one hand, human beings are "desiring animals," programmed by nature to preserve their own lives and to pursue their own interests. As Hobbes puts it, human beings are pieces of matter subject to the same causal laws of nature that all other material in the universe obeys. We have no exempt status but must apply the same scientific method to the study of the motions of the human body that Galileo applied to observing the orbits of planetary bodies. In time, this side of Hobbes gave rise to utilitarianism and contemporary behavioral psychology. These schools of thought share the view of human behavior as reducible to the motivating force of pleasures and pains on the "desiring" animal.

On the other hand, in the rival vision of human nature, human beings are moral animals capable of laying down the law to their desires. We are

170

the authors of our own behavior, with freedom to choose. As moral animals, we have obligations as well as motivations. We make promises and keep our word, sign and enforce contracts, make choices to perform our duty rather than our desire, give our consent to laws and obligations. Hobbes captured this vision of the moral animal in his central idea of a social contract as the source of our political obligations. This side of Hobbes gave rise in time to Rousseau and Kant and to visions of politics as transcending mere service to self-interest in favor of the moral and common good.

It is not easy to see how a body rigged to pursue its own self-interested desires can also be a body capable of making and keeping promises to do one's duty. Does the human animal enter into agreements only because the agreements are calculated on the basis of self-interest? And even if our motives are inescapably self-interested when we make agreements in the first place, are we nonetheless capable of responding rationally to the force of obligation to keep our agreements, even when doing so threatens self-interest?

The genius of Hobbes was to keep together the desiring and moral aspects of human behavior—what he tellingly calls alternate views of man as but a chunk of matter versus man as the artificer or creator of other matter. It is a high-wire act, and a lesser intellectual acrobat could never have kept his feet on the two different wires as long as Hobbes did. In the end, I do not think it possible to hold together the view of persons as determined matter and the view of persons as morally free agents. But the excitement of reading Hobbes is to confront full force the fundamental question of human freedom.

Hobbes's Introduction to *Leviathan*

I want to begin with a sustained look at Hobbes's own introduction to his masterwork, the *Leviathan*. That introduction consists of a sustained two-page metaphor comparing human works of art to God's work of art: nature.

In the seventeenth century the name for such an exaggerated metaphor was, appropriately, a conceit. Comparing nature to art was, in Hobbes time as in ours, a familiar metaphor. We are used to complimenting a painting of a sunset, for instance, by saying it looks like the real thing. But we usually stop the aesthetic praise short of claiming that human beings can "create" sunsets in the way God does. We accept that some unbridgeable chasm distinguishes God's creativity ("nature") from human artistic creation. But Hobbes stands the familiar metaphor on its head, reworking it into a radical claim that the "natural" animals which God creates are but machines that we can duplicate and even go one better.

A current joke captures the daring of Hobbes. Bragging about the power of science, a scientist claims that he and his colleagues can make anything God made. Hearing the boast, God challenges the scientist to make a human being. "That's easy," says the scientist, bending down to scoop up a handful of dirt as raw material. "Get your own dirt," God balks. The joke speaks to the still lingering sense that the mystery of creation is beyond our science.

It is worth proceeding step by step through Hobbes's opening conceit. He begins by closing the usual gap between nature and art with the observation that while God alone makes "natural" animals, we make animals of a certain artificial sort. Hobbes singles out watches as an example of an "Artificial Animal" that has moving hands just like God's animals. The comparison is apt, Hobbes insists, because what is "life but a motion of Limbs?"[2] To find one of God's animals no longer capable of movement—heart not beating, lungs not breathing, brain not emitting waves—is to find a dead animal. But if motion is the sine qua non of life, then art can imitate God's creation of animals by designing engines that bring watches to life, or gears, springs, sprockets, or wheels that put other objects into motion. From the functional point of view, the spring inside a watch "animates" it in much the same way that the heart animates the man machine.

But Hobbes is not content to describe art in natural terms. His real purpose is to describe nature in artificial terms. To this end Hobbes takes a series of natural body parts and describes them by reference to their mechanical equivalent. Thus the heart is but a spring; the nerves are "but so many Strings; and the Joynts, but so many Wheeles, giving motion to the whole Body, such as was intended by the Artificer."[3] By insisting on this interchangeability of natural and mechanical terms, Hobbes means to deny to nature its uniqueness.

Not even God's "most excellent worke of Nature, Man" is exempt from Hobbes's demotion of nature. "Art goes yet further," apparently, than God did in creating an "Artificial Man . . . of greater stature and strength than the Naturall."[4] This artificial man is the state, the true Leviathan, the largest entity to roam the earth. Hobbes's reaching for the term "Leviathan" is purposeful: it is the biblical name for the whale or sea monster, the largest of God's creations. And yet here again the artificial animal rivals and outstrips the natural in its size and power.

Why is the Leviathan we create of "greater stature" than even God's most excellent creation of human beings? Hobbes's answer is that God's creatures, their very lives, stand in need of protection and defense. By our art—by our politics—we create, design, and manufacture solutions that make nature work.

Later on, Hobbes will argue that political scientists should not use metaphors ("senslesse and ambiguous words") but rather should strive to emulate the cold, objective language of natural science.[5] But it is doubtful that anyone has ever been able to write a book on politics entirely free of metaphor. Hobbes certainly did not, once he titled his most famous book *Leviathan*. After all, we have never "seen" a state. And in the absence of a vocabulary drawn from sensory experience, we invariably turn to metaphors to express what a state is "like."

In the Middle Ages the favorite metaphor was the state as a "body politic." Medieval writers such as John of Salisbury gave us long descriptions of the parts of the state as parts of a body. Just as a body has a head, so the state must have a head, writes John. Just as the body has hands, so the state must have hands to carry out the commands of the head. Now, metaphors constrain thought, influence the imagination, and create pictures for the mind's eye. And the habit, before Hobbes, of thinking of the state in organic or biological terms—as if it were a body—had certain obvious effects on political thought. First, just as the body can have only one head, so too the state. The metaphor tilts toward monarchy. Second, the metaphor tends to promote a cyclical view of history. States are born, sicken, and die, just as bodies do. There is no escape from this cycle; no state can outlive its lifespan. Third, and perhaps most important, the old metaphor of the body politic tended to encourage the view of the state as natural—as if it were not a human invention to tinker with but a body like any other, subject to the invariable laws of nature.

Hobbes accomplishes a decisive shift from organic to mechanical metaphors for describing politics. At first, in calling the state a "Leviathan," Hobbes seems to be staying with organic metaphors. He even describes the state as a body with a head (the sovereign), joints to move its parts (magistrates and officers), nerves to communicate motion to the parts, and so on. But in typical Hobbist fashion, he replaces the older organic implications of the metaphor with mechanical implications. The state may be a body, but it is a mechanical body, not a biological one. The state is not natural but artificial; it is not so much born as it is built. This shift to mechanical language was to have profound and lasting influences on the study of politics. Let me list some of them.

First, the movement of a machine is purposive; it is given a definite purpose by those who make it. Now, if we ask what the purpose of the human machine is, if we inquire into God's intention in creating human beings, Hobbes gives no answer. No doubt God put our parts together and into motion with some end in view. But we can never be privy to what God's purposes are. Hobbes is at his most nasty in ridiculing those scholastics—those schoolmen and theologians—who think they can apprehend the reason why we have been placed on earth. This is simply not a question for scientific knowledge. Or, as Hobbes writes, "[w]hat kind of felicity God hath ordained to them that devoutly honour him, a man shall no sooner know, than enjoy; being joyes that now are as incomprehensible, as the word of School-men *Beatificall Vision* is unintelligible."[6]

And yet we can know the ends of those machines, those artificial animals that we make for ourselves. The purpose of politics is simply and strictly to create state power sufficient to protect and defend the lives of the state's members.

There is nothing sacred, static, or divine in this political mission. Therefore we can afford to be experimental with how to build the better mousetrap, taking apart the state at will, tinkering with it, rearranging its parts. Mechanical metaphors open up a new daring toward political change and reform. If one imagines the state as a body politic, then one may well hesitate about amputating the hands of this body, or cutting off its head. But if one is talking about parts of a machine rather than hands on a body, then there seems more freedom to imagine chucking out one part and building another.

Second, Hobbes's leading metaphor frees the study of politics from prevailing religious notions about divine right of kings and God's anointed. Politics becomes exclusively a human creation marching to human purposes.

Third, Hobbes moves the study of politics away from the Greek notion of the state as natural. Aristotle's emphasis on the polis being "natural" to the human condition gave a certain warmth, if I may put it that way, to political life. The state did more than merely protect us; it completed us, fulfilled our natures, provided us with a home and a community of shared lives. By contrast, machine language is cold language. It is difficult to feel much of a communal attachment to the state when it is considered impersonally as a piece of artificial machinery, dead metal. Conceived in Hobbes's terms as a mere tool to be used to protect our separate homes and hearths, the state ceases to be a place of belonging. Hobbes would have considered it a victory for the "science" in political science that his approach dispensed with emotive attachments to the state. But it is a question to keep in mind as to what happens to the human desire for belonging when politics shuns it.

Fourth, consider this comparison of Machiavelli and Hobbes. Machiavelli insisted that states cannot be founded by just anyone. It takes a truly great man, possessed of power and cunning, to accomplish lasting acts of political creation. This Machiavellian necessity for the great man disappears in Hobbes. The prince in the flesh is replaced by a disembodied system or blueprint that can create stability without the help of charismatic leaders. One might expect that Hobbes would lean toward democracy, since he eliminates the need for the prince in politics. But without getting ahead of the story, let me note at this point that the opposite is the case. Somehow Hobbes ends up supporting absolute government, and we will spend considerable time figuring out why this should be so.

Let me now return to Hobbes's metaphor. To describe the state (this "Artificiall man"), Hobbes says he must consider "[f]irst, the *Matter* thereof, and the *Artificer,* both of which is *Man.*"[7] This dualism—this two-pronged view of human beings as both pieces of matter and creators of matter—reappears throughout Hobbes's writings. On the one hand, Hobbes introduces man as a tremendous creator, an "Artificer" rivaling God in creating Leviathans, artificial animals, and the like. On the other hand, Hobbes describes human beings as created just like any other pieces of matter in the material world. The body is but an elaborate machine driven by springs and wheels. This mechanical description of the man machine suggests a deterministic view at considerable odds with the view of human beings as creative artificers.

In the concluding paragraph to his introduction, Hobbes confronts this tension between his views on human nature and the proper way to study it. Newton and Galileo devised scientific methods that enabled them to prove and verify the assertions they made about bodies in motion. Is an equivalent proof available in the human sciences? Hobbes hesitates. To study ourselves is different from studying things outside us. We verify the truth of claims about human nature not through some distant process of deduction but by introspection. Planets cannot be asked whether claims about their nature make sense to them, but human beings can, and the best available proof is whether we see in ourselves what Hobbes says about human beings in general. A person who wishes "to govern a whole Nation, must read in himself, not this, or that particular man; but Man-kind." Necessarily he "looketh into himself, and considereth what he doth, when he does *think, opine, reason, hope, feare, &c,* and . . . he shall thereby read and know, what are the thoughts, and Passions of all other men." The last line of the introduction is particularly surprising for a man who wishes to apply methods of natural science to political science. Referring to introspection as a method of proof in political science, Hobbes concludes that "[political] Doctrine admitteth no other Demonstration."[8]

In the *Leviathan,* Hobbes for the most part tries to emulate natural science in deducing political theorems from more basic axioms about individual human behavior. He starts from the most basic natural laws governing the motion of the man machine and derives laws of politics from these imperatives of human nature. But the tension he admits to in his introduction between introspection and demonstration as forms of proof, and the larger tension he does not admit to between his view of man as but matter and man as a creator of other matter, continue to shadow his arguments.

The Imperatives of Nature

Part One of the *Leviathan* has the feel of a dictionary, as Hobbes sets out to translate our familiar but careless vocabulary for describing human behavior into the exact terminology fit to describe the scientific truth of the matter. In the original editions of the work Hobbes wrote the common vocabulary terms out in the margin—words such as "appetite," "aversion," "love," "hate," "good," and "evil"—and proceeded to explicate what such terms really mean. The act of translation is ruthless and driven by one overriding observation. Everything about the man machine is programmed or hardwired to pursue self-preservation and self-interest; absent defective equipment, we cannot choose other than to do that which secures our life.

The crucial work of translation takes place in the great Chapter 6 of the *Leviathan.* To be alive, as we have seen, is to be in motion. At the most basic level, these motions are involuntary and interior: the blood courses, the heart beats, the lungs fill. Not to be in motion in these ways is to be dead, and the purpose of life is simply to do that which is conducive to preserving our vital motions, what we still call our vital signs. To do so, we engage in voluntary motions; we walk, talk, move our limbs toward or away from objects. These voluntary motions become apparent only when they achieve gross form, but they start invisibly inside with the small tug provided by imagination.

Voluntary motions are instrumentally in service to our vital motions. We do not *choose* to move one way or the other, but are determined to move toward that which preserves our vital motions and away from that which threatens them. The words "appetite" and "desire" properly signify movement toward objects that serve our vital motions, as when have desires to eat or drink. By contrast, "aversions" cause us to flee fire and the like.

With this clear, Hobbes can offer two immediate conclusions. First, desire is the motive force in life. Just as motion, not rest, is the natural condition of the planets, so too human life is restless. While we live, there can simply be no cessation of desire. Second, all desires are self-interested: we can desire only that which is good for us.

Two questions now arise. The first is what it means to call some desires "good," others "bad." Hobbes's accommodation with desire as the brute motive force of life leads him to offer a radical redefinition of such moral terms. *Whatever* we have an appetite or desire for is, by definition, good: good in the sense that the objects of our desires preserve our vital motions. Conversely, the only thing we mean when we judge an object as "bad" is that it is bad from our self-interested point of view. All moral judgments are relative and subjective. Nothing is objectively good or bad in and of itself; it is simply a question of whether a particular object serves our self-interests or not. Human beings have no ability to arrive at unbiased or impartial notions of what is good or bad. The human machine is strictly rigged to judge as good whatever protects us. To speak as if we have the capacity to pass objective judgments on the desires we are wired to have is to speak nonsense. Here, in Hobbes, we have the intellectual origins of modern skepticism about moral life and insistence on a scientific approach that reduces moral life to the self-interested sources of all human behavior.

One immediate question to ask is how Hobbes would explain the obvious instances of altruism when human beings prove capable of acting against their self-interests. Firefighters rushed into the burning World

Trade Center towers knowing they were risking death. Soldiers go to war to defend their nations, and strangers stop to administer first aid on the side of the road to accident victims. If we are as self-interested as Hobbes insists, then how are we to explain the good soldier, the compassionate altruist, or the Good Samaritan?

Hobbes tackles this question head-on. He allows that his dictionary needs terms such as "pity," "grief," "sympathy," "fellow feeling," and "compassion." But Hobbes is at his most nasty in translating such terms into the hidden self-interests that always motivate us: "Griefe, for the Calamity of another, is Pitty, and ariseth from the imagination that the like calamity may befall himselfe; and therefore is called also Compassion."[9] In other words, all seemingly altruistic and other-regarding acts start when the imagination sets in motion before the mind's eye a re-visioning of someone else's suffering as if it were our own suffering. Only because the imagination can perform this work of translation can our limbs be set in motion in altruistic or charitable ways.

Consider how charitable giving seems to rise when images of the human toll extracted by an earthquake, cyclone, or flood are seen around the world. This would hardly have surprised Hobbes; it fits his suspicion that we are imagining ourselves in that flood or under that earthquake rubble.

In lecturing on Hobbes, I often ask my students to offer a counter-example of altruistic behavior that resists Hobbes's reduction of compassion to self-interest. With regularity they offer me the twin examples of having and raising children. They make the argument that self-interest cannot explain the desire to have children, or to nurture and sacrifice for them once born. As to childbearing, the class posits an interest in species preservation, not self-preservation, as the motive. I let the class find its own level of Hobbist comfort with the biological fact that we are programmed to achieve pleasure in the act of procreation: why did God design us so that (until recently) the only way to propagate the species was through the sexual act?

Examples of caring for offspring, often at considerable personal sacrifice, are indeed harder to explain in purely egotistical terms. Hobbes conceivably could fall back on his stock answer that we protect the small and vulnerable only because we can imagine changing positions with them. But the science of evolution provides a disenchanted answer that does Hobbes one better. In a particularly Hobbist reworking of evolutionary theory aptly titled *The Selfish Gene,* biologist Richard Dawkins argues that the unit of evolution is not the body as a whole but the individual gene: the body is but an elaborate machine designed to pass on its genetic makeup. Thus, over time, evolution has selected for those forms of human behavior—nurturing being among them—that are in the interests of the genes' survival, the preservation of *their* vital motion. Hobbes in his day thought that the human body was rigged to preserve *its own* life as a unique entity; Dawkins argues that the deepest imperative is not to preserve my own particular embodiment of genetic material but to behave in the interest of the genes to be passed on. This is heady and frightening stuff, but it shows an intriguing continuity between Darwinism and Hobbism.

Consider a particularly odd but telling example of Hobbes's reductionism and behavioralism. Turning to the definition of laughter, Hobbes observes that laughter is a motion of muscles into grimaces and smiles. But what causes us to be capable of responding to humor? Hobbes answers: "*Sudden Glory* is the passion which maketh those *Grimaces* called LAUGHTER; and is caused either by some sudden act of their own, that pleaseth them; or by the apprehension of some deformed things in another, by comparison whereof they suddenly applaud themselves."[10] This is my favorite example of just how nasty Hobbes can be. Either we laugh at the expense of others or we smile to congratulate ourselves at just how clever we are. The typical *New Yorker* cartoon would be an example of the latter category; we smile when we "get" the joke, when we figure it out, and feel on the inside of the writer's cleverness. All kind of jokes fit the other, poking fun or put-down possibility (*Question:* Did you know that Helen Keller had a dollhouse in her backyard? *Answer:* No. *Response:* Neither did she).

For Hobbes, there is no third way to humor, no such thing really as innocent or good humor at all; the joke has to be on somebody, or it has to be an inside joke. As the saying goes, in every joke there is a *little* bit of humor.[11]

The Purposes of Life

Are there no limits to Hobbes's purging from his dictionary all talk of things being good in and of themselves? Are there no objects that are universally judged as good, which all persons desire despite their differences? Hobbes allows one, but only one, such object, and that is life itself, the perpetuation of our vital motions. But if we were to ask, as

Aristotle asks, what is the ultimate purpose of life, beyond staying alive, Hobbes famously answers that there is none, or at least there is none that we can know or attain in this life, "[f]or there is no such *Finis ultimus,* (utmost ayme,) nor *Summum Bonum,* (greatest Good,) as is spoken of in the Books of the old Morall Philosophers." All Hobbes can see on the horizon is the perpetual and "continuall progresse of the desire, from one object to another." Life is an infinite regress, with no end to desire in sight, no plateau where desire achieves its purposes and all is rest—that, to repeat, would be death.[12]

Even if one could imagine accomplishing all one's desires, there would still be a problem. How could we possibly know that we have stockpiled enough resources so that, in the future, whatever fortune or change brings, we will still have the power to remain content and to fulfill our desires? The felicity of this life, Hobbes writes, is always contingent and precarious. The cause is not that we are naturally greedy and always after more "intensive delights." This might be true of some persons; but even the modest among us cannot "assure the power and means to live well, which [we have] present, without the acquisition of more." Our lives must obey the insurer's logic: we can never know when "enough" is enough. So "I put for a generall inclination of all mankind, a perpetual and restless desire of Power after power, that ceaseth onely in Death."[13] The psychology Hobbes describes may be "power hungry," but the motives for seeking "power after power" turn out to be anxiety rather than aggression, defensive rather than offensive, fear of loss rather than a search for gain. *If* we could know that we had already squirreled away enough to satisfy the future course of our desires, then we would have no rational reason to pursue power for power's sake. But we cannot know this. And since there is no end to desire in life, but only one desire leading to the next, then there is also no limit to the means necessary to accomplish desires without end.

What Hobbes is describing here is a troubling inversion of means and ends in life. I find over the years that my students recognize the trap Hobbes is describing. I suspect we all do. You study hard in high school as a means to get into a good college. But once in college, you cannot rest; success in college turns out to be but a means toward the further end of getting into law school. You imagine that, once in a fine law school, you can quit the rat race, you will have arrived and can coast. But this turns out not to be true. You have to do well in law school to get to the end of finding a good job. But is getting that good job with a high salary your end in life? It turns out, of course, that making money is not an end but a means to further ends such as buying a nice house, taking great vacations, raising your kids well, and sending them to the right schools, so that they can race the race just as you did. There is no escape from this mentality, according to Hobbes; our behavior is entirely rational.

Rational though our life plans be, reason takes a backseat to desire. For Plato, the proper hierarchy of the soul is for reason to command desire. But Hobbes turns the tables. Reason, in Hobbes's famous phrase, "scouts" for the desires.[14] As a matter of prudence, we send our reason ahead to figure out the best means, the best course to pursue to realize our desires. But reason is limited to instrumental logic; it can figure out means to our ends, but there is no process of reasoning that can dictate what ends to pursue in life. These ends, such as they are, are given by desire, programmed into the man machine as part of its nature, and the best reason can do is to mull over the means for carrying out the program.

More than 350 years after Hobbes wrote the *Leviathan,* his means/ends logic is so familiar to us that we miss its revolutionary significance. The means of life—the stockpiling of the instruments and tools and power, the money and resources to accomplish our purposes in life—become by default the ends of life. The default kicks in because there are no ends in life, nothing beyond the continual pursuit of desire after desire. The great sociologist Max Weber captured the Hobbist logic in his phrase "The Kingdom of Means." In some topsy-turvy but rational way, the supposed means of life become the ends of life. We commonly use the phrase to "make a living." Or sometimes we ask, "What do you do for a living?" We take for granted the Hobbism in these throwaway lines. Aristotle talked of "living well," but somehow that question retreats forever before the imperatives of "making" and "doing."

An old television commercial for Miller beer captures the point I am trying to express. A group of men in work clothes and smudged faces emerge from a factory after an obvious hard day's work. The voiceover intones: "You've worked hard all day and now comes your reward. It's Miller time." But however enjoyable Miller time is, it does not promise to replace factory time. Far from it; one has to return to work to buy the next round of Miller time. Now, it might be good for beer sales that this cycle continue unbroken, but it is hardly an appealing prospect that there is no "end" to factory time, only the occasional break for Miller time.

Hobbes's view of human psychology is deeply troubling, even—or especially—when it seems accurately to describe our condition. On the one

181

hand, he elevates desire to the primary moving force in life. On the other hand, he tells us that we can never finally achieve our desires; we can only make "continuall progresse" from one desire to another. The achievement of pleasure constantly recedes before us and escapes our grasp, much as happiness eluded Jay Gatsby in *The Great Gatsby*, despite his wealth. The consequence is that the Hobbist desiring animal is an anxious and fearful one, perpetually concerned about "making" a living, to the exclusion of living "well."

Here we come to a certain paradox in Hobbes's insistence on casting desire as the primary motive force in life. One might have thought that such a radical accommodation of desire would lead to a philosophy of hedonism. But with Hobbes we get the opposite. Man the desiring animal is more often in pain than pleasure, constantly fearful, anticipating loss, worried about the future, restless, unable to achieve satisfaction, forever moved by desires that have no end and no real purpose.

What is life like in the Kingdom of Means? Hobbes now moves the discussion ingeniously from psychology to politics according to the following plan. First, we should trace out what kind of life human beings live in a perfectly natural condition—a so-called state of nature prior to any restraints of government or law. The state of nature will tell us what human psychology leads to *naturally*. We can then go on to deduce political theorems from the axiomatic truths of the state of nature.

The State of Nature

The paramount feature of the state of nature is that it is competitive and warlike, a veritable state of war. It *must* be this way, because human machines are rigged to seek power after power. Once we grant this truth, it follows that human beings left to their own devices end in conflict and violence.

Let me review the logic that led Hobbes to the starting axiom that men seek power after power. Hobbes is *not* saying that human beings are naturally greedy or instinctually aggressive. He does not argue for any affirmative desire to steal from or to kill other people. The axiom Hobbes starts with is far weaker and less controversial. The mere basic instinct for self-preservation will cause a person to attack others first.

Consider it this way. In the state of nature, I need—as you need—to gather fruits and nuts to stay alive. Now, I might be content with a modest gathering, if only there was some way—some assurance—that I could secure the supply I had gathered, from you and from others who might take it away from me. This being a state of nature, I cannot (yet) claim that the fruit and nuts I have gathered are mine, that they are my property, that they belong to me because I worked for them. No such rights to private property exist naturally. They have yet to be invented or agreed upon. The rule of the state of nature is simply that everyone has an equal right to everything.

In such an anarchic and lawless environment I therefore become "diffident" or fearful: I am constantly anticipating that you might attack me, take from me what I need to live, even kill me. Reason scouting for my desires informs me that the only way to defend myself against your anticipated attack is to attack first: the preemptive attack is rooted in the logic of the state of nature. That logic is a defensive one, a search for security. But it turns out that offense is the best defense. Even to secure myself requires me to take from you before you take from me.

Strictly speaking, Hobbes's conclusions about natural conflict do not follow from his starting assumptions. What if the state of nature were a place of plenty? Given sufficient abundance, it would always be easier, and safer, for the man machine bent on self-preservation to pick up another apple rather than steal mine. So Hobbes must be assuming, without saying so, that the state of nature is a state of scarcity.

How about if human beings are so unequal that rulers would naturally emerge, ending the violence by subjecting others to their power? To eliminate this possibility, Hobbes make explicit that "Nature hath made men so equall" that despite differences in body and mind, "the weakest has strength enough to kill the strongest."[15] This rough equality means that no one is exempt from the grip of fear of attack.

Surviving notes from lectures I once heard Michael Walzer give indicate that he spied a third flaw in Hobbes's logic. Walzer imagined a state of nature in which all individuals were poets. Unfortunately my notes stop there, but I imagine Walzer was arguing that we could envision a state of nature in which all persons were constitutionally unable to steal or kill—pacified by, or satisfied with, the contemplation of poems. Hobbes has to rule out such a possible utopia of poets; he has to assume that it is in some of our natures to act violently when necessary.

If we factor into the state of nature assumptions about scarcity and equality, and if we rule out Walzer's utopia of poets, then we can describe

183

Hobbes's argument for the state of nature as already a state of war according to the following steps:

1. Scarcity breeds competition.
2. Competition leads to theft and conflict.
3. Theft and conflict instill fear in persons.
4. Fear leaves persons in perpetual anticipation of attack.
5. Anticipation of attack leads persons to attack first.

Hobbes adds another argument for the state of nature being a state of war. Although most of us hanker only for security, some will always want more; they seek "glory" and take "pleasure in contemplating their own power in the acts of conquest, which they pursue farther than their security requires."[16] The existence of such men forces the rest of us into war, even though we might on our own have been content to live at peace and write poetry.

Hobbes can then conclude with his famous description of the state of nature as a "warre of every man against every man." War enforces "continuall feare" on all equally, and raises the imminent "danger of violent death" from every vista. The result is that "the life of man [is] solitary, poore, nasty, brutish, and short."[17] Solitary not because we are hermits but because there are no commitments we can trust. Poor because the standard of living is low. Nasty because reason demands we destroy or be destroyed. Brutish because the human species could not develop any refined passions in such circumstances. And above all short because the threat of violent death is everywhere.

Hobbes claims to have deduced these features of the state of nature from the passions that nature programs into the man machine. He concedes it seems strange that nature would design us so poorly, but he invites readers to check out the truth of his views by "introspecting" and considering their own passions. There is the testimony of personal experience, as when one travels to a foreign country uncertain about the protections offered by government: the first thing we do is to arm ourselves. Even in our own homes, we declare constant fear of attack by locking doors and chests, thus "accusing" mankind by our acts every bit as much as Hobbes accused in words.

Lastly, Hobbes offers history as proof. "It may . . . be thought, there was never such a time" as a state of nature, and Hobbes concedes that "it was never generally so."[18] Still, examples of a state of nature survive. Hobbes wrongly alludes to "the savage people in many places of

America" as one such example. Civil war temporarily ushers us back to the state of nature. And the absence of international government leaves nations precisely in a perpetual state of war, obeying the logic that leads from national security to preemptive attack.

Escaping the State of Nature: The Social Contract

All state of nature theorists face a problem. If our most basic passions are responsible for making the state of nature a state of war, then how do we ever get out of it? For Hobbes this is a special problem, since he is emphatic that the man machine is deeply programmed to obey its passions. As he has forcefully concluded that our passions incline us to war, how is it possible for Hobbes—staying within his determinism—to argue that our passions can nonetheless incline us to peace?

Hobbes is up to the challenge. The most elementary of human passions is for life itself, for the preservation of vital motions. But life in the state of nature is short. Fear of death gives persons a passion for peace, if only they could have it. In this way the specter of death enters into our deliberations, creates a pain that outweighs the pleasure of anarchy, and *makes* us will peace.

How does this happen? Reason, scouting for the desires, discovers "laws of nature" that human beings "ought" to obey in their own interests. Brutish though they are, Hobbist persons are philosophers enough to figure their way out of the state of nature. They reason out laws based on the fundamental law of nature whereby "a man is forbidden to do, that, which is destructive of life, or taketh away the means of preserving the same." This is to say that "every man, ought to endeavor Peace, as farre as he has hopes of obtaining it; and when he cannot obtain it, that he may seek, and use, all helps, and advantages of Warre."[19]

Moved by fear of death, rational human beings would agree on this fundamental precept that peace is in their collective, and individual, best interests. But this first agreement is purely contingent: if it is possible to have peace, then we should seek it; but if it is not, then we retain our natural right to remain at war. In Hobbes's special vocabulary, "natural rights" are what we have already in the state of nature: a right to do anything that protects our vital motions. "Laws of nature" are what we puzzle out with our reason in order to overcome the insecurity of life lived with the "natural right" to kill or be killed in turn.

Hobbes derives the first law of nature from the fear of death in the state of nature. He derives the second law from the first: I should be willing to surrender my natural right to wage war against you, to the extent that you are reciprocally willing to surrender your natural right to wage war against me. This mutual disarming, this mutual surrender of natural liberty is in each person's self-interest. Each individually seeks "some Good to himselfe" in agreeing to surrender the rights of war, and this Good is "nothing else but the security of a man's person."[20]

With whom do I make this contract? In the first instance, the social contract is made between and among individuals. Anyone who does not agree to enter into the contract remains in the state of nature; the rest of us move out of the natural state by our own consent. By our own art we create a civil society with a law of nature to govern it.

This civil society in turn appoints a single voice, a single Sovereign, henceforth to represent it and to act on its behalf. To achieve the requisite unity required to end the strife to which our natures are prone, the agreement must grant absolute power to the Sovereign; the Sovereign must be authorized to do whatever is necessary to carry out the ends for which we enter society, namely, to keep the peace.

Granting such absolute authority makes the Hobbist social contract alarmingly one-sided. We promise to obey the Sovereign, but the Sovereign promises precious little in return. The Sovereign promises to protect us, but the Sovereign is to be the sole and undisputed judge of the means necessary to achieve the ends of peace. In Hobbes's view the social contract becomes a blank check, as it were: we authorize the Sovereign's acts in advance and cannot afterwards complain that the Sovereign breached the terms of the contract, since we agreed that it was in our individual best interests to invest the Sovereign with absolute authority.

When I first make this agreement, as a good Hobbist calculator I am predicting that the absolute arrangements will serve my individual interests. It may not turn out so, but I cannot complain about anything the Sovereign does, since it acts with my voluntarily given permission. In a moment we will see that Hobbes does place some limits on the Sovereign's power, but for the most part he insists that *whatever* the Sovereign does is just, in the special sense that every act of the Sovereign is authorized by the consent of the governed.

Obligations versus Self-Interest

Hobbes's insistence that the social contract binds individuals to near absolute obedience to government creates a problem, of which he is well aware. How is it possible for individuals who are programmed to obey their own individual interests to agree instead to obey the Sovereign's will? At the moment I sign the contract, I do so no doubt because I am calculating that creating an all-powerful government will work to my individual advantage—at least as compared to my precarious hold on life in the state of nature. But what if, after I sign, events occur so that the contract no longer works to my personal advantage? What if occasions arise when obeying the Sovereign will not be in my interest?

To deal with such situations, Hobbes adds a third law of nature: "that men perform their Covenants made."[21] Once we give our word, we are bound by it; we are obliged to keep our promises regardless of consequences. Hobbes knows that his entire system depends on this proviso. Without the moral obligation to keep one's promises, "Covenants are in vain, and but Empty words."[22] Given our self-interested psychology, we would run away from our agreements the moment it was expedient to do so.

Still, it is a mystery how the Hobbist person can possibly feel these sorts of obligations to "keep one's promises." The deterministic psychology with which Hobbes starts now seems to straitjacket him. While Hobbes can explain the weaker, prudential calculations men make—I ought to do this because of the benefits that will flow to me—he cannot explain the stronger moral obligation that I ought to do this because I said I would, because I promised, because I consented. Machines cannot promise; there is no "I" in the box. So a dichotomy exists between Hobbist psychology and Hobbist morality.

Let me pause to go over this dichotomy or tension in Hobbes's thought in some detail. On one interpretation of the *Leviathan,* the key point about Hobbes's concept of obligation is that the laws of nature are not moral commands of a categorical sort at all ("Thou Shall Not Commit X"). They are more like hypothetical imperatives or prudential maxims ("If you desire Y, then you should do X to get Y"). The question why we should obey laws of nature of this sort answers itself: reason is but scouting for the desires. Understood only as hypothetical maxims of prudence, "obligations" are perfectly consistent with the tyranny of self-interest over all human behavior.

But why should we think, in the state of nature, that everyone would arrive at the same maxims, the same prudential calculations, for how to achieve their personal desires? It seems more likely that persons in the state of nature, even if rational, would devise different and shifting routes for getting to different desires. Moreover, if my "obligation" to obey the laws of nature is rooted merely in strategic calculations, then what if the prudent thing to do on occasion is to flout the laws of nature? Given Hobbes's psychological views, it would seem as if all obligations are contingent and last only so long as they prove useful in reaching my egotistical ends. And yet obligations so weak could hardly cement persons into the permanent and stable obedience to the Sovereign that Hobbes is counting on to keep the peace. Presumably Hobbes added the third law of nature, obliging us to keep our contracts absolutely, to deal with this problem. But it is still difficult to understand how we could morally condemn a person for breaking his contract and acting on self-interest, since Hobbes tells us we are determined to so act.

Reflecting on these problems, some scholars distinguish between the *motives* persons have for obeying the laws of nature and the *grounds* that make it right to obey those laws. On this view, Hobbes's portrait of human motivation is meant to show only the incentives that self-interested human beings have to obey the laws of nature. But the status of the laws of nature is not reducible to these incentives. Some of these scholars argue that Hobbes grounds the moral force of the laws of nature on God's commands and seeks only to explain how to devise a politics whereby self-interested persons will come to obey the laws that they ought to obey.[23]

I have never found this distinction between motives and grounds persuasive as an interpretation of what Hobbes is about. Take an example the political philosopher Thomas Nagel has crafted. A particular person suffering from hydrophobia, or fear of water, stands by and watches a person drown. In this case we might be lenient when judging the person's moral failure, since we understand that the person was clearly incapacitated from acting as a moral person would have in such circumstances. But the hydrophobe is morally incapacitated in one arena only; in other aspects of her life, presumably she would be able to act as she ought to.[24]

The difficulty with Hobbes, Nagel goes on, is that he views human beings as constitutionally incapable of ever acting except in accord with self-interest. The malady that the hydrophobe suffered in one area we bear everywhere. There never arises for Hobbes, there never could arise, a pure example of human beings acting on the basis of moral obligation: every act is reducible to self-interest. Likewise, when human beings fail to meet their obligations, as soldiers do when fear of death causes them to desert, Hobbes has to mitigate his condemnation, much the way we do with the hydrophobe. The hydrophobe fears water; the soldier fears death, and this means we can hardly blame him for running away. And yet Hobbes's system requires him to somehow hold the soldier in obedience.

Hobbes has to perform quite an intellectual tap dance to reconcile a soldier's obligations with human psychology. Although we created government to protect us, in times of war the government asks us to protect it. What can we expect from Hobbist persons in such upside-down circumstances? Is the man machine obliged to risk his life to defend that which was supposed to defend him? Hobbes's system requires his strange dance. On the one hand, the power of government to draft soldiers to fight is implicit in the social contract: without such power, the establishment of government was in vain. On the other hand, allowance has to be made for the "naturall timorousnesse" of the man machine programmed to preserve its own vital motions. Not only women but also "men of feminine courage" are constitutionally incapable of dying for the sake of country. Thus when they run away from battle in fear, they cannot be said to act unjustly, since they are only doing what their nature compels them to do. And yet government has the right to punish, even to put to death such deserters.[25]

A similar situation occurs domestically when government comes to arrest, imprison, or execute a person. Even a person justly condemned retains the right to defend himself. That is why we "lead Criminals to Execution, and Prison, with armed men, notwithstanding that such Criminals have consented to the Law, by which they are condemned."[26] There is only so much consent can do to alter the natural propensity of persons to defend themselves as they are led to the gallows or to prison. Hence Hobbes characteristically says that government has the right to execute and imprison criminals (for violating the social contract), and yet criminals retain the natural rights of self-defense against enforcement of the social contract.

Deterrence

These two examples—of leading persons to war or to prison—show once again Hobbes's struggle to resolve the tension between his psychology (persons are causal machines programmed to pursue their own will) with his morality (persons are obliged to obey the Sovereign's will). But there is something new here as well. In his social contract theory Hobbes grounds political obligations on the duty of persons to keep their promises once made. But with soldiers and criminals, he sees the weakness of arguing that the man machine can be asked to go off to prison or war voluntarily. The mere "force of Words [is] too weak to hold men to the performance of their Covenants." Instead the better way to extract obedience is to motivate persons through fear, awe, terror, and punishment. With soldiers, we let deserters know that fleeing the risks of battle will only expose them to the more certain risks of being shot if they desert. With criminals, we escort them with ample armed guards so as to nip in the bud any desire they might have to escape. Here we have the origins of modern deterrence theory. We cannot change the self-interested ways in which all persons deliberate, but we can change the surrounding "facts" that affect our calculation of pleasures and pains.

After Hobbes, the emphasis on deterring human behavior by manipulating positive and negative reinforcements will fly apart from the emphasis on controlling human behavior by appeals to doing our duty, keeping our promises, and the like. Utilitarians will pursue the Hobbist image of the pleasure-pain calculus. Social contract theorists will pursue the alternate Hobbist image of socializing man through the sheer force of promise keeping. The remarkable achievement of Hobbes was to have held together competing visions of political obligation as well as he did.

Absolutism

To prevent the social contract from being mere words, it "is no wonder if there be somewhat else required . . . to make their Agreement constant and lasting; which is a Common Power, to keep them in awe."[27] Awe requires awesome powers, and thus Hobbes arrives at his insistence that the Sovereign be invested with virtual unchecked authority to render persons obedient. The authority of the state must be "as great, as possibly men can be imagined to make it."[28] Trying to reserve some rights would be like trying to keep one foot back in the state of nature and hence no solution to conflict at all.

To those who would complain about the dangers of so radical a surrender to political authority, Hobbes answers: "And though of so unlimited a Power men may fancy many evil consequences, yet the consequence of the want of it, which is perpetuall warre of every man against his neighbor, are much worse. The condition of man in this life shall never be without Inconvenience; but there hapeneth in no Commonwealth any Great Inconveniences, but what proceeds from the Subjects

Disobedience."[29] Hobbes's preference for absolute power in the Sovereign is peculiar. The Sovereign does not achieve its absolute power by force, coercion, claim of divine right or blood inheritance: the power of the Sovereign rests purely on the consent of the governed. In the later history of political thought, Hobbes's vision of a social contract as a basis of government's origin will be divorced from his absolutist conclusions. The notion that government rests on the consent of the governed will be reworked to limit the power of the state by specifying core rights that human beings would never consent to surrender. But Hobbes is Hobbes because he wields the social contract to empower rather than limit the Sovereign. So great is our fear of death through the violence of the state of nature that we consent to authorize the Sovereign to do whatever it takes to keep the peace.

As long as the Sovereign is absolute, Hobbes does not care whether we invest absolute power in one person, a few persons, or many persons.[30] Given the civil wars of his own time, the preference for absolute monarchy as a solution to discord seems evident, but strictly speaking, Hobbes's system permits an "assembly of men" to be Sovereign, provided they rule as absolutely as a monarch would. What matters to Hobbes is less to whom we grant sovereignty and more that, wherever we invest sovereignty, we invest it absolutely and without reservations.

Or almost without reservations. In liberal versions of the social contract after Hobbes, the list of inalienable rights we would never agree to contract away can be fairly extensive and typically includes protecting our individual property rights, our freedom of religion, and our freedom of speech. In Hobbes's vision the only right that reasonable persons would not contractually surrender to government is the right to defend one's own life. Since the single-minded reason why individuals agree to obey government is to protect their individual lives, it would be a contradiction in terms for persons to surrender their basic rights to self-defense. Thus a "Covenant not to defend my selfe from force, by force, is always voyd," for "no man can transferre, or lay down his Right to save himselfe from Death, Wounds, and Imprisonment."[31]

In the chapter of the *Leviathan* titled "Of Liberty," Hobbes reiterates that "Covenants not to defend a man's own body, are voyd," and he gives the examples of a Sovereign commanding a person "to kill, wound, or mayme himselfe; or not to resist those that assault him; or to abstain from the use of food, ayre, medicine."[32] For analogous reasons, we may justly refuse to accuse ourselves of crimes or to bear witness against ourselves in ways that threaten punishment or execution. But beyond these limited reservations, we willingly surrender our liberties to give government the power it needs to keep the peace.

Hobbes's empowerment of the Sovereign is extraordinary. Once we agree to obey the Sovereign, there is no going back; there is no right of revolt no matter what the Sovereign does. There is not even a way of accusing the Sovereign of breach of contract, since the contract grants government unchecked authority to determine how to carry out its contractual obligations to protect the people. If individuals could dispute justice with the Sovereign, then such disputes would perpetuate the very conflicts from which we wish to flee.

Moreover, since we authorize the government to achieve the end of peace, we authorize government to be the sole judge of what means are conducive to that end, and to use all means necessary to keep the peace. From experience with civil war, Hobbes knew that disputes over religious opinions and doctrines were a prime trigger of violence. Thus "it is annexed to the Sovereignty, to be Judge of what Opinions and Doctrines are averse, and what conducing to Peace."[33]

This is an important moment in the history of political thought, when Hobbes dares to claim that human beings, for all their religiosity, would be willing to surrender religious freedom for peace. His proposals for bringing about religious peace do not include separation of church and state. But he lays the groundwork for taking religion out of politics by insisting that persons do not need religion for their well-being and would be happy enough to abandon such matters to the Sovereign in exchange for peace.

Contracts and Fear

Hobbes is what we may call a "contractual enthusiast," insistent on enforcing contracts even in situations in which most of us would balk. Take the example of a kidnap victim's family agreeing to pay a ransom for the person's release. Lawyers today would consider such a contract null and void, given the obvious fear and duress under which it was made. But for Hobbes, "Covenants entred into by fear . . . are obligatory"; he could hardly conclude otherwise since it is the great fear of death that motivates persons into the social contract in the first place.[34]

From the lawyer's point of view, a contract made under fear and duress is an involuntary act and hence no contract at all. From the Hobbist point of view, "Feare and Liberty are consistent; as when a man throweth his goods into the Sea for *feare* the ship should sink, he doth it neverthelesse very willingly."[35]

Needless to say, this is a cramped view of "voluntary" action. The coercion in the kidnap example is so grave as to rob my "volunteering" or "consenting" to pay a ransom of any moral significance. But Hobbes's system requires him to offer a flat and formulaic distinction between "voluntary" and "involuntary" action. Recall that we are but machines programmed to behave in ways determined by our desires. Thus even when we act voluntarily, we act out of necessity for Hobbes. The ransom case is but an extreme example of the way human beings always calculate: we add up the pleasures and pains, fears and joys, and act to maximize pleasure and to minimize fear.

Contracts and Liberty

In what sense, then, are human beings ever free? In what sense are any of our actions truly voluntary? I suggest that Hobbes places so little value on human freedom to begin with that he can readily endorse a political system that surrenders liberty for obedience to an absolute state.

In a famous chapter (21) of the *Leviathan,* Hobbes turns explicitly to a definition of liberty. He triumphantly announces that "Liberty, or Freedome, signifieth (properly) the absence of Opposition; (by Opposition, I mean external Impediments of motion)."[36] This simple definition has had lasting influence in the history of political thought. It is commonly known as a statement of negative liberty. I am free as long as I am not interfered with, as long as I behave according to my own will and not according to the will or dictates of another. Of course, it may turn out that my own will is not free, that factors internal to my nature determine me to behave in definite ways. But as long as the determinants of my will are internal rather than external, I am "free" in the only way human beings can properly be said to be free.

Take the case of rivers. We commonly say that a river flows freely downstream. We say this, even knowing that rivers have no choice but to flow in the direction they do flow. We also know that rivers have banks that channel and contain the flow of their waters. But still we say rivers flow freely in their banks and channels. Compare this to a river, such as the Colorado, whose natural flow is obstructed by a dam, that is, by a manmade interference. Now we say that the Colorado no longer flows freely, and some environmentalists campaign to restore the Colorado to its wild and free state. What is the difference between a river obstructed by its own banks and a river obstructed by a dam? In Hobbes's view, the first river is free: whatever obstacles to motion the water meets are obstacles that are internal to the river's own nature. The fact that by nature rivers obey certain natural laws does not deprive them of freedom. All we say is that "freedom and necessity" are consistent when the river is obeying only its own will. But the Colorado is no longer free, because it is obeying not the necessities of its own nature but the force of someone else's will.

Or take another example. Every river east of the North American Continental Divide flows into some body of water that eventually drains into the Atlantic or the Arctic Ocean; every river west of the Continental Divide eventually drains into the Pacific. These are necessities of river flow imposed by nature. For Hobbes, the mere fact that rivers west of the divide have no choice but to flow toward the Pacific rather than the Atlantic is no reason for denying their freedom. As long as the rivers obey only their own natures, they are free—even if they are determined by their natures to move the way they in fact move.

Human freedom for Hobbes is analogous to river freedom. It makes perfect sense to speak of human beings as having "free will" even if human beings are determined by their nature to will what they in fact do. As long as a person's behavior is directed by his own will, and not dammed or channeled by someone else's will, the person can be said to be free. Thus for humans as for rivers, liberty and necessity are perfectly consistent.

I suggest that this rather cramped view of human freedom explains the peculiarities of Hobbes's use of the social contract. Even in the state of nature, the human condition is to be a person whose choices are dictated by the program for self-preservation hardwired into the man machine. To be a human was always to be a person incapable of motion other than the motives of self-interest allow. Given this understanding of the deterministic underbelly of natural liberty, the prospect of surrendering *that* liberty (with all the difficulties it bred in the state of nature) for obedience to the Sovereign's will (with its promise of peace) suddenly seems a reasonable rather than a dreadful outcome.

Life within the Kingdom of Means

What is the life of the ordinary individual like inside the Leviathan? For one thing it is safer, and presumably longer. But what do we do with our

194

newfound security and longevity? Frequently Hobbes writes as if the sole task of government is to provide safety. But in Chapter 30 of the *Leviathan* he advises that "by Safety here, is not meant a bare Preservation, but also all other Contentments of life, which every man by lawfull Industry, without danger, or hurt to the Commonwealth, shall acquire to himselfe."[37]

What are these "contentments" that civil society can provide, once the struggle for existence is pacified? One possibility is that life inside a community changes our natures so that we strive for shared pleasures and public delights. In this vision, politics moves beyond security concerns to give us festivals and holidays, loyalties and allegiances unknown in the natural state. Aristotle's polis was no Leviathan precisely because its people cherished public celebrations. Machiavelli likewise stressed the peculiar contentment that Romans found in citizenship. Later in the history of political thought, Rousseau will pick these threads up and weave them into a political tapestry adorned with public celebrations, meetings, entertainment, marches, and the like.

When Hobbes says that the state should bring "contentments" to its residents, his vision of what politics can do to make us happy is far more limited, even cold. Characteristically, Hobbes speaks about those "contentments of life" which every man "shall acquire to himselfe."[38] The use of the reflexive pronoun here is haunting. Even after we move from the state of nature into civil society, we remain the same unchanged persons seeking only our own private delights. We keep company with other persons for instrumental reasons, only because social cooperation gets each of us to our own private stations. Thus for Hobbes, the task of politics is never to change our separate paths in life until they converge. It is simply to arrange laws as so many "Hedges" along the byways, so that each of us can best travel on our way without interference from others.[39]

Paradoxical as it sounds, for Hobbes we agree to enter society as the better way to be left alone. In the state of nature there were no hedges to protect my travel from thieves, marauders, and murderers along the way. We devise government and grant it awesome powers only to protect us and then to leave us alone.

This is why Hobbes can conclude that the individual subjects of the Leviathan remain free despite the absolute power of the state. The liberties most of us want are domestic and economic rather than public or political. In Hobbes's list, persons want the "Liberty to buy, and sell, and otherwise contract with one another; to choose their own aboad, their

own diet, their own trade of life, and institute their children as they themselves think fit; & the like." Such "bourgeois freedoms," as they came to
be known, are entirely consistent with the unlimited power of the Sovereign. The Sovereign can "praetermit" persons to choose the private occupation they think "most profitable to themselves," as long as all decisions
affecting the direction and defense of the public sphere remain under its
exclusive control.[40]

Of course, the fact that an enlightened absolute Sovereign *may* grant
us our private freedoms is no *guarantee* that the Sovereign will use its
discretion wisely. Repeatedly Hobbes comes back to the bottom line that
the Sovereign can do what it wants, without injustice. Such a view strips
the concept of justice of any capacity to limit the raw power of the Leviathan and leaves Hobbes unable to provide private-minded persons with
any recourse should the government's reach exceed expectations. It will
take John Locke's reworking of Hobbes's theory before the social contract emerges as a way of limiting, as well as legitimizing, the authority of
government.

10

LOCKE, LIBERALISM, AND THE
POSSESSIVE LIFE

I first read about John Locke in a book that everyone seemed to be reading in my college days—Louis Hartz's *Liberal Tradition in America*.
Hartz offered a scholarly defense of what otherwise would have seemed a
storybook version of a liberal and inclusive American society. Referring
to American founding principles of legal equality, rights of property, and
religious freedom, Hartz described a widely shared consensus in national
politics that made all successful political movements "Lockean." The
reigning Lockean paradigm in the United States was already present
in the language of the Declaration of Independence, with its references
to inalienable rights and the right of the people to rebel against any
government that violated their basic liberties. In fact, Locke's language
justifying revolution against tyranny appears almost verbatim in the Declaration's recital of the "long train of abuses" that made revolution necessary.

Hartz conceded that liberal inclusiveness and equality in America
had its limits, but these mostly had to do with the enduring problem of
race or with confrontations with foreign nations. The book had little to
say about discrimination against women and immigrant groups. These
omissions were most likely due to Hartz's focus on what made American
politics "exceptional" compared to European politics. In European nations, before and after Locke, it was possible to mount genuine conservative movements in defense of class hierarchies and against the norms
of equality. Likewise, socialist parties found European constituencies
that rejected Locke's defense of private property rights and fought for
public rather than private ownership of property. But for Hartz, the distinction of American politics is that neither socialism nor genuine conservatism ever gained much of a toehold. Everyone who seeks political success in the United States must do so largely within Lockean terms that

regard religious and economic liberty as "self-evident." This consensus, Hartz argued, has long muted the supposed differences between Republicans and Democrats, liberals and conservatives, even employers and employees.

In the heady and optimistic days before the Vietnam War, Hartz's thesis about American exceptionalism was welcomed not only as accurate historical description but also as an endorsement of the moral superiority of American over European politics. Where the United States did go wrong—as in race—the country needed only better practice of the Lockean language in the Declaration of Independence, that all "are endowed by their Creator with certain unalienable rights, that among these are life, liberty and the pursuit of happiness." No other ideas were needed.

I do not think I exaggerate by claiming that few scholarly books achieve the same influence and wide acceptance that met Hartz's account of the triumph of liberalism in America. In my day students could still afford to buy books, and *The Liberal Tradition in America* was ubiquitous on the shelves of college dormitory rooms. There were other books that marked my generation. I can think off the top of my head of Herbert Marcuse's *Eros and Civilization,* Philip Roth's *Portnoy's Complaint,* Kurt Vonnegut's *Cat's Cradle,* and Norman O. Brown's *Love's Body,* all lined up on college bookshelves alongside the equally obligatory record albums—*Rubber Soul, The Wicked Pickett, The Freewheelin' Bob Dylan.* And there in the midst of all these cult classics was Hartz's volume, the rare scholarly book that spoke to a generation at once worried about the race problem in America and about nuclear brinksmanship with the Soviet Union. Hartz offered a synthesis that put the two concerns together: we had work to do at home to complete the liberal project, but we also needed to defend the principles of the open society against the Iron Curtain abroad. And the necessary ideas for "getting it right" were all in John Locke, though I managed to graduate from college without ever reading Locke in the original. It was as if Locke's ideas had become so self-evident in American culture that we no longer actually needed to read him.

When I arrived at graduate school, I immediately registered for Hartz's course on American political theory, but sadly he fell seriously ill, the course had to be canceled, and Hartz never returned to teaching. I continue to wonder what he might have said to defend his views as events soon unfolded that tested the hold of liberalism on American politics.

Since Hartz's death, revisionist historians have argued that American domestic politics were never as singularly liberal, as exceptional, or as egalitarian as Hartz claimed.[1] As to foreign policy, Hartz's "exceptionalist" thesis stands in danger of lending an air of self-righteousness to our dealings with the world, as if we alone got it right. In short, it is difficult today to make the case quite as Hartz made it for the moral uplift Locke gave the New World.

A different problem stems from the difficulty most of us have in feeling moved or inspired by Locke's own vision. In his day Locke generated great excitement by daring to attack the "Ambition, Fear, Folly or Corruption" that cause established governments to violate the trust of their own people.[2] He dared to ask who was responsible for "all those mischiefs of Blood, Rapine, and Desolation, which the breaking to pieces of Governments bring on a Country." Was the blame to be put on people brave enough to resist the "robbers or pirates" or on the thieves themselves who run off with the state as if they owned it and not the people?[3] This is bold language, and yet it is accompanied by another vocabulary entirely, a constant stream of references to property as what we would ultimately be moved to fight to protect.

Locke treats the right to private property as if it were the paradigmatic case of what it means for a person to "possess" freedom—as if freedom itself were just another possession. When I finally got around to reading Locke in the original, I remember the considerable deflation I felt upon seeing his opening description of what politics is all about. The state, he writes in his *Letter Concerning Toleration,* exists merely to protect our "possession of outward things, such as money, lands, houses, furniture, and the like."[4] My eyes became glued to this word "furniture." Where had all that glorious Platonic talk gone about politics elevating the self to a higher moral plateau, taking responsibility with others for sustaining a common life? How did the state come to be reduced to a furniture-insuring business? With time, and I daresay with more furniture to cushion me through life's ups and downs, I have more appreciation of why Locke embedded his defense of freedom so thoroughly within a defense of the propertied life. But that Locke saw possession of property as a crucial means to liberty, and that he was comfortable with wide inequality in wealth, tells us much about the historical origins of liberalism. I suggest, then, that we begin our study of Locke by examining his vision of politics as providing protection for the possessive life.

Locke and the Idea of Self-Ownership

In his most influential political work, the *Second Treatise of Government,* Locke repeatedly returns to his grand theme that the "great and chief end . . . of Mens uniting into Commonwealths, and putting them under Government, is the Preservation of their Property."[5] But lest he be misunderstood by making protection of property the primary task of politics, Locke adds that he uses the general term "property" to refer to our "Lives and Liberties" as well as our "Estates."[6]

This is an odd twist of phrase, to refer to our interests in life and liberty as if they were a species of propertied interests. But Locke is serious about this: our basic relation to ourselves is a property relationship; we should think of ourselves as owning ourselves, as owning our own body.[7] Or almost owning our own body. In fact God owns our bodies, and we have at most a lease on them, a kind of life estate, on condition that we treat the preservation of both our bodies and those of others, all of which are God's property, as a duty, as a law of nature.[8] Locke expresses this point first in religious terms but then secularizes it, true to his property language. In a feudal society, of the sort from which England and European nations derived historically, some persons could be owned by others; hierarchy, class, rank, and subordination were the organizing principles of society. But such arrangements, however historically common, did not derive from nature and were inconsistent with the first and most indisputable law of nature: that every person owns himself. To own oneself is to be master, not serf. To own oneself is to be a free and equal human being, an end, not a means. Later in the history of political thought Kant will carry this analysis of treating persons as ends and not means to a higher level of abstraction, but the notion of natural equality is fully present in Locke.

Locke allows that human beings have interests other than property interests. But moral and spiritual life—the inner life—is not what we are after when we devise government. To have an inner life is to understand why it would be illogical for persons to assign the salvation of the soul to government. Governments are in the business of wielding the sword and the purse; by the use of such means they can compel persons to conform their outward behavior to the commands of law, but they cannot reach the inner judgment on which faith depends. In this way Locke offers separation of church and state as a solution to religious warfare: civil society uses civil means to protect our civil interests, while the church wields only spiritual means to serve spiritual interests.[9]

In contrast to the long history of hierarchy in feudal Europe, Locke uses his property metaphors to sketch out a state of nature in which equality, not rankings, is our natural condition. If we start with the notion that we own our own bodies—or at least that we have title to them from God while we live—then it follows that equality, not subordination, is the original and natural condition.[10] No human being was made to be a mere instrument of someone else's pleasure. God made the lower animals precisely to be used for the good of human beings; as the biblical account of Genesis puts it, God created the land and the sea, and all the inhabitants therein, with the intent that the inferior creatures be used as a means to the ends of *human* good. By contrast, no such principle of inferiority exists among the human species. All human beings "are made to last during his [God's], not one anothers Pleasure."[11] Reason would prompt discovery and obedience to a law of nature decreeing that each person preserve both his property in his own preservation and the like and equal property another human being has in his preservation: put simply, no one has the right to destroy property belonging to another.[12]

Locke saw human beings as sufficiently rational to be able, prior to government, to live in some degree of peace in accordance with this basic property perspective. Here we can see how he is already "flipping" the Hobbist logic. In Hobbes, we begin with a natural right to everything—including the right to take another's life and everything else along with it. We reason ourselves, for Hobbes, into laws of nature to escape the violence and anarchy of natural liberty. For Locke, there never was any such natural right to destroy others. Hobbes confuses the state of nature as a state of "liberty," which it is, with a state of "license," which it is not.

Locke begins his reclamation project by laying out the moral possibilities inherent in the human condition even prior to government. On their own, free human beings would have laid down a law for themselves in the state of nature. This is not a law which they made but one which they discovered already there, a principle of reason that teaches "all who will but consult it" that we have no right to the property of another.[13]

But I *do* have a right to the property of myself. From this basic axiom Locke derives his justly famous argument on behalf of the "naturalness" of private property. Locke aims to establish two major points. First, the right to property is a natural right, a right that preexists the establishment of government and in fact limits the power of government once established. Second, the acquisition of private property would not have led to the violence and competitive warfare Hobbes thought it would.

Locke's Defense of Private Property

It is well worth the effort to go through the steps in Locke's defense of a natural right to private property. In the first step, Locke makes it hard for himself by conceding that "originally" the earth was one vast "commons" whose bounty lay open to all.[14] No one starts with title from God to any particular piece of the common earth. How, then, could human beings ever have become entitled to take out of the common stock and, by taking, make it theirs as of right? Hobbes's answer was simple: human beings certainly would have taken grain, apples, or animals out of the common stock to stay alive, but that is just it—they would simply have taken, fought, stolen, without any concept that some takings were "right" and others were "wrong."

Locke sets out to show that rational human beings would have come to recognize that some ways of taking actually do create an entitlement to that which is taken. Although God gave the land to us in common, he gave it with the intent that it be useful to mankind. For it to be useful, there must be some way to take, to appropriate out of the common stock for personal use.[15] For instance, it would be a crazy deduction from the land's originally being an undivided commons to conclude that I cannot slake my thirst at the lake or pond or river. So Locke reaches his first conclusion: that I may rightly appropriate out of the common stock, notwithstanding that I do not own the common stock. Hobbes, of course, reaches the same conclusion. But again, the act of appropriation for Hobbes is a kind of theft; it creates no title, and others can appropriate from me what I just appropriated from the commons. It is this anarchy of appropriation that Locke wants to dispute.

Here is the crux of his argument. Remember that I start by owning one thing and one thing only: I own my own body. But this means I own the power, the labor of my body and the work of my hand.[16] When I appropriate land or produce from the common stock, I do so by working on the land, by removing rocks, by plowing and sowing fields, by carrying water to drink, by diverting streams to irrigate crops, and so on. The result is that I have now "mixed" what I own (the labor of my body) with the commons. Since there is no way to separate what is mine from what is common, I justly am entitled to own the mixture.

The first time Locke expresses his argument, he stresses the brute fact of "mixture" as the source of private property's origin. But it is easy to refute this logic, as the philosopher Robert Nozick did in a famous example, an example so perfect in making a complex idea accessible that it has stayed with me for more than a quarter century now.[17] Imagine going down to the waters of Boston Harbor. By sheer dint of labor, you open a can of tomato juice; you work to pour the red juice into the brackish waters of the Atlantic, watching the red mix in with the brown, creating a bounded pool of red-brown water. Does Locke really mean to suggest that you now own fifty cubic centimeters of the Atlantic Ocean simply because you poured tomato juice into it? Presumably not. As Nozick put it, it seems more likely that you have foolishly forfeited any right to the spilled tomato juice at all.

In the very next paragraph Locke anticipated Nozick's refutation by making clear that his argument did not root private property in the fact of "mixture" per se. The significant point is what happens when we mix our labor with God's land. We add value to the land by working it; we make fertile what once lay fallow. In this sense it is our labor that is the source of the value, or the added value, of the land. This value-creating power of my labor makes it right that I own the piece of land which I have made valuable by clearing it, the well I have made full by digging it, the animals I have raised and fattened.[18] Of course, in the tomato juice example or in the case of graffiti spraying on subway walls, no value is created, and hence no property rights arise.

Locke's view became known as the labor theory of value, an economic theory that is shared by Adam Smith and his free market analysis and by Karl Marx and the socialist tradition. With Locke, *Homo faber*—the man of labor—becomes for the first time in the history of political thought a central rather than peripheral figure. In Greek culture, to labor was to be enslaved to a life of sweat and necessity in ways that made the full flowering of a free human being impossible. In Locke's world, status and honor still flowed to the aristocrats, who were entitled to vast landholdings but were letting history pass them by precisely because new economic realities were in the process of shifting wealth to a bourgeoisie that actually created value by work. In time, Locke's elevation of the significance of labor was bound to appeal to the rising bourgeoisie. But in time as well, Locke's labor theory of value would appeal to the socialist critique of his conclusions, since Locke never systematically addressed the question of how and why some persons become entitled to own the labor of another.

In Locke's vision, the state of nature would have hosted for a time a modest and peaceful regime of property owners, each reciprocally recognizing the right of others to that amount of property taken out of the common store. But why would property acquisitions in the state of nature have left persons at relative peace? Why wouldn't competition break out, with Hobbes-like violence trailing in its wake? Take one of Locke's favorite examples. He considers it self-evident that I acquire a property right in the water I carry away from the common well. Nothing, Locke writes, could be more self-evident, or else we would be likely to die of thirst in a state of nature, notwithstanding plenty.[19] But what if that drop of water I take is the last water in the well; what if I take so much that there is not enough left for the next taker; what if one has to walk one hundred miles to the next water supply?

Or consider a shipwreck example discussed in law school classes for over one hundred years now. Two shipwrecked sailors, A and B, are struggling to stay alive; a plank floats by big enough to support the weight of only one of them. Suppose A clambers aboard first. Does that give A the exclusive "right" to it, such that A can attack, even kill B, if B tries to climb aboard? Would it be reasonable for B to concede to A the only foreseeable means of survival simply because A got to it first?

To deal with issues in which scarcity would likely propel men in Hobbist directions, Locke adds two important codicils to the natural right to private property. Together the codicils make clear that for the very same reasons individuals have a right to acquire property, they have but a *limited* right. Both my right to take and the limits on that taking are rooted in nature and hence would have permitted the natural property regime to be modest and moderate.

The first limit flows from the fundamental right of human beings to take that much out of the common stock that they need and can use. It follows that I have no right, and no incentive, to take more than I can use. In a pure state of nature I would therefore gather only as much of the bounty of the earth that I could use before it spoils.[20] The shelf lives of fruits, vegetables, and the like, as it were, enforce an external limit on how much property in goods subject to spoilage we would want to accumulate.

The spoilage limit is probably not much of a limit at all. First, Locke notes that persons have rights to use property not merely for bare preservation but also for "the greatest conveniences of Life."[21] We may take out of the common store as much as we can use "to the best advantage of Life."[22] But in a state of nature, who judges what is to a person's advantage? Presumably each of us judges his or her own advantage.

The second limit is that I have a right to take out of the common stock only if I leave behind "as much and as good" for those who come after me.[23] If, by reducing the common stock to remnants, I prejudice others by my taking, then according to Locke the right to take has ceased. But why should persons in a state of nature subscribe to such a limit? Why care about the plight of those behind me in line? Locke does not make an argument here, but perhaps he had in mind that each individual has to worry that he or she might find himself or herself at the end of the supply line on some future occasion. For purely self-interested reasons, the principle of leaving "as much and as good" behind might have emerged as a rational compromise in the state of nature.

So long as these limits hold, Locke is an optimist about the ability of persons devoted to "preservation of their Property" to live in relative harmony even without government and civil law to constrain their behavior. The Lockean individual is "possessive" in his approach to life, but it is a modest possessiveness.[24] Why have more than one can use? This makes no sense in a state of nature. Why take and exhaust the common supply if tomorrow you also are dependent on its containing "as much and as good?"

With the invention of money, the modesty of property accumulation in the state of nature gives way to more extensive and unequal property holdings. The spoilage limit no longer applies in a world where stored crops can be converted into "a little piece of yellow metal, which would keep without wasting or decay." Money makes it possible for persons to desire more than they need; it gives humans for the first time an incentive to accumulate property beyond what can be used presently. Locke makes these points not to criticize the growing inequality within the state of nature but to justify it. For what money makes valuable is ultimately the "different degrees of industry" that bring more to those who labor most.[25]

The invention of money also alters the significance of the requirement that we leave "as much and as good" behind for others to take from the common store. But here we have to unravel an ambiguity in what Locke meant by leaving "as much and as good" to others. One possibility is that we leave others with as much and as good *land* to take. But another possibility is that we leave only as much and as good *produce* or *yield* from the land for others to use. That Locke may have had in mind this second, and weaker, limit is suggested by his argument that I do not prejudice but in fact further the welfare of others when I enclose and culti-

vate one acre of land, since that tilled soil now yields ten times "the provisions serving to the support of humane life" as an acre of land lying
fallow.[26] Since this is so, then God's plan that the earth be of *use to all* is
served by individuals' appropriation of land, even if all land is taken out
of the common stock. The industriousness of some in enclosing the land
so increases the bounty from the land that even those unable to own "as
much and as good" land themselves nevertheless find their welfare rising.

Money also makes it possible for an economy based on wage labor, or
the exchange of one's labor for cash, to take root in the state of nature.
Almost in passing Locke makes this telling jump: "Thus the Grass My
Horse has bit; the Turfs my Servant has cut . . . become my *Property,*
without the assignation or consent of any body."[27] How did the master-
servant relation get smuggled so quickly into the state of nature? Locke
hardly pauses to defend the right of some persons to "own" the labor of
others. He moves without comment from his initial assertion of equality—that every person owns the work of his own body—to the passing
remark that somehow in the state of nature some persons rightly came to
own the work of others. Presumably Locke saw no need to justify the
emergence of wage labor; he may have thought it obvious that owning
one's own labor implied the right to sell it. But this assumption considerably weakens the formal equality Locke otherwise insists on for persons
in the state of nature. Prior to the invention of government and the signing of a social contract, relations of domination and subordination have
emerged that claim the support of the law of nature.

Suppose we ask this question. In the state of nature, C acquires large
tracts of land by mixing his labor with them. But C finds that he cannot
cultivate them all by himself, so he makes use of D's labor by paying D a
wage to labor on land C cleared first. But now it is D's labor that is mixing with the land, it is D's labor that is making the land of use and adding
value to it. Why should the mere fact that C labored first give him title to
the fruit of D's labor? Presumably D sold his labor to C only because
there was no longer as much and as good land remaining in common
stock for D to come upon first. This only adds to the problem Locke has
in making the jump from C's owning his own labor to C's owning D's labor. On Locke's own theory, it would seem that the first taker of land
should share the property with anyone he hires to make use of it.

Locke assumes that the right to own property carries with it the right
to bequeath one's property to one's heirs. But he never defends this assumption, and it is not clear how he could on his own theory. After all,

the heirs did not mix their labor with the property; they are not the ones who made it useful or created the value. Moreover, it is not readily apparent how the basic premise—I own the work of my own body—survives the death of my body. Nonetheless, Locke assumes that possession of title to property includes the right to pass that title on to whomever one wills.

Locke's Version of the Social Contract

So what goes wrong? In large part the answer is nothing dramatic, nothing pressing. Human beings have succeeded in discovering a law of nature to govern them, but they have difficulties in executing that law for themselves.[28] Locke stresses that the law of nature gives every person not only a natural right to defend oneself against those who violate the law but also a right to punish the transgressors.[29] But how to carry out those punishments? How to avoid conflicts of interest, since even reasonable human beings would run into practical difficulties when judging their own cases. To deal with conflicts of interest, we would have spied the need for "a known and indifferent Judge, with authority to determine all differences according to the established Law," and for a "Power to back and support the Sentence when right, and to give it due Execution."[30] In other words, while the state of nature had a law to govern it, it had no executive to enforce the law. We invent government to deal with this problem, thereby hoping the better to secure our lives and estates.

How does Locke structure the social contract? Since our own understanding of constitutional government descends from the Lockean rather than Hobbist version of the social contract, we should pay special attention to how Locke reworks the notion that government derives its powers from an original compact so as to minimize rather than maximize the authority of the state.

If you recall, I referred to Hobbist persons as "contractual enthusiasts," uncommonly eager to barter away their natural liberties. But their enthusiasm is decidedly pessimistic, the flipside of the fear and despair that make them willing to accept the lopsided bargain that the Hobbist Sovereign drives.

Locke is what I will call a contractual minimalist. Lockean natural persons are already living the life they wish to continue living and preserving. For them, contractual behavior is not so much a matter of brute survival as it is a continuation of the propertied existence they already enjoy. In place of fear as a primary incentive for escape from the state of nature, Locke places the confidence of relatively contented individuals that they can work out a cooperative arrangement among themselves the better to keep on living pretty much as they already are.

Hobbist persons enter into the social contract with a desperate sense that they have little to lose. But Locke's men, by virtue of being less needy, reason more freely; they are not willing to gamble with their possessions, nor is everything up for negotiation. Off the table are any social arrangements that would fundamentally alter the equality of rights that humans enjoy in the state of nature: rational self-interested actors could not agree to any such arrangements.

Locke's social contract moves through two major steps. In the first, by my own individual consent, expressly, personally, and deliberately given, I take myself and my properties out of the state of nature and agree to join with others into one community.[31] Locke is clear that nothing less than an explicit and express act of consent will do. It is a necessary condition for owing obedience to the community.

What is it that I consent to? In this first step I consent henceforth to be bound by the consent of the community. Unless I bind myself in this way, I have not agreed to join with others "to make one Community" at all.[32] I make this agreement the better to protect my individual life and property. My sociability, as it were, is quite thin. I seek from civil society only a means, an instrument to preserve the life I am already living. I find that I share this much of a "common interest" with other individuals, and this makes the social contract possible.

Still, who speaks for the community? Locke concludes that the only practical and moral answer is that "the Majority have a Right to act and conclude the rest."[33] Practically speaking, a requirement of unanimous consent is not feasible and would reduce the social contract to a meaningless exercise. Morally speaking, the principle of majority rule is the only practicable procedure that free and equal individuals could agree to follow, consistent with preserving their initial equality. In majority decisions, everyone's consent counts the same. Thus by our own mutual individual consents we agree to the fairness of being bound by the majority.

Of course Locke, unlike Hobbes, sees the fundamental rights recognized by the law of nature as surviving the social contract. Each of us enters into civil society for the sole purpose of protecting our own lives and estates. Thus Locke's intuitive and plausible idea is that there are some rights that rational persons could never consent to surrender. Members give to the majority "all the power, necessary to the ends for which they unite into Society."[34] This language hardly implies an unlimited grant, and yet Locke can be infuriatingly unclear on this.[35] On the one hand, he speaks as if the social contract empowers the majority to make binding decisions in the name of the common interest and public good.[36] On the other hand, he speaks as if individuals preserve rights that even the majority's good cannot override.[37] Locke's system seems to demand some distinction between the majority good and the common good that we will have to explore.

In the second step of the social contract, the majority forms and empowers the government to act on its behalf.[38] Strictly speaking, the relation between civil society and government is not an act of contract. Locke describes it as a fiduciary arrangement, a matter of trust, with government functioning as a trustee for the purpose for which individuals joined society in the first place, which is nothing other than to protect and preserve the lives and properties of its members.[39] Locke does not dwell particularly on the form government should take. The only form of government he rules out is absolute monarchy: it has the particular vice of perpetuating the vice of the state of nature, where there was no fair or impartial umpire to enforce the laws.[40]

Whatever form of government the majority empowers, that government must rule by declared, settled, and standing laws.[41] If government violates this trust, then the majority is free to dissolve it and place its trust in another.[42] This dissolution of government does not threaten the social order, since the one community we formed through the social contract survives even the death of government.[43]

Locke's version of the social contract is recognizable to this day and has had profound influence on the course of history, enshrining a principle that legitimate political authority can stem only from the consent of the governed. Still, Locke's vision of society as resting on a contract masks two large problems that continue to roil the theory and the practice of politics today. The first has to do with what counts as consent. I want to trace out how Locke waters down his original strong and unambiguous concept of consent into something so vague and vacuous as to leave "consent of the governed" without any real meaning.

The second question has to do with Locke's way of resolving inherent tensions between two poles of his thought: the natural rights that individuals take with them into society versus the agreement to be bound by majority rule. This is probably not a tension that democratic politics should ever seek to resolve, but we will have to ask how Locke would have us live out the tension.

Consent: Express and Tacit

Let me take up the first problem. In the beginning, when Locke imagines the first generation's agreement to quit the state of nature and form a civil society, he insists that consent be expressly and individually given.[44] To make his point clear, Locke uses the grammatical singular: "[N]o one can be . . . subjected to the Political Power of another, without his own Consent."[45] Or again, the "only way whereby any one devests himself of his Natural Liberty, and puts on the bonds of Civil Society, is by agreeing with other Men to joyn and unite into a Community, for their comfortable, safe, and peaceable living one amongst another, in a secure Enjoyment of their Properties."[46]

Surprisingly, and against our modern notions, Locke treats express consent as irrevocable, creating a permanent allegiance that cuts off the founding members' right to emigrate. The use of the social contract to cut off a right of emigrating is so contrary to contemporary views that it is worth quoting Locke directly: "[H]e, that has once, by actual agreement, and any *express* Declaration, given his *Consent* to be of any Commonweal, is perpetually and indispensably obliged to be, and remain unalterably a Subject to it, and can never be again in the liberty of the state of Nature; unless, by any Calamity, the Government he was under comes to be dissolved; or else by some public Act cuts him off from being any longer a Member of it."[47] Of course persons do not have to consent; upon coming of age, they are free to emigrate instead. But once they expressly declare their allegiance, that declaration is irrevocable.

Locke seems concerned that recognizing a standing right to emigrate would destabilize the commonwealth and subject it to "dismemberment" were persons free to leave, taking with them their property (which, after all, belongs to them by natural right). Thus the social contract subjects both the *person* and the *property* of the contractor to irrevocable membership in the new society. Of course, as many commentators have pointed out, a solution would seem to have been at hand. We could conceptually distinguish between a state's jurisdiction over property and its jurisdiction over the person. Locke could have then quieted his fears of dismemberment by arguing that individuals remain free to take their persons, but not their properties, out of the commonwealth.

Once civil society is established, what binds future generations? Locke concedes that the father's consent can hardly bind his sons (Locke's vision is male specific).[48] Each person is born free of any obligation to established authority and must consent on his own: otherwise the cardinal notion that we are born free collapses. Thus, for profound reasons going to the essence of individual freedom, Locke rules out the possibility that persons come to be citizens merely by being born in the territory controlled by a government or to parents who are citizens.[49]

But now Locke runs into a problem. If succeeding generations have to consent anew expressly, in order to assume voluntarily the rights and duties of citizenship, then presumably we should notice all "these expressions" going on. But we do not.[50] To handle this difficulty, Locke (at first) qualifies the original (express) notion of consent to allow for "tacit" forms of consent. Sometimes, accepting the benefits of government's protection is a way of making a contract without words. This seems reasonable enough; lawyers today still find implied contracts when one party's behavior signifies that an offer has been accepted. The tricky question, as Locke puts it, is "how far" tacit consent binds us.

The first time Locke introduces the notion of tacit consent, he writes as if it substitutes for express consent in making persons citizens or full members of civil society.[51] Locke singles out the example of inheriting property as carrying with it agreement to become a member of the society where the property is located. Locke reasons as follows. A father may dispose of his estates as he sees fit. This is implicit in the natural right to own property. He may thus "annex such conditions to the Land . . . as may oblige his son to be of that Community, if he will enjoy those possessions which were his Fathers."[52] Locke is at first prepared to go even further. The founders not only annex themselves to the community but attach their properties as well, in a fixed and irrevocable way. Therefore, to prevent the commonwealth from disintegrating, inheritance must be understood as implying that "the son cannot ordinarily enjoy the Possessions of his Father, but under the same terms his Father did, by becoming a Member of the Society."[53]

A passage such as this suggests that, at least "ordinarily," (male) persons living under an already established government become full members of the community by inheriting property, without ever having to consent formally. But then Locke for good reasons draws back from this conclusion. Harking back to the question of "how far" tacit consent obliges, Locke finally settles on the argument that tacit consent obliges one to *obey* government but is not sufficient to make one a full member of the community. Only "actually entering into it [the Commonwealth] by positive Engagement and express Promise and Compact" can make one a member of the community.[54]

Locke arrives at this whittled-down force of tacit consent by considering the common sense of the matter. Foreigners after all can own property within the realm without signifying any intent to join themselves as members to that society. The obligation created by owning property within an established state is more akin to the obligation to pay homage and obedience to the established authorities that make possession and enjoyment of property possible.[55]

Once Locke is clear that tacit consent makes one a subject of government but not a citizen, he can see that tacit consent comes in all kinds of forms other than inheriting or owning property. He specifically mentions the person who takes lodging for a week, or the traveler along the highway, or the temporary resident, or even the permanent resident alien.[56] All these forms of behavior are contractual; they silently declare that one is exchanging obedience to the law for accepting the benefits of living under the protection of the law. Merely by going about the business of daily life within an established commonwealth creates duties of obedience. As the philosopher John Plamenatz puts it, Locke's notion of tacit consent leads to the conclusion that we agree to obey by obeying.[57]

Locke's consent theory ends in an odd two-tiered kind of system. Some of us are full members of the commonwealth by virtue of expressly volunteering to assume the rights and duties of membership. Others have never actually consented to anything but nonetheless are obliged to obey the government simply by virtue of going about the daily business of living. For members of society, there is no right to emigrate. For subjects of society, obedience "begins and ends," as Locke puts it, with their enjoyment of the property, the lodging, the travel in the realm.[58] Merely by quitting their lands or their acceptance of hospitalities, they are as free as ever to leave and to join another society.

Why should any of us care to go into such detail about Locke's theory of consent? We take for granted that government derives its legitimate powers from the consent of the governed, and yet it turns out that difficulties abound once we ponder what is to count as consent. Locke puts a great deal of moral weight on actual or express consent: for him it is the sign of a free person that nothing less can trigger political obligations. But the "actuality" of consent is its weakness as well as its strength.

Those of us who are born under an established government do not typically "actually" consent to our political station, and Locke knows it. So he ends with the considerably watered-down notion of tacit consent: without any deliberate choice but simply by residing where we do, we become subjugated to government. Consent, which promised to declare our freedom, ends up suggesting our subjugation.

Majority Rule versus Individual Rights

I turn now to a second problem with Locke's social contract: the tension between majority rule and individual rights. In my brief summary of Locke's theory I mentioned that he makes both a practical and a moral argument for majority rule. The practical argument justifies majority rule by default, since there seems no other feasible procedure for determining a group's decision. To insist on unanimity would be to give each individual veto power over the community's preferences and thus would perpetuate rather than solve the difficulties of the state of nature.

With my own students, I find that they are persuaded by the *practical* reasons for settling on majority rule. But each year I ask them to give me a *moral* justification for majority rule. I tell them that I know they can mount passionate arguments for minority rights, for protections against living under the thumb of the majority. But can they give me moral reasons for why majority rule is preferable to any other procedure for government? I remind them that there must be some such argument for the moral superiority of majority rule in politics over other possibilities; otherwise we could hardly explain our objections even to benevolent minorities' excluding majorities from political participation.

Typically my students have trouble thinking of majority rule as resting on moral grounds. They revert to purely practical considerations that eliminate other procedures: unanimity is not to be expected, supermajorities would be cumbersome to achieve, and the like.[59] At best they seem lukewarm in their majoritarian sympathies. They can make out the necessity for it, the way it is better than the other possibilities, but they have little to say as to what is *positive* about rule by the majority.

Locke does provide a moral justification for majority rule, alongside the practical defense. The value of majority rule is that (other than unanimity) it is the only procedure that rests on the equality of individuals.[60] In majority rule, every person's consent or vote counts as one, every person has an equal say in what the group decides. Any departure from majority procedures ends up giving us a system of weighted voting, whereby some person's vote counts more than another person's vote.

But is majority rule always consistent with the equal liberties of individuals? What if the majority proves intolerant or legislates tradeoffs between the interests of the few and the many? Some scholars have seized on these issues to argue that Locke's endorsement of majority rule creates its own form of absolutism, namely, the tyranny of the majority.

This criticism ignores Locke's insistence that certain individual rights are reserved against the majority, that basic principles of justice, already recognized in the state of nature, must be understood as continuing to hold in society and to limit even what majorities may do to individuals.[61] But the criticism is right that Locke is frequently not clear about these limits or where to draw the line between the rights of majorities to set policy and the rights of individuals to be free from majority rule. On the one hand, Locke writes that "Men give up all their Natural Power to the Society which they enter into."[62] On the other hand, it cannot be supposed that persons seeking to protect their own life and property meant to grant "absolute Arbitrary Power over their Persons and Estates."[63] Were the community to be a Leviathan in this sense, "this would be in effect to leave them no Property at all."[64] The laws of nature are not abrogated by the social contract but are incorporated into it and serve as a limit on the sovereignty that even a majority can muster.

Here is a passage in which Locke seeks to hold together individual rights and majority rule even as they threaten to fly apart:

> But though Men when they enter into Society, give up the Equality, Liberty, and Executive Power they had in the State of Nature, into the hands of Society, to be So far disposed of by the Legislative, as the good of Society shall require; yet it being only with an intention in Every one the better to preserve himself, his Liberty and Property . . . [,] the power of the Society, or Legislative constituted by them, can never be suppos'd to extend farther than the common good; but is obliged to secure every ones Property by providing against those . . . defects . . . that made the State of Nature so unsafe and uneasie.[65]

Left unanswered in a passage such as this is what to do if the community's decision about the common good is in conflict with a particular person's good. Does a just society permit the interests of the many to outweigh the interests of the few?

In the history of political thought following Locke, a great debate will break out over how to answer this question. One school of thought, known as utilitarianism, will argue that societies rightly aim to maximize the overall or aggregate or net happiness of its members; therefore "imposition of disadvantages on a few can be outweighed by a greater sum of advantages enjoyed by others."[66] The other school of thought, building on the idea of a social contract, will argue that justice prohibits certain kinds of tradeoffs, that each person is an end in himself and has a right against merely being used as a means to majority welfare. Locke seems committed to this latter notion. As John Rawls, the greatest contemporary proponent of social contract theory, puts it, "the role of equal rights in Locke is precisely to ensure that the only permissible departures from the state of nature are those which respect these rights and serve the common interest."[67]

Of course, what it means for political society to "respect" the equal liberties of its members is not an easy question to answer. But the crucial point is that Locke is among the first to use the idea of a social contract to express the intuitive notion that justice gives persons as individuals certain inviolable or inalienable rights that not even the general welfare can override. If, to take an example posed by the British philosopher Bernard Williams, there were many, many more pagans in first-century Rome than Christians, and if the pagans were made intensely happy by throwing Christians to the lions, would that practice have been justified in the name of "the greatest happiness of the greatest number"? I remember my own professors unnecessarily apologizing for using this example: sure it makes light of historical cruelty, but sometimes a bit of black humor makes the horror comprehensible.

But although Locke gestures toward robust reservation of individual rights in civil society, I am not persuaded that he always delivers on the promise. Let me offer two troubling cases, one involving religious liberty and the other protection of property.

In his justly celebrated *Letter Concerning Toleration*, Locke fashions an argument for tolerance, at least among Protestant sects. The most persuasive of his arguments is actually mounted from the point of view of the faithful.[68] To have faith is to understand that belief cannot be coerced, that force and punishment may make a person conform on the outside but cannot touch or transform a person's inner convictions. Religion by its very nature has to be a voluntary association of persons who believe. Thus intolerant practices are inherently self-defeating: they sub-

215

stitute fear for faith. Locke's argument for tolerance is actually two-sided, imposing equal obligations on church and state. For reasons already mentioned, the *state* must be tolerant of religion, leaving the faithful to find their own faith. Conversely, the *church* must not interfere with the legitimate powers of the state. The church by its very nature is limited to serving the spiritual interests of its members through spiritual means. It should seek neither to control the civil interests of society nor to use the means of civil government (the coercive force of the sword and of the law) to dictate spiritual ends. Thus Locke arrives at a kind of two-by-two matrix to express the idea of separation of church and state:

	Civil interests	*Spiritual interests*
Coercive means	state	[nothing]
Spiritual means	[nothing][69]	church

It turns out, however, that Locke's theory of tolerance has severe limits. In the case of Catholics, atheists, and Muslims, Locke thought that the state had factual evidence to conclude that the substantive doctrines of these groups made them a threat to public order. The threat was that they could not be relied on to obey their obligations to civil society in cases of conflict between fidelity to law and allegiance to religious authority or the authority of individual conscience. At a time of bloody war between Protestants and Catholics in England, Locke disqualified Catholics from the community of the tolerant since they supposedly could not agree to a social contract that bound them to obey the law rather than the pope. Locke offered a parallel caveat about Muslims. He disqualified atheists since lack of belief left them free to break their contracts when it suited them without fear of divine retribution.

Thus there are insufficiently strong or stable "rights" to religious freedom in Locke's version of the social contract. An individual's religious freedom is precarious and contingent, open to empirical findings by civil authorities that a given religion at a given time is a threat to public order. But these empirical findings are left to majority rule, and hence Locke has not established as firm a basis for religious freedom as his own theory required.

As Rawls notes, "greater historical experience and a knowledge of the wider possibilities of political life" have persuaded Locke's successors to expand the bounds of tolerance. Since intolerance of Catholicism was not dictated as an article of faith ("God ordains it") but reflected a factual judgment about threats to civil order, Locke's theory left room for expansion and inclusiveness.[70] Still, for the same reasons that Lockean tolerance can expand in certain historical circumstances, presumably it is open to contraction upon sufficient evidence, say in a post–9/11 world, that certain doctrines are a threat to law and order.

Of course, even rights-based theories of individual religious liberty draw the line somewhere and limit noxious religious doctrines when they threaten direct and imminent harm to others. Famous cases abound about refusal of Jehovah's Witnesses to vaccinate their children for a contagious disease such as smallpox, or Christian Science doctrines that keep parents from seeking medical care for their sick children, or the religious practice of female circumcision in certain Muslim nations, or the ancient requirement that a Hindu woman immolate herself on the funeral bier of her dead husband. But Locke goes beyond the uncontroversial claim that religious liberty is never absolute and needs to be balanced against the rights of others. He suggests that the majority's interest in public order goes beyond intolerance of a *particular* practice within Catholicism or atheism to a wholesale refusal to accept such persons as signers of the social contract to begin with. This is why there is some force to the claim that Locke's theory could very well justify tyranny of the majority in certain historical circumstances.

A second instance of tension between majority rule and individual rights occurs in Locke's theory of property. Consider two different societies, both organized on Lockean principles. Each society starts with a social contract that recognizes principles of justice antecedent to government which no government can violate, not even one authorized by the majority. One of the agreed-upon principles of justice is that individuals are entitled to own the fruit of their own labor. In the first society, the majority entrusts supreme power to a permanent and unelected "Legislative"—a choice Locke allows.[71] The characteristic danger in such a legislature is that it might come to see itself as having "a distinct interest . . . from the rest of the Community."[72] This distinct interest, in turn, might prompt legislation that arbitrarily takes property from individual members. Locke is clear that such legislation violates the antecedent principles of justice which limit government's power. The supreme power, Locke remarks, "cannot take from any Man any part of his Property without his own consent."[73]

Consider now a second possibility. The majority entrusts its power to a legislature whose members vary and who therefore move in and out of the society that will have to live according to the rules legislated. In such a representative body it "is not much to be fear'd" that the legislature will "dispose of the Estates of the Subject arbitrarily, or take any part of them at pleasure"—since those who legislate are themselves equally subject to the legislation.[74] In this way Locke relies on the procedures of majority representation to provide, ordinarily, adequate protection for individual rights of property.

I think it is fair to say that, in response to the dangers of his own time (seventeenth-century England), Locke was mostly concerned with protecting the majority—what he tellingly refers to as "the people"—from the arbitrary and oppressive rule of a government that served the interests of a few, specifically the danger that the ascension of a Catholic to the crown would create. He therefore tended to write as if it was "the people's" property at large that was at political risk, rather than individual entitlements to property being threatened by the people (that is, the majority).

Trusting in the reasonableness of human beings, Locke saw the majority as a force for reason, and he never fully developed a theory of rights against the majority.[75] Indeed, the *Second Treatise* is full of passages in which Locke's ambition is to justify the political rights of majorities, including the final passage of the *Treatise*, which trumpets that the "Power that every individual gave the Society, when he entered into it, can never revert to the Individuals again, as long as the Society lasts, but will always remain in the Community; because without this, there can be no Community, no Common-wealth."[76]

Nevertheless, Locke's majoritarianism stopped short of a demand for democracy or representative government. Government is initially established only by the consent of the governed, but the majority may invest it in institutions that do not require going to the people's representatives on particular issues. The one major exception is taxation, where there can be no justice without representation. Taxation raises the problem of whether government may lawfully take property from its members when the sole reason government was established was to preserve the members' enjoyment of their property. Locke accepts that government can do its job only if it is supported, and hence taxation is implicit in the social contract. Still, on this issue, the property-taking aspect of taxation requires government to get a person's "own consent." But then, in telling fashion, Locke clarifies that by "own consent" he means "the Consent of the Majority": "'Tis true, Governments cannot be supported without great Charge, and 'tis fit every one who enjoys his share of the Protection, should pay out of his Estate his proportion for the maintenance of it. But still it must be with his own Consent, i.e. the Consent of the Majority, giving it either by themselves, or their Representatives chosen by them."[77] So here Locke is clear that the social contract works to substitute majority consent for individual consent. We get the protection that the consent of our representatives gives us from the arbitrariness of "no taxation without representation," but we do not get to preserve living by individual consent once we consent to join a community and establish a government.

Arguably, in the passage just quoted, Locke meant to limit as well as to recognize government's taxing authority. The purpose of taxation is to defray the costs of running the policing and law enforcement aspects of government. What if the majority authorizes taxes for other purposes— say, for redistributive purposes, to take money from the rich in order to support the poor or the unemployed? Some philosophers, notably Robert Nozick, argue that redistributive programs violate core Lockean notions of liberty. Suppose a person chooses a certain lifestyle, and she finds it takes n hours of work per week to maintain this lifestyle. The effect of taxation is to force a person to work an extra y hours per week for free. The y hours are those additional hours of labor a person must put in, in order to pay the taxes and still have the same amount of property left that n hours used to net. In this sense, Nozick argues, a taxed person is working as a slave laborer for those y hours per week. Since Locke strongly argues that I am entitled to own the fruits of my labor, government violates my property rights, according to Nozick, when it forces me to work those extra hours to put money in someone else's pocket.[78]

Nozick certainly had a way of making political theory lively and relished the strength of arguments that called into question even the most settled of convictions, for instance, the justice of a progressive tax system. To this day I love giving Nozick's examples to my class and seeing what they make of arguments that cut against their political grain. No one has ever actually accepted his overheated equation of taxation with slave labor. But Nozick does highlight an issue Locke leaves unresolved. It is one thing to argue that individuals give tacit consent to narrow uses of taxation to support the policing functions of government. It is another to argue that the familiar income redistributions brought about by the welfare programs of the modern state could possibly find their justifica-

219

tion in the individual consent of persons who join the state only to protect their individual property entitlements. Once again, Locke envisions the majority as necessarily in synch with the interests of property, and hence he never ponders the details, as it were, of what to do if the majoritarian procedures he authorizes come into conflict with the entitlement theory of property.

Right of Revolution

Ultimately the people find their protection from oppressive government in the right to revolution. Locke's writings on revolution are bold, even in our own time. It is one matter to recognize that governments may turn oppressive or tyrannical. It is another to leave it to the people, or some part of the people, to judge when governments so violate the trust placed in them that they can be rightly dissolved. Locke takes the position that the people can be trusted to exercise the right of rebellion reluctantly.[79] "Revolutions happen not upon every little mismanagement in public affairs," Locke opines, adding that the people are more likely to bear even "great mistakes" than to overthrow an established government.[80] In language that the authors of the American Declaration of Independence essentially cribbed, the only government vulnerable to rebellion is one that undermines its own foundations by provoking a recalcitrant majority through "a long train of Abuses, Prevarications, and Artifices."[81]

Did Locke place the right of revolution only in the majority, or did he mean to permit individuals to resist with violence the acts of government against them, even when the majority did not necessarily support their grievances? In principle, Locke seems prepared to defend an individual right of resistance.[82] In practice, he counsels prudence: when government's unlawful acts extend no further than "some Private Mens Cases," rebellion is an exercise in futility, since the "Body of the People do not think themselves concerned in it."[83] Rebellion should be resorted to only when a government's "illegal Acts have extended to the Majority of the People" or if the few aggrieved can persuade the majority that the "consequences seem to threaten all."[84]

One of the reasons why Locke can contemplate a right to dissolve tyrannical governments is that the collapse of government does not mean we are thrown back into the state of nature. Locke carefully distinguishes between the dissolution of a government and the dissolution of civil society.[85] It was his expectation that the community we form by contract would withstand even acts of rebellion or revolution or collapse of government due to other causes; without government, there would still remain a common interest sufficient to maintain civility and enable the community to form a new government.

Nowhere does Locke seem more wrong and Hobbes more right. In a number of recent instances—Iraq, Yugoslavia, and Rwanda, to name just a troubling few—the fall of an authoritarian government led to civil war and dismemberment of the social condition entirely, as religiously or ethnically divided peoples sharing a territory fell into something approximating Hobbes's state of nature. It would not have surprised Hobbes that it takes the strong arm of the Leviathan to maintain the peace, that there is no social condition other than that maintained by fear of coercive authority. But the regressive tendencies of these societies are not readily explainable in Lockean terms: it does seem as if, to take the case of the former Yugoslavia, the existence of an authoritarian government was indispensable to holding various peoples together in one community.

I do not wish to pursue this point further. It may be that these examples are not to be explained by the fall of government so much as by the deliberate choice of new rivals for power to instigate and inflame violence for their own ends. But whatever the explanation, Locke's core distinction between the dissolution of government and the dissolution of the underlying civil society hardly seems useful to capture the regressive tendencies of history today.

Where did Locke go wrong? Even after persons move themselves by contract into a community or civil society, they remain for Locke the same atomized individuals they were before. They share a "common interest" that is little more than building better fences and outposts to permit them to lead their lives and protect their properties without interference. But is society just a collection of individuals? Politically, Locke was keenly aware of the Catholic-Protestant divisions of his own England. Theoretically, however, he reverted to a sociological individualism that saw "the people" as but an aggregation of individuals.

In the absence of government, Locke wrote, power reverts to the community, which, by majority decision, establishes a new government. Relying on the majority seems reasonable if one views society as composed only of individuals. But it is a recipe for provoking, not preventing, civil war in territories inhabited by diverse peoples, with sharp distinctions between the majority and minorities. Locke's individualism kept him from exploring the "social" in society and makes him seem quaintly optimistic in an era when the prospect of various peoples' being able to maintain their civility through a social contract seems bleaker than ever.

11

ROUSSEAU AND THE RUSTIC

When I was an undergraduate, Rousseau was my favorite. He still is. Rousseau is the proverbial poor kid from the provinces (Geneva) who takes the big city (Paris) by storm. Son of an itinerant watchmaker and of a mother who died in childbirth, Rousseau was a self-made and self-taught man who remained raw, angry, and unruly throughout his life, both in his personal relations and in his thoughts.

If you recall my earlier discussion of Aristotle, Rousseau is the opposite of Aristotle's privileged gentleman practicing the virtues of moderation and singing the praises of the status quo. Rousseau certainly knew such types—the swells and luminaries of the Paris scene. Diderot, D'Alembert, Voltaire, and Hume: these are a few of the leading lights of his day with whom Rousseau was first friends, then enemies. On the one hand, Rousseau desperately wanted admittance to this elite world, and he was constantly seeking introductions, entering prize contests given by French academies in hopes of being discovered. On the other hand, he despised himself most when he was living inside a world whose hypocrisy he hated. Not surprisingly, Rousseau therefore remained an outsider, what Dostoyevsky would later call an underground man, who turned his resentments into a revolutionary indictment of the status quo.

No one has ever penned a more fierce *j'accuse* against the privileges of the rich ("they have nerve endings in their property"),[1] the logic of commerce ("every man finds his profit in the misfortunes of his neighbor"),[2] the depravity of actors and actresses (they show themselves off "to the public for money"),[3] the fakery of women (full of "counterfeited sweetness"),[4] the wickedness of reason ("it is reason that makes [man] keep aloof" from the suffering of others),[5] and the inhumanity of philosophers (they would sleep through a murder committed outside their window).[6]

Rousseau's indictment of modern life is wholesale, a sweeping condemnation and unmasking of the pretenses of the so-called "civilized" or "cultured." Consider, for instance, Rousseau's first major breakthrough. The staid and stately Academy of Dijon sponsored an essay competition on the question of whether progress in the arts and sciences contributes to the purification or corruption of morals. Rousseau's winning entry laid out a template he was to follow throughout his career, in which he contrasted the original innocence of mankind to its corrupt version once we wander through the labyrinthine mazes of so-called "progress" and "civilized" society. This essay launched Rousseau's career as a friendly critic of the Enlightenment and its faith in progress.

As we shall see, Rousseau struggled to keep two contradictory strains of his thought in conversation with each other. In one voice, Rousseau is a romantic—a utopian who turns to "natural man" as his ideal of all that is good and pure, as compared to the dis-ease that is civilization. Some persons heard that voice and assumed Rousseau was a pied piper leading them back to a lost golden age. Marie Antoinette, for instance, re-created an entire rustic village (the Petit Trianon) on the grounds of Versailles. Others were inspired by the tales of noble savages whom explorers of the seven seas brought back with them. In 1769 Louis Bougainville became the first French explorer to circumnavigate the globe. Diderot penned a fictional supplement to Bougainville's account, idealizing Tahiti as a place where nature still reigned pure.[7]

With Rousseau, the surprise is that he praises the state of nature only to tell us, in another voice, that it never existed, that we neither can nor would want to go back there even if it did exist, and that the solution to the ills of society is to become more thoroughly absorbed into the community, rather than less. This other Rousseauist voice is intensely political, and it holds up the life of the citizen, rather than that of natural man, as the highest ideal. But how is it possible for one and the same philosopher to idealize *both* the natural condition and *also* the most fully politicized condition? What sense can we make of Rousseau's famous remark that "we must force people to be free"? How is that even possible—to *force* persons to be *free*—and how did the Rousseau who praised natural goodness end up endorsing such a thoroughgoing politics?

Reading Rousseau can be frustrating, even maddening, as we follow his attempts to stave off the tension between his romantic and political streaks. But when I say Rousseau is my favorite, I say this not despite the tension but because of it. In the end, I think Rousseau failed to explain how human nature can be good and yet politics goes right only when it radically takes aim at our natures, manipulating and molding us into citizens. But it is a spectacular failure, and I would much rather keep company with a political thinker who wrestles with the tension between individual and community, nature and society, than with one who senses no strain at all.

The *Confessions*

Before turning to Rousseau's political writings proper, I pause by way of introduction to consider a few passages in Rousseau's autobiographical *Confessions*. In our Oprah-fied world we are used to confessional literature, and it no longer has much capacity to shock. We have heard it all— the inside stories of murderers, wife-beaters, child abusers, heroin addicts, thieves, prostitutes, and so on. But Rousseau was a pioneer of this literature, and he set out to write a no-holds-barred, warts and blemishes account of Jean-Jacques Rousseau, Exhibit Number One of the moral degradation of modern man. Augustine's *Confessions* had been a story of triumph; Rousseau's autobiography traces a more ambiguous moral trajectory.

Of course, Rousseau counts on receiving the reader's congratulations for the honesty it takes to confess one's darkest secrets, and the *Confessions* often seems self-serving. The deeper the secret he confesses, the more pure and trustworthy a character he is supposed to emerge in our eyes. In this sense the *Confessions* mirrors the tension in Rousseau's political thought. He sees himself as both socially corrupt and yet naturally pure underneath it all.

Still, some of the confessions are bound to disturb. And having said Rousseau is my favorite, I feel an obligation to point out that he was not a very admirable person. While it is certainly possible to admire a writer's work without liking him as a person, in Rousseau's case it is an intriguing question whether some of his personal deficiencies are reflected in the contradictions of his thoughts.

I limit myself to three confessions Rousseau makes. The first is an episode that he had never before told anyone about and that had caused him remorse for more than forty years. When he was about nineteen, Rousseau stole a rather worthless pink and silver ribbon from the household where he was living. Upon discovering the missing ribbon in Rousseau's room, the master of the house asked how it came to be there. Rousseau says he "grew confused, stammered and finally said with a blush that it was Marion who had given it to me." Marion was a young servant girl whom Rousseau knew to be a total innocent and to whom he had taken a fancy. When Marion was brought in, she denied the charge and pleaded with Rousseau not to bring this ruin upon her. Rousseau persisted in bearing false witness. Unable to tell where the truth lay, the master dismissed them both, virtually assuring that Marion would never again find employment.[8]

Why did he do it? Rousseau excuses himself from any "deliberate wickedness." Marion's name just popped into his head because he thought of her so much, especially in connection with the ribbon, which he intended to give her. Of course, his persevering in the lie was quite calculated and expedient, but this only shows how social pressure overcame his better impulses. Had he been taken aside and interrogated in private, Rousseau assures us he would have immediately confessed and taken his punishment.[9] The problem was that he was confronted in public, before all eyes, and could not bear the humiliation, disgrace, shame, and dishonor that the *reputation* for being a thief would bring.

Rousseau is not proud of how he chose to protect his own reputation at the expense of another, but he tells the story not to reveal a character flaw peculiar to him but to fault social life in general. This emphasis on reputation will color all of Rousseau's political writings.

A second confession shows Rousseau's same tendency to condemn his social corruption while insisting on the underlying purity of his heart. He is smitten by Guilietta, a common girl or prostitute. Rousseau wants us to know that there is good enough in him to have overridden social conventions and to have opened his heart to the "charms and graces of this enchanted girl." Once he responds, he elevates her from prostitute to goddess. "Young virgins in the cloisters are not more fresh, ... the hours of paradise are less enticing." Or as he also writes, "I entered a courtesan's room as if it were the sanctuary of love and beauty; in her person I felt I saw the divinity."[10]

But then he looks again and sees that this woman has a defect, a withered breast or malformed nipple. All of a sudden, "instead of the most charming creature, . . . I held in my arms some kind of monster, rejected by Nature."[11] Guilietta now sinks below even the level of a courtesan in his view. Sensing his disgust, she dismisses him with great nobility, and Rousseau comes to his senses when it is too late.

This confession is one among many that illustrate Rousseau's deeply troubling attitudes toward women: he expects them to be goddesses, and any imperfection or blemish reduces them to the category of a prostitute or worse. But this particular story about Guilietta illustrates more. Rousseau congratulates himself on being sufficiently in touch with natural love as to fall in love with her despite her profession. This was his good side. But what kept him from acting on it? Why did he throw away a genuine chance at happiness? Rousseau does not answer this in his *Confessions,* except to suggest that the physical defect triggered disgust and undercut his idea of the perfect woman he was trying to find in the prostitute. Throughout his life this basic pattern reasserts itself: women have to be perfect, and if they are not the Madonna, then they are the whore. For the most part this kept Rousseau from ever forming a satisfactory relationship with a woman.

The one exception ends up proving the rule. Sometime around 1774 Rousseau met and fell in love with a laundry servant of twenty-two or twenty-three, Thérèse Le Vasseur. Thérèse was to remain Rousseau's lifelong companion, although he steadfastly refused to marry her until late in life. At first Rousseau thought to "improve her mind" but then gave up the effort: "Her mind is as Nature made it; culture and teaching have no effect on it." Thérèse never learned to read or write properly, but "I lived as pleasantly with my Thérèse as with the finest genius in the world." As in the Guilietta story, we see Rousseau offering his love of the "natural" Thérèse as an example of the surviving force of natural goodness in him. By virtue of escaping the corruptions that stalk all learned women, the unvarnished Thérèse fit Rousseau's image of the naturally good woman.[12]

But there is another, darker dimension to their relationship. When Thérèse is pregnant with their first child, Rousseau confesses to looming "embarrassment" at the prospect of fathering and raising a child out of wedlock. He happily seizes on what he describes as the prevailing social custom for men in his situation, which is to abandon the child at a foundling hospital. He himself had no "scruples" to overcome in acting in this socially expedient way, but the good Thérèse had to be talked into giving up her child. Not once but four more times Rousseau would father children with Thérèse, only to take each of them to the foundling hospital.[13]

In his political writings Rousseau will assign great importance to the love of parents for their children, calling such love the "finest sentiment" of which we are capable. Yet in his own life Rousseau contradicts his philosophical beliefs and attaches little importance to fatherhood. Once more Rousseau uses his confessions to turn his own life into disturbing evidence—and he knows it is disturbing—of how the purity of natural impulse gives way to the morality of civilization, a morality that sanctioned abandonment of so-called bastard children in foundling hospitals as proper behavior from so-called gentlemen.

As to all three of these confessions, we are left to wonder: Is the problem really with society, as Rousseau would have it? Or did Rousseau have more to confess than the ordinary civilized man? I turn now to his philosophical writings to see how this tension between individual and society, natural goodness and social corruption, plays out.

The Romantic Rousseau and the Love of Nature

I begin with Rousseau's most passionate work, his *Discourse on the Origin of Inequality*. Commonly known as the *Second Discourse,* the essay was written for yet another prize contest sponsored by the Academy of Dijon, although this time Rousseau did not win. The question posed was "What is the origin of Inequality among Men, and is it Authorized by the Natural Law?" To answer the question, Rousseau makes use, but novel use, of the state of nature/social contract methodology of Hobbes and Locke.

Unlike his two predecessors, Rousseau reworks the social contract into an attack on the injustice of the status quo; he denies that historical societies rest on any sort of fairly bargained social contract at all. Rousseau's attack drives home two related points. First, the origin of inequality is far more social than it is natural. People may differ naturally in qualities such as strength, speed, dexterity, height, or even beauty. But natural differences matter only when social conventions assign more value to one set of attributes than to another. Second, most social and economic inequality is unjust. Philosophers think they can legitimize existing unequal distributions of property by tracing them back to some sort of first contract where we pledged to protect one another's property. But they forget that the terms of contract always favor the rich and that the rich never surrender their privileged status voluntarily. Whatever else one makes of Rousseau, he cared deeply about equality and saw through the prevailing arguments defending the privileged ranks with a clarity that has rarely been matched.

The State of Nature

To persuade us that existing inequalities are socially constructed and morally unjust, Rousseau begins with a detailed examination of the state of nature. Right off he stresses how his account will differ from that of the likes of a Hobbes. Hobbes failed ever to get back to the state of nature at all. He merely described the plight that civilized men—seventeenth-century Englishmen—would find themselves in were they to wake up one morning and learn that all the restraints of government had vanished overnight.[14] To Hobbes's great discovery that persons with all the avarice characteristic of society would fall into aggression if suddenly deprived of government, Rousseau waves off the supposedly shocking conclusions as banal. The Hobbist approach reveals only the obvious fact that civilized men have come to depend on government to keep the peace. Beyond the obvious, Hobbes tell us nothing about how truly natural human persons might have behaved before they became bloated with the artificial desires for luxury, reputation, and power that sow the seed of so many quarrels.

To get back to the state of nature, we must strip the world of more than government and law. We must strip human beings of all the passions, ideas, imaginations, and relationships they acquire only in society. We want to know, for instance, what hunger necessitated before human beings acquired a taste for cooking, dining, condiments, and dessert (recall that Glaucon ridiculed such an image of a state of nature as a state fit only for pigs). We want to know what contact men and women kept before there was any notion of a family; what behavior the sexual drive caused before it became violent with emotions such as jealousy and possessiveness.

But now Rousseau says something surprising. To find the state of nature in this precise sense, we must begin by "laying aside facts, for they do not affect the question."[15] Instead Rousseau takes us on a "thought experiment" in search of a state of nature that is only "hypothetical" and never really existed. Kant will say as much after Rousseau, but Hobbes and Locke had come close to describing the state of nature as a real and original place. For Rousseau, the state of nature is not some ancient period of prehistory that fossil evidence could one day conceivably unearth. Nor does it survive in the deepest rainforests of the Amazon, among some long-lost tribe that anthropologists might discover someday. For Rousseau, the state of nature is a fiction.

Why invent a fictional story? How does it help us understand what is natural, what is social in us, if Rousseau concedes that his account of the natural is mythic? Rousseau's point seems to be that, although his state of nature is historically a myth, it nonetheless captures a moral truth that can guide our political practices. It does so, first, by giving us an ideal against which to judge and to criticize existing political arrangements once they are deprived of the cover that comes from seeing them as founded on nature. But the ideal of a "state of nature" does more than this. Instead of a treasure map to guide us on a voyage of discovery into the past, it is an expression of the ideal toward which we want to move politics in the future. Like Aristotle in some ways, Rousseau argues that we achieve our natural human condition only by building a political community finally in tune with human nature. Such a community never existed and probably never will exist. But the utopian ideal of politics in tune with human nature is worth trying to practice, even when we know we will constantly fail to reach it.

Here, then, is how Rousseau imagines his state of nature, populated by hypothetical human beings who have yet to develop any ideas or passions from social contact of any sort. To begin with, the state of nature was a state of plenty rather than scarcity.[16] The earth was fertile enough to sustain the basic and spare set of needs generated by the instinct for self-preservation. Rousseau's initial point here is that the natural necessities of life are few, modest, and easily met. Human beings would have stood in no original need of one another to gather acorns or to hunt animals, and they would have lived dispersed among the animals, "with no fixed habitation nor . . . scarcely [encountering one another] twice in their whole lives."[17] As Rousseau puts it, far from our being born with social natures, "it is impossible to conceive why, in this primitive state, one man should have more occasion for the assistance of another than one monkey or one wolf for that of another animal of the same species."[18]

The solitary and self-sufficient lifestyle kept the peace in the state of nature; there simply was no reason for human beings to attack one another to feed themselves. Hobbes, of course, thought that the state of nature was a state of war from the beginning. But this was only because "he had injudiciously included in that care which savage man takes of his own self-preservation the satisfaction of numberless passions which are the work of society, and have made laws necessary."[19]

What else besides a spare instinct for self-preservation characterizes natural man? Rousseau's answer is—not much. Self-preservation "was almost his only concern."[20] This concern sharpened *some* human faculties, developing the savage's skills for preying rather than being preyed on by other animals. But all else about the human condition lay fallow and undeveloped. Items such as clothing and dwellings were unknown, however much today we think of such things as "necessities."[21] Above all, the savage's days were an endless succession of regularity, there being no occasion for change or progress.

Apart from constantly being alert to danger, the natural man was idle and fond of sleep—of necessity a light sleeper but a frequent sleeper, much like the other animals, who "think but little and may, in a manner, be said to sleep all the time they do not think."[22] I often illustrate Rousseau's point by asking a student who has left a dog at home to speculate about what the dog does when left alone. Almost invariably the student answers that the dog is probably asleep. No one ever imagines the dog lying awake thinking or anxious or planning the next day. This is Rousseau's point about the natural human. With every day being a repeat of the same familiar foraging in the woods, "his imagination paints nothing to him, . . . his soul, which nothing disturbs, gives itself up entirely to the consciousness of its own present existence."[23] Savage man, in short, has nothing to do or think about once he has eaten. Should he plan tomorrow's foraging? Natural man has no concept of the future or of time. Where would he have developed such ideas? He has neither curiosity nor forethought, nor the capacities it takes to foresee his own needs in advance. Life is entirely static.

Rousseau continues in this vein to portray the barrenness of the state of nature and to insist that most of what we take for granted in the human condition is social rather than natural. There was no discovery of fire yet, no knowledge of agriculture, no tools, no use of metal, no private property, no family life, no language, no grammar. For Rousseau it is a mystery as to how human beings ever made such discoveries or "how many thousands of ages" it took for the human mind to evolve the operations of which it was capable.[24]

Natural Goodness

I said earlier that Rousseau was a romantic when it came to nature. But so far the picture hardly seems romantic. All we have is a crude (male) creature whose "[d]esires never extend beyond his physical wants," whose only pleasures in life "are food, a female, and rest."[25] But now Rousseau makes a sly move on the chessboard. Natural man may be a creature without any moral capacity; he may lack any sense of good or evil other than to value self-preservation. But "let us beware of concluding with

Hobbes, that man, as having no idea of goodness, must be naturally bad; that he is vicious because he does not know what virtue is."[26] Hobbes has it backwards. More evil has been committed in the name of morality, and more bloodshed has been shed by men of culture than was ever spilled in nature. Enveloped in their primitive innocence, human beings were "naturally good" and immune to the "thinking evil" that spreads in civilization.

Rousseau makes two different arguments on behalf of our natural goodness. The first is that natural man was good by default, since he remained innocent of the "enlightened" ideas and specious reasoning that sets civilized men apart. Natural man is a stranger to social vices; his goodness reflects not thought but "the calm of the passions." Rousseau gives many examples of the calm of the natural passions, for instance, the moderation built into quenching thirst or slaking hunger in creatures who had no reason to drink or eat in excess. But sexuality is the example he returns to time and again for the peace of nature. In civilization the sexual drive is agitated and "impetuous"—a "terrible passion" often threatening "brutal rage" and "which, in its transports, seems proper to destroy the human species which it is destined to preserve."[27] To control the violence of sexuality, civilization depends on law and custom to restrain what nature seems to leave wild.

Rousseau again suggests that we have it backwards. The disorders traceable to sexuality "come into being with the laws themselves." The natural or physical aspect of sex "prompts one sex to unite with one another," but not toward any permanent coupling. "Their need once gratified, the sexes took no further notice of each other."[28] The "moral" aspect is the socially originated custom or insistence that we fix our sexuality on one particular person.

Once we make this distinction between the natural and the moral elements of love and sexuality, we will see that the physical aspects of sexuality are moderate and peaceful, easily satisfied. It is ridiculous, Rousseau admonishes, to think of savages slaughtering one another to achieve satisfaction of a periodic drive, extinguished for a time by the act, and renewable without trouble. But things turn ugly when we lay over biology a moral and artificial desire to have a particular mate, to possess her and to prevent competitors from possessing her, to win admiration from others for possessing the most beautiful or desirable partner, or to feel or cause jealousy. The combination of the natural passion and the social passion to treat the sexual partner as one's own property makes sex in so-

231

ciety "lethal." By contrast, the natural man enjoys the goodness (inno-cence) of sex in its pre-moral condition.

Rousseau's point is gender specific. It is the social male who becomes violent, but it is the social female whom he blames for practicing the civi-lized arts that call out the violence of sexual possession.

In ways that parallel his separation of the physical and the social in sexuality, Rousseau traces the warped socialized version of other natural passions. Thus "savage man, when he has dined, is at peace with all na-ture." But "with man in society it's quite another story: in the first place, necessities are to be provided, and then superfluities; delicacies follow, and then immense riches, and then subjects and then slaves." Natural man sleeps; social man is restless and "does not enjoy a moment's relax-ation." Natural man knows satisfaction; social man always wants more. Natural man has no morality but even so lacks any reason to attack oth-ers. Social man knows it is wrong to kill but "will end up by cutting every throat, until he at last finds himself the sole master of the universe."[29] Natural man has yet to discover medicine, but he is rarely ill because his appetites are modest. Social man is surrounded by doctors and yet is per-petually sick on food adulterated for profit by the greedy, or by the spread of epidemics in crowded cities. (I was recently reminded of Rous-seau when reading that one worrisome scenario for the spread of the avian virus, the so-called bird flu, from birds to humans is through the il-legal poaching and smuggling of pet birds to line someone's pockets.)

Rousseau summarizes this first argument on behalf of natural good-ness with a marvelous passage, worth quoting at length:

> We must not confuse selfishness with self-love; they are two very distinct passions. . . . Self-love is a natural sentiment, which in-clines every animal to look to his own preservation, and which, guided in man by reason and qualified by pity, is productive of hu-manity and virtue. Selfishness is but a relative and factitious senti-ment, engendered in society, which inclines every individual to set a greater value upon himself than upon any other man, which in-spires men with all the mischief they do to each other.[30]

Sympathy in the State of Nature

Rousseau makes a second argument on behalf of natural goodness. Nat-ural man is good not just by default, not only for being pure of the evils of society. On the positive side, there is an inherent goodness in the natural passions that Rousseau summarizes with the French word *pitié,* in English "pity" or "sympathy." Pity is "another principle that has escaped Hobbes."[31] It instills in the savage an "innate abhorrence to see beings suffer that resemble him."[32] The remarkable thing about pity is that it precedes "all manner of reflection; and [is] so natural that the beasts themselves sometimes give evident signs of it."[33] (A 2006 experiment showing mice responding to the pain of other mice makes Rousseau seem prescient in this regard.)[34]

The sad fate of pity is that it is eclipsed by reason, which teaches man new forms of self-awareness and self-love that destroy the primal capacity to identify with the species as such: "[I]t is reason that makes man shrink into himself; it is reason that makes him keep aloof from everything that can trouble or afflict him."[35] Echoing this Rousseauist point, Karl Marx was later to lament the increasing alienation of modern man from his "species-being." Marx thought that alienation was specific to certain antagonistic organizations of society, but Rousseau considered alienation from our natural fellow feeling as one among many prices we pay for social and moral progress.

Part One of the *Discourse* ends by putting the two arguments together. "With passions so minimally active," on the one hand, and with the "salutary restraint" of pity not yet drowned out by selfish reasoning, on the other, the state of nature was a state of peace.

Equality in the State of Nature: A Psychological Account

But was it also a state of equality? No doubt some persons were stronger, taller, more agile or fleet of foot. Perhaps as a kind of pre-Darwinian, Rousseau might admit that nature selected, say for height, at least in circumstances where the food supply was mostly to be found on tall trees, or for speed when the only available prey were swift animals. But mostly Rousseau thought the fertility of the earth sufficient to mute the importance of these sorts of natural inequalities. One point he is clear on: the inequality of rich and poor is not some legitimate inheritance bequeathed by natural differences. The very idea of private property would have been foreign to natural man, since he lacked any incentive to accumulate more than he needed at the moment.

Natural inequalities were benign and of limited importance for a *psychological* reason as well. Remember that each person is an isolate in the state of nature, observing no one else and noticed by no one in return. Living apart from one another, natural persons had not yet developed the mental capacity it takes to *compare* persons, to rank them according to height or speed or strength.

The absence of comparisons from the state of nature is crucial to Rousseau. By insisting that creatures who lived apart from sustained relationships could not yet have evolved the mind it takes to rank persons, Rousseau draws two great conclusions. First, natural inequalities come to matter only when a quality we happen to possess wins us respect, praise, worth, or value in the eyes of others. Once other persons start to observe my strength and think that I am somehow a better person or a person to be esteemed more highly than others because of it, then and only then do natural differences in strength matter. In society not only do I possess my natural strength abilities, but also I rank higher in public opinion and enjoy a loftier reputation.

The other great conclusion Rousseau draws from the pre-comparative stage of our brain in the state of nature is that natural man—and natural man alone—is honest. In society we are always concerned with what others think of us; we are motivated to do what will win us honor and the respect of others. It gets to the point where my sense of myself is derived from the impressions other people have of me. My behavior is unmoored from expressing my inner desires and anchored to currying favor with others.

I find that this is a part of Rousseau that my students most take to heart. I ask them to think about the process they went through in deciding which colleges to apply to and which one to attend. I ask them whether they pored through the guidebooks with their rankings of the reputation of particular colleges, whether they were concerned with what other people would think of them because of where they were accepted or rejected. I ask whether it was even conceivable that they could have distinguished the "inherent" quality of a college from its reputation, or whether they could have chosen to go to a college with a lesser reputation but more appeal to them personally. In posing all these leading questions, I do not mean to criticize them for paying heed to ratings and rankings; we are all in the same boat. I am, however, asking them to mull over the insight that Rousseau provides when he zeroes in on how dependent we have become on what others think of us.

In an influential book from the 1950s, *The Lonely Crowd,* the sociologist David Riesman distinguished between persons who were "outer directed" and those who were "inner directed." Rousseau's point is that society harnesses us to outer direction, and this orientation necessarily involves deceiving others, as well as ourselves. We become role players, calculating what pose we should assume in different social circumstances.

Back in the state of nature, we could not help but be honest. Since there was no such thing yet as reputation or public esteem, behavior reflected a person's own desires, primitive though these desires were. As Rousseau writes, "savage man lives within himself." In other words, natural man had the merit of *authenticity,* or what the French critic Jean Starobinski called *transparency.*[36] Savage man knew nothing about cunning, deceit, or hypocrisy, about catering to the opinions of others or of engaging in calculations or strategies designed to make one appear other than who one was. What there was to natural man was not much, but at least it was honest.

Social Inequality and Its Psychological Roots

What happened to natural man? Where and how did he become extinct? Part Two of the *Discourse* tells the story of how social life would have inevitably emerged after "thousand of centuries" of static and solitary existence in the state of nature. Once again Rousseau is frank that his account of social origins is hypothetical. When it comes to key steps in human progress, such as the discovery of fire or the origins of language, Rousseau throws up his hands at the essential mystery of it all.[37]

What he does insist on is that social relationships emerge not just as some network *external* to our human nature; for better or worse, social contact *changes* human nature and becomes embedded in the very way the mind works, in the structure of consciousness. In a manner of speaking, Rousseau is a forerunner of evolutionary psychologists in offering a history of mind or consciousness. Rousseau's starting point is that even in the state of nature, there were two features that distinguished the human relation to nature from that of the other animals. The first is a basic "consciousness of liberty," an awareness of our free will or of our capacity to choose. Other animals are dictated to by natural impulse; only man has the capacity to master his own nature and to exercise dominion, even tyranny, over nature.

The second distinguishing feature of human nature is what Rousseau calls in French, *perfectibilité.* The other animals are today what they ever will be, but humans alone have the capacity for improvement, for progress, for perfectibility. Emphasis on human progress would have been much in keeping with the Enlightenment faith of his day. But Rousseau adds a distinctive twist: with "melancholic necessity," he regards the human drive to master nature as a mixed blessing. It "raises us up above the animals" and makes possible all of the moral and material refinements that make life worth living. But "progress" is also a matter of sliding backwards, until we regress and "fall back even lower than the beasts themselves." (Could it be, Rousseau parenthetically remarks in ways that he knows will be shocking, that the Orinoco Indians are onto something when they bind the temples of the young so as to produce imbeciles?)[38]

In Rousseau's account, sooner or later—and for him it was later—the long duration of the state of nature had to end, as the human mind noticed regularities in nature, figured out how things worked, and used that knowledge to free itself from the stimulus and response of instinct. Such knowledge included fledgling awareness that creatures around us were similar and a new desire to have contact with like persons. Rudimentary relationships developed, and for the first time persons lived under the same roof. Men and women discovered not only their similarities but also their differences, and they begin to form the first families. At this point Rousseau lavishes praise on the moral uplift wrought by the shift from solitary to social life. The family gives "birth to the sweetest sentiments" of which humans are capable: "conjugal and paternal love."[39]

Other improvements follow. A capacity to make tools develops, and we labor productively on the raw material of nature, introducing agriculture and metallurgy. We make music; we keep warm with furs and tame lightning into fire. We adorn ourselves with ornaments. In short, in place of the indolence of the state of nature, human beings are busy transforming themselves and their environment. Rousseau calls these early societies the "happiest and the most durable epoch, . . . the real youth of the world."[40] At this point humans bask in the moral and material benefits that come from social cooperation, and they have not yet degraded cooperation into ventures for domination and subordination. But they will, and they do.

The Birth of Social Psychology and the Origins of Inequality

Even as progress improves the human condition, it is sowing the seeds of our degradation. Rousseau offers a prosaic and yet subtle portrait of the mixed blessings of early civilization. Imagine a small group of persons who have shaken off enough of their original wildness to be enjoying the purest forms love and leisure will ever take. They "assemble round a great tree" and begin to sing and dance. Even so,

> [e]veryone began to notice the rest, and wished to be noticed himself; and public esteem acquired a value. He who sang or danced best; the handsomest, the strongest, the most dexterous, or the most eloquent, came to be the most respected: this was the first step towards inequality, and at the same time towards vice. From these first distinctions there arose on one side vanity and contempt, on the other envy and shame; and the fermentation raised by these new leavens at length produced combinations fatal to happiness and innocence.[41]

This seemingly simple passage requires careful analysis. Rousseau does not deny that some people in fact sing or dance better than others, that still others have the most beauty or superior dexterity. Take beauty, for instance. Many people believe that beauty is relative, that beauty is in the eye of the beholder, as the saying goes, or a socially constructed ideal that varies from culture to culture. Rousseau certainly shares this view, insofar as it highlights the crucial role society plays in determining what *value* to attach to a quality such as beauty. But he can acknowledge this social feature while also acknowledging that nature distributes a quality such as beauty or musical talent unequally. Indeed, when he writes that "the handsomest" began to be noticed by the rest, Rousseau seems to accept that beauty is not democratically distributed. But this level of inequality did not trouble Rousseau. Even if some persons are endowed by nature with more singing talent or more physical beauty, persons in the state of nature took no notice, for the simple reason that they took no notice of other persons at all.

What it means to live in society, by contrast, is to develop a consciousness of oneself and of one's worth *only* in relation to other people. The birth of comparative thought makes the benign natural inequalities turn malignant. Now, inequality of beauty or skill in singing or dancing triggers another layer of inequality altogether, differences in the distribution of respect and reputation. It is no longer merely a matter of my being naturally the better *singer*. It is now that I am also considered a better *person* across the board, at least if I happen to live in a time and place where singers are greatly esteemed. Fairly soon, I move from singing merely as an authentic and honest expression of my own desires to singing precisely in order to impress other persons. I no longer live within myself, as natural man did. Instead social man lives "constantly outside himself, knows only how to live in the opinion of others." In a marvelous phrase Rousseau writes, "[I]t is, if I may say so, merely from [others'] judgment of him that he [social man] derives the consciousness of his own existence."[42] Equally marvelous is this passage:

> It became to the interest of men to appear what they really were not. To be and to seem became two very different things, and from this distinction sprang haughty pomp and deceitful knavery, and all the vices which form their train. . . . [M]an, hitherto free and independent, was now, in consequence of a multitude of new needs, brought into subjection, as it were, to all nature, and especially to his fellows, whose slave in some sense he became, even by becoming their master.[43]

Why is our natural independence so sorely compromised by "progressive" entrance into civil society? One of the jarring features of Rousseau's account thus far is that he locates the problem not in this or that set of social institutions but in the logic of social relationships as such. To live with other persons is to become dependent on *their* judgment for our own sense of self-worth. Public esteem controls self-esteem and reputation dictates behavior. This logic of social life, moreover, does not remain outside the person as so much background; instead social relationships enforce a transformation on the human mind itself. In creatures whose sense of self is dependent on social acceptance, reason develops in competitive and antagonistic ways as each seeks to raise his relative fortune and standing at the expense of others. If he were to go into all the gory details of our ultimate corruption, Rousseau writes,

> I could show how much this universal desire of reputation, of honors, of preference, with which we are all devoured, exercises and compares our talents and our forces; how much it excites and multiplies our passions; and by creating an universal competition, rivalry, or rather enmity among men, how many disappointments, successes, and catastrophes of every kind it daily causes among the innumerable aspirants whom it engages in the same competition. I could show that it is to this itch of being spoken of, to this fury of distinguishing ourselves which seldom or never gives us a mo-

238

ment's respite, that we owe both the best and the worst things among us, our virtues and our vices, our sciences and our errors, our conquerors and our philosophers; that is to say, a great many bad things and a very few good ones.[44]

And as if this were not enough of an indictment of the antagonisms of reason in social man, Rousseau concludes: "I could prove, . . . that if we behold a handful of rich and powerful men seated on the pinnacle of fortune and greatness, while the crowd grovel in obscurity and want, it is merely because the first prize what they enjoy but in the same degree that others are deprived of it; and that, without changing their condition, they would cease to be happy the minute the people ceased to be miserable."[45]

Private Property and Social Inequality

In my summary of Rousseau's account of our fall from grace, I have deliberately emphasized the leading role he assigns to changes in human consciousness. But ideas do not work in a vacuum, and Rousseau reserves his harshest criticisms for the introduction of private property and the full flood of inequality that follows in its wake. In the pre-property world, there were still limits on the kind of power one man could exercise over another. But

> [t]he first man who, after enclosing a piece of ground, took it into his head to say, *this is mine,* was the real founder of civil society. How many crimes, how many wars, how many murders, how many misfortunes and horrors would that man have saved the species, who pulling up the stakes or filling up the ditches should have cried to his fellows: Beware of listening to this imposter; you are lost, if you forget that the fruits of the earth belong equally to us all, and the earth itself to nobody![46]

Why is private property such a snake in the Garden of Eden? Without private property, natural differences in talent or industriousness do not much matter. But "from the moment it appeared an advantage for one man to possess enough provisions for two," then the stronger or the most industrious or dexterous or ingenious get more.[47] You might say—Rousseau does not but free market enthusiasts do—that this is all fair and just. Those who work harder or those who invent ways of being more productive with their labor have a right to keep the fruit and profit of their labor. Rousseau agrees with Locke before him, and Marx after him, that labor is the source of economic value, that there is all the difference in the world between the value of the tilled and untilled field.[48] This is why he singles out the discovery of agriculture as one of the great revolutions that made progress possible.[49] But it also ruined mankind, as "boundless forests became smiling fields, which had to be watered with human sweat, and in which slavery and misery were soon seen to sprout out and grow with the harvests."[50]

Already conscious of how they compare and rank vis-à-vis others, humans now fall into conflict over competition for property. Not necessity but an "insatiable ambition" to outstrip others "inspires all men with a wicked inclination to injure each other . . . and always a secret desire of profiting at the expense of others." At this point, but only at this point, do social men fall into the brutal state of war Hobbes so accurately described but wrongly located in the state of nature. Perpetual conflict, battle, bloodshed, terrible disorders, usurpations, and pillaging: these are the results of the fatal marriage of the changes in human consciousness and the pursuit of private property. Inequality spins out of control, as the rich continually aggrandize themselves at the expense of others. And once they taste the pleasure of commanding or dominating others that their wealth allows, the "rich . . . [prefer] it to every other [pleasure]." They behave toward the poor "like those ravenous wolves, who having once tasted human flesh, despise every other food, and thereafter want only men to devour."[51] It is doubtful that anyone has ever surpassed Rousseau in the flourishes with which he tells the story of how the rich got rich.

At this point in the evolution of society, government and law do not yet exist. The rich protect their holdings through brute force, violence, and war. But the perpetual precariousness of their fortress existence (again well described by Hobbes) ultimately inspires them to conceive an ingenious solution, what Rousseau describes as "the deepest project that ever entered the human mind."[52] The rich cunningly play a trick on the poor that philosophers excuse by giving it the high-sounding name of the "social contract." For the rich and poor did not enter into the social contract from equal starting points or with equal bargaining power. The formal terms of the contract seem fair enough as all equally agree to obey a government that will protect our property rights. But the contract serves only the interests of those who already own the property. Instead of having to protect their takings by force, the rich con the poor into protecting it for them and into believing that justice demands such mutual assured protection. Through this sleight of hand, politics, government, and law take the social condition to the next level. But so-called justice for Rousseau is nothing more than a kind of car wash, through which the rich send their self-interest to make it come out squeaky clean and smelling of roses. Rousseau smells a rat.

With the invention of government, Rousseau ends his account in the *Discourse* of our odyssey from natural to socialized persons. He has followed humanity out from the wilderness into first associations, families, economic units, and finally political communities. Through every successive stage, inequality grows until finally it is allegedly justified or legitimized in the idea of a social contract. But Rousseau sees no legitimacy in the social contract, at least as it has so far been written.

If the existence of inequality is said to be just because it is natural, Rousseau is satisfied that he has decisively punctured that myth. If the social contract is lauded for securing persons their freedom, Rousseau dissents here as well. From the moment we first entered social relations, we lost our independence and became psychologically dependent on the opinion of others for what we think of ourselves. The social contract community is the pinnacle of our loss of freedom. It pretends to treat persons fairly, but in reality it is a devious device for imposing the domination of the rich on a submissive and enslaved poor. According to one of many Rousseauist aphorisms that set fire to future revolutionaries in France and in America, "Man was born free and everywhere he is in chains."[53]

Ideas as Driving Forces in History

As a way of finishing our look at the *Discourse,* I want to say a few words about how it came to influence later thinkers. In Rousseau's account of social change, both ideas and material developments matter. But do ideas have independent historical force, or do they merely reflect the material circumstances or economic interests of various classes and actors? Influenced by Rousseau, Karl Marx approached moral and political ideas as inevitably "ideological," in the sense that they arise after the fact to justify or to rationalize what is in the economic interest of a particular class.[54]

We can see something of this Marxist approach to change in the *Discourse.* For instance, the theory of a social contract comes into play at a particular period of history to reflect the interests of the rich in securing their property. Or take what Rousseau says about agriculture. It represented a new technology for creating wealth from the land, and it inevitably caused new relations and new ideas about enclosure and private property to emerge so that the potential of agriculture could be tapped.

Nevertheless, the *Discourse* is most striking for its emphasis on the psychological, not economic, preconditions, for shifts in human consciousness. As insistent as Rousseau is about the evils of economic dependency, he is equally troubled by the density of psychological dependency among social persons, who cannot escape being conscious of, and responsive to, the opinions of others. The abolition of private property will not free persons from this deeper surrender of freedom.

So what is to be done? If the obstacles to freedom and equality in society are internal and psychological rather than external and institutional, how is change possible at all? I take up Rousseau's surprising answer to this basic question in the next chapter.

12

ROUSSEAU AND THE POLITICAL

I left off in the last chapter asking "what is to be done" to recover our lost freedom and equality. The *Second Discourse* gives us grounds to doubt that the tragic loss of natural innocence can ever be reversed. After uncountable eons, social relationships have embedded dependent ways of thinking into the structure of the human mind, putting a premium on antagonistic forms of reasoning and on hyperconsciousness of what others think of us. At the deepest levels, social psychology is one consuming desire for social acceptance, and there seems to be no way to cut the chains that bind us to the altar of public opinion.

One way out is to escape from society altogether, to flee back into the woods and live in splendid isolation from others. I have to admit that the first time I read the *Discourse,* and maybe even the second and third times, I wanted this to be Rousseau's prescription. I loved those passages where Rousseau condemned even the most successful of social creatures for their false and fictional identities, for the hypocrisy that masquerades as morality. Rousseau's condemnation of social relationships was so sweeping, surely it implied that dropping out of society altogether was the only honest thing to do. Of course I was first reading Rousseau in the 1960s, when the phrase "dropping out" was much in vogue and countercultural types were establishing "far out" communes in the mountains of New Mexico, the beaches of Kauai, the canyons of California, and other would-be last vestiges of the state of nature.

In a famous footnote to the *Discourse,* however, Rousseau rejects "back to nature" as a viable solution:

> What, then? Must societies be abolished? Must *meum* and *tuum* be annihilated, and must man go back to living in forests with the bears? This would be a deduction in the manner of my adversar-

ies. . . . As for men like me, whose passions have irretrievably destroyed their original simplicity, who can no longer live upon grass and acorns, . . . all such [men] will . . . respect the sacred bonds of those societies to which they belong.[1]

Rousseau's refusal to escape back into the state of nature is hardly surprising, since it was he who warned us that there never was such a place. But what *is* surprising is the lengths to which Rousseau goes the other way, calling for a politics that will bring us further into the social condition than ever before, molding and transforming human nature from the moment we first taste a mother's milk. Rousseau triumphantly announces the political necessity to "deaden" and "destroy" our human natures, to reduce to nothing the powers we enjoyed in the state of nature.

What happened to all that romantic depiction of natural goodness and honesty and independence? Rousseau's short answer is that the psychology of the savage cannot possibly coexist with social psychology. What was appropriate for solitary men who were "complete and individual wholes" no longer works in society, where of necessity we must learn to behave as "part of a greater whole." In a chilling passage from *Émile*, Rousseau dismisses as monstrous the life of someone who tries to live in society as if he were alone: "Under existing conditions a man left to himself from birth would be more of a monster than the rest. Prejudice, authority, necessity, example, all the social conditions into which we are plunged, would stifle nature in him and put nothing in her place. She would be like a sapling chance sowed in the midst of the highway, bent hither and thither and soon crushed by passers-by."[2]

Since there is no going backwards, the only solution is to give up on the natural ideals entirely, or if not give up on them, then use them to fashion a politics that can yet provide the moral equivalent of the freedom and equality natural man enjoyed effortlessly. Of course, political freedom can never be the mirror image of natural freedom: the latter is a matter of independence, and the former, if it is possible at all, would have to be the sort of freedom that resides within conditions of social dependency.

The New Social Contract

Hitherto social and political dependency has been of a virulent sort, a form of tyranny rather than freedom. This was precisely Rousseau's critique of the social contract in the *Second Discourse*. He summarizes that critique in his most political work, *The Social Contract*, as follows. The equality offered by the creation of government is "only apparent and illusory." The invention of government "serves only to keep the poor in their misery and the rich in their usurpations."[3]

But could there be a new social contract that invented a liberating form of dependency?[4] Is there some way to make the authority of government legitimate and equality real? In *The Social Contract* Rousseau presents this as a kind of riddle. How is it possible to be free and yet obedient to government? How is it possible to be equal if we are enmeshed in dependent social relations? The answer for Rousseau—and he delights in how paradoxical it sounds—is that we will find our freedom and equality by becoming more absolutely dependent on others than ever before. We become free by becoming nothing as individuals and everything as self-governing citizens of a political community.

Here is how Rousseau unravels the seeming paradox. Any social contract that results in my surrendering my freedom to obey myself (my own "particular will," as Rousseau puts it) only to obey the will of some other particular person or persons is inherently flawed. If all that happens when we move from the state of nature into civil society is that we surrender our natural independence in exchange for obedience to the authority of someone else, then let's call this arrangement what it is: a form of slavery, a system of domination and subordination.

But the social contract could be reimagined so as to reconcile freedom with obedience to authority. As paradoxical as it sounds, there could be a social contract that establishes a community in which "each, coalescing with all, may nevertheless obey only himself, and remain as free as before." But how can I possibly obey only myself if I agree to join with others to establish a government? Milking the paradox for all it is worth, Rousseau says that the key clause in the new social contract must be "the total alienation to the whole community of each associate with all his rights."[5] In other words, we reserve none of our natural freedoms; we give them away entirely.

In the Lockean version of the social contract that historically came to undergird liberal politics, reservation of rights is a key term of the contract. While we see that it is in our interest to obey government, we simultaneously see that it would be irrational to surrender the right to arbitrary seizures of our person and our property. The modern constitutional state rests on this understanding that only limited government is consistent with government's deriving its authority from the consent of the governed. But Rousseau disagrees and insists that the social contract must invest the sovereign government with absolute authority and that we must totally surrender to this authority whatever privileges of *independence* we enjoyed in the state of nature. It is almost as if Rousseau relishes the counterintuition in his claim that surrender of rights to the community is the key to an individual's freedom.

In explanation of how freedom and absolute authority go together, Rousseau makes three points in rapid succession, which I present in a different order than he does. First, I am agreeing to obey not "you" but "us"; that is, I am agreeing to obey only the sovereign authority of the community of which I am an equal part. In this sense of popular sovereignty or power to the people, "each giving himself to all, gives himself to nobody."[6] My freedom resides in collectively authoring the laws I agree to obey. Second, the conditions of obedience are equal for all, and thus no person could have any interest in making unjust laws. The procedural arrangements work to make *me* worry about how the laws affect *you*, since they affect us equally. This equality of circumstance staves off the tyranny we might otherwise fear from absolutist government. Third, since everyone engages in the same act of mutual surrender to everyone else, I acquire the same rights over my fellow community members that I concede to them over me. Reciprocity means that my promise to obey is actually a form of empowerment rather than surrender.

So far Rousseau has explained and defended his proposed new social contract in quasi-legal language. The social contract can make political authority legitimate only if that authority is lodged in the community as a whole, with each member of that community entitled to an equal say in what the "will" of the community is.

Still, there is a problem here. Even Rousseau's contract has me surrendering my former freedom to obey only my own will in favor of obeying the collective will, the sovereign authority of the community. What if I disagree with others about how the sovereignty of the community should be exercised? Do we vote? Does majority rule? Can't the majority be tyrannical? Can't the majority or even the whole community be wrong? In short, Rousseau has not yet explained how placing absolute sovereignty in the community as a whole or in a majority is any guarantee at all of *individual* freedom. From the point of view of the individual who holds unpopular views or belongs to a minority religious sect, for instance, there might be as much to fear from the tyranny of the people as from any other tyrant.

246

The General Will

Quite aware of these issues, Rousseau shifts from a legalistic to a psychological sketch of how the social contract works. The metaphor of a social contract can mislead us into thinking of political community as a very weak form of association, in which we all remain "independent contractors," as it were, and join loosely with others to devise schemes of cooperation that serve our mutual individual interests. A political community of this weak sort may have a "common good," but it is "common" only in the restricted sense of being the space where our individual self-interests happen to overlap.

Rousseau wants us to think of ourselves as *citizens* rather than independent contractors. But we are not born citizens; we have to be fashioned into them. We must undergo a radical psychological transformation whereby we morph from narrowly self-interested actors into moral persons whose new senses of self are wrapped up with the virtues of belonging, allegiance, patriotism, solidarity, and fraternity. This emphasis on the transformative effects of the social contract is what decisively distinguishes the Rousseauist version from the models favored by Hobbes and Locke. For them, individuals are fully formed rational agents *before* they sign the social contract, and they enter society merely to serve the individual interests they already have. For Rousseau, not unlike Aristotle, the individual comes into being only *by joining* a community and changing from a self-interested calculator into a citizen devoted to the public good.

Among such transformed citizens, political community is a strong union in which the common good emerges as more than, something different from, the sum of individual interests. The common good is a genuinely shared good that changes the interests we have as individuals. Outside of political community we may be free to pursue our own particular will, but this freedom is enslaving in its own way, yoking us to the narrow confines of amour propre. Inside strong communities, we experience for the first time the elevated moral freedom that comes from exercising another kind of willpower, another kind of free will altogether. Rousseau calls this the "general" will.[7] The general will is my own best will, but a willpower of which I am capable only when I live together with fellow citizens and am inspired by ties of citizenship to choose what is good for us, what is for the common good rather than what is merely in my self-interest.

The general will is Rousseau's solution to the riddle of how the social contract can yet reconcile freedom and authority. I surrender my former freedom to pursue my own particular will and agree to obey the sovereign authority of the general will of the community. But the general will is not obedience to someone else's particular will. It is not even obedience to some mysterious group mind or collective entity. It is the promise to obey my own best will, and this is why Rousseau can maintain that in promising to obey the authority of the community, I am nonetheless promising to obey only *myself*. This "self" is my "real" self, and yet it was not available to me in the state of nature. It is, in a sense, a social creation. And yet the general will re-creates for social man the sympathies and fellow feeling that instinct generated in natural man.

Rousseau clarifies what he means by the general will by contrasting it with the "will of all." The will of all is "merely a sum of particular wills" and is what passes for a common good in weak communities.[8] In communities with only a thin sense of a common good, individuals undergo no psychological transformation. They continue to pursue the same interests they had before signing the social contract, and their union simply establishes the cooperative framework within which they can safely pursue individual interests. If you like, the "will of all" community assigns to government the mechanical task of aggregating self-interests into public policy, as if government were little more than some gigantic adding machine or calculator.

The general will is different. It is inside me, or at least it is inside me when I have undergone the "very remarkable change" that makes me choose not what is good for *me* but what is good for *us*.[9] Ideally, therefore, we do not discover what the general will is by aggregating the different interests of different individuals. If a community genuinely shares a common good, then each citizen expresses the exact same general will. The more harmony and unanimity there are in what each of us thinks the general will is, the more the general will in fact reigns. By contrast, and this is troubling, Rousseau regards disagreement and dissent as obstructions that "proclaim the ascendancy of private interests" and the decline of the general will.[10]

To be sure, Rousseau does think that we find the general will by voting. In investing sovereignty in the community, we are investing sovereignty in ourselves as a collective body, and we all have an exactly equal say in what the will of the sovereign community is. But Rousseau's view of voting is peculiar in several regards. First, although practically speaking the majority gets to determine what the general will is, it is never really the number of voices that "generalizes" the will as it is the common interest that unites them. So ideally, voting should tend toward unanimity; the mere fact that voters disagree or dissent is already a sign that the common interest is weak and that private interests are contaminating the process. If I find myself in the minority on a vote, "that simply shows that I was mistaken, and that what I considered to be the general will was not so."[11]

Rousseau's insistence in keeping the general will pure from corruption by private interests is so strict that he displays remarkable hostility to politics of any ordinary sort. Partisanship, political parties, campaigns, coalitions, brokering deals: these wrongly mobilize persons to capture the state on behalf of factional interests. Voting will best express the general will when there is no communication among citizens prior to the vote. The need for "long discussions" and debate indicates either confusion or else compromise among private interests. For Rousseau, the common good is unitary; it is one thing and leaves no room for competing views, much less compromise among views.

The Ideal of Citizenship

Like Machiavelli, Rousseau loved stories about the public devotion the Roman republic inspired in its citizens. He retold the story of Cincinnatus, the yeoman farmer who repeatedly abandoned his fields and his family to answer the military call of the state. He was even fonder of the story of the Spartan mother who sent her two sons off to war and waited breathlessly for news from the front. When a slave messenger returned, she hurriedly asked him, "[W]hat news of the war?" The slave replied that he was sorry to report her sons had been slain. "Vile slave, was that the question I asked of you?" the mother retorted. When the reply came that Sparta had triumphed, the woman ran off to give thanks to the gods. In praise Rousseau writes, "[T]hat was a citizen."[12]

By contrast, Rousseau takes "puny" modern man to task for letting "private concerns become all-absorbing." The "bustle of commerce," the "greedy pursuit of gain," the "love of comfort" and the distractions of art have crowded out attention to public affairs.[13] No one hastens to the assemblies or takes much interest in what goes on there. People prefer to pay others to perform the necessary work rather than do the work of governing themselves. Such persons belong to no country; they "know no passion except . . . for money," and "[t]heir fatherland is any country where there is money for them to steal."[14]

Rousseau saves special ridicule for the watered-down version of citizenship that characterizes representative democracies. The general will is not something you can sensibly ask *another person* to represent; as soon as you use your freedom to deputize others to act for you, you have lost your freedom. For Rousseau, citizenship can never be a spectator sport. It requires participation together in the heavy lifting that makes self-government a reality rather than an idle phrase. But our participation has to be of the right sort, we have to be transformed into citizens who ask not what will be of benefit to me personally but what is good for the public.

The story of the Spartan mother-citizen shows just how demanding Rousseau's model of citizenship is. Speaking for myself, I wonder whether I am up to the task or even find the ideal appealing. In university communities professors are expected to be good citizens, regularly attending faculty meetings. I trust it will not shock if I confess that I would rather not go to such meetings (often); I have other things to do with my time, just as Rousseau lamented. I remember one of my undergraduate professors gently testing my self-proclaimed belief in all things Rousseau by asking how often I raced off to student meetings on campus, what choice I made on a Saturday night, as it were.

Most of us are too busy living our lives to be the model citizen Rousseau adored. Truth be told, there are times when I would like to be a better citizen of the university and of the national community. I would like to feel that sense of belonging that Rousseau's Romans got from devotion to the common good. But not always and every day; I would still want time for moneymaking, career moves, hiking holidays, Boston Red Sox games, family get-togethers, and the like. Rousseau does not permit me to opt in and out of citizenship or to set my own civic schedule.

Citizenship, Rousseau advises Polish patriots desirous of securing national independence from foreign threats, has to "fill up every moment" of the citizen's life. It has to be fixed upon us like a "yoke of iron."[15] To be a genuine citizen is not to juggle my public and private roles; it is to inhabit the role of citizen so thoroughly that I am always a citizen first, in the way the Spartan mother was even at the most inopportune time.

Comparing the Ideal of Citizenship and the Ideal of Natural Man

The story of the Spartan mother illustrates the distance between Rousseau's political ideals and his adoration of naturalness. Sparta made a citizen of this mother only by extinguishing or overwriting her natural impulses to care first for her own. Most of us would find it natural that a parent would care, not necessarily more for the fate of her children than for the fate of the republic, but at least to hear first about them and to mourn their deaths in ways that would mute her celebration of national victory. But citizenship in Rousseau requires eliminating all those conflicts of interest that stem from being part mother, part citizen. The price we pay for good citizenship is to stamp out the natural person in us and make the equality of the public voice drown out the preferences of the private person.

Rousseau praises Moses and Lycurgus as two ancient lawgivers who understood how to mold persons into citizens and did not hesitate to adopt the extraordinary measures it takes to pull off the remarkable psychological transformation of self-interested creatures into lovers of the common good. Lycurgus fixed the attention of Spartans on their nation every waking moment, making sure "that the image of the fatherland was constantly before their eyes" and in "their games, in their homes, in their mating, in their feasts." Moses rigged matters so that the Hebrew tribes could never be absorbed into other peoples, by "weight[ing] them down with rites and peculiar ceremonies" that gave them an impenetrably different national identity. "Hebrews" and "Spartans" do not exist by nature; Moses and Lycurgus understood that national identity has to be forged, and they stopped at nothing to instill "burning love of country" as "the strongest—or rather the only—passion" of these peoples.[16]

The Great Legislator

Rousseau's emphasis on the political making of citizens creates a "chicken and egg" sort of problem. It takes good citizens to make good laws, but it takes good laws to make good citizens in the first place. Facing up to this problem, Rousseau once more agrees with Machiavelli that the founding of a decent community requires the presence of an extraordinary legislator, of the likes of a Moses or Lycurgus, to lay down enduring laws. Only then can the scheme envisioned by the social contract— empowering the citizenry at large to be the sovereign legislature—work.

One can appreciate why Rousseau relies on the figure of the "great legislator" to get things started. Still, it involves him in inconsistency. As long as we are obeying the laws laid down by the original legislator, we are obeying the authority of someone else and not our own general will, collectively expressed. Rousseau's response is that certain persons are so extraordinary, so God-like, that they essentially embody the "general will." But if he allows the great man to embody the general will in order to found a republic, what is to stop other persons at moments of crisis from claiming that they too embody the "general will" and speak for us?

The Molding of Citizens

However citizens are made, Rousseau's general point remains that the psychology of the citizen has to be crafted; it does not come naturally to any of us. Yet as unnatural as the life of the citizen is, a moral vision connects it back to the idealized portrait Rousseau once drew of the natural savage. Love of country instills in the citizen that sense of being at one with the people around him which the savage achieved by ignoring them. In the *Second Discourse* Rousseau starts with a vision of the self at peace through splendid solitude. In *The Social Contract* he ends with a political re-creation of the same ideal, only now selves are at peace with one another through merging their separate identities into a common life. The very thickness of their bonds does for social man what the total absence of bonds once did for natural man.

Rousseau's writings are peppered with descriptions of how citizenship overcomes the history of social antagonism and restores to persons the benign forms of selfhood that once reigned in the state of nature. My own favorite passage in all of Rousseau describes the state of nature–like feeling that citizenship at its best attains. In his *Letter to M. D'Alembert,* Rousseau has been excoriating the famous French *philosophe* for suggesting that Geneva, Rousseau's own beloved native country, needed to develop a theater to entertain its residents. But look at how theatergoing has corrupted Parisians, Rousseau replies, in ways that hark back to Augustine's criticisms of catharsis and theater. Among the vices the professional theater brings to a city, Rousseau singles out the way Parisians flock to the playhouses but disdain attending public meetings. And what do Parisians do in the theater? They sit in the dark and cry copious tears for the fictional miseries of imaginary persons, all the while neglecting the actual miseries of real citizens of Paris. "People think they come together in the theatre," Rousseau writes, but "it is there that . . . they go to forget their friends [and] to concern themselves with fables, in order to cry for the misfortunes of the dead, or to laugh at the expense of the living."[17] And yet, even knowing that all is imitation on the stage, these Parisians nonetheless exit the theater feeling purified and uplifted, as if they had somehow satisfied the demands of justice by watching a play. Geneva does not need to import such corruption. Rousseau issues the same warning to Poland.[18]

Entertainment should not be a spectator sport in a republic; it should be a participatory enterprise in which ordinary citizens are the actors. The content of the festivals does not much matter; it is the very assembling together of persons "who have so many reasons to like one another" that provides "sweet bonds of pleasure and joy."[19] Recalling being "struck in my childhood" by one such moment of simple civic entertainment, Rousseau lovingly calls to mind a day when a local regiment was in town. Having finished their exercises, the men broke ranks and started to dance:

> A dance of men, cheered by a long meal, would seem to present nothing very interesting to see; however, the harmony of five or six hundred men in uniform, holding one another by the hand, . . . the sounds of the drums, the glare of the torches, a certain military pomp . . . , all this created a very lively sensation that could not be experienced coldly. . . . My father, embracing me, was seized with trembling which I think I still feel and share. "Jean-Jacques," he said to me, "love your country. Do you see these good Genevans? They are all friends, they are all brothers. . . . You are a Genevan; one day you will see other peoples; but even if you should travel as much as your father, you will not find their likes.[20]

A passage such as this romanticizes Geneva for the same reasons Rousseau romanticized the state of nature. The savage was innocent; so are Genevans. The savage did not yet know luxuries; Genevans eschew luxury and practice the austerity fitting republican citizens. The savage's natural instinct for self-love had not yet bred selfishness. The citizen's moral commitment to the common good restores selflessness to the self. The savage was an honest and transparent creature who did not know how to dissemble or disguise his desires; goodwill makes citizens once again transparent to one another, their "hearts are . . . in their eyes as they are always on their lips."[21]

Rousseau specifically remembers that it was only the men who danced; the women remained spectators. This does not bother him, nor does he pause to reflect on the contradiction between his idyllic memory of citizen entertainment and the exclusion of women. One is tempted simply to expand Rousseau's memory to include women on equal terms; but including women in that entertainment would in Rousseau's eyes vitiate not only the military pomp of the moment but also the asceticism he believed was necessary to turn men into citizens.

Rousseau as a Critic of Liberalism

Rousseau's portrait of the citizen living the life of the common good is both appealing and frightening. The appeal is in belonging to a community which is worth belonging to. The danger is that not all communities are worthy of belonging to, and Rousseau's praise of loyalty, allegiance, and patriotism can be used—has been used—to support malignant and malicious forms of closed and intolerant communities. Let me expand on this claim that what is most appealing about Rousseau is also what is most alarming.

In previous chapters on Hobbes and Locke I have traced the philosophical and historical foundations of what we today call liberal or open societies. It is a hallmark of such societies that persons are left free to "choose their own good in their own way," absent harm to others. Rousseau *knows* what life is the *best* choice—the life of the citizen—and he does not hesitate to use the muscle of politics to promote the virtues of citizenship and public devotion while denigrating the vices of those who choose lives devoted to private and business interests. Liberals, by contrast, do not know what life is best for us, or what the "virtuous" choices are to make in life. So a liberal society is one in which the state treats the diversity of lifestyles chosen by persons as equally worthy of respect, as long as no one threatens harm to others.

What kind of community can such "choosing" selves share? Nothing very demanding or permanent, since what I choose today I am free to undo tomorrow. In an open society no one has to stay put; people and ideas are constantly shifting about; we are mobile and migratory, in both a geographical and a mental sense. No traditions, no allegiance to the past, no loyalty to one's religion or ethnicity or homeland is so valued as to prevent one from dissolving ties and picking up stakes. In short, in liberal societies identity itself is portable and reinventible. I am a pioneer setting out into the new frontier in search of a new life. I am Huck Finn saying, "I can't go back, I been there before." I'm a young person leaving home, spreading my wings, trying to "find myself" now that I've escaped from parental authority.

Rousseau does not give sufficient due to the eloquence of this liberal vision of individuals left free to be the authors of their own differing life plans. I, at least, would never want Rousseau's alternative model of citizenship to do away with the restraints on obedience to the "fatherland" that liberalism has historically accomplished. Still, liberalism itself will always need a critic such as Rousseau, lest its members fly apart entirely and there is no sense of public duty or service. If members of a liberal society are linked together merely by overlapping self-interests, then politics is but selfishness writ large, and winners in social competition have little obligation to care at all about losers. It is difficult to understand how a society with no sense of a common good could be stable, let alone just. It is certainly difficult to understand how a society of radical individualists could be a *democratic* society, inspiring persons with sufficient sense of citizenship and civic virtue to vote, attend meetings, and take into consideration the interests of others. Rousseau, or someone like him, will always be necessary to check the excesses of individualism to which the liberal ethic of leaving persons alone may tend.

Still, in the end, Rousseau's own notion of the common good is frighteningly undemocratic. In the Rousseauist state there is precious little room for any diversity or plurality in the common goods we might share. There is room for only one community, one unity, and that is the state itself; every other kind of association or group belonging Rousseau reviles as the triumph of factionalism and the mere pursuit of private interests. But sometimes we join with others to maintain a common way of life—a religious loyalty, a charitable undertaking, a cultural project that does not reduce to merely self-interested behavior. A democratic understanding of the common good would permit this plurality of common goods and ways of life to flourish under the big tent of the state; in fact a large part of the common good we share in a democracy is precisely respect for the diversity of common goods that persons can share. In other words, one can agree with Rousseau's moral vision of moving persons from the narrow confines of self-interested behavior into the virtues that come from allegiance to a shared good *without* accepting the unitary and homogenized version of the common good which Rousseau offers.

Moreover, even at the level of the whole community, Rousseau's politics have a tyrannical edge to them. In robust democratic politics, popular deliberation about what the common good is matters, precisely because the common good does not "exist" prior to and independent of this deliberation; in some powerful sense, bringing persons together to deliberate about the common good *is* what produces the common good. I do not mean to suggest that there are no limits on what the people can decide. There are certain ways of mistreating individuals or excluding them that give the lie to the existence of a common good. But within the bounds set by liberal respect for the freedom and equality of all members of a community, there are many different common goods these members could choose for themselves without there being one definitively right answer.

Rousseau misses this point, and in the end his remarks about the general will take on a spooky character. Rousseau loved to say that the general will can never err, that only you or I can be mistaken about what the general will "is." Such phrasing bestows on the general will an objective status that transcends the wills, opinions, and interests of the people in whose name the general will speaks. Rousseau wants to make us into citizens who fly to the assemblies and attend to public business. But once there, his citizens are remarkably deferential to the authority of the sovereign community. If I dissent from the assembly's views on the general will, then I must be wrong and presumably should reeducate myself to understand and accept what the "true" general will is. There seems no room for opposition politics in Rousseau's ideal republic, no grounds for mobilizing and marching to protest what the sovereign has legislated in my name.

As an individual I need and get no rights, no protection against the general will, because it expresses my real self, if only I knew it. This explains Rousseau's odd and telling phrase that obedience to the general will is but a way of "forcing persons to be free." This juxtaposition of coercion and freedom works only if we accept the lordly and apolitical perfection Rousseau mystically assigns to the general will. Otherwise Rousseau's community may be a community of equals, but equal only in being equally submissive to the authority of the group that is supposed to be themselves but somehow develops a life and a will of its own.

If we think back to the *Second Discourse,* we may recall that one of Rousseau's chief complaints was the way social man is enslaved to matters of reputation, allowing the opinion of others to dictate one's own choices. But rather than freeing the citizen from the controlling force of public esteem, Rousseau makes the passion to win public honor into the defining desire of the good citizen. In *The Government of Poland,* Rousseau expresses his wish that citizens "shall become as completely dependent upon public esteem as to be unable to do anything, acquire anything, or achieve anything without it."[22] Institutions should be arranged so that "every citizen shall feel the eyes of his fellow-countrymen upon him every moment of the day; that no man shall move upward and win success except by public approbation."[23]

Here then we have the ultimate irony about Rousseau's politics: the very concern for public reputation that historically corrupted us can yet save us. I suppose Rousseau would say that there is no irony, that his republic honors citizens for the right reasons, as compared to the vices rewarded in a city such as Paris. But raising persons to care passionately about their public persona is dicey business, as Rousseau well knew from that moment he let another take the rap for stealing a ribbon in order to protect his own reputation.

At one point in *The Social Contract* Rousseau describes the mindset of the ideal citizen as follows. As an individual he regards himself as nothing, as a mere cipher. He derives his identity only from who he is "in combination with all the rest."[24] To my mind, this is going too far. In any community there will always be some tension between the common good and individual interests. Rousseau is a worthy critic of political practices that try to resolve the tension by eliminating the tug toward community entirely. But it is no better for him sometimes to go to the other extreme and subsume individual identity totally into national identity. In the end, we do best by accepting that the tension between the value of individualism and the value of community is not a tension we would be happy to see resolved.

I started by saying that Rousseau is my favorite. My hope is that his passion for equality and his unmasking of the hypocrisies and pretenses of all manners of elites—the wealthy, the artists, the pious, and the philosophers—will kindle in others the same fire for change it once kindled in me. Those fires in me have died down over time as I have come to worry more about the dark purposes to which nationalism and devotion to the state can be—and have been—put. But I would never accuse Rousseau himself of going over to the dark side. He was insufficiently careful in his portrait of the devoted citizen. But perhaps he could not be careful and angry at the same time. Rousseau understood what there was just cause to be angry about: the inequality between rich and poor; the misuse of philosophy to justify that inequality; the sacrifice of the common good to greed and private ventures. When the march comes through town to protest the continuing stranglehold of these injustices on politics, I still hope to be marching alongside Rousseau.

13

It is common but mistaken, I believe, for American universities to omit teaching Immanuel Kant in political theory courses. In part this omission stems from an understandable division of labor, whereby Kant's towering status in the history of ethics makes him central to courses on moral philosophy. But it also reflects an unfortunate bias toward Anglo-American philosophers at the expense of acquainting us with the tradition on the European continent that leads from Kant to Hegel to Marx.

Even within the Anglo-American tradition, Kant is indispensable to understanding the insistence of classical liberalism that individuals have rights which not even the general welfare can override. His theories provide the major alternative to utilitarianism as a way of thinking about justice. In large part because of John Rawls's brilliant revival of the social contract tradition in *A Theory of Justice,* Kant's version of the social contract has now taken its rightful place, alongside those of Hobbes, Locke, and Rousseau, in our ongoing conversation about politics and justice.

For a philosopher famous for his separation of ethics from empirical considerations, Kant's political writings are surprisingly oriented toward the practical achievement of justice in imperfect conditions. While he continues to hold to an ideal in which ethics and politics go together, his most systematic account of the state in the *Metaphysics of Morals* develops the notion of a constitutional or "juridical order" which embodies principles of justice that persons can practice, even when their behavior does not conform to the more transcendental demands of morality. Nevertheless, since Kant's practical philosophy cannot be understood except in the context provided by his ethical ideals, I begin with a detailed account of Kant's moral theory.

Kant's Ethics and the Rejection of Consequences

Kant's inquiry into ethics begins with the odd claim that the morality of conduct is to be judged without regard to what effects, results, or consequences the conduct brings. To hinge the rightness of an act on whether it happens to bring about good or bad results is, in Kant's view, to deprive morality of its sublime purity, of its absolute correctness, of what he calls its "unconditioned necessity." After all, the same conduct—say, telling the truth—can bring about good results in certain circumstances and harmful effects in others. Once we introduce this sort of calculation into moral reasoning, all is lost, according to Kant. The morally right thing becomes "contingent and precarious," varying according to circumstances.[1]

If the "right" is not to be judged according to whether it is "good," then what is the alternative? For Kant, the moral person not only always does her duty but also does it for the sake of duty. She *wills* the good not because it will make her happy, not because it will benefit others, not because she has interests or inclinations to satisfy, but simply from the pure motive of doing one's duty.

Take, for example, Kant's example of the grocer who refrains from overcharging an inexperienced and unsuspecting customer.[2] The mere fact that the grocer "conforms" his conduct to the right course of action does not give moral worth to his behavior. He may simply be acting out of self-interest, knowing that competition in the marketplace makes honesty his best policy. Or it may be that the grocer happens, by luck of nature or nurture, to love his neighbors, and so he does the right thing out of his natural inclinations. This too fails to answer to morality for Kant. Inclinations can be overclouded. The moral grocer *wills* the right thing to do, and finds the ability to so will, by the sheer force of reason. His behavior is impartial and disinterested, almost as if morality takes us from one identity, in which our behavior is rooted in experiences we do not control, to another and purer identity, in which our behavior is *willed* as a free choice dictated by reason alone.

Kant has his own specialized vocabulary for developing this basic intuition. One way he frequently puts it is to distinguish the study of anthropology from the study of morality. In anthropology we are concerned with understanding the nature of human beings as creatures in the natural world, subject to all the physical and causal laws of nature. Here we can learn about human nature only empirically, only by experience with how human beings actually behave in the empirical world.[3]

But morality has nothing to do with inquiries into human nature, into what we learn from experience is natural to us, or even what is good for us, or fulfilling, or perfecting of our talents and capacities. The distinction of moral maxims is that they "have an origin entirely and completely *a priori,*" meaning that their truth comes from a pure act of reasoning abstracted from anything we learn from experience.[4] It is basic to Kant's ethics that, in addition to inhabiting the empirical world, human beings qua rational beings are capable of reasoning in this wholly disembodied, abstract, and formal way. In fact it is precisely the ability of reason to legislate moral maxims in a disinterested way that gives human beings their freedom or autonomy. As empirical creatures, we behave in a way that Kant calls "heteronomous," subject to the forces of nature, to the accidents of experience, and to the will of others.[5] As rational beings, we are capable of living according to laws we choose or author for ourselves. For Kant, the very possibility of morality is tied up with the possibility of becoming free persons of this sort, our own self-sufficient moral authority.

Kant is well aware that his views on ethics represent a frontal challenge to the classical tradition and in particular to the "virtue ethics" of Aristotle. Three particular points require elucidation.

First, for Aristotle as for Plato, the ultimate purpose of morality was to make persons happy, in the broadest sense of that term. But then we could know what was right to do only if we first had some knowledge of what was good for human beings, what fulfilled their natures and made it possible to live well by doing well. Kant is insistent on severing this connection between morality and psychology, and with it the promise that morality and happiness necessarily go together. Here is a peculiarly chilling statement of this rejection of the classical tradition: "[T]he more a cultivated reason concerns itself with the aim of enjoying life and happiness, the farther does man get away from true contentment. This is why there arises in many . . . a certain degree of *misology*—that is, a hatred of reason; for when they balance all the advantages they draw, . . . they discover that they have in fact only brought more trouble on their heads than they have gained in the way of happiness."[6]

Second, Kant rejects the Aristotelian emphasis on inculcating good habits and character in a person, habits that condition a person to take pleasure in acting in virtuous ways. To root morality in good habits is to rob right conduct of its sublime and transcendental nature by making it expressive only of the inclinations we happen to have. For Kant, the disposition to act in virtuous ways has to be a matter of pure reason directing one's will according to the concept of duty. If this results in self-denial rather than self-fulfillment, then so be it. Hegel was to refer to this disposition toward duty as that of an "unhappy consciousness." Kant would have thought the description beside the point, which was to achieve the indifference or impartiality toward one's own happiness that marks the steadfast character of the moral person.

Third, Aristotle did not aspire to elevate ethical principles to universal application. Instead he emphasized that living in a community capable of sustaining a shared concept of the good life was a precondition of an individual's ability to practice the full range of moral virtues. Only communities of limited size and diversity could support a common good, according to Aristotle, and hence moral life was necessarily local rather than universal.

For Kant, there is a necessary connection between morality and universal applicability. Reason works purely only when it breaks the hold of the merely customary or traditional or cultural; the correctness of a moral maxim is to be judged precisely by whether it can be defended as true for rational human beings as such, irrespective of their cultural or historical circumstances. Kant expresses this connection between morality and universalizability in his famous concept of the "categorical imperative." Some imperatives are merely hypothetical in force and take the form of prudential maxims such as "If you wish to get Y, then do X." But morality is categorically imperative because its maxims take the form of unqualified, or unconditional or absolute, commands ("Thou Shall Not Lie").[7]

How does reason discover these categorical imperatives? For Kant, there is a logical or formal test: "Act only on that maxim through which you can at the same time will that it should become a universal law."[8]

The categorical imperative does not tell us what to will but only how to will. It does not provide substantive answers to the content of moral life but offers only procedural or formal answers for how to reason morally. Hegel regarded the "content-lessness" of the categorical imperative as its defect, arguing that only "discontent-ed" persons could live by so unspecific a formula. Kant thought it a virtue that his method specified a *procedure* for determining what was right that did not depend on *substantive* agreement over whether a given aim was good or bad. By rea-

261

soning in the form of categorical imperatives, we achieve a kind of impartiality toward our own behavior, asking whether we could consistently and publicly will, without contradiction, that the principles on which we act be followed universally by others.

Kant gives this example. Suppose a person in dire circumstances borrows money, promising to pay back the loan within a fixed time but knowing he will not be able to make the payments. Such behavior solves the person's problems and serves his welfare, but can the person "transform the demand of self-love into a universal law" to be followed by others in similar straits? The answer is that, if it were openly acknowledged that everyone in need can make any promise without any intention of keeping his word, then "the very purpose of promising [would be] impossible, since no one would believe he was being promised anything, but would laugh at utterances of this kind as empty shams."[9]

In a way this example calls to mind the case that started the discussion about justice in Plato's *Republic*. Socrates asks Crito whether it is always right and just to pay back what is lent. He gives the case of a friend who stores his weapon with you when sane but asks for it back when crazy. This example is supposed to illustrate that we cannot define justice in the abstract but must know first what is good and what is harmful to a friend. But Kant denies this; from the moral point of view, consequences never matter.

In addition to expressing his moral theory in terms of the categorical imperative, Kant puts forward his views in three other formulae that are supposed to amount to the same thing. The first he calls "the Formula of the End in Itself."[10] The one good that has absolute or ultimate moral value in and of itself—and so the one substantive end that is synonymous with living according to universalizable law—is that every person is an end in himself, rather than a mere means or instrument to be used for the purposes of someone else's good, even the good of the majority. This absolute moral value provides an objective principle for reason; it means that the categorical imperative can be reexpressed in the practical maxim "Act in such a way that you always treat humanity, whether in your own person or in the person of any other, never simply as a means, but always at the same time as an end."[11]

It is this formula that Kant uses to expose the morally untenable conclusions to which utilitarian doctrines lead. Since utilitarianism aims at maximizing the overall or aggregate social welfare, it can entertain certain tradeoffs where the happiness of the many compensates for the deprivations imposed on the few.

The second formula Kant offers is "the Formula of Autonomy."[12] Underlying the formal logic of the categorical imperative is the notion that every person gives the moral law for herself, that each is the author or legislator of the moral imperatives to which she is subject. In other words, the sheer idea of human beings as moral agents necessarily involves freedom; unless we are capable of willing or choosing the moral good for its own sake, we are merely conditioned and determined creatures.

If I say, "I ought not to lie if I want to maintain my reputation," then I am acting heteronomously. I am willing only as a self-interested calculator; those calculations do not hold categorically and universally but only hypothetically and contingently. Presumably my duty not to lie holds only as far as not lying is a means to the ends of reputation. For Kant, this robs my conduct of any moral worth, for the very reason that I am not genuinely free in my choices. I am dependent on my desire for reputation.

By contrast, when I will not lie "even if so doing were to bring me not the slightest disgrace," then my will has "abstracted" itself from the influence of my personal interests, and I achieve my freedom precisely by doing my duty.[13]

Kant's views here show the influence of Rousseau's concept of the general will. Like Rousseau, Kant poses the question of how a person can be subject to law and moral duty and yet remain free. The answer for Kant, as for Rousseau, is that we are our own lawgivers. By willing the general will or by willing the universal maxims implicit in the categorical imperative, man "is subject only to laws which are made by himself and yet are universal."[14] It is the very achievement of impartial reason that frees us to define our own identities, rather than having an identity chosen for us, by the force of nature or nurture.

Kant offers one final formulation for the categorical imperative. Practically speaking, when each wills in ways that are capable of being universal law followed by all, then a "kingdom of ends" comes about. In such a kingdom, rational human beings achieve a *social* union without surrendering individual autonomy, since each mutually stands "under the law that each of them should treat himself and all others, never merely as a means, but always at the same time as an end in himself."[15] In this ideal kingdom, each individual is both member (subject to the law) and head (maker of the law). Although admittedly only an ideal, this practically serves to direct morality to the making of laws whereby alone such a kingdom of ends is possible.[16]

The vision of a kingdom of ends provides a transition for Kant from ethics to politics. Interestingly, for all Kant's emphasis on the individual's subjective freedom and the autonomy of the choosing self, reasoning pure of any cultural constraints, his ethics end on a pronounced social note. Instead of turning persons inward, ethics makes respect for others the cardinal duty of a moral person.

Kant's Politics: Justice as a Practicable Ideal

As with his moral philosophy, Kant's political philosophy derives from universal principles of right or justice that hold true regardless of the interests, history, or circumstances of a particular state. These principles of right are a working out of what it means to treat persons as ends in themselves, and they provide a framework for regulating the acts of individuals so that "the free use of your will is compatible with the freedom of everyone."[17] The "rights of men must be held sacred," Kant wrote, "however much sacrifice it may cost the ruling power."[18]

Kant was uncommonly aware that his insistence on grounding politics on binding principles of justice would be dismissed as unrealistic. In his most practical essays he takes on those who treat theory with scorn, dismiss justice as an "empty thought," and argue that justice needs to bend to accommodate reasons of state, national customs, and the public's welfare.[19] In general, Kant defends the practicability of his political ideals, displaying the Enlightenment era's faith that human reason "grows pragmatically" and works toward realizing the idea of the state as based on objective principles of justice. Kant is at his most intrepid in exposing the "political moralist . . . who forges a morality in such a way that it conforms to the statesman's advantage."[20] The vaunted practical mindset of such a politician boils down to "flatter[ing] the power which is then ruling," and makes his supposed practicality a danger to "the nation, and, possibly, the whole world."[21]

But Kant does attend to ways in which politics must make do with less than ideal conditions; principles of right do not apply so sternly as to require their immediate execution in circumstances which would be self-

264

defeating.[22] As we shall see, Kant favored world government but understood the necessity of working through the existing system of nation-states to achieve international justice. What is needed, Kant argues, are politicians who have the good practical judgment to "distinguish . . . instances where the rule applies from those where it does not."[23] Kant calls persons capable of that sound judgment "moral politicians."[24] Moral politicians differ from, and are preferable to, political moralists since they aspire to make politics conform to morality rather than the other way around.

Kant's awareness that political theory is a branch of practical rather than pure philosophy leads to one major difference between ethics and politics. In the ideal moral kingdom of ends, legislation is "internal," authored by each person and rooted in the subjective disposition to do one's duty. No other incentives operate and no coercion is permissible, consistent with morality's being an expression of self-determination. But political legislation is "external."[25] It regulates the *actions* of persons, not their intentions, motives, or inner states. Thus just laws never coerce or even concern themselves with a person's inner moral life; this must be left free for a person to choose according to her own free will. While moral life can never be coerced, external acts can be subject to legitimate lawful coercion—coercion made lawful by providing procedures for harmonizing one person's freedom with another's.

For an idealist, Kant is refreshingly frank about the connection between law and coercion. Moral life must be self-determined, but our external acts are subject to uses of reward and punishment to provide incentives for carrying out our duty, even when the pure moral will is lacking. Thus while Kant's moral philosophy points to the ideal of a kingdom of ends, in his political writings he typically invokes the less grandiloquent paradigm of a constitutional or "juridical" order, in which law conforms to, and enforces, principles of right.[26]

Of course, as with Rousseau, Kant's understanding of freedom as self-determination requires him to show how a legally coercive order can buttress, rather than undermine, my status as a free person giving the law to myself. To show how public law is harmonious with individual freedom, Kant followed Rousseau in having recourse to the concept of a hypothetical social contract. But his conception of a contract is original in using it to capture the priority of justice over any competing ends, even ends that promote a nation's wealth, advantage, aggrandizement, or welfare. And

265

Kant is among the first to push the idea of a social contract beyond national borders to conceive of a covenant or league of nations based on principles of international justice.

The Kantian Version of the Social Contract

Like Rousseau, Kant is clear that the idea of an original contract is a fiction, a heuristic device useful for capturing "an idea of the state as it ought to be."[27]

The ideal of a social contract to whose terms free persons *could* have given their consent "provides an internal guide and standard" against which to test the justice of actual political arrangements and laws. In other words, existing statutory laws have to pass a test of "rightness" framed as follows: could free and equal persons possibly or hypothetically have agreed to be bound by such a law?[28] If they could have, then the law is just. Obedience to the law secures rather than undermines the individual's freedom, since the person is the author or legislator or the giver of the very laws to be followed. Just as in moral life the individual achieves self-governance by willing to do one's duty, so in political life freedom is a matter of the self-governance made possible by living in a constitutional order in which citizens give the law to themselves. These laws will mutually restrict our freedom to act as we please but, by coercively enforcing those restraints, provide each person with the greatest freedom consistent with like freedom in others.

Though an ideal, the social contract "nonetheless has undoubted practical reality," since "it can oblige every legislator to frame his laws in such a way that they could have been produced by the united will of a whole nation."[29] Kant gives two examples. Can a law privileging a certain class of citizens as a hereditary ruling class be just? The answer must be no, since the whole people could not possibly have consented to such an unequal arrangement.[30] Or take the case of a constitution which creates a theocracy, in which the state establishes one religion for the people. Such a law cannot possibly be based on individual consent, since it requires persons to surrender their moral freedom to choose for themselves as reason dictates. Citizens in a theocracy are subject to the will of the ruler on matters of conscience, and this is something that no rational being could authorize.[31]

Everyone reading this book will be aware that Kant has yet to carry the day politically when it comes to ruling out theocratic politics. Regimes that legally enforce religious codes of conduct are hardly fading from history's stage but show surprising resilience. Some theocracies treat religious dissenters not only as unequals but also as unworthy of any sort of respect at all; these regimes seem unjust in ways Kant specifies. But what about regimes which, while shaping public space around a preferred religion, nonetheless give minorities the right to practice their religious beliefs? Such societies seem decent, even if they do not fit the Kantian ideals of justice.[32]

The Question of Civil Disobedience

One might think that the social contract leaves citizens with a right to disobey or even to revolt against a government that violates the terms of the contract. But who judges when such violations occur? This question stymied Kant and led him to deny that there is ever a right to disobedience or rebellion.[33] The people retain the right to protest acts of injustice, in word or pamphlet. But once they have rendered disagreement, "[i]t is the people's duty to endure even the most intolerable abuse of supreme authority."[34] Kant does not follow Hobbes in arguing that anything the sovereign commands must be seen as authorized by the people. He more squarely faces the possibility that the sovereign may act in unauthorized ways. Still, he follows Plato's *Crito* in arguing:

> [E]ven if the power of the state or its agent, the head of the state, has violated the original contract by authorising the government to act tyrannically, . . . the subject is still not entitled to offer counter-resistance. The reason for this is that the people, under an existing civil constitution, has no longer any right to judge how the constitution should be administered. For if we suppose that it does have this right to judge and that it disagrees with the judgment of the actual head of the state, who is to decide which side is right? Neither can act as judge of his own cause. Thus there would have to be another head above the head of state to mediate between the latter and the people, which is self-contradictory.[35]

It is not clear how Kant, consistently with his own principles of justice, can condemn all rebellions, even those waged in opposition to a government based on violence rather than consent. In his last complete piece of writing, Kant praises the French Revolution, for instance, as a "moral cause" justified by the right of a nation to secure a republican constitution for itself. But then Kant draws back and notes that the revolution "may be so filled with misery and atrocities that no right-thinking man would ever decide to make the same experiment again at such a price."[36]

Hypothetical versus Actual Consent

Kant insists on the difference between the people's "possibly" agreeing to an original contract and their "actually" or "currently" agreeing with government policy. Let's take up his example of a war tax proportionally imposed on all subjects. It may be that the people consider the tax oppressive because the war is unjust or unnecessary in their opinion. Still, the tax is just according to Kant, since it is "possible" that the war was unavoidable and the tax indispensable. In other words, the governing principle is not whether the people *actually* support the particular war and the war levy but whether, hypothetically speaking, they could have originally authorized government to levy taxes to fight wars the government declared. By contrast, a war tax levied on only one class would be an example of an unjust law, since the whole people could not possibly have agreed to empower government to proceed in such an arbitrary fashion.[37]

In rough outline, Kant understands the social contract in Rousseauist terms. Each person contracts with all to be mutually bound by the general will. As Kant expresses the point in the *Groundwork of the Metaphysic of Morals,* "[a] rational being belongs as a member to the kingdom of ends when, although giving universal laws in it, he is also subject to these laws. He belongs to it as sovereign when, while giving laws, he is not subject to the will of any other."[38] Closely echoing Rousseau's formulation of the general will, Kant argues that the individual does not sacrifice his freedom by obeying a lawful state; rather he abandons "wild, lawless freedom in order to find . . . whole freedom again undiminished in a lawful dependency . . . since this dependency comes from his own legislative Will."[39] Put negatively, freedom is independence from the constraints of another's will. Put positively, freedom is the will voluntarily subjecting itself to the moral law and acting on the basis of universal maxims that make one's own freedom compatible with treating others as equally free.

Three Principles of Right

Kant specifies three principles of right or justice that hold true and can never be overridden by concerns of necessity, expediency, national interest, or even the general welfare.

Freedom

The first is the freedom that members of the state preserve simply as human beings. As free or autonomous persons capable of choosing their own ends and purposes in life, individuals have rights that protect them from being compelled to follow some orthodox conception of what ends are truly good to choose, what plans of life will make them happy. Such legal paternalism, Kant insists, is incompatible with the status of human beings as self-legislators, able to be their own moral authority. In a particularly eloquent passage that captures the rights-based liberalism which flows from his doctrines, Kant writes, "No one can compel me to be happy in accordance with his conception of the welfare of others, for each may seek his happiness in whatever way he sees fit, so long as he does not infringe upon the freedom of others to pursue a similar end."[40] This freedom belongs to individuals as of right and does not depend on whether persons benefit from possessing such rights. Freedom has unconditional moral value as inherent in the dignity of a human life; its value is not proved from experience but is an absolute given, if we are to be capable of the self-governance that alone makes moral life possible. In one of his sternest passages Kant bluntly writes that "[n]o generally valid principle of legislation can be based on happiness."[41] People's understanding of happiness sufficiently varies that respect for the capacity of persons to choose their own ways of being happy is the foundation of what it means to be treated as free.

It is thus a hallmark of Kant's liberalism that the state must be neutral among the competing conceptions of the good life which it is possible for persons to entertain. It is not the state's job to make persons moral; this is something that only individuals can do for themselves by willing to do the right thing regardless of consequences. For the state to legislate morality is a contradiction in terms, since it takes away from human beings the very autonomy that makes moral conduct possible.

Equality

The second principle of right or justice is the equality of all persons as *subjects* of the state. Each of us is obligated to obey the same law, and we receive from the law equal treatment.[42] It is this equality of treatment that makes the coercive rule of law just. The only exception is that the head of the state, in Kant's view, cannot be subject to the rightful coercion of the others, since this would contradict what it means to be head of state. From the American constitutional point of view there is something odd in Kant's conclusion that the rule of law cannot be extended to govern the sovereign, but Kant thought that this exception was logically required for there to be "order" in a system of law and order. Otherwise there would be an infinite regress when it came to the question of who enforces the law against whom, and the difficulties Locke spied in there being no executive of natural law in a state of nature would continue.

Legal equality entails the important conclusion that careers and rank must be open to everyone on the same terms. Kant's formulation, similar to contemporary notions of "equality of opportunity," is that all members of the commonwealth must be entitled to reach any degree of rank which they can earn "by their talent, industry and good fortune."[43] Since birth is not a voluntary act on the part of the one who is born, it is absurd, Kant notes, to think that it can create any inequality in legal position. Only the commission of a crime could do that. Thus the "*birthright* of each individual . . . is absolutely *equal.*"[44] While persons can inherit property, they cannot inherit legal rank.

But, as Marx was to make his central criticism of liberalism, this notion of legal equality is permitted to coexist with inequality in the economic sphere. Kantian equality means that no one may justly prevent me from achieving whatever social station my talents and industry bring. And no one can undermine equality of opportunity by making legal advantages of rank inheritable. But within these limits, equality of opportunity is "perfectly consistent with the utmost inequality of the mass in the degree of its possessions."[45]

In recent years the American philosopher John Rawls offered a criticism of Kant on equality from within Kantian premises. For Rawls, Kant's remark about birth not being a moral act implies a more general conclusion that the skill, talents, and intelligence with which we are born carry with them no moral significance; they simply show brute luck in the natural lottery. Therefore it does not follow for Rawls that persons have earned whatever their brute luck in being born strong, industrious, adventuresome, or intelligent brings to them. Justice should correct for economic inequalities that stem from starting points which are arbitrary from the moral point of view.

Echoing Kant's concept of a hypothetical social contract, Rawls poses this question: what inequalities in the distribution of primary goods, such as income, wealth, and education, would free and equal individuals agree in advance to accept, if they had to reach agreement in an "original position" behind a "veil of ignorance" that kept them from knowing what their social fate would be or what luck they had in the natural lottery's distribution of talents? Rawls offered, in what he specifically referred to as a "Kantian interpretation" of the social contract tradition, a far more expansive principle of equality than Kant's own limited principle of equality of opportunity. I defer to a subsequent chapter on contemporary political theory the grounds Rawls gave for using Kant's own premises to push beyond Kant's politics. But it is worth noting here that many of the most lively debates today about justice and income inequality have their roots in the contract tradition Kant best exemplifies, a tradition that constantly requires the status quo to justify itself as if we were starting over again.

Independence

Kant calls the third principle of justice the independence or self-sufficiency that human beings achieve only as citizens or full voting members of the commonwealth. Kant's discussion of legal equality focused on persons as subjects of the law. Kant's discussion of citizenship focuses on persons as givers of the law.[46]

In part the term "independence" seems misleading, since Kant is concerned with the *interdependence* of citizens in willing universal law to govern their union. But Kant raises the question of which persons, in their economic lives, have the independence and self-sufficiency it takes for them to cast votes as citizens which express their free choices. Here Kant imposes stringent conditions that depart from contemporary liberalism. He reasons that persons who serve others by selling their labor for a wage do not have the independence that is a precondition for citizenship.[47] Since they are servants dependent on the will of a master, their vote on legislation cannot give us a true expression of their own will. By contrast, small farmers and artisans can be voting citizens. Although they sell a piece of work or a crop to others, they do not sell themselves. Kant gives the example of a tailor: such an artisan owns the product of his labor until it is paid for, and hence can be a citizen. But a person I hire as a day laborer to chop my firewood is paid for as a servant, and I own the person's labor as well as the product.[48]

Kant's limits on universal rights of citizenship are difficult to reconcile with his insistence that each human being has an equal capacity for self-determination. In the Kantian state, some subjects of the realm must live by laws given by the will of others. As *subjects* of the law, we may be equal in living under its protections, but only some of us participate in

271

making the laws we are asked to obey. Kant reconciled his views on the inequality of citizenship rights with the equality of subject rights by arguing that in a just society, there would be no legal impediment preventing laborers and servants from changing their economic status and thereby qualifying as voting citizens. But Kant did not sufficiently attend to the social and economic roadblocks to social fluidity that remain even when legal roadblocks are removed.

Kant's Republicanism

When it comes to the form of government, Kant is an advocate of republicanism but not democracy.[49] To an American ear the difference may seem cryptic, but Kant operates within a tradition that extends from the Roman republic through Machiavelli to Mill and the framers of the American Constitution.

The distinguishing feature of a republic is a separation of powers among the executive, legislative, and judicial branches.[50] The persons who administer the law are not the same as the persons who make the law. Without this separation, any form of government—even, or especially, democracies—will veer toward despotism, Kant argues. Democracies invest sovereign power in the many. But the crucial question is *how* sovereign power is exercised, not *who* possesses it. When a democracy is organized without separation of powers, the people carry out the laws they themselves decreed, and this makes them think of themselves as the masters of the state rather than as servants. The will of the many is taken automatically to represent the general will, and thus "'all' decide for or even against one who does not agree; that is, 'all,' who are not quite all, decide, and this is a contradiction of the general will with itself and with freedom."[51]

By contrast, in a republic the system of government is necessarily representative. The supreme authority resides in the people, who, in the idea of an original contract, give their consent to laws consistent with freedom. The executive carries out not its own will but the laws given with the consent of the governed through their elected deputies.[52] Only when government takes this form of representing the consent of the governed is freedom reconcilable with legal coercion. The problem with pure democracies that do not take this representative form is that "the people" become a law unto themselves.[53]

It is not clear why Kant counts on representation and separation of powers to stave off the dangers of majoritarianism for which he faulted pure democracy. I suppose it could be said, in a purely formal sense, that representative institutions assure that the consent of all is solicited, but this has no practical import when majorities simply outvote minorities.

Kant's Cosmopolitanism

One of Kant's lasting contributions to the canon of political thought was to expand the reach of justice from the domestic to the international sphere. Near the beginning of this book I expressed concern that Plato glided over the moment when his ideal republic's need for land triggered war with its neighbors. Kant is different in making obligations to peace and to universal justice paramount over domestic politics.

Kant's ethics, with their insistence on the universal reach of moral obligations, already suggests that politics should ideally tend toward world government, or at least an international regime governed by global principles of justice. In his writings on the purpose or end of history Kant suggests that history is a progressive realization of the ideal of a "universal cosmopolitan existence" in which a world republic governs individuals directly, without the nation-state as an intermediary.[54] Just as individual persons overcame their lawless condition in the state of nature by devising a government that put all equally under the law, so for "states in their relation to each other, there cannot be any reasonable way out of the lawless condition which entails only war except that they . . . should give up their savage (lawless) freedom, adjust themselves to the constraints of public law, and thus establish a continuously growing state consisting of various nations . . . which will ultimately include all the nations of the world."[55]

Although Kant presents world government as the theoretical end of history, he does take notice that there are reasons to fear the tyranny that world government could spawn. When various states combine under one power, "law always lose[s] in vigor what government gains in extent; hence a soulless despotism falls into anarchy."[56] Given these tyrannical dangers, Kant suggests a lesser form of cosmopolitan politics in his most famous practical essay on achieving peace. He proposes that there should and will emerge a federation of free states or a league of nations governed by an accepted body of international law. Kant specifies several principles that such a federation must follow. First, membership would be limited to states that are internally well governed. For Kant this means that member states must adopt republican constitutions and require the consent of their citizens for making war. When the citizens who will fight and suffer from war are the ones who must declare it, "nothing is more natural than that they would be very cautious in commencing such a poor game, decreeing for themselves" the costs and calamities of war.[57]

Kant then sees such internally well-governed states as federating around agreed-upon principles for resolving their differences without warfare. They do *not* surrender their sovereignty to a world government, in the way individuals surrender their freedom to the nation-state; but they form an alliance for the purposes of achieving their mutual interests in avoiding war.[58]

Although it is a moral duty for each state to seek the peace, Kant does not count on this duty as sufficient motive for the emergence of a league of nations. Rather, in well-governed states that seek the general good, the "spirit of commerce, which is incompatible with war, sooner or later gains the upper hand." Thus, without any moral urge, but only through economic incentives, republics domestically generate the will to promote peace.[59]

The members of this international society are states rather than individuals directly.[60] Nonetheless, as a final point, Kant would require international law to recognize a limited kind of universal citizenship, which he suggests is more like universal hospitality. Individuals do not have the right to take up permanent residence anywhere they wish on the globe but only the right of "temporary sojourn" in foreign lands.[61]

Kant sees this hospitality as working both ways. Under the guise of visiting, European traders cannot use the welcome given them to conquer territory and enslave native populations. From experiences such as these, China and Japan were justified in refusing entry to guests who behaved unjustly after entry. But the opposite violation of hospitality happens when nations such as the Barbary Coast rob ships that visit their seas or when nomadic Bedouin tribes plunder stranded travelers.[62]

Kant sees human history as bringing about ever-increasing contact of persons across the face of the globe. Under conditions of hospitality, "distant parts of the world can come into peaceable relations with each other [and] [t]hus the human race can gradually be brought closer and closer to a constitution establishing world citizenship."[63] World citizenship would be the *right* ideal for Kant, even if our natures and history did not underwrite its possibility. But it is a cause for future optimism to find that the actual course of history and commerce are creating the circumstances that make the ideal practicable.

Kant and Utilitarianism

Kant once quoted with qualified approval the proverb "fiat iustitia, pereat mundus" (let justice reign even if the world should perish).[64] The remark captures Kant's unqualified opposition to the utilitarian school of ethics, with its leading claim that we judge the rightness of an act in reference to the goodness of its consequences or results. But perhaps one does not have to be a utilitarian to think that surely at *some* point numbers and consequences matter. This is the force of the ticking bomb scenario and the problem of dirty hands long discussed in philosophy classes: if it were the case that you could save a thousand children's lives by torturing a prisoner into revealing the whereabouts of the ticking bomb, is it still wrong to torture? Empirically, of course, it may be that torture does not work, that we never really know whether the prisoner is privy to the bomb's location, but Kant's doctrines rest on principled arguments about rights, not these sorts of prudential calculations of costs and benefits. However much the formulation that we should never use persons as means to serve the welfare of others captures moral life under ordinary circumstances, it does not take into account the political dilemmas that could justify dirtying our hands.

It may be that specifying the extraordinary justifications that torture must meet would strengthen the presumption against its use. It may be that we want to acknowledge the wrong done by the use of torture, even when we find it necessary. But should we actually punish the persons whose use of torture saved a thousand children's lives, or should we congratulate them? Hegel remarked that Kant was correct in saying that "welfare without right is not a good" but incorrect in asserting that "right without welfare" could be the good. That is why, for Hegel, "fiat justitia should not be followed by pereat mundus."[65]

Let us consider two famous examples of Kant's nonconsequentialism. One was taught to me the first day in my first philosophy class by a professor who knew that the example would make us both resist and come back to Kant in the future. Kant starkly poses a test case for his own stern ethic: to save the life of a friend I am hiding, am I permitted to lie to a murderer who asks me if I am hiding my friend? Kant reasons that the maxim "Lie when it is necessary to protect your friends" cannot be universalized without undermining the worth of honesty, since everyone would have carte blanche to practice dishonesty when necessary to promote partisan interests. I therefore do the right thing by telling the truth, even though my friend perishes. The moral responsibility for my friend's murder would rest on the murderer and not on me for telling the truth.[66]

Way back then this seemed to me, as it still seems today, an implausible conclusion. Here enforcement of the rule on truth telling so divorces morality from human psychology as not to resonate with our intuitive understanding of ethical conduct. The dire consequences count as a reason why a good person (and not just a good friend) would suspend the rule. It may be, as some scholars have argued, that Kant's conclusion does not follow from his own premises and that the maxim "Lie to prevent an imminent murder" is indeed universalizable. But the very requirement that I may lie to save my friend only if I can reformulate the moral impulse into a rational and abstract duty seems to drain the impulse of its humanity.

The second example is drawn from Kant's writings on punishment, one often invoked today in arguments over the justice of capital punishment. Consistently with his moral theory, Kant argues that the purpose of punishment can never be to bring about deterrence or to set an example for others; this would be tantamount to using the individual criminal as a means toward serving the general welfare. The moral purpose of punishment must be strictly retributive—to hold the person to account for having chosen of his own free will to do wrong. Not to punish a criminal suggests a denial of the prisoner's humanity, as if he were not the author of his own behavior.

For Kant, the retribution due a criminal had to be equal to the crime done. Thus the only punishment sufficient to right the wrong done by a murder is to execute the convicted. Only the "sameness" between what the murderer did and what we do to him speaks to the equality of persons. In this sense Kant views equality in punishment as "negating" the original crime, restoring the moral balance disturbed by the condemned. Thus his theories lead to this stern and strange example: "Even if a civil society were to dissolve itself by common agreement of its members (for example, if the people inhabiting an island decided to separate and disperse themselves around the world), the last murderer remaining in prison must first be executed, so that everyone will duly receive what his actions are worth." Failure to carry out this penultimate duty before abandoning the island would leave the moral universe permanently out of kilter and make the people "accomplices in this public violation of legal justice."[67] But what exactly is accomplished by emptying death row of its prisoners through execution as we leave the island? Suppose we change Kant's example to picture the island as home for many years to a shipwrecked crew, who suddenly are about to be rescued. As they rejoice over their rescue and prepare to return home, Kant would still have them carry out any pending executions. But why? Kant does not cite any particular benefits to be gained from such rigor; he does not, for instance, invoke fear that the murderers upon repatriation might become a future danger. He simply says that it is an absolute duty of justice which admits of no exception. The jubilation felt upon being rescued and the temptation to declare a general amnesty might be understandable, but these "mere sympathies" stand in the way of doing one's duty to the letter of the law.

To my mind there is something bloodthirsty, almost vengeful, in the prospect of islanders carrying out every last execution before boarding the rescue ships. I could well understand an argument that the condemned persons should be left behind, that they are too dangerous to repatriate. But Kant does not rest the duty to execute on these sorts of calculations. Even though the island society is to be no more, the books on it cannot be closed until the executions are completed. At this point Kant's ethics demands a rule-abidingness and a legalistic mentality that stand in the way of good judgment. For what kind of moral persons are these islanders who are so duty bound as to be incapable of recognizing when the rules do not apply? The convicted murderers represent one sort of danger, the moral islanders, bent on retribution even against ordinary human impulses, quite another.

Kant and the Disembodied Self

Kant places on every person the burden of authoring his or her own morality. Moral principles must be the object of free and rational choice. They can never be right simply because they rest on tradition or custom; likewise, when we act simply to achieve the specific desires we happen to have, we lack the freedom to choose our own ultimate ends in life, expressing merely the influence of the circumstances in which we find ourselves. Unless a moral imperative or law floats free of the incentives and motives that we have as particular persons, it does not achieve the impartiality and generality on which moral life depends.

But what shape would our moral and political lives take if we followed Kant in "reasoning out"(the phrase comes from Alasdair MacIntyre) all our obligations? There is both a great liberation in Kant's doctrines and an accompanying danger. The liberation is that Kant secures for individual rights a firm basis, resting on the mutual respect that persons have for one another. The danger is that Kant's views on individual autonomy make it difficult to explain in what sense a state respectful of personal freedom can have a common good at all.

Shortly after Kant's death, Hegel criticized Kant for leaving persons aimless and adrift in their freedom. Hegel credited Kant with giving the fullest, most moral expression possible to those modern understandings of freedom that treat the individual as a complete whole. It was Kant's considerable achievement to take Hobbes's self-interested and egotistical person and elevate him into a person of conscience and duty. But conscience found its freedom only in disembodied ways, only by detaching oneself from culture—its history, custom, and traditions—and floating above all this, reasoning purely and universally. According to Hegel, this ability of Kantian persons to turn themselves into pure reasoning minds, attractive as it is, nonetheless condemned them to have "identity without content" and to remain without any definite character. They could never be "situated anywhere," permanently belong to a place, since the very act of putting down anchor would be a loss of freedom.[68] Thus for Hegel, as glorious and modern as Kant's emphasis on individual freedom was, it was finally one-sided. Gone for modern men were the ethical attachments to community that the polis once had provided Greek citizens. Indeed for Hegel, the problem with Kant is the problem Aristotle identified when he compared the isolated individual to a hand severed from the body.

This dispute between the "situated" or communal view of freedom endorsed by Hegel and the more "rootless" or individual view of freedom in Kant is a dispute that echoes through the entire history of political thought and continues unabated today. In the next chapter I take up the great defense of individual freedom made by John Stuart Mill in England. I then return to Germany to consider the case Hegel and Marx were to make against the liberal political ethic.

14

JOHN STUART MILL AND THE
DEMANDS OF INDIVIDUALITY

When he was twenty, John Stuart Mill fell into a deep depression. He lost all interest in work and reading, and wondered whether he had any reason to go on living. Mill had been raised as a child prodigy by his father, James Mill, a leading philosopher of his day. The elder Mill was a follower of Jeremy Bentham's utilitarian school of thought. James Mill took an avid interest in political reform, hoping that legal and public policies could be revamped to serve "the greatest happiness of the greatest number." One of his projects was his own son, whom he educated in languages, logic, and philosophy from an early age.

By the time he reached twenty, the younger Mill was an avid Benthamite and set his sights on using his learning for "the good of mankind." But in his *Autobiography* Mill recalls the painful period of his youth when he came to realize that his love for mankind was entirely abstract and divorced from any capacity to *feel*. The *Autobiography* follows in the tradition of Augustine's and Rousseau's *Confessions,* but it is more recognizably modern in exploring intellectual crises as rooted in mental depression. Mill describes his own education in utilitarianism as turning him into a "mere reasoning machine," competent at cost-benefit calculations but with a pronounced "under-valuing of feeling." One day, as clouds began to gather in his mind, Mill asked, "Suppose that all your objects in life were realized; that all the changes in institutions and opinions which you are looking forward to, could be completely effected at this very instant: would this be a great joy and happiness to you?" Mill reports an "irrepressible no" welling up, at which "my heart sank" and "the whole foundation on which my life was constructed fell down." Crushed by the realization that he did not *actually* care about the happiness of others—it was all an intellectual exercise for him—the young man fell into a profound depression:

I seemed to have nothing left to live for. At first I hoped that the cloud would pass away of itself; but it did not. A night's sleep, the sovereign remedy for the smaller vexations of life, had no effect on it. I awoke to a renewed consciousness of the woeful fact. I carried it with me into all companies, into all occupations. Hardly anything had power to cause me even a few minutes oblivion of it.

Mill describes a pain so deep that he did not see how he could go on living for any length of time feeling, in words he quotes from Coleridge, a "grief without a pang, void, dark and drear." Finally, after about six months of near incapacity, Mill was reading a poem that described the death of a father; as he read of the son's determination to save the family by stepping into the father's place, the younger Mill was moved to tears. He felt, for one of the first times in his life, a direct and emotional connection to human suffering and long dammed-up avenues of emotional being sprang to life inside him. Mill tells this story without betraying any awareness of its Oedipal dimensions or any sense that it might have something to do with feelings toward his own father. The most he ever admits is that his father's methods of education, with the best of intentions, may have developed the rational while dwarfing the emotional in the son.[1]

I start with this story because it presages two great contributions Mill came to make to moral and political thought. Although the son always remained loyal to the utilitarian philosophy he inherited from his father, Mill found a way to add some romance and poetry to what hitherto had been a rather quantifiable, cost-benefit approach to weighing pleasures and pains. In Bentham's hands, the principle of "the greatest happiness of the greatest number" had profound democratic and egalitarian implications. Each person's pleasure counted the same; there were to be no qualitative judgments about which pleasures were "higher," only quantitative judgments about matters such as intensity, duration, and costs. Bentham's famous tagline for the equality of all people's happiness was that pushpin (a child's game) was as good as poetry.[2]

Perhaps in homage to what reading one poem did to restore his mental health, Mill introduced into the utilitarian calculus a qualitative element reminiscent of Socrates' distinction between "higher" and "lower" pleasures. Human happiness, Mill remarks, is the happiness enjoyed by a free and progressive being who has "arrived at the maturity of his faculties." Instead of living an "ape-like" existence, slavishly imitating the customs of the day, a progressive human being exercises the full range of human faculties to make free choices for himself. Indeed it is only when persons choose their own life plans that both the individual and society become capable of progress and development. Choosing for oneself is always a high-wire act, and we are bound to fall. But the risks involved in choice at least make life exciting and dynamic, as opposed to a stale and static existence locked into unquestioning obedience to custom and tradition: "He who does anything because it is the custom makes no choice. He gains no practice either in discerning or in desiring what is best. The mental and moral, like the muscular, powers are improved only by being used."[3] When happiness is muscular in this sense, human beings become energized and spontaneous. They become original rather than conformist. In fact they become *individuals* for the first time, marching to their own drum, rather than fungible commodities no different from a thousand others. It is in this spirit that Mill offers his remark that it is "better to be Socrates dissatisfied than a fool satisfied."[4] Better because at least Socrates experienced strong impulses that flowed from his own being. Even if his choice of a life plan frustrated Socrates, his very struggle to think for himself gave him an experience of freedom that the nonthinking person can never enjoy.

In its Benthamite form, utilitarianism had difficulty coming up with a coherent defense of the importance of freedom. Bentham was insistent that any defense of freedom must do without "rights" (which he considered "nonsense on stilts") and justify freedom in terms of its utility to maximizing happiness in society. But suppose I could make all of the people happy by slipping them a drug, as was done in the dystopia Aldous Huxley fictionalized in *Brave New World*. Or consider Robert Nozick's example of maximizing happiness by hooking everyone up to an "eternal bliss" machine that could be programmed to provide each individual with the perfect state of pleasure. Examples such as these illustrate that freedom does not seem a necessary condition for happiness.

Mill understood these problems. In his most famous work, *On Liberty*, he set out to provide a more absolute defense of individual liberty than utilitarianism had produced thus far. Mill is insistent that his defense does not require resurrection of the ghostly apparition of "rights" that Bentham, in his view, had rightly buried. He sets out, rather, to show that freedom is indispensable to the muscular and energized individuality he identified with happiness. Still, Mill's case for freedom in *On Liberty* is finally not wholly instrumental; freedom emerges as an end in itself, the inviolable core of human dignity.[5] It is this defense of liberty as *the* human good that made *On Liberty* the most influential of all nineteenth-century statements of liberalism.

Summarizing his own argument, Mill offers "one very simple principle" to draw a bright line between the sphere of individual liberty and the sphere of proper governmental regulation:

> [T]he only purpose for which power can be rightfully exercised over any member of a civilized community, against his will, is to prevent harm to others. His own good, either physical or moral, is not a sufficient warrant. He cannot rightfully be compelled to do or forbear because it will be better for him to do so, because it will make him happier, because, in the opinions of others, to do so would be wise, or even right.[6]

Concern for the welfare of another, Mill continues, might provide good reason for "remonstrating with him, or reasoning with him, or persuading him, or entreating him." But to justify legal compulsion, the state must show that a person's conduct is "calculated to produce evil to some one else. The only part of the conduct of anyone for which he is amenable to society is that which concerns others. In the part which merely concerns himself, his independence is, of right, absolute."[7]

Mill's principle is commonly referred to as the "harm" principle, or a principle of noninterference or antipaternalism. Mill assumes that our acts divide rather neatly into two distinct categories. Self-regarding acts are those which affect only us and our own good. In this sphere, individual freedom is absolute. We should be left alone to "choose our own good in our own way," reaping the pleasure that comes from the very act of being authors of our own destiny.[8] Other-regarding acts affect the interests of others; here government rightly regulates to prevent harm to others.

Sweeping in its rejection of paternalism, *On Liberty* is frequently cited in debates on a host of issues, including abortion, assisted suicide, same-sex marriage, hate speech, surrogate motherhood, pornography, gun control, tobacco regulation, public nudity, prostitution, and gambling. Without bothering to count court citations, I would hazard the guess that *On Liberty* is referred to more often in contemporary American legal debates than any other book in the long canon of political theory.[9]

The intuitive appeal of Mill's principles goes something like this. Society is composed of individuals, each with his or her aims, aspirations, values, and purposes in life. In the face of this diversity of life plans, government respects the freedom of individuals only by treating every person's beliefs and values as worthy of equal respect. This is to say that government should treat citizens as adults capable of making informed choices on their own.

As long as my behavior affects only myself, I should be treated as capable of being the author of my own moral values. This is so because there is no one right way to live, no orthodox set of values and views that government should enforce on persons for their own good. There are only diverse ways of living, and freedom is respected only by respecting the capacity of persons to choose for themselves. This very act of choosing is what makes us progressive human beings, as we develop the capacities to author our own life plans. Expressed in these terms, the similarity between Kant and Mill on liberty comes to the fore, though Mill obscures it by talking about the empirical utility of freedom, whereas Kant rejected such contingent arguments.

We need, however, to ask two questions about Mill's theory. First, the empirical issue is whether any acts are self-regarding in the way Mill assumes or whether all acts affect the interests of others in nontrivial ways. Second, even if we can isolate self-regarding from other-regarding acts, the ethical issue is what value is served by standing aside and permitting persons to harm themselves. What is so good, or useful, about permitting persons to make choices that are bad for them? How does that serve the collective happiness? In considering these questions, we run into a third issue implicit in the other two. Mill sees his principles as establishing a "big tent" within which individuals are free to choose their own aims and aspirations in life (as long as no harm to others results). But are Mill's principles as inclusive or neutral as they claim to be? What if I am deeply religious and my view of the good life is doing God's work on earth, establishing a city upon a hill where citizens are brought into the good graces of the Lord and saved from evil? I address each of these questions separately.

Are There Any Self-Regarding Acts?

Some critics take the position that there are no purely self-regarding acts, that the category constitutes a null set. In making this argument, these critics hark back to Rousseau's point that self-regarding acts stop when we exit the state of nature; everything we do in society affects the interests of someone else.

We might put Mill's theory to the test by considering a number of cases in which self-regarding action is arguably at stake.

First, Mill took up the question of whether a legislative prohibition on eating pork in certain Muslim nations was consistent with freedom.[10] The typical law prohibited not only Muslims but non-Muslim residents and visitors as well from consuming pork within the national boundaries. Mill's position was that such legislation improperly invaded the sphere of liberty and amounted to coercing obedience to the state's morality. Since eating pork affects only the person eating it, individuals should have been left free to make their own choices.

Against Mill's position, many commentators argue that eating pork can just as well be classified as other-regarding. Viewed from the perspective of the Muslim majority, the consumption of pork is offensive and repulsive, an injury and insult not just to the faithful but to divine dictates. On this argument, law can prohibit an individual from consuming pork in order to prevent harm to the religious sensibility of others.

Mill rejects this kind of argument as fallacious—rightly so in my judgment. It works by counting as "harm" *any* behavior of which the majority morally disapproves. Were this kind of "harm" to justify government regulation of conduct, then government could in principle regulate everything.

To avoid such misuse of his "harm" principle, Mill in effect distinguishes between two different kinds of preferences individuals have. One set (internal preferences) are about what *I* prefer to do; the other set (external preferences) are my preferences for what *you* do. For Mill, the fact that my internal preference (for eating pork) offends your external preference (for what I do) does not count as a reason for classifying my behavior as "other-regarding." The individual eating her pork is minding her own business. It does not become the state's business merely because some or many persons would prefer to choose my preferences for me.

Implicit in this first example is a general feature of Mill's theory. Mill believes that the state should remain neutral as between competing conceptions of the good, letting persons choose for themselves. In this case the law should be neutral as between those who say it is good to eat pork and those who say it is bad. When the law is neutral, then those who wish to abstain from eating pork are entirely free to do so, just as those who wish to eat pork are free to act on their morality.

But is Mill's principle neutral? It could be argued that Mill's principle fits the beliefs of Western-style democracies that value individual freedom, but not that of theocratic states that believe their laws are dictated by the Almighty. Put it this way: if a nation and its people sincerely believe that God dictated the ban on eating pork, then leaving persons free to eat or not eat pork hardly seems neutral. Mill's solution sides with the liberal view that it is good for individuals to choose for themselves, and it rejects the theocratic view that it is good for individuals to obey divine commandments.

I think this objection to liberalism's neutrality is wrong. Consider the central case of religious tolerance. It remains the case that a society practicing the Mill principles is neither choosing the religious good for individuals nor prohibiting them from choosing their own religious values. Individuals remain free to be religious or not, and to practice whatever religiosity they have. The same cannot be said of a theocratic society. There the state dictates to members that the only good in matters of religion is what the state says (God says) it is.

Consider a second example of seemingly self-regarding behavior. Many states have laws requiring individuals to wear a helmet while riding a motorcycle.[11] These laws are frequently challenged, on the grounds that their sole purpose is to protect cyclists from injuring *themselves*. In college I had a motorcycle-riding friend who steadfastly refused to wear a helmet. He had been ridiculed so often by the rest of us for his foolishness that he developed a rather eloquent defense that went something like this: "Look, I'm tired of this bourgeois life; I'm out for a little adventure, that's why I ride a bike in the first place. I *want* it to be dangerous; the thrill is the risk. And the more I risk, the bigger the thrill."

To this day I doubt that my friend had really thought seriously about whether the thrill was worth the risk of ending up a paraplegic, or brain-dead. If he *did* think it worth that level of risk, then I would have to think there was something wrong and irrational about him. But Mill does not want me to go down that path. Mill specifically noted that the sphere of freedom includes "liberty of tastes and pursuits, of framing the plan of our life to suit our own character." He went on specifically to note that the mere fact that we find someone's tastes "foolish, perverse, or wrong" is no grounds for state interference.[12]

But was my friend's decision to ride sans helmet a decision that affected only himself? Stones or other objects might fly up from the road, causing him to swerve into others. Even were he to injure only himself, that injury might involve head trauma that could have been avoided by wearing a helmet. My friend would then expect not to be left alone but to be ministered to by ambulance drivers, medics, and EMTs. Valuable time and money would be expended to subsidize his thrill seeking. The medics might not get to another victim in time because they were busy working to stuff brain tissue back inside his cracked skull. Hospital space and resources would also be taxed, doctors called upon, and medical and auto insurance rates pushed upward for all of us.

It would seem that the helmet-free motorcyclist is engaged in other-regarding conduct after all. It is not that the public cares much about what happens to the motorcyclist; we care about the costs to the rest of us that flow from daredevil behavior. Not all lifestyles are equal in terms of the burden or tax they place on public resources. Helmetless bikers seem a particularly extreme example of egoists asking the public to *support* their choices, not just leave them alone.

Perhaps there might be some way to require those motorcyclists who wish to ride without a helmet to sign a "death wish" contract, in which they waive any right to have public authorities come to their assistance in case of accident, or else they agree to reimburse the public treasury for all expenses incurred on their behalf. But such contracts seem unrealistic and even immoral. Medics could hardly be expected to check and see whether there was such a contract in existence before administering emergency assistance. Moreover, we do not treat other examples of reckless driving in this way; the norm is for medics to treat the injuries sustained by drunk drivers or by minors driving without a license, regardless of fault. Of course, in the case of the drunk driver or minor, we *do* criminalize their behavior, but this may be due to the fact that their recklessness threatens direct physical harm to others in ways that helmetless riders do not.

Motorcycle helmet laws raise a general problem for Mill's theory. In modern complex societies, virtually everything a person does affects the interests of others to some degree. If all else fails, there is always the catchall argument that injury to myself diminishes to that extent the gross national product. Less attenuated is the argument that wage-earning parents threaten the welfare of their children when they risk harm to themselves; that harm in turn could impose costs on the public treasury were families to be thrown onto welfare. Mill was quite aware of this and acknowledged that "[n]o person is an entirely isolated being; it is impossible for a person to do anything seriously or permanently hurtful to himself without mischief reaching at least to his near connections, and often far beyond them."[13] He turned to this argument to deny persons with family responsibilities the right to attempt suicide.

But the entire distinction between self-regarding and other-regarding acts collapses if we treat every possible social effect traceable to an individual's behavior as sufficient to justify state regulation, no matter how marginal, remote, or improbable the impact. As one court mockingly noted, worker productivity might indeed increase if the state required all employed persons to be in bed by 10 PM on work nights!

Mill dealt with these difficulties by introducing a distinction between "direct and indirect" effects. By a self-regarding act, he meant conduct that "directly and in the first instance" affected only the person doing the act. The mere fact that personal behavior indirectly imposed costs on others down the road was not a sufficient warrant for reclassifying the act as other-regarding.[14]

Mill never specified the criteria for separating direct from indirect effects. His language suggests a focus on causation. Thus, in the case of motorcyclists, the absence of a helmet threatens to cause direct harm only to the person making the risky choice; harm to others occurs, if it occurs at all, as an unintended, second-order or indirect consequence of the harm to the motorcyclist. Some American courts have relied on this interpretation of Mill's principle to strike down motorcycle helmet laws as infringing on personal liberty.

But as a theory of causation and moral responsibility, Mill's reliance on distinguishing direct from indirect effects does not seem persuasive. If the driver of Car A negligently hits Car B, causing Car B in turn to ram into Car C, surely legal blame can be assigned to Driver A for any injury to Driver C, whether or not we consider the linkage to be direct or indirect.

The spirit of Mill's own principles requires a clearer way than the "direct versus indirect" distinction provides for drawing the line between the sphere of liberty and the sphere of permissible state police power. In judicial decisions on motorcycle helmet laws that turn for guidance to *On Liberty,* American courts frequently consider two different factors in deciding the cases.

First, judges ask a question Mill is committed to *not* answering. They inquire into how substantial, basic, or fundamental is the individual's asserted interest in being left alone to ride a motorcycle without a helmet. Here many courts make a substantive distinction between the fundamental importance, say, of religious worship in an individual's life and the marginal importance that helmetless motorcycle riding plays in any rational person's life choices. But Mill disdains such substantive judgments about the good to which a person puts freedom. In fact he considers it a credit to his position that it protects personal quirks or eccentricities against the tide of mass conformity.[15] For Mill, only the individual can judge the sufficiency of the good that motivates risking harm to self.[16] To refer again to my friend, he *claimed* that the pleasure of riding a cycle without a helmet was high among his life plans, and Mill pushes us to respect that choice, and to require society to defray the indirect financial and medical costs that personal freedom sometimes imposes on others.

The second factor that courts consider in motorcycle helmet cases is the significance or substantiality of the public interest at stake. The factor of substantiality actually seems to rest on two different calculations. The first is an assessment of probability of harm: the more remote it is, the less substantial is the state's interest in policing the individual's behavior. The second calculation is about the significance of the public interest. Courts distinguish between "compelling" interests and lesser ones. In general, where an individual's basic liberty is at stake—as it is when the state seeks to regulate religion or speech—courts require an extraordinarily compelling public interest that cannot be met except by interfering with a person's fundamental right to be left alone on matters of speech or religion. When the individual interest in being left alone does not go to basic liberties, then courts engage in a more relaxed scrutiny, permitting any rational state interest to outweigh the individual's lesser claim on noninterference.

Such inquiries require courts to engage in delicate acts of *balancing* individual autonomy against social welfare. In theory, Mill's distinction between self-regarding and other-regarding action promised to avoid the need for such balancing tests by pointing out an absolute, unwavering line separating the sphere of liberty from the domain of state police power. But in practice, in ways foreseen by Mill when he introduced the distinction between direct and indirect effects, drawing the line is difficult and leaves reasonable persons to disagree.

In regard to motorcycle helmet laws, a minority of American courts have declared such laws an unconstitutional infringement on fundamental liberty, finding that the conduct "directly" affects the rider's own head and only indirectly affects others through the risk the rider imposes only on himself. A majority of courts have made a similar inquiry and yet concluded that, given the substantial costs to the public versus the marginal benefits to the individual, the conduct is sufficiently "other-regarding" to be regulated.

My purpose is not to arbitrate this dispute but to discover in it a general problem with Mill's theory. Mill rested his defense of individual liberty on a debatable sociological claim that human conduct falls into the separable spheres of self-regarding and other-regarding behavior. But even Mill had to admit that matters were more complicated, and he resorted to the "direct versus indirect" distinction to deal with cases straddling the line. It may be better, in the end, to dispense with Mill's sociology altogether and to acknowledge the web of social relations that makes Mill's separation of the spheres unrealistic. This does not defeat Mill's defense of individual liberty, since the self- versus other-regarding distinction is not necessary to that defense. It is not necessary because some liberties are so basic to human dignity and equality that they cannot be overridden even to achieve desirable consequences for others.

A third case, that of tobacco regulation, is particularly revealing of the fluidity of the self- versus other-regarding distinction. At first, smoking was considered a purely self-regarding act and was largely unregulated. But as evidence of the health risks of smoking mounted, the state justifiably required cigarette manufacturers to place warnings on cigarette packs in order to make sure that smokers knew the risks they were assuming. Once warned, however, smokers were left free to make their own choices.

Discovery of the harm smoking caused to nonsmokers—the problem of secondhand smoke—changed the paradigm. What had seemed an example of self-regarding behavior now became an other-regarding public health threat, responsible for the death of thousands of *non*smokers annually in the United States. To deal with the hazards of secondhand smoke, bans on smoking in public places and accommodations were put into place. Smokers remained free to harm themselves in the privacy of their own homes, but they could not smoke in places where their behavior threatened harm to others.

I remember a particularly ingenious student a few years back, a nonsmoker, who tried to convince the class that bans on smoking in public violated *his* right as a nonsmoker to choose his own good. He loved going to bars with friends, some of whom smoked. But it was all less pleasurable than in the old days, since his friends either suffered, or stepped outside, or refused to go at all. My student claimed that he preferred sitting in a smoke-filled bar with friends enjoying themselves to going to a bar without his friends or with friends not able to smoke. The class thought he was joking, but he protested his sincerity. Matters stood at a standstill until another student pointed out that the argument foundered on exposing bartenders and waiters to secondhand smoke. But it was intriguing to watch the class struggle with whether or not to accept the basic argument that a nonsmoker might rationally prefer to be in the company of smokers.

In the United States, the other-regarding aspects of smoking have been invoked successfully by state governments and the federal government in various lawsuits against the tobacco industry. Although tobacco companies sell a legal product to willing consumers, their business imposes tremendous indirect costs on public treasuries, as governments are left to foot the health bill for patients receiving Medicare or Medicaid benefits. Governments and the tobacco companies resolved the litigation with a settlement that required the industry to pay back billions of dollars into the public treasuries.

In and of itself, there is nothing alarming in finding that the line between self-regarding and other-regarding behavior shifts in light of new scientific knowledge. But it is telling that, depending on what aspects of smoking one focuses upon, the behavior can be described as either self-regarding or other-regarding. At least in the complicated web of social relations that constitutes modern life, what is true of tobacco is true about helmetless motorcycle riding and a host of other behaviors described as merely self-regarding. Mill's atomistic sociology seems outdated in this respect.

Are There Any Self-Regarding Acts That Government May Regulate?

So far we have been concerned with difficulties in drawing a line separating self-regarding from other-regarding acts. But let's assume for argument's sake that the line can be drawn somewhere. Are there any justifiable examples of legal paternalism for Mill in which government ought to interfere with self-regarding acts to protect persons from harming themselves? Consider the following possibilities.

First, a person voluntarily wishes to sell herself into slavery for life, or for a period of years. Even Mill would not permit a person to choose slavery as her own good. The reason we can prohibit a person from making such a choice is that it contradicts the very principle of liberty invoked to defend the choice. The slave surrenders the right to remain a free person; if we believe that liberty involves the capacity to choose for oneself, then a choice to surrender that capacity cannot be consistently defended in the name of liberty.[17] Thus when government prohibits contracting oneself into slavery, it does so not to enforce one particular conception of the good life on a person but simply to preserve that person's inalienable autonomy to continue to choose and to revise her own life plans.

Second, drawing parallels to Mill's argument about slavery, many argue that government should similarly intervene to uphold the foundational value of individual liberty against cultural and religious traditions and other forms of socialization that—while falling short of slavery—nonetheless make it impossible for persons to exercise genuine freedom of choice. Consider an example from France, which prohibits young Muslim girls from wearing the traditional *hijab*, or headscarf, while attending a public school.[18] The French government has defended this legal prohibition of a religious practice as follows. What we want to do is to give these young Muslim girls the level of education that will make it possible for them to decide for themselves one day whether to wear the *hijab* or not. Many if not most of these children come to school under parental dictate to wear the *hijab*; so segregated by dress, they cannot in reality be integrated into the open and secular classroom experience that would give them a vantage point from which to freely consider alternative futures. If, after being democratically educated, a Muslim girl chooses to wear the *hijab*, then we respect that choice and her freedom to make it. But the state owes it to such children to intervene against parental and religious authorities who would prohibit them from ever making free choices about religion.

Since we are dealing with children, the applicability of Mill's principles is complex. Mill noted that children are generally not yet of the age sufficient to make free choices for themselves.[19] But, especially on matters of religion, who should choose for children until they can choose for themselves? In liberal societies it is generally the practice to make parents, not the state, the proxies for their children's religious freedom—absent a showing that parental choices threaten physical harm for the children. Parental choice, as opposed to governmental control, seems more in tune with maintaining equal respect for the diverse religious choices made in a heterogeneous society. But France has taken the opposite position, for the reasons already discussed.

In the United States, authorities for the most part regard the wearing of religious garb or insignia in class as quintessential self-regarding behavior. This has long been the case with Jewish skullcaps, Latin crosses, ashes on foreheads on Ash Wednesday before Easter, Sikh turbans, and the like. In all these cases, presumably including the *hijab,* American schoolchildren are seen as minding their own business and harming no one; for the state to say it is "bad" for a girl to wear religious garb in a public school classroom is to dictate moral choices to children and their parents.

Consider, for instance, the way a religious dispute between the state of Wisconsin and the Amish religious sect was resolved by the United States Supreme Court in 1972. At the time Wisconsin had a typical law requiring children to be educated in some state-certified school until the age of sixteen. The justification for the law was that the state has a compelling interest in providing children with at least the minimal level of education necessary for them to take their place as informed, self-governing citizens in a democracy. The state also cited economic reasons for insisting that children receive sufficient education to support themselves in the market. An Amish family refused to obey the law and kept their fifteen-year-old daughter at home to work on the family farm.

The Amish are a long-established, highly cohesive, and economically self-sufficient community whose religious beliefs rest on a sweeping rejection of modern life and its technologies in favor an agrarian lifestyle lived on the land. The Amish argued that, by fifteen, it was time for a young girl to practice the spiritual life that comes from agrarian work. The Amish also argued that public high schools taught values antithetical to the practice of their religion and that the very survival of their religion was threatened when children went to high school, exposed to the relentless peer pressures or even mockery that made them ever after misfits for a return to life on the family farm.

Wisconsin countered that children's development into free and progressive human beings required a minimal education to the age of sixteen and that the religious autonomy of *groups* such as the Amish should not trump the liberty interests of *individuals* within that religion. But the Supreme Court ruled in favor of the Amish. Although the case does not squarely fit Mill's principles, since children are involved, still the gist of the Court's opinion was that parents, not the state, should decide what is in the best interests of the child when it comes to balancing religious values and secular education. The Amish had a proven track record in providing for their children, and this pushed the Court to decide that Wisconsin should accommodate the alternative understanding of "the good life" practiced by the Amish.

It could be argued, on Millian grounds, that the Court should have reached the opposite conclusion. Mill was clear that the decision to have children imposed legal obligations on parents to take care of their children's basic welfare, including their health and education.[20] In fact he specifically objected to the misuse of his principles of liberty when it came to issues of a parent's duty to provide compulsory education for his or her children. For Mill, the decision to have children imposed a legally enforceable obligation on parents to ensure instruction and training for their offspring up to a decent minimum. He regarded the conclusion in favor of compulsory education laws as a "self-evident axiom" and had little patience for protecting parental despotism as if it were a deduction from liberty.[21] Given Mill's strong pronouncements on the subject, it is intriguing that the United States Supreme Court could reach an opposite result.

Consider a third example. Despite his strong stance against paternalist legislation, Mill does permit the state to protect persons from making some sorts of mistakes. Mill poses the example of a person about to cross an unsafe bridge unaware of the risk he is assuming. If there is no time to warn the unsuspecting person, a bystander may stop him bodily, "since liberty consists in doing what one desires, and he does not desire to fall into the river."[22] Where there is time, government should limit itself to posting warnings of the danger. Once the person has the facts necessary to make an informed decision, then the choice remains his, since "no one but the person . . . can judge of the sufficiency of the motive which may prompt him to incur the risk."[23]

Mill's solution to the unsafe bridge example is rather peculiar and unpersuasive. While the state can post warnings about the hazard, and stop a person from crossing who has not been forewarned, once the warning is posted and there is a *risk* but not a *certainty* of harm to oneself, then Mill would allow the person to choose to cross, since no one but the person can calculate whether it is worth running the risk. But surely at some point the risk is substantial enough that, for the same reasons Mill allows intervention to prevent certain injury, he should also permit the state to stop persons from recklessly crossing dangerous bridges. Should they fall, they expect rescue, and this is a sign that they did not seriously choose to risk dying for the benefit of crossing the bridge.

The philosopher Gerald Dworkin points out that Mill's position rests

293

on a distinction between two different kinds of mistakes persons may make. The first are "cognitive" errors, or demonstrable errors of fact or understanding about the physical world: here the person thinks the bridge is safe, but it is not. Or to take another example posed by the philosopher Robert Nozick, a person is about to jump out of a thirtieth-floor window. When you seek to stop her, she says, "Don't worry, I can fly."[24] In such a circumstance we can be certain that the person is making a cognitive mistake and that, but for the mistake about the law of gravity, the person would not desire to jump. Mill's theory leads to the conclusion that individual freedom is underwritten rather than undermined when we act to prevent persons from doing what they would not do were they in full possession of the facts of physics.

But suppose we correct the mistake by posting the warning, and some persons—be they thrill seekers, persons in a hurry, or melancholics—still want to cross the unsafe bridge or jump out windows. We might be tempted to think they were still making a mistake, but it would be an evaluative rather than a cognitive mistake. The person who knows the bridge is unsafe but runs across for the thrill of it is like my helmetless motorcycle rider: each seems to be placing the wrong weights on temporary thrill versus life and bodily integrity. The melancholic seems constitutionally incapable at the moment of rationally weighing the value of going on living.

As I understand Mill's antipaternalism, he allows for limited intervention in the case of cognitive mistakes but rarely in the case of evaluative mistakes. This is the upshot of his bridge example: once the warning is posted, the cognitive mistake has been cured, and the person must be left free to weigh the risks for herself knowingly. If a person were actually "delirious, or in some state of excitement or absorption incompatible with the full use of the reflecting faculty," the state might be justified in intervening. Absent such circumstances, the individual's choices must be respected.[25]

Much of Mill's position on mistakes and warnings is reflected in current American law on informed consent and medical practice. If patients are to make truly voluntary choices, then doctors and medical professionals must inform us of the risks involved in taking a particular drug or undergoing elective surgery. In anticipation of a day when we may be comatose or mentally incompetent, we are encouraged to draft living wills, specifying in advance what medical procedures we wish in the event of falling into a vegetative state, and which we wish to forgo. Likewise, no competent and conscious adult has to accept any medical treatment, even a life-saving one. These instances are all straightforward applications of Mill's liberty principle.

There are some cases, however, in which Mill's antipaternalism seems implausible. I am in the habit of crossing the railroad tracks at an unmarked crossing every day during my afternoon run. I could alter my route to wind around to the official crossing, but that would take time that I would rather spend in more open spaces. The place where I cross has "Danger" signs prominently posted and a chain-link fence to keep persons out. I depend on someone else to keep on cutting a hole in the fence, and I run across despite the warnings. I do this knowing that I am assuming a certain risk. I am aware that on average one person dies every day somewhere in the United States crossing railroad tracks at unmarked intersections. But I am careful; I look both ways; I don't expect to be hit, and consider the joy of running my own route to outweigh the ascertained risk involved.

Does Mill mean to say that a police officer who happened to be in the vicinity could not prevent me from crossing? Perhaps the solution in this case is that I am trespassing on private property and could be arrested not for my own good but merely to protect the private property rights of the railroad. Or perhaps my act is other-regarding because I impose risks on the crew and passengers aboard the train, should the engineer brake suddenly upon seeing me. But these seem rather roundabout ways of justifying the police authority to prevent me from crossing at places marked "Dangerous—Do Not Cross." A state does not seriously erode my freedom when it insists that it is in my own interests to be coerced out of the habit of crossing railroad tracks surreptitiously. And yet Mill does seem to say that only I can make the cost-benefit analysis of whether to cross at risk. Here his utilitarianism leads him to think that a sane person is the sole judge of the consequences of his acts, once there is only a statistical probability of harm rather than certain injury.

Take another example raising the issue of mistake. At the time of the first publication of On Liberty in 1859, the Mormon church still endorsed the practice of polygamy, whereby Mormon men could take multiple wives. (Under considerable pressure from the U.S. government, Mormon authorities recanted the doctrine in the late nineteenth century.) "No one has a deeper disapprobation than I have of this Mormon institution," Mill remarks.[26] And he proceeds to attack Mormon polygamy as inconsistent with liberty, as "a mere riveting of the chains of one half of the community."27 From Mill's point of view, Mormon women are making some sort of evaluative mistake; the religious education given to Mormon women persuades them that it is preferable to be one of many wives than to be no wife at all. But a mistake of this sort does not render the Mormon woman's choice involuntary or coerced, according to Mill. If, educated and socialized to be the person she is, she makes such a choice, it must be respected as an example of pursuing one's own good in one's own way. Nor does it do harm to others. Like the Amish, the Mormons had at the time, as they do now, an enviable record of providing for their children; there was no empirical evidence that polygamous marriages led to greater incidence of child neglect or abuse than occurs in monogamous families.

It could be argued that Mill's distinction between so-called "voluntary" slavery and polygamy is inconsistent: why does not the foundational principle of liberty prohibit both? Interestingly, Mill remarks that he does believe that one-way polygamy is inconsistent with a woman's freedom, but he nonetheless thinks it must be tolerated in the way slavery must not. Presumably Mill is depending on the fact that the contract which binds a woman to a polygamous marriage is dissoluble at the woman's own will, while the slave has no way out of slavery. The mere fact that the Mormon woman is socialized into making the choices she makes does not mean that she should not be regarded as responsible for those choices. If one were to reason otherwise, it would seem as if the Mormon woman were being treated as a child, to be protected as a ward of the state since she is not capable of protecting herself.

For the most part, I find Mill to be persuasive when he argues that a person's choices do not become unfree simply because they are a product of socialization into a particular community or religious tradition. But there are choices and there are choices. One wonders what Mill would make of the custom of some communities to circumcise young women; in one form of the custom, the circumcision involves the virtual cutting off of the clitoris, specifically to diminish the woman's capacity to experience sexual pleasure. Suppose (which is not often the case today) a community limits the ritual circumcision to *adult* women who consent to it from religious belief? Is Mill committed to the notion that the state cannot intervene in the name of the woman's own good, that the state cannot bar the procedure on the grounds that it cannot be good for the woman, whatever she may think at the time, to sustain irreversible physical injury? Is the argument that the capacity to experience clitoral sexual pleasure is basic to a woman's selfhood a mere "Western" preference that adult women should be free to reject? Here, I think, Mill's principles lead to a conflict. On the one hand, Mill is insistent that the state cannot enforce one particular view of the good life on an adult against her own choices. On the other hand, Mill is equally insistent that the state can prohibit those choices which make it impossible to choose freely in the future. Slavery is the clearest example to him of a choice that negates choice, but undergoing *irreversible* genital injury also prohibits a woman from ever revisiting or changing that choice in the future. Mill does not provide us with any way to resolve this tension in his thoughts in cases such as these.

The Legacy of *On Liberty*

On Liberty remains one of the great statements of liberal tolerance. It puts forward in unsurpassed ways the core conviction that government owes equal respect to the diverse answers free individuals give to the meaning of the good life. There is no *summum bonum* beyond this diversity of choice; the end of a free society is precisely to support the habits that make it possible for diversity, difference, and pluralism to flourish in place of homogenization and conformity. A society can find unity within this diversity, but it can only be a unity based on the shared respect individuals have for their mutual rights to be different.

And yet, despite its enduring power to persuade and to inspire, *On Liberty*'s case for tolerance has two difficulties. The first has to do with the status of tolerance as an end rather than a means. The second has to do with Mill's understanding of individual psychology.

First, Mill treats tolerance both as an end in itself and as a means to other ends. As an end, tolerance for Mill already defines the good life—a life that brings energy, vitality, and spontaneity to human existence by virtue of exposing each individual to the different choices and life plans of others. Tolerance is the end state for Mill precisely because it *is* the state of mind of a fully developed individual, navigating through life's choices in the spirit of adventure, without the narrow-mindedness characteristic of the morally judgmental person, whose self-righteousness leaves the muscular faculties of choice to atrophy.

But it proves difficult for Mill, or for anyone, to offer a pure defense of tolerance as an end. Should we tolerate the intolerant? Should we welcome, in the name of the beauty of the freely choosing self, ideas and doctrines that, if followed, would stamp some selves as inferior, not entitled to education, unworthy of respect? When confronted with issues such as these, Mill tends to retreat and to write as if tolerance is not so much an end but rather a means to the higher ends of truth, knowledge, progress, and genius. He argues that in the robust competition of a marketplace of ideas, truth will triumph over falsity, and justice will win out over prejudice in the long run. Arguments such as these are the spine of the book and constitute the specific arguments Mill makes for freedom of speech and freedom of religion. Tolerance of ideas and beliefs, no matter what they are, no matter even if they are noxious or demonstrably false, is said to be the best way to correct error through trial with the truth.

The trouble with Mill's argument, to pursue Kant's line of reasoning, is that it is purely contingent, leaving the value of tolerance to depend on whether it happens to be the best means in particular circumstances to combat error with truth. Mill's argument could justify departures from tolerance when it is not productive of socially desirable results. Moreover, there is precious little evidence supporting Mill's optimism that truth will prevail in the marketplace of ideas. Mill himself was an early diagnostician of the conformist tides in mass society that "regulate" thought even when law does not. In the march of history since Mill's death, propaganda and prejudice have proved capable of persuading masses of humanity to act on barbarous propositions. Conversely, as Isaiah Berlin pointed out, truth and even genius have flourished in the bowels of authoritarian societies. As great as Mill's defense of tolerance is, he makes it too easy, as if there is little risk "in the long run" that injustice will win out over justice in any fair competition for people's minds. But in our own times, those of us who make Mill's arguments for tolerance have to do so knowing full well that tolerance of certain ideas and sects is a dangerous proposition.

One reason why Mill downplayed the danger is that he regarded free speech and freedom of religion as wholly self-regarding matters, in and of themselves threatening no public harm. He drew familiar distinctions between speech and action, arguing that society can ordinarily protect its interests by regulating the actor and not the speaker. There may be good reasons for maintaining this distinction between speech and action as an argument for tolerance. But one of the reasons is not that truth and reason always triumph over falsity and prejudice in conditions of freedom and tolerance.

The second difficulty with Mill's defense of freedom is that at times it rests on an unpersuasive account of individual development. Like Kant,

Mill regards the self as a portable entity whose very detachment from any customs, traditions, and belongings is the best assurance that the rational will triumph over the irrational in the development of the individual personality. Moreover, Mill tends to regard the formative experiences leading to autonomy as ones that an individual experiences alone and internally rather than in connection to other persons. But it may be that mobility and detachment can be carried too far, that a thoroughly rootless person, with no firm commitments, situated nowhere, is too easily preyed upon by those who offer a home, a community, a sense of belonging to something larger and more permanent than the peripatetic life, the perpetually moving self. Mill's case for mobility as integral to freedom—the readiness always to pick up and move one's allegiances and start anew—is an important and inspiring one. But mobile freedom of the sort Mill and Kant idealize needs to be augmented with what Hegel called "situated" freedom—the freedom that gains content and definition from having a place to call home.

Mill could not make room for the solidarities of life consistently with his regard for freedom of choice as the highest moral value. The idea that an individual might find freedom through allegiances to a way of life with others, judged so worthwhile as to anchor the person to a group and oblige him to duties that restrict personal choice and freedom of movement, was foreign to him. Theoretically, Mill's theory allows that some persons could *choose* to make the non-choosing life their own good. But this would have to be one choice among many, supported by society but not institutionally enforced.

It is in the nature of Mill's case for freedom and mobility to call out an alternative vision of freedom found by sometimes staying put. Unless the liberal case for the importance of uprooting oneself and choosing open-ended futures is combined with Rousseau's sense that freedom and belonging to a community are consistent, liberalism in practice would threaten a vast atomization of social relations, assigning little value to virtues such as loyalty and solidarity, destructive of the virtues of sharing a common good with other human beings. The free person is Mill's choosing self, but the free person is also Rousseau's citizen, capable of putting down anchor in a community that makes it possible for individuals to have a particular and defined identity in the first place. There will thus always be reasons to read and to be persuaded by On Liberty, just not entirely.

On the European continent, Kant rejected the utilitarian defense of liberalism but put forward a compatible case for the autonomy that comes only to the person free to choose his own conception of the good life. Mill himself took inspiration from other German liberals, noting in the frontispiece to *On Liberty* the work of a contemporary, Wilhelm von Humboldt. But this moment of convergence of German and Anglo-American liberalism was soon to pass. With Hegel, and then Marx, German intellectual thought centrally explored the deficiencies in the ethic of individualism held to characterize liberal societies. Their thought was to push the canon of political theory in dramatically new directions. To that story I now turn.

15

HEGEL, MARX, AND THE
OWL OF MINERVA

A great flourishing of political thought took place in nineteenth-century Germany as Hegel took on Kant, and Marx in turn set his sights on Hegel. The transmission of ideas from Kant to Hegel to Marx is so dramatic as to rival the initial flow of thought from Plato to Aristotle to Augustine, with which our study of the canon of political thought began. Karl Marx is a revolutionary figure in the history of political thought, but he forged his politics in confrontation with Hegel, just as Hegel formed his thoughts in dispute with Kant.

In certain moods Marx was restless in reading his predecessors, waiting for the philosophizing to end and the politicking to begin. As to the German intellectuals of his day, Marx found them often too esoteric and deliberately obscure to be *political* thinkers. Hegel alternately inspired and infuriated him, a mixture of feelings bound to be shared by anyone who has struggled with the notorious difficulty of Hegel's language. Chafing at the limits of study, Marx deliberately set out to change the canon of political thought so that the great distance between philosophy and politics—a distance Plato first staked out when he stalked away from political life—could finally be bridged.

But even as he rebelled against traditional ways of doing political philosophy, Marx studied it, and remained a student his entire life. A series of notebooks he kept as a young man record his early confrontations with Hegel in particular. These notebooks were discovered and published only long after Marx's death. They make it clear that Marx's economic criticisms of capitalism grew out of a political critique he first began developing as he studied Hegel. To understand Marx, then, we need to go back to Hegel.

The density of Hegel's writing and thinking, however, is an obstacle to even the most intrepid of readers. The vocabulary is beyond our ordinary use of terms, the references to world literature require encyclopedic wisdom, and the political points are embedded in a dense and strange philosophy of history, metaphysics, and theology. I confess to having never found a way to teach Hegel. Years ago Judith Shklar hired me to proofread her manuscript on Hegel's *Phenomenology of Spirit*. I say she hired me, but the truth is more that I pleaded to read the manuscript and she obliged me. I was not a very good proofreader. Shklar, who was unfailingly frank, let me know this when the book came out with typographical errors. My excuse was that I was too busy trying to understand the book to pay attention to my job as proofreader. Even so, I found the reading tough and said so, not out of courage or rudeness but because Shklar insisted I should be as frank with her as she was with me. She was not terribly surprised or upset that her commentary did not immediately help me. It was to be expected, she said; there was no good way to "introduce" or "explain" or "summarize" Hegel. He resists such approaches and rewards only persistence, patience, and the passage of time.

Since my aim in this book is to make political theory accessible, I have been sorely tempted to leave Hegel aside and proceed directly to Marx. But Hegel is too important a figure in his own right, and too much the philosopher against whom Marx cast his politics, to be purged from the canon. What I propose, therefore, is to approach Hegel indirectly, only through Marx's own reading of Hegel. One need not vouch for the correctness of Marx's reading of Hegel to see the importance of the confrontation that altered the future of politics.

Given what I have just said about Hegel's inscrutability, it may seem strange that in the years after Hegel's death, German university students became passionately caught up in disputes over which were the true disciples of Hegel. Philosophy departments were dominated by professors dubbed the "Old Hegelians" by their students. These established figures understood Hegel largely in theological terms and echoed the master's pronouncement that man was but Spirit or God alienated from itself, an alienation that will end with the end of history itself, when Spirit comes to be aware that all of creation is an emanation from its own "Absolute Mind."

Organizing into "Young Hegelian" societies and meeting outside of classes, students experimented with using Hegelian concepts to dispute the Hegelianism of their professors. One such young Hegelian was Ludwig Feuerbach, who originated what became known as the "transformative method" of criticism. What was needed was to invert Hegelian categories as they were then understood. Thus, instead of man being alienated from God and striving to overcome that alienation, Feuerbach argued that "reversing Hegel" was closer to the truth: God is simply man alienated from himself, an illusory projection outwards of our own human essence. The goal must be to recover that alienated human essence from the spurious religiosity in which it is lost in Hegel.

Around the time Feuerbach made his criticisms, Marx was writing his Ph.D. thesis on Epicureanism and Greek philosophy. But he was among those who flocked to the meetings of the young Hegelians. To judge from the notebooks in which he recorded his reactions to Hegel's most systematic political work, *The Philosophy of Right,* Marx took away from his young Hegelian phase three lifelong influences. The first had to do with the purpose of political theory itself. Here, as much as Marx belongs in the tradition of political thought as I have described it, he also set out to end that tradition, to "abolish" philosophy, in his word, by practicing it.

The second influence of Hegel on Marx came from Hegel's criticism of liberalism, and of the sphere of civil society where the liberal bourgeois lifestyle is played out. In time Marx would develop his own critique of liberal society in economic terms, but he always stayed with Hegel's moral objection to liberal societies for lacking any robust common good or genuine concern for the welfare of others.

Third, even while absorbing Hegel's critique of liberalism, Marx balked at Hegel's own political solutions—solutions that Marx saw as typical of political theory ever since Aristotle created the myth of the polis as some heavenly place where human beings perfect themselves. Hegel represented to Marx a high-water mark in the mystique of the state, and Marx set out to demonstrate that the reviled sphere of civil society, and not the revered sphere of the state, carried with it the germ of a better future.

The Purpose of Philosophy

Philosophy, Hegel famously remarked, "is its own time apprehended in thoughts."[1] From the beginning, Marx seems to have been intrigued but disturbed by this aphorism. To be able to reflect critically on the nature of one's own society: this appealed to Marx's sense that philosophy could make a difference in the real world, if only it would leave the ivory tower and engage "its own time." But Marx was perturbed by the quietism suggested by Hegel's remark. For one thing, Hegel made it seem as if philosophy's imagination is shuttered, never able to look beyond "its own time" to see new times. Expressing his disdain for utopian speculations, Hegel remarked that the task of the political theorist is to understand the actual existing state, not to "construct a state as it ought to be."[2] The construction in thought of a state "supposed to exist, God knows where," can only be a "one-sided, empty ratiocination."[3] It can express our subjective freedom to dream, but it cannot make that freedom concrete and definite in the world as it is lived.

To illustrate his point about the limits of philosophy, Hegel reached back in the canon to reinterpret the ambition of even the most seemingly utopian of political philosophers: Plato. Even Plato's *Republic* should not be read as the construction of an ideal state in some Beyond. Plato's achievement was to clarify the nature of Greek ethical life, just as another ethical principle was breaking into that world and shattering its unity. This is the way all great philosophy works. In a manner of speaking, it always comes on the scene too late to give "instruction as to what the world ought to be."[4] As Hegel puts it, referring to the Roman goddess of wisdom, the "owl of Minerva spreads its wings only with the falling of the dusk."[5] Only when a given period of history is about to pass is its spirit finally comprehensible in thought, thrown into relief by the challenge to an old ethic from a new one.

As the young Marx reflected on the purposes for which he studied philosophy, he chafed at the notion that philosophy and politics were fundamentally different enterprises and that thought could do its work purely only at some remove from the world. This notion of a gulf between philosophy and politics, between the ivory tower and the cave, was hardly peculiar to Hegel: it had been a large part of the canon of political thought ever since Plato withdrew from politics in disgust at Socrates' execution. But Marx deliberately set out to change that tradition, to overthrow it. In one of his famous theses on Feuerbach, his fellow young Hegelian, Marx congratulated Feuerbach for taking on Hegel philosophically, intellectually. But this was not enough; it was not enough to "apprehend" the world "in thoughts." As Marx pithily put it, "the philosophers have only interpreted the world. . . . [T]he point, however, is to *change* it."[6]

In support of closing the gap between philosophy and politics, the young Marx found some support in another of the aphorisms with which Hegel prefaced his *Philosophy of Right:* "What is rational is actual and what is actual is rational."[7] Such a remark suggested that philosophers did not have to escape history or the cave in order to realize ideals: in some fundamental way for Hegel, whatever is present and actual already contains, or at least gestures toward, the ideal. To study the state as it actually exists in history is to study "the state as something inherently rational."[8] Not every state, not every moment in the life of any actual state, is the embodiment of reason. But as one translator of Hegel puts it, philosophy's "task is to find joy in the present by discovering reason within it. . . . [It] may 'dance' for joy in this world [and] need not postpone its 'dancing' until it builds an ideal world elsewhere."[9] Or to put the point another way, Shakespeare had Macbeth, upon hearing of his wife's death, dismiss life as a bad play, "a tale told by an Idiot, full of sound and fury, signifying nothing."[10] By contrast, Hegel saw reason as working through history to manifest itself.

The notion that the state is inherently rational can have conservative, even reactionary implications, insofar as it legitimizes the status quo by anointing it with the quality of Reason. But it can also have, as it did for the young Marx, profoundly revolutionary significance, suggesting that political ideals are realizable in history if we dare to act to change the actual.

State versus Civil Society

One of the great themes running throughout Hegel's *Philosophy of Right* is the difference between two competing conceptions of freedom. The first, central to Hobbes, Locke, Mill, and the liberal tradition, frees the *particular* in the person, leaves persons free to express the individual desires and aspirations they happen to have. These desires do not have to be especially rational or worthy; what it means to be a free person is to be left alone to express one's own personality, no matter how capricious, whimsical, or arbitrary that personality happens to be.

As opposed to Rousseau, Hegel is more or less accepting that notions of freedom which tilt toward the individual are here to stay; in irreversible ways, modern persons can understand themselves as free persons only if they see themselves as wholes in and of themselves. It was not always this way; Hegel understands Greek culture to have been "organic" in ways that made persons feel free only when they understood themselves as parts of a larger whole. But the day of the polis is gone.

Still, Hegel did agree with Rousseau that the particular self is not the highest or most ethical self we can achieve, that there is a freedom we attain only by calling out the universal in us, only by using reason to free us from merely slavishly following whatever desires or opinions we happen to have.

Much of the notorious difficulty in reading Hegel has to do with the intricate ways in which he wields this vocabulary about "particular" freedom versus "universal" freedom, "subjective" versus "objective" freedom. For instance, Hegel makes the dense remark that freedom for the particular persons we are can support a "moral" life but not an "ethical" life. His point seems to be that, insofar as the moral life places the accent on individual conscience and each person looking inward for standards of right conduct, then morality and individuality go together. Hegel credited Kant with giving the best possible expression of this link between moral life and individual freedom. But a higher "ethical" plane is reached when we understand that the source of right is not ours to define individually, but comes only from living in a community whose values, institutions, and norms are indeed universally or objectively good.

For our purposes, we can put these difficulties aside. Hegel's more accessible point, and the one that engaged the young Marx, was that in modern societies, the difference between civil society and the state more or less corresponds to the difference between the particular and the universal in mankind. In civil society, the realm of bourgeois man, we pursue our own self-interests, our own economic needs and material desires. The norm of behavior is self-satisfaction, and this can create the famous "war of all against all" that Hobbes analyzed and that liberal politics superintends without seeking to transform. Hegel was not entirely critical of civil society. He thought that a limited sociability emerged in the market, when "men are . . . dependent on one another and reciprocally related to one another in their work." Under such conditions, "subjective self-seeking turns into a contribution to the satisfaction of the needs of everyone else."[11] And thus a kind of ethical and universal life is spun out unintentionally even among self-interested economic actors. But it is a limited kind of sociability, more about overlapping self-interests than about deeper commitments to one another.

To achieve that deeper commitment, we have to move from civil society to state, from the realm of self-interest to the realm of universal interests. For Hegel, the state is distinctively and ideally "the embodiment of Reason," the concrete expression of the rational will of its people, the locus of the individual's "true identity." The state alone frees individuals by investing an individual's particular will with a rational and universal ethical content. This is not an ethical elevation individuals can accomplish on their own; we elevate self-interest into a commitment to the universal good only by living in a community whose norms in fact embody Reason. Of course, not every actual state embodies Reason. The state "stands on earth and so in the sphere of caprice, chance, and error.[12] Still, there is a direction to history such that the actual does contain the rational, and Hegel was not above casting the emerging Prussian state as the coming carrier of universal world history and the vehicle for giving individuals their "true" and "ethical" identity for the first time.[13]

No serious reader of Hegel would suggest that he favored the murderous and racist ways in which the Nazis came to have the German state embody the supposed one true essence of its people. Still, any political theory that speaks of the individual "identifying" with the state is likely to sound dangerous, mystical, or both to a liberal ear.

Marx's ear was not especially attuned to liberal fears, but he did criticize, in his notebook, the "mystique" with which Hegel wrote about the state, the aura and halo that Hegel granted the state. It was by reflecting on this key question about the supposed ethical superiority of "politics" over "economics" or of the state over civil society that Marx came into his own, as a critic of both Hegel and contemporary liberals.

Marx's Critique of Hegel

Marx rested his critique of Hegel on an unmasking of the pretensions of the Hegelian state to universal status. The notion that persons live a universal life through the state, Marx argued, was an illusion conjured up only by standing the state over civil society in the same way that religion stands God over man. The Hegelian state was but an empty abstraction, a "mystical substance," a projection or alienation of our "practical, sensuous activity" onto an ideal but mythical realm.[14] The concrete person is bifurcated into two existences, one as a person in civil society, the other as a citizen of the state. In this double life, man is supposed to find his freedom, but for Marx the separation merely made the state "otherworldly" and, like any religion, "infused with an unreal universality." That is, "[t]he political state, in relation to civil society, is just as spiritual as is heaven in relation to earth. It stands in the same opposition to civil society, and overcomes it in the same manner as religion overcomes the narrowness of the profane world."[15]

The problem, according to Marx and his fellow young Hegelians, was that the Hegelian state is an "inverted reality." In one of Marx's most famous phrases, the relation of civil society to the state "is standing on its head" in Hegel and "must be turned right side up again, if you would discover the rational kernel within the mystical shell."[16] That is to say, Marx accepted that there was great insight in Hegel's struggle to tease a "universal" existence out of the clash of interests in civil society, but the truth can be gotten at only by an immanent critique that restores order to Hegel's topsy-turvy conceptions.

To understand what was at stake, we have to detour briefly into the metaphysical debates consuming German professors of the day. In some complicated sense, Hegel was an "idealist" who taught that mind—human consciousness—constructed the external world as it appears and is known to us. Marx thought that this philosophical idealism led Hegel to invert the proper relation of the human subject to its own experiences, properties, or "predicates." Take, for example, the simple claim that "Jeff had thoughts." For Marx, it is clear that "thoughts" do not have some independent, disembodied existence; they have to be thought by someone, such as Jeff. But in Hegel it gets turned around. Instead of starting with the flesh-and-blood person who has thoughts, Hegel bestowed on thought and consciousness a "mystifying subjectivity," as if activities such as will, consciousness, and thought had an existence outside of their embodiment in concrete individuals.[17] This is why Hegel can strangely refer to the state as "the *self-knowing* ethical actuality of spirit."[18] But states aren't the kinds of entities that have wills or thoughts or consciousness in the way human beings do. It is as if, Marx suggests, Hegel saw the world through some kind of "camera obscura" that turns images upside down. Ordinarily we think that the material world exists and we form ideas about it. But with Hegel, Marx wrote, ideas somehow have godlike power to create reality:

> To Hegel, the life-process of the human brain, i.e., the process of thinking, which, under the name of "the Idea," he even transforms into an independent subject, is the demiurgos of the real world, and the real world is only the external, phenomenal form of the "Idea." With me, on the contrary, the ideal is nothing else than the material world reflected by the human mind, and translated into forms of thought.[19]

I will come back shortly to what sort of "materialist" Marx is, and is not. But first let me illustrate his point about the upside-down nature of the

Hegelian world with two political examples well analyzed by the philosopher Shlomo Avineri.

In the *Philosophy of Right,* Hegel defended constitutional monarchy as the ideal form of government. This would have been a considerable and progressive reform from the direction the Prussian state came to take, but it was still, in Hegel's own time, a halting suggestion that put Hegel at some distance from liberal reformers pushing for more representative government. Marx questioned Hegel's rather peculiar defense of monarchy. The thrust of that defense was that the monarch does not really express or rule on the basis of his "particular will" at all but somehow in his royal person expresses the "universal" and "true will" of the people.[20] So Hegel can say that the will of the monarch *is* the will of the state. Marx brilliantly debunks this claim by again focusing in on the oddity of talk about states as if they were like persons in having a "will." It is true, Marx remarked, that in "the historical context of the early 19th century, the will of the monarch finally decides" what the state does. But Hegel expresses this historical truth only in inverted form, so that it comes out mystically in a cryptic formulation such as "the final decision of the will is the monarch."[21] But this makes no sense to Marx. The only sensible way to read Hegel is to see that he is offering only a very pretty rationalization for subjecting persons to the will of another person.

A second example, equally conservative, is Hegel's argument in favor of granting one class of persons—the landed gentry—special political status. Hegel's particular recommendation was that the gentry should form the upper house of the legislature, since their ties to the land made their interests more permanent and substantial, less shifting and quixotic, than the interests of the industrial classes.[22] In making this suggestion, Hegel in his own day sided with those classes that did much to stymie the modernization process in Germany; in time, as Barrington Moore's classic study of dictatorship and democracy shows, the political dominance of the landed aristocracy in Germany gave us not the universal politics Hegel predicted but the militaristic and nationalistic politics of the Prussian state.[23]

Marx was acutely aware that Hegel's politics once again had this "mystical" quality. What was it that made Hegel think that the gentry would have "universal" rather than "class" interests? Hegel pointed out that the practice of primogeniture assured that the estates of the nobility passed intact to the firstborn male son. So encumbered or entailed, the estates could not be sold or otherwise transferred as property in the normal market sense. It was this arrangement, Hegel argued, that gave ethical and universal content to the gentry, as against the riot of particular interests that attach to property when it is transferable at will. One supposed benefit of primogeniture to the landed gentry was that it kept families together on the land, preserving estates intact and thereby preserving the ethical value of family life even as it collapsed elsewhere in bourgeois societies. But Marx attacked the spuriousness of the equation of the nobility with some higher and more universal ethic. What Hegel had done was to take what Avineri calls the "accidental fact of a person's birth as the oldest son" and elevated this accident into a moral claim for holding political office.[24] Marx thought it obvious that firstborns viewed the world from the particular vantage point of their station rather than from some universal perch. And he disputed the claim that primogeniture served to keep families intact rather than tearing them apart by privileging the firstborn.

Marx's Critique of Liberalism

Had Marx merely debunked the spurious universality of Hegel's politics by exposing the cover it gave to the particular classes that were dominant in Prussian society, this would already have been a considerable achievement. But Marx's genius was to see that the problem with Hegel was a problem with liberal politics as well. In Hegel there was this dualism between civil society and the state, between the particular life individuals live in the economic realm and the supposedly more universal life they lead as citizens in the state. But this same dualism is characteristic of modern liberal societies. Consider, for instance, the characteristic split expressed in the very title of the French Revolution's Declaration of the Rights and Man and of the Citizen. (Marx treats the various state and federal constitutions of the United States as expressing a similar theory in even more perfect form.) As citizens, individuals enjoy political rights that do not depend on who the person happens to be in civil society, whether Protestant, Catholic, or Jew, whether a property owner or not. In a fully realized liberal state, for instance, there is no religious or property qualification for voting. The liberal constitutional state is necessarily secular and could be called "atheistic" in the limited sense that the state has no official or established religion. It is the same with property, as the state treats each citizen as equal, regardless of the prevailing inequalities in civil society.

Compared to the Prussian state, Marx regards the liberal state as delivering "great progress" in human freedom.[25] In *On the Jewish Question,* an essay alternately brilliant and perverse, he takes the German state to task for not developing a constitutional order in which the "Jewish question" is resolved by separating church and state. But despite its achievement, liberalism delivers only a partial liberation that Marx, clearly influenced by Hegel, calls "political emancipation," as distinguished from true or "human emancipation." In political emancipation, the state is freed from the influence of religion and property, but man in his actual life in civil society is not. *There* religion still matters, and the other side of the constitutional abolition of state religion is protection for the "free exercise of religion" in the private sphere. Marx astutely points out that it is precisely under the conditions of separation of church and state that religion flourishes in the United States.[26]

The same can be said for private property. Although the state formally works its way pure of property qualifications on the right to vote, real-life prospects continue to depend on possession of property in civil society. The liberal norm is for the citizen to be "politically emancipated" from forces that the individual in civil society is not "humanly" emancipated from:

> Where the political state has attained to its full development, man leads, not only in thought, in consciousness, but in *reality,* in *life,* a double existence—celestial and terrestrial. He lives in the *political community,* where he regards himself as a *communal being,* and in *civil society* where he acts simply as a *private individual,* treats other men as means, degrades himself to the role of a mere means, and becomes the plaything of alien powers.[27]

In this early essay one can see the drift Marx's political thoughts are taking. Working within a Hegelian paradigm, Marx faults liberalism for leaving man in his actual lived life (in civil society) mired in the "war of all against all," Jew versus Protestant versus Catholic, rich versus poor. Liberalism does not speak to the universal in us—what Marx calls our "species-being," our social being, whereby, unlike the other animals, we are aware of ourselves as alike. Hegel does speak to our species-being, but only by divorcing it from actual social existence and locating it ethereally in the state. The task that Marx sets for progressive politics, different from liberalism and Hegelianism alike, is to heal the breach between our social being and our particular interests by freeing persons *in civil so-*

ciety—in their concrete daily lives—to express the universality that citizenship in the state is supposed to express.

Unfortunately, *On the Jewish Question* ends by pandering to, if not endorsing, anti-Semitism. To be fair, Marx attacks *any and all* religious differentiation as an obstacle to the species-consciousness he hopes will emerge. In this sense he calls for man to liberate himself from religion generally and for the abolition of Jew and Christian alike. But Marx singles out Judaism to equate with the spirit of "huckstering" that is at the heart of the problem of the war of all against all. Alongside political and human emancipation, Marx refers to the particularly Jewish way of emancipation, which turns out to be acquisition of money. Despite the nominal dominance of Christianity, the Jewish love of money "has become the practical spirit of the Christian nations," and in this sense "Christians have become Jews."[28] Given this "effective domination of the Christian world by Judaism," by "Money . . . [,] the jealous god of Israel," Marx can conclude that human emancipation waits upon "the emancipation of society from Judaism."[29] The Holocaust makes chilling any suggestion that Germany should have resolved its "Jewish question" by overcoming the pernicious influence of Judaism.

Materialism versus Idealism

In rejecting Hegelian idealism as "humbug," Marx does not slip into a crude sort of materialism. By a crude materialism I mean a view that (1) posits a world of matter (nature) as having a permanent and ahistorical existence wholly apart from human thought or creativity; (2) sees human beings as having a definite and static nature embedded in physically given needs, like other pieces of organic matter; and (3) regards human consciousness, ideas, religion, culture, and politics as merely the product of circumstances, with material factors being the prime mover in history, and human thought merely reflecting the force of nature and the external environment. We shall struggle in a moment with ways in which Marx does approach politics in a reductionist manner, but let me begin with a simple example Marx gives in *The German Ideology* to distinguish his views from the materialism of Feuerbach, his fellow young Hegelian. Feuerbach spoke of the "true essence" of things and described the "sensuous world" around us as if it were "a thing given direct from all eternity, remaining ever the same." To rebut such a view, as Avineri shows, Marx offered the example of cherry trees. However much the cherry tree is a given of nature, nonetheless human beings interact with cherry trees only in historically conditioned circumstances:

> Even the objects of the simplest "sensuous certainty" are only given [to human beings] through social development, industry and commercial intercourse. The cherry-tree, like almost all fruit-trees, was, as is well known, only a few centuries ago transplanted by *commerce* into our zone, and therefore only *by* this action of a definite society in a definite age it has become "sensuous certainty."[30]

Thus nature is not something that stands outside of and over human beings; in any particular historical era it is what it is by force of the work that the "sensuous human activity" of previous generations has done on matter. In one era, the countryside around Rome consists of pasturelands and swamps; in another, there are only vineyards and villas.[31]

It is true, as the materialists say, that we must begin with human beings who eat and drink before they think or do anything else. But a primary difference between humans and animals is that we satisfy our needs actively, by working on nature and producing the means to satisfy those needs. In other words, we come to produce material life itself. And in the process of re-creating the natural world to satisfy our needs, we also create ourselves: "[T]he satisfaction of the first need (the action of satisfying, and the instrument of satisfaction which has been acquired) leads to new needs; and this production of new needs is the first historical act."[32] This is what Marx is driving at in oft-repeated phrases about man's having a "historical" nature: who we are, and what needs are human, cannot be discovered by studying biology alone. Human nature is dynamic and develops through the interaction between the physical world and our labor on it. Marx *is* a materialist, in the sense that he insists that the starting point of historical analysis must be with "the material conditions under which [human beings] live."[33] But his position mediates the normal tension between materialism and idealism, since for Marx these material conditions are not objective things beyond human mind and activity but are in large part "produced" by human activity.

It is against this background that one must consider the central Marxist thesis that the means of production are the primary mover of history and that forms of human relationships, and the "echo" of those relationships in law, art, religion, and philosophy, are driven by changes in the means of production. It is common to read this Marxist thesis as implying a kind of economic or technological determinism. Such a reading disregards Marx's reminder that the means or forces of production are not objective things out there in nature but are shaped by human activity. Avineri offers the example of Niagara Falls to illustrate Marx's point. Niagara Falls no doubt exists as a particular moving body of water in nature, prior to human thought about it. But it does not become a means of production by virtue of its natural properties alone; it must be viewed as such and acted on purposively. Thus, Avineri concludes, the famous Marxist aphorism about ideas being merely "superstructural" and derivative from underlying material circumstances must be understood not as asserting a brute opposition of mind and matter but as setting up a dialectic between "conscious human activity, aimed at the creation and preservation of human life, and human consciousness, which furnishes reasons, rationalizations and modes of legitimization and moral justification for the specific forms that activity takes."[34]

One of the reasons why Marx opposes a pure materialism is that he is aware of its passive political implications, as if human beings must necessarily wait for material conditions "out there" to change. In a phrase, Marx derides what he calls the quietism of "contemplative materialism." Or, as he succinctly puts it in his third thesis on Feuerbach: "The materialist doctrine that men are products of circumstances and upbringing, and that, therefore, changed men are products of other circumstances and changed upbringing, forgets that it is men who change circumstances."[35]

Political Theory as Ideology

It is through the concept of ideas as "ideology" that Marx issues a decided challenge to the long tradition of political theory. For Aristotle, there was a wide division between the life of labor and the life of thought. Labor mired one in the necessities of life; leisure enabled persons to think freely. The Aristotelian polis, therefore, is never merely an economic organization; it is an association around a distinctly *political* concept of the good that private persons cannot experience alone or in families or in economic activity. The capacity of persons to live together in responsibility for a common good is what makes Aristotle claim that human beings are not merely *social* animals, in the way ants and bees are, but *political* animals who come together to create a moral good higher than and qualitatively different from the material goods enjoyed in social and economic life.

For all the changes in political theory since Aristotle, this vision of politics elevating us from the limited lives we live in family, in the market, in society has persisted, along with the pejorative view of labor. Aristotle considered slaves and laborers as necessary to the polis but as disqualified from full citizenship. Likewise Plato reserved political rule for guardians who had no relation to family or private economic life at all. Even Kant reasoned that working for a wage disqualified a person from citizenship, since such employment put one under someone else's will. Rousseau distinguished between the will of all that is triumphant in civil society and a truly general will that can be expressed only in public activity. Hobbes had an absolute Sovereign keep the peace, since we cannot on our own end the war of all against all in civil society. Hegel entrusted executive power to a bureaucracy whose work for the state assured that bureaucrats, as opposed to industrialists, had "universal" as opposed to class interests.

Against this long tradition of contrasting the "commonwealth" or "res publica" that politics can bring about with the Thrasymachean, self-interested, desiring individuals we otherwise are in private, Marx argues that the general will comes out of the crucible of civil society itself. It is his location of the universal will *in* the life activity of labor that moves Marx decisively outside the tradition of political philosophy as I have described it in this book.

Recognizing his own dissent from political theory, Marx lay down two challenges. The first is that the state as a distinct "political" or "public" space must be abolished and its universal aspirations absorbed back into our real lives in civil society. The state as embodiment of the universal is a myth for Marx, an ideological screen behind which class interests continue to operate. Only by ending the class struggle can the universal in our natures be liberated to express itself in the one and only life we actually live—in civil society. Marx's second challenge is to the enterprise of political theory. Its task is to abolish itself by realizing itself. When "reality is depicted," Marx writes, "philosophy as an independent branch of knowledge loses its medium of existence."[36]

The Primacy of the Social over the Political

Let me take up first the way in which Marx dismantles the category of the "political." Thus far I have been at pains to show that Marx is no crude determinist, reducing human consciousness to the predetermined results of underlying material forces. Nonetheless, Marx does see the human mind as developing in interplay with those material circumstances of labor that Aristotle criticized as unfree. The creative and revolutionary force in history is *Homo faber,* and it is through the power of labor to change the material world that persons eventually may come to free themselves.

To see that work is the premier form in which human beings act creatively on their surroundings is to see that the traditional separation of the "political" from the "social" is false: "The social structure and the State are continually evolving out of the life process of definite individuals, but of individuals not as they may appear in their own or other people's imagination, but as they *really* are; i.e. as they operate, produce materially, and hence as they work under definite material limits . . . independent of their will."[37]

The mistake of political philosophy is to ground political analysis on "what men say, imagine, conceive." But these conceptions of the state, Marx argues, are "echoes" or "phantoms" or "sublimates" of the way in which thought is concretely shaped in individuals by their activity as workers, not thinkers:

> The production of ideas . . . is at first directly interwoven with the material activity and the material intercourse of men, the language of real life. Conceiving, thinking, the mental intercourse of men, appear at this stage as the direct efflux of their material behavior. The same applies to mental production as expressed in the language of politics, laws, morality, religion.[38]

The Abolition or "Withering Away" of the State

In *For a Ruthless Criticism of Everything Existing,* Marx wryly notes that "[r]eason has always existed, only not always in reasonable form." One example is the political state. In form the state "contains . . . the demands of reason." But "everywhere [the state] comes into contradiction between its ideal mission and its real preconditions." The state appears to us "sub specie rei publicae"—as a public thing. But in reality it only gives *political* expression to "the rule of private property."[39]

In *The Poverty of Philosophy* Marx similarly notes that "political power is precisely the official expression of antagonism in civil society."[40] It does not transcend but reflects class interests, so that "[p]olitical power, properly so-called, is merely the organised power of one class for oppressing another."[41] In capitalist society the state is "but a committee for managing the common affairs of the whole bourgeoisie."[42]

As a solution to the partiality and class biases of the state, it will not do for political philosophers to propose yet another ideal republic, new social contract, or bigger Leviathan. The solution must be to give up the utopian aspiration entirely that political power can ever speak to the universal. "Freedom," Marx wrote, "consists in converting the state from an organ superimposed upon society into one completely subordinate to it."[43]

How is freedom to emerge from *within* the tensions and class struggles of civil society? Since the state exists to superintend the class struggle, the end of that struggle would permit the abolition or "withering way" of the state as such. As Marx, joined by Friedrich Engels, put the point in 1851: "The abolition of the state has a meaning only for the Communists, as the necessary result of the abolition of classes, with which the need for the organized power of one class for the suppression of another ceases of itself."[44]

The classic Marxist thesis on the abolition of the state actually comes from Engels: "The proletariat seizes the state power and immediately converts the means of production into state property. But it thereby abolishes itself as proletariat, abolishes all class differences and antagonisms, and abolishes the state as state."[45]

The state, however, does not disappear overnight. In the first stages of postrevolutionary society, private property has been "universalized" only by being nationalized. This is a necessary step, but Marx refers to the emerging society only as "crude" or "vulgar" communism. Although the state is now the sole property owner, it functions only as a "universal capitalist." Far from abolishing wage labor, the egalitarian accomplishment of crude communism is simply to make everyone a wage laborer.[46] In one of his great rhetorical flourishes, Marx compares what crude communism does to workers to what prostitution does to women.

Given these conditions, Marx envisions a transition period in which "the annulment of the state [is] still not complete" and communism is "of a political nature." The state becomes "nothing but the revolutionary dictatorship of the proletariat."[47] Since class has not yet been abolished, politics in the sense of coercion remains necessary, and the "proletariat will use its political supremacy to wrest, by degrees, all capital from the bourgeoisie."[48]

The Russian anarchist Mikhail Bakunin pounced on phrases such

as "dictatorship of the proletariat" to accuse Marx of authoritarian leanings. Bakunin offered that any state, even a "people's state," necessarily
means domination. His alternative and anarchist solution was to accomplish the revolution by immediately smashing government. Marx's response was to accuse Bakunin of mistakenly thinking that a social revolution could simply be "willed" into existence. As long as economic
conditions leave the proletariat in struggle with the bourgeoisie—a struggle that would continue after the revolution—then the proletariat must
organize politically and "use measures of *force,* hence governmental
measures," to consolidate the revolution against its enemies.[49]

It was Marx's expectation, however, that a socialist society could
evolve "beyond politics." All preceding social revolutions have been partial, with one class seeking to gain the "upper hand" over other classes.[50]
But the proletariat cannot free itself without freeing everyone; it represents the "last form of servitude" and comes to be conscious that its own
dehumanization is the dehumanization of all.[51] In Marx's phrase, the
proletariat is a "universal class," since "[t]he condition for the emancipation of the working class is the abolition of every class."[52] Although the
proletariat's immediate goal is to destroy its own living conditions, "[i]t
cannot do so without destroying *all* the inhuman living conditions of
contemporary society which are concentrated in its own situation. Not in
vain does it go through the harsh but hardening school of *labour.*"[53]

Precisely because the proletariat cannot free itself without freeing society from the very idea of class, its victory coincides with the end of the
need for politics. As Marx puts it, after the fall of the old society "there
will be [no] new class domination . . . and there will be no more political
power.[54]

The New Society

What is life like in a socialist society that achieves this "positive transcendence" over the state? The key for Marx is in the changed conditions of
labor. Labor in a socialist society has the potential to be "life's prime
want" rather than a "means of life."[55] When labor is a mere means rather
than an end in itself, the worker experiences time spent in labor as unfree
time, an alienation from self and from other human beings. Work comes
to be associated with envy, competition, and antagonism. But a socialist
society can build on the tremendous, wealth-creating productivity unleashed by capitalism not only to shorten the workday (as an antidote to

labor's misery) but also to reconnect laboring activity with joyous expression of our own humanity.[56]

To achieve its joyous potential, labor must be free from the phenomenon Marx calls "alienation." It may seem as if all work is drudgery, but Marx thinks that capitalism rests on a particular organization of work that "alienates" the worker in three different ways. First, the worker is estranged from the products of his own labor; he cannot afford the very things he produces. Second, the worker is alienated from himself, exploited in ways that treat him as if he were a thing rather than a person. Third, each is alienated from his fellow workers and from his own social or "species-being." Instead of work expressing our common humanity, under conditions of capitalism it perpetuates Hobbes's notorious war of all against all.[57]

The key to ending alienation is to end "the enslaving subordination of the individual to the division of labor," which sets up an antithesis within each worker (able to express only one part of his being) as well as among workers.[58] How a modern industrial economy can abolish or even minimize the division of labor Marx does not say, but he offers this portrait of the nonauthoritarian nature of labor choices in a socialist society where the state has withered away. Under existing conditions, each of us is compartmentalized by the division of labor into working at one thing. We are "a hunter, a fisherman, a shepherd, or a . . . critic," and we would lose our livelihood were we to flit from one occupation to another. But socialism will make it possible "for me to do one thing today and another tomorrow, to hunt in the morning, fish in the afternoon, rear cattle in the evening, criticise after dinner, just as I have a mind, without ever becoming hunter, fisherman, shepherd or critic."[59] Here we have Marx's characteristic description of the emergence of the universal *within* the activity of labor. It is precisely when labor expresses our social being that the state, organized to superintend a vanished class struggle, can vanish as well. And when the state disappears, its passing, like the passing of God, permits humanity to experience its species-being in the practical activities of everyday life.

The Abolition or Realization of Political Philosophy

It is not merely the state but also political philosophy that must wither away. Marx quite self-consciously set out to end the tradition of political thought as I have described it in this book.

I do not wish to exaggerate this point. Marx is well aware that before the revolution, "the work of our time [is] to clarify . . . the meaning of its own struggle and its own desires." Alongside those who fight are those who "show the world what it is fighting for, and consciousness is something that the world *must* acquire, like it or not."[60] Thus Marx could express his motto as "Reform of consciousness not through dogmas, but through analyzing the mystical consciousness, the consciousness which is unclear to itself, whether it appears in religious or political form."[61] A political philosophy along these lines need not be merely "ideological," meaning that it need not reduce to offering rationalizations for the status quo and the ruling class. Marx even went so far as to stress that, because of the power of ideas, some "portion of the bourgeois idealists, who have raised themselves to the level of comprehending theoretically the historical movement as a whole," will go over to the proletariat, "in times when the class struggle nears the decisive hour."[62]

Still, Marx never quite abandoned the view of philosophy he first offered in his notes for his doctoral dissertation, where he wrote that philosophy's "relationship to the world is that of reflection."[63] If there is a purpose to political theory, it is to criticize itself, and by exposing the way in which it has historically been used, uncover the ugly truths about civil society long given window dressing by philosophers.

Marx argued that philosophy and politics had a reciprocal relationship. On the one hand, an adequate philosophical understanding of the status quo was a prerequisite to changing it. On the other hand, changing the world would, by realizing philosophy at long last, abolish philosophy—abolish it in the sense of turning theory into practice. This is the significance of Marx's statement I quoted earlier, that hitherto "philosophers have only *interpreted* the world; the point, however, is to *change* it." Unless political theory leads to its own transcendence, it is just another religion idolizing heaven rather than practically bringing heaven down to earth.[64]

By contrast to the tendency of political philosophers to think in heavenly terms, Marx praises the practical thinking of workers

in the Manchester or Lyon workshops, [who] do not believe that *"pure thinking"* will be able to argue away their industrial masters and their own practical debasement. They are most painfully aware of the *difference* between *being* and *thinking*, between *consciousness* and *life*. They know that property, capital, money, wage-labor and the like are no ideal figments of the brain but . . . must be abolished in a practical, objective way.[65]

When I say that the tradition of political theory met its match in Marx, I have in mind his distinction between the ways in which workers and philosophers think. It is not that Marx is some Philistine with no appreciation of the indispensability of political theory; his own lifework is in *interpreting* the status quo precisely so it can be understood enough to be changed. But Marx judged the merits of a political theory in terms of whether it leads to practical change. Political theory has no intrinsic value for him; its reason for being ends when labor permits persons to express in practical activity the freedom that political theory preserved alive as a critique of alienated labor.

At the beginning of the canon of political thought I have traced in this book, Plato placed political power in the hands of philosophers. Revolting against the canon, Marx places political power in the hands of the proletariat. Both claim universal status for their chosen vehicle, the philosophers because their very removal from social and economic life permits them the distance to *know* what justice is, the proletariat because their place at the bottom of the social ladder has made them suffer *injustice.*

In Marx's new social order there will no longer be any need for politics, since the class struggle, and hence injustice, will have been overcome. But until that day, neither politics nor political theory can be abolished. In fact for Marx, the *political* struggle over political theory—over the best interpretation of the status quo—remains vital to changing it. Marx means what he says: that philosophy should work toward abolishing its theories by realizing them. It is just that, in his time and no doubt in ours, much work remains to be done.

16

THE REVIVAL OF POLITICAL THEORY

History did not put an end to politics in the way Marx planned. In his own day, Marx opposed so-called left-wing adventurers bent on forcing a revolution on a people not yet ready for it. He warned that without popular preparation, socialist revolutions would spawn terror and reprise the fate of the French Revolution.[1] There can be little doubt that Marx would have regarded Bolsheviks, Leninists, and Maoists as latter-day Jacobins who did more to empower the state than abolish it.

Not revolutionary utopia but reactionary regimes, world wars, the Holocaust, terror, nuclear fear, and religious violence turned out to be in humanity's future. Politics remained, and sometimes seems destined to remain, deeply burrowed into Plato's cave. And yet, in hopes of shedding light into dark places, we comb the classics that have mapped that cave for so long. Such study need not be an act of despair or resignation; it can keep alive those criticisms and alternative visions which promise that all caves have exits.

Harking back to my own "From Plato to Marx" course in college, I remember fondly the respect my professors felt for the texts they passed on to us. Even today I feel the full force of their scholarly devotion to preserving the accumulated learning of the past. Reverence alone, however, can obscure that even the greatest of political philosophers is still making *political* arguments, open to response and lively debate. No political theory, however brilliant, can solve or leave behind the riddles of politics. Politics is a permanent part of the human condition.

Happily, political theory is in the midst of a great revival today. Without any loss of respect for the philosophical depth of the classical texts, we engage them once more to engage in political life. The study of political philosophy will always lead at first to that detour away from immediate political involvement which Plato took, carrying with him along the way the memory of Socrates' fate. But the detour need not trap us in the cave or release us only into some ivory tower. We study political arguments to make them, and to live by them.

The Rawlsian Revival

In our own time no one did more to keep the canon alive than John Rawls. Rawls's contribution is so immense and so likely to endure that it is not too early to say his writings now enter into the canon we pass on. When Rawls began his work on a theory of justice, the idea of a "social contract"—once so central to Hobbes, Locke, Rousseau, and Kant, among others—was close to moribund. Indeed, doubt surrounded the entire notion of "justice"—as if the mere fact that justice varies from place to place meant that there was no way to think rationally on the subject at all. This suspicion about justice was greatest when it came to claims about individual rights that might "exist" prior to law and form the basis for law's justice. The central paradigms in political science were adopted from economic analysis, with its preference for cost-benefit analysis, tradeoffs, and efficiency calculations of how best to maximize the overall or aggregate public welfare. From the economic point of view, rights were notoriously inefficient and an irrational obstacle to charting public policy so as to achieve benefits for the greatest number of persons. The same utilitarian paradigm dominated law schools, with legal scholars urging judges to abandon "rights talk" in favor of weighing the public policy costs and benefits of alternative decisions.

It was in such an atmosphere that Rawls began his revival of the core political theory tradition which had always "taken rights seriously," in Ronald Dworkin's phrase. But how to defend the notion of rights in an age when theological derivations of rights from divine law or even from what used to be called "natural law" were likely to be divisive from the start? In articles dating back to 1957 and 1958, Rawls began his lifelong attempt to unpack the basic meaning of "justice as fairness." According to Rawls, the basic intuition we share about the fairness of justice starts with—and largely ends with—a claim about fair *procedures*. What we are looking for is a decision rule, a procedure that permits persons who do not share *substantive* views on justice nonetheless to live together on terms that treat each person's views and values as equally worthy of re-

323

spect. Modern constitutional democracies, in Rawls's view, are marked by a "reasonable pluralism." The task of justice is to fashion a practical response to the irreducible diversity of reasonable ways of living.

To take one example, we may not agree on our ultimate moral values or life plans; we may be sharply divided when it comes to belief in a religion or any religion at all. A theory of justice cannot possibly resolve disputes among competing conceptions of the good life if it prefers the views and values of some over others. Rather, a theory of justice must bracket resolution of these ultimate substantive moral views—put aside any attempt to answer what is in fact good for human beings and accept that there will always remain a diversity of answers worthy of mutual respect.

This very bracketing, or refusal of the democratic state to arbitrate ultimate moral disputes, *is* what makes a decision rule or procedure right and fair. The fairness is the initial agreement to seek a purely procedural way out of our substantive differences. *If* there were a procedure that could generate agreement or consensus on basic social institutions—*without* siding with any one side's ultimate moral values—then the agreement reached would be fair and right by virtue of its ability to generate consensus across the diverse starting divides. In other words, we do not know beforehand *what* justice is, substantively speaking. And we do not have some independent, objective criterion against which to compare the agreement reached through the "bracketing" procedures. Instead, in what Rawls calls "pure procedural justice," the agreement reached through a fair or just procedure *is* just.[2]

Such an approach to justice obviously requires coming up with a persuasive account of what such a fair procedure for decision making among diverse peoples might be. And, in a testament to the continuing power of the canon to inspire, Rawls found his model in the idea of a social contract, of an initial meeting or constitutional convention where participants are charged with agreeing on the design of the basic social institutions. The brilliance of Rawls's achievement is to take a concept such as the social contract, which seemed so arcane and dated at the time, and give it fully modern dress.

Rawls begins by imagining an "original position" from which persons deliberate about the design of just social institutions. From the procedural point of view, the deliberation is likely to be fair and impartial only if done behind a "veil of ignorance." The veil keeps parties to the deliberations from knowing certain things about themselves or the positions they will occupy when the society is up and running. Thus persons do not know which natural talents they happen to have, physical or mental; they do not know whether they will end up rich or poor, in the majority or minority, healthy or disabled. They have no particular race, sex, or ethnicity but are "representative persons." Perhaps most crucially, they do not know what values they hold, what "concept of the good" stands at the center of their life.[3]

Psychologically, people in the original position are mutually disinterested with regard to one another. But precisely because they cannot know who they are to be once the society is up and running, they are motivated to consider the quality of life for the "least advantaged person" in that society. In other words, the veil of ignorance ratchets up the generality and impartiality of deliberations in the original position, *despite* the fact that persons do not start with interests in the welfare of others.

Here is Rawls's central argument with the Platonic tradition. Plato's *Republic* is founded on a particular conception of the good life, a notion that the philosopher kings know best and benignly enforce on a population that does not necessarily know what is good for them. But for Rawls, in modern constitutional democracies trying to find practical and fair ways to harbor diverse views about the good life, the state should remain strictly neutral as between these differing views. To elevate the moral preferences of some over those of others is to violate the fundamental right that persons have to equal respect for their capacity to choose their own ends in life.

Rawls has his own special vocabulary for explaining the place of his theory of justice in the history of political thought. For the Greeks, the "good" was "prior" to the "right"; that is, only if we *first* know what is morally good for persons and fulfilling of our human natures can we determine what rights persons have, what it means to treat them justly. But for the Kantian tradition of liberalism that Rawls seeks to illumine, the "right" precedes the "good." This priority of the right over the good is absolutely crucial for Rawls's vision of liberalism. A just state is a morally neutral state, and a morally neutral state is one founded on the bedrock principle of equal respect for the right of individuals to choose their own ultimate aims, ends, and aspirations in life, consistent with a like right for others.

Rawls's intuition is that if persons had to reason about justice from behind a veil of ignorance, they would agree on this core notion of equal respect. The veil of ignorance accomplishes for Rawls what the idea of the "general will" once did for Rousseau—and Rawls does all this while avoiding the controversial psychological claims that Rousseau made in postulating a general will. We become agents of disembodied reason, since we do not yet know which life in the flesh we are to lead, which among many permissible life plans we will pursue. We *do* know that there is a natural lottery, as it were, and that nature distributes skills and talents, physical prowess and mental intelligence, even industriousness and interests, differently and unequally. Knowledge of the fickleness of the natural lottery makes it rational for me to worry about my social fate should I happen to be unlucky at birth or born without the particular skills and talents society happens to value. As Rawls puts it, from the moral point of view, a person's natural talents are arbitrary, a matter of brute luck rather than attributes that one earns. Thus, behind a veil of ignorance, we each would reason in ways that cushion against bad luck in the natural lottery.[4]

As many commentators have pointed out, Rawls makes the rationally self-interested person decidedly "risk averse." Even though persons could calculate that the odds are against *their* happening to end up in the worst-off position, still the horror of such a fate is sufficiently grave as to preclude taking the risk at all. Here is the ingenious sleight of hand accomplished behind the veil of ignorance. I enter the deliberations worried only about my own individual situation. But precisely for that reason, I worry about the fate of the least advantaged person.

Rawls adds one qualification to this portrait of how mutually disinterested persons can nonetheless represent one another's interests. He takes it that a just society must have some direct interest in the fate of the next generation. Thus representative persons in the original position should think of themselves as heads of households, interested at least in the well-being of their immediate descendants.[5]

With these starting points Rawls then gets down to work. His core political claim is that persons in the original position would reach agreement on two fundamental principles of justice. The first principle is that "each person is to have an equal right to the most extensive total system of equal basic liberties compatible with a similar system of liberty for all."[6] Among the basic liberties Rawls names are the right to vote and to hold office; freedom of speech and assembly; liberty of conscience; freedom of thought; freedom of the person from psychological oppression and physical assault; the right to hold personal property; and freedom from arbitrary arrest, searches, and seizures.[7] The list is meant not to be exhaustive but to capture the basic rights and liberties that are foundational in a constitutional democracy.

In works subsequent to *A Theory of Justice,* Rawls made clear that he did not mean to defend his account of basic liberties as holding true universally. His aim is more limited and more political: to provide a persuasive account of the principles already implicit, however imperfectly, in our settled democratic convictions.[8] The problem with utilitarianism, according to Rawls, is that it cannot provide a satisfactory account of the "absolute first importance" democracies attach to the free and equal status of persons. Instead, utilitarian calculations justify tradeoffs, whereby the loss of a few persons' liberty is justified by greater liberties afforded the population as a whole. Or utilitarians may justify restrictions of liberty if they permit persons to enjoy greater economic advantages. But the principle of equal liberty is meant to rule out such tradeoffs between individual liberty and the general welfare. Basic liberties can be restricted only for the sake of liberty itself.[9]

The second principle of justice that persons in the original position would agree on has to do with democratic equality. Here Rawls meant to prod the liberal tradition in a far more egalitarian direction than those who preceded him had taken. Known as the "difference principle," the second principle states that "social and economic inequalities are to be arranged so that they are . . . to the greatest benefit of the least advantaged."[10]

Unlike the principle governing distribution of basic liberties, this second principle does *not* insist that income and wealth have to be distributed in equal shares. But Rawls does make the case that inequalities in wealth and property are justifiable only to the extent that they make "everyone better off" than they would be were property to be distributed in equal shares. This concern for *maximizing* the economic and social status of the *minimal* or least advantaged position in society grows from the nature of deliberation behind the veil of ignorance: when we imagine the society being founded as a going concern, we have to be able to "prefer [our] prospects with the inequality to [our] prospects without it."[11]

Clearly the difference principle is meant, once more, to rule out utilitarian defenses of inequality. Rawls is clear that "[o]ne is not allowed to justify differences in income or in positions of authority and responsibility on the ground that the disadvantages of those in one position are outweighed by the greater advantages of those in another."[12] Such utilitarian compensations could not possibly appeal to self-interested actors in the original position, worried that they might occupy the disadvantaged position. In this way persons in the original position would arrive at the core convictions of justice as fairness: that society is not a game with winners and losers but a joint venture or social union in which the fate and earnings of each is dependent on the social cooperation of others. No one has a moral claim to the skills and talents arbitrarily given her in the natural lottery; everyone is exposed to the social contingencies of family life and historical patterns. Economic justice for Rawls is a matter of mitigating the influence of social contingencies and natural fortune on the distribution of income and wealth.[13]

As to whether capitalism or socialism is a better way to meet the demands of economic justice, Rawls believes there is no one answer but that each might be preferable, depending on circumstances and the traditions of a particular society.[14]

One way to appreciate the significance of Rawls's views on equality is to contrast his difference principle with competing conceptions of equality. So-called meritocrats argue for only a formal equality of opportunity, in which careers and occupations lie equally open to talents. But for Rawls, such formal equality leaves persons' social fate to the arbitrariness with which nature distributes talents. Classical liberalism saw this difficulty and developed a principle of *fair* equality of opportunity, requiring society to give persons a fair and equal chance to develop their natural talents, by opening up education and other cultural assets to all regardless of their class. But while mitigating the effects of social position on opportunity, classical liberalism still left social fate to be buffeted by the luck of the draw in the natural lottery.[15] The difference principle distinctively offers what Rawls calls a "democratic" concept of equality—a concept that reflects the "intuitive idea . . . that the social order is not to establish and secure the more attractive prospects of those better off unless doing so is to the advantage of those less fortunate."[16]

Rawls's Significance

Rawls's theory at once had the merit of capturing our settled convictions in a constitutional democracy about fundamental rights and unsettling our views on equality. The significance of his achievement was recognized not only in academic circles but in the popular press as well, with the *New York Times* singling out *A Theory of Justice* as one of the ten most notable books of 1971—a rare designation for a work of academic political philosophy.

Just how much Rawls's approach to justice resonated with the times can be seen by considering the Supreme Court's 1973 decision in *Roe v. Wade*, finding that the right to choose an abortion is a fundamental liberty belonging to women. Justice Harry Blackmun did not refer to Rawls in his opinion for the Court, and I have no reason to believe that he had read *A Theory of Justice*. Nevertheless, his approach is a perfect illustration of the "bracketing strategy" and of the ideal of the morally neutral state. Justice Blackmun begins by taking note of the intractable moral controversy that abortion presents, depending as it does on ultimate and often theologically derived views about when human life begins. Justice Blackmun does not suggest that the Constitution resolves that ultimate moral debate; rather, in the name of due process of law, it brackets or puts aside that controversy in favor of leaving individual women free to choose according to their own moral convictions. Some women will elect abortion; others will continue a pregnancy. As between these competing choices, the state and law remain perfectly neutral. The state is neither pro-abortion nor anti-abortion. It is simply "pro-choice" in leaving the woman alone to make the decision.

Constitutional lawyers were quick to see that the Rawlsian ideal of the morally neutral state was implicit in a great number of civil liberties cases. In the area of free speech, the Supreme Court had long hewed to a principle of "content neutrality" that prohibited government from regulating speech on the basis of agreement or disagreement with the content, the substance, the message, the viewpoint of the speech. In cases about religion, a parallel principle of neutrality prohibited the state from acting in favor of one religion over another, or even on the basis of morally endorsing the value of religion over nonreligion. The same principle of neutrality explained core convictions about why race was generally irrelevant to government action: a just state never premises action on the basis of preferring one race over another. In sum, Rawls's ideal of the neutral state, devising fair procedures for permitting individuals to choose their own moral ends in life free from discrimination or favoritism, seemed to express theoretically what already was driving the practical resolution of legal disputes in a number of areas.

Rawls's difference principle did not square so readily with prevailing law, in which ordinary market transactions, even when they lead to vast accumulations of wealth while leaving others in poverty, do not trigger obligations to redistribute income. For a time, a number of prominent legal scholars turned to Rawls to craft novel constitutional arguments in favor of treating the right to welfare as a fundamental liberty on a par with other basic civil liberties.[17] But these arguments never convinced a majority of Supreme Court justices. Legal protection of the poor remains in the United States a matter for electoral politics to debate, not a fundamental matter of justice at the level of constitutional protection.

Interestingly, in a preface to the revised edition of *A Theory of Justice*, Rawls expresses the wish that he had more clearly declared his preference for a "property-owning democracy" over the idea of a welfare state. A welfare state protects persons passively, as it were, primarily by redistributing income to those with less. By contrast, a property-owning democracy seeks "to put all citizens in a position to manage their own affairs." It does this ideally by dispersing "the ownership of wealth and capital, and thus . . . prevent[ing] a small part of society from controlling the economy and indirectly political life itself."[18] For Rawls, welfare rights do not capture the ideal of fair equality of opportunity that justice requires; they compensate those who lose out without giving them the wherewithal to participate in society as free and equal citizens.

Critiques of Rawls

Rawls's influence on political philosophers has, not surprisingly, been greater than his influence on lawyers and the judiciary. It is hardly an exaggeration to say that all contemporary political theorists find it necessary to comment on Rawls.

For the most part I have avoided entering into discussions among academics, preferring to engage the classical writers directly. But as we move toward a conclusion, I want at least briefly to survey the way in which Rawls has become the fulcrum around which political theory turns today.

Some theorists—the libertarian Robert Nozick is a prime example—have argued that Rawls's theory of distributive justice wrongly empowers the state to override the property rights and entitlements of individuals. Turning back to Locke's theory of private property, Nozick conjured up an exquisite example of why the more limited power of the Lockean state over property was preferable to the constant interferences and redistributions of property a Rawlsian state would have to authorize. Let's suppose, says Nozick, that we are living in an ideal state of justice according to Rawls, where any inequalities in income distribution work to the benefit of the least advantaged person. But then what is life like in such a utopia? Presumably persons have preferences and enjoy the freedom to act on the basis of those preferences. So imagine that some persons enjoy watching basketball games and are willing to pay to watch those play who are lucky enough in the natural lottery to be talented basketball players. Suppose, further,

> that Wilt Chamberlain is . . . a great gate attraction [and] signs [a] contract [whereby] twenty-five cents from the price of each ticket of admission goes to him. . . . The season starts and people cheerfully attend his team's games; they buy their tickets, each time dropping a separate twenty-five cents of their admission price into a special box with Chamberlain's name on it. They are excited about seeing him play; it is worth the total admission price to them.[19]

At the end of the season, 1 million persons have attended the games, and Wilt Chamberlain has $250,000 in his pocket. (Nozick was writing in 1974; in 2008 the average salary of a professional player in the National Basketball Association was $5.3 million.) The initial Rawlsian distribution has been skewed, but it has been skewed by the free and voluntary choices of persons. *Liberty* has upset the pattern that Rawlsian justice seeks to maintain.

The initial distribution of property in a Rawlsian utopia could be maintained only by a politics of the Procrustean bed sort, a politics that twisted human behavior until it fit the pattern. Nozick offers the Wilt Chamberlain example to persuade us that voluntary property transfers do not threaten justice simply because they result in inequality. And Nozick is committed to saying this, regardless of whether the Wilts of the world end up with $250,000 or $250,000,000. From the historical point of view—the point of view we take when we follow good title passing from one person to another over time—transactions remains just, no matter how much they upset some "ideal" of how property ought to be distributed. For it is human beings who, by acting on their preferences, have disturbed Rawls's initial, utopian distribution of property. The mere fact that some become wealthy and others poor is no warrant for taking away from the Wilts what they are individually entitled to through their own efforts.

Whereas Nozick argued that Rawls was insufficiently protective of individual entitlements, others have argued that Rawls was too individualistic and insufficiently attentive to the virtues of belonging to a political community that sustains a common good and that makes self-government possible. In *Liberalism and the Limits of Justice*, Michael Sandel persuasively and eloquently argued that Rawls's theory of justice rested on a particular theory of the self that ultimately derives from Kant.[20] This is the view of the "unencumbered" or "disembodied" self, who attains a moral life precisely by detaching herself from the parochial influences of who she happens to be by birth or culture, or by the force of belonging to a particular religion or clan or tradition. Kantian freedom is a matter of the self conceiving of itself as fully migratory or portable, perpetually ready to pull up anchor and move on, should reason dictate it. As attractive as this view of autonomy is in some respects, Sandel finds it limited when it comes to shaping politics around the virtues of loyalty or allegiance, of sharing a common good with fellow citizens, of feeling implicated in a way of life that makes it possible for us to be the "embodied" or "situated" selves that real people always are.

Sandel makes his point by focusing on those passages in which Rawls speaks of the "self as prior to [its] ends."[21] What Rawls means by this difficult turn of phrase is that we enjoy a stable identity over time, even though we can change our life plans, abandon some ends or goals in life, and take on new purposes. For Rawls, the self's identity is wrapped up with its freedom to choose ends, and to choose new ends, and is not given or limited by the ends we happen to pursue at any one stage of life. Any constraint that anchors the self to ends not of the self's own choosing is a loss of freedom in this view.

For Sandel, such a self is incapable of forming and sustaining the binding attachments to others that in fact give definition and location to a self, make a particular lived life out of what would otherwise be a mere string of arbitrary choices. These deep and permanent attachments to others are the ones Sandel singles out as "constitutive attachments." They are those that are not just external to my personality but in fact enter into my makeup, make me the particular person I am. In her great rumination on nature in *Pilgrim at Tinker Creek*, Annie Dillard remarked that there are no trees in the world, only this tree or that one. This captures Sandel's point about all lives being embodied or situated lives. To find a self with no constitutive attachments is to find no self at all, or at least a shriveled and dwarfed self incapable of friendship and citizenship, incapable of feeling those bonds or loyalties to others that community life built on shared or common goods alone makes possible. Sandel's description of the virtues we attain only through deep attachment to a community harks back to Aristotle's comparison of the individual living apart from community being like a hand severed from the body.[22]

Sandel does not make the silly mistake made by others and accuse Rawls of having no sense of community at all. Rawls's egalitarianism resists the atomizing description of society as but a marketplace with winners and losers; it calls out our sense that society is a collective enterprise, that we are involved in a joint enterprise in which the advantaged owe their success as much to the cooperation of others as they do to their own efforts. But Sandel wants communities of a stronger sort than Rawls's emphasis on society as a cooperative or joint venture can deliver. It is one thing to see individuals as yoked by their mutual overlapping self-interests in maintaining schemes for social and economic cooperation. It is another to see individuals as forming one another's psyches, so implicated in sustaining their community life together—their particular traditions, customs, religions—that they stay put, stay at home, stay loyal, even when rational self-interest might lie elsewhere. Not every community, in fact very few, can rightfully claim this deeper moral obligation from its members. But Sandel argues that democratic communities in particular stand or fall on whether they can support constitutive attachments among citizens. For democracies are governments according to the common good. And the common good can thrive only when individuals have those virtues of abiding allegiance, loyalty, and solidarity that the Rawlsian person, ever open to choosing new ends and purposes in life, cannot attain.

Beyond Rawls, Sandel faults liberalism in general for two parallel reasons. First, the liberal state can never be as neutral in practice as its theory demands. Second, even if the ideal of a neutral state could be practiced, it would be singularly unattractive.

Sandel takes the abortion decision of *Roe v. Wade* to be an example of the first problem. *If* one happens to believe that the fetus is not yet a person, then the decision of the Court to let individual women make the decision as between abortion and pregnancy will seem perfectly fair. But *if* one believes that the fetus is already a human being, then permitting the individual woman to make a decision as to the life or death of another human being will hardly seem neutral: it will be seen as authorizing murder. Thus, whether one agrees with the decision in *Roe v. Wade* or not, Sandel's point is that the Supreme Court did not succeed in bracketing or remaining neutral on the underlying substantive moral dispute about how to balance respect for the woman and respect for the fetus. Rather, the very permission given the woman to choose is already a decision that tilts against the view of those who feel that the fetus must be respected as being already its own person.[23]

What is true about the abortion controversy is true about politics generally for Sandel: even the liberal state cannot stave off taking a stance on substantive moral disputes. And it is a good not a bad thing that liberalism cannot deliver on the promise of moral neutrality, since such a politics would be arid and demagogues would rush in to satisfy our human thirst for belonging. To take just one example, democratic politics cannot afford to be neutral between the value of an individual life plan based on satisfying the consumer in us and a life plan based on the value of calling out the citizen in us. Democracy requires at its very foundation the promotion of the civic virtues that alone give moral value to self-government. Without those civic virtues we get only crude or vulgar democracy: rule according to self-interest writ large. With those virtues we get rule according to the common good. To say as Rawls does that the state cannot prefer one life plan to another would be to erode the specific moral virtues that make democracy possible.

The political life of the "situated self" is also what Michael Walzer sets out to explore in his *Spheres of Justice*. The problem with Rawls's theory is a problem Walzer sees in any political philosophy that aspires to "walk out of the cave, leave the city, climb the mountain" in order to gain "an objective and universal standpoint."[24] The view from atop the mountain or the ivory tower is bound to lose sight of the "particularities" that always attach to political life. We always live in some actual city, not "in a utopia located nowhere," and the task of political theory is to make arguments to fellow citizens on the basis of the "world of meanings that we (already) share."[25] That these "shared understandings" are historically specific to a particular time and place, and not applicable everywhere, is a good thing for Walzer, not a cause of lament—as long as the understandings are indeed shared. It is the very specificity of the understandings that makes it possible for a people to share them in a meaningful way, to recognize them as their own, their human construction, and to argue for change from within a world toward which they feel special affinity and responsibility. In other words, the very fact that justice is a human and political construction is what makes democratic politics possible, once we see that a society is just only if it can be understood and appreciated as such by the persons who live in it.

But there "are an infinite number of possible lives, shaped by an infinite number of possible cultures, religions, political arrangements, geographical conditions, and so on." Pluralism *is* the political condition, and the justice of societies has to be judged internally for the most part, by its own members, arguing over whether a given arrangement for distributing goods is consistent with their shared understanding of the local principles for fair distribution. There "are no external or universal principles" that can replace the principles that are internal and implicit to a given society. Every account of how to distribute goods justly is, Walzer concludes, "a local account."[26]

Consider, for instance, contemporary debates in the United States over health care. Walzer has a political position: he argues that inequalities in income should not translate into inequalities in obtaining high-quality medical care. But in making this argument, he believes that he is merely reflecting back to his fellow citizens their own views about what counts as good reasons why a doctor should treat one patient before another. We (here in the United States) already share an understanding that the doctor should treat the sickest person first, not the richest. Walzer can imagine some other society organized on caste lines where persons understand justice differently and where the lower-caste members might conceivably share the view that all sorts of goods, from the harvest to medical care, must go to the purer castes first. But this only goes to show that all political argument is local; it does not alter the fact that, in the United States, the rich already understand that they are not a caste and that persons should not go without good medical care simply because they are too poor to afford it.

Consider another famous example Walzer gives to illustrate that all political argument is local. My generation came to political consciousness over Vietnam; but what the Vietnam War was to us, the French-Algerian war of the 1950s was to Walzer's generation. Long after that conflict ended, Walzer tended to ruminate about it. Both the French colonial forces and the Algerian rebels had the blood of innocents on their hands, and in this sense the war was a precursor of Vietnam. Given what it took for France to maintain its rule over Algeria, the justice of the French cause was difficult to make out. But suppose Algeria could have been turned into a liberal democracy without spilling any blood, without firing a shot—for instance, by dropping a magic political pill in the water supply? Would France then have been justified in determining Algeria's politics for Algerians? The answer for Walzer was still emphatically no. Even the value of liberal democracy is not a "universal" value sufficient to justify a colonial power in deciding the fate of another people. If Algerians were to become democrats, they would have to reach this understanding among themselves. For Walzer, there is no "original position" where "we" can go to decide the fate of "them."

Walzer did not mean his Algerian example to rule out the justice of all wars or humanitarian interventions abroad, but he did mean to set the bar high. The renegade state's aggression has to be so clear or its internal violation of human rights has to be so grave as to justify the international community in concluding that the people inside the renegade state consent to the intervention.

By the time Walzer, Nozick, and Sandel had contributed their critiques of Rawls, it was apparent that political theory was enjoying a rebirth, once more central to confronting actual political and legal questions, ranging from abortion to property rights, welfare reform, war, and humanitarian interventions. Rawls's sternest critics often tried to cabin him as "relevant only for American or at most Anglo-American audiences."[27] But this has hardly proved true. In Germany the significance of Jürgen Habermas is in part attributable to the way in which Habermas reflected on Rawls as part of his larger project for buttressing constitutional democracy in a post-Holocaust Germany. On many issues Habermas is quite distant from Rawls. Whereas Rawls emphasizes the autonomy of the self, Habermas emphasizes the ways in which an individual's identity is formed intersubjectively, in relation to others, and in the act of communication with and recognition by others. But he is at pains to consider Rawls's understanding of a constitutional democracy as one which is a "social union of social unions." That is to say, the democratic state is not *the* community or even *a* community in a strong sense of sharing common values. Nevertheless, it proves capable of supporting a shared sense of mission in a people when *what* they share is respect for the diversity of communities to which they may belong. Habermas understood the aptness of this version of liberalism for contemporary Germany.

In Israel, Yael Tamir's book *Liberal Nationalism* is an extended consideration of whether Rawls's basic paradigm of the "neutral state" is compatible with a state that has a particular conception of its mission regarding the Jewish people. In Greece, my fellow graduate student and longtime professor at the University of Athens, Pascal Kitromilides, has toiled out of the limelight, through periods of military rule, to make the Rawlsian case for civil liberties in Greece. I suspect that this pattern holds true for political argument throughout the newly emerging republics in eastern Europe and Asia, as Rawls provides inspiration for arguments about the drafting of constitutions from something arguably akin to an "original position."

In international relations, scholars such as Charles Beitz and Thomas Pogge began to think imaginatively about what the implications of Rawls's views on domestic justice might be for global justice. If the difference principle requires that economic inequalities work to the advantage of the least well-off person, should there be an "international" difference principle requiring distributions of wealth from nations with plenty to nations with little? So-called cosmopolitans have argued that international justice parallels domestic justice in limiting the extent of economic inequality among nations.

Interestingly, in his book *The Law of Peoples,* Rawls emphatically rejected the notion of an international difference principle and argued, more in line with Walzer, that justice imposes particular responsibilities at home toward those with whom one shares a politics which it does not impose on relations with those who are properly governed by their own politics.[28] If, for example, a nation makes theologically driven choices to protect a culture that inhibits the growth of business, the mere fact that such a nation is "worse" off economically than others is no grounds for requiring international redistributions of wealth. For Rawls, wealthy nations do owe a serious "duty of rescue" triggered by grave humanitarian disasters in another country, but this is a far cry from the more extensive income redistributions that nations should practice domestically.

For the same reasons that liberal democracies at home grant equal respect to the differing life plans of citizens, they should respect the diversity of ways in which societies abroad organize their politics, even when those politics are not liberal or democratic. Rawls's point was that societies can be decent and well ordered without being liberal democracies of our sort. As long as a state is peaceful and not expansionist, and has a legal system that honors basic human rights and is seen as legitimate by its own people, then international law should honor the sovereignty of that state and welcome it into international society.[29]

Some societies, however, are "outlaw states" whose sovereignty international law need not recognize. The difference between an outlaw state and an illiberal but decent state comes down to this: both societies may reject the notion that all citizens are free and equal. But in a decent society, those who are not respected as equals are still tolerated, and their views and needs are taken into consideration. In an outlaw society, even this basic tolerance of reasonable ways of living, other than the approved way, is lacking.

The Straussian Alternative

The great dissent from acknowledgment of Rawls's singular importance comes from those political theorists who trace an intellectual debt to Leo Strauss. So-called Straussians have been much in the news in recent years, thanks to rather silly media hyperbole about how many of President George W. Bush's key advisers came out of the Straussian camp. These accounts were silly insofar as they reduced Strauss's complicated teachings to an ideology the press liked to call "neoconservatism." And then just as Socrates was once held responsible for every wrong committed by his pupil Alcibiades when the student became an Athenian general, so too Strauss was somehow responsible for the advice his pupils (more accurately the pupils of his pupils) gave to the president about the war on terror.

The in-house disputes between academics who studied with Rawls or with Strauss is of little interest to anyone but the academics involved. But I do want to say something about Strauss's considerable achievement. Strauss was a prolific writer, but his writings cohere around reviving ancient political theory as a way of exposing the dead end he thought modern rationalism, across the board, reaches, done in by its own worst impulses. By rejecting the concept of natural right as the ancients understood it, modern philosophy and especially social science convey a dangerous moral relativism that is said to threaten nihilism. For the ancients, nature provided an objective and enduring standard of justice against which to judge laws and governments. Plato and Aristotle taught that men, or at least some men, can "acquire . . . genuine knowledge of what is intrinsically good or right." But for moderns, according to Strauss, law is merely positive: its authority derives from the mere fact that it has been legislated. No principle is inherently true, and everything is seen as merely a product of circumstance. History supposedly teaches us that "all principles of justice are mutable," that any value is relative to some passing moment, some ephemeral stage of culture or civilization. Contemporary thought is thus bound to Plato's cave in inescapable ways; the idea that political philosophy can transcend its time in history and apprehend transcendental truths is regarded as mythic.[30]

Strauss paid particular attention to the reigning "fact/value" distinction in modern social science. Ever since Max Weber, social scientists have aspired to make their inquiries "value neutral." A scholar studying the sociology of religion has no business evaluating the worth of the religion; she should limit herself to offering factual knowledge about things that can be scientifically known, such as the causes and effects that various religious ideas have had in history. But as to evaluating the worth of the ideals themselves, this is said to be a subject that reason cannot tackle. There are, and always will remain, a variety of ultimate values. The choice among those values is apparently subjective and nonrational; there is supposedly nothing that reason or science or philosophy can do to make value choices any less arbitrary than they are, a matter of personal preference in the end. Thus in precisely the ways Rawls epitomizes, a student of society and politics is supposed to "bracket" value questions from the factual questions that exclusively can be made a subject of rational inquiry.

For Strauss, this view of values as merely personal preferences leads modernity to its characteristic predicament. While we can have knowledge of things of lesser import, "we have to be resigned to utter ignorance in the most important respect: we cannot have any knowledge regarding the ultimate principles of our choices, i.e., regarding their soundness or unsoundness; our ultimate principles have no other support than our arbitrary and hence blind preferences."[31]

The core purpose in studying ancient political theory is to recover the possibility of asking the question what is truly or inherently or intrinsically good for human beings. But here Strauss's approach to political theory was distinctive in two further regards. He taught that many of the greatest works of political theory were deliberately obscure or esoteric, written in ways that distinguish the surface meaning offered to the public from deeper and hidden meanings. These meanings are not meant to be discovered by the many or to serve as blueprints for political change; they will always be the province of the few, and they will always leave unresolved a tension between politics and philosophy, between the "opinions" that rule politics and the genuine knowledge that philosophy spies only when it scrambles out of the cave and into the light.

In *Spheres of Justice*, Walzer described himself as meaning "to stand in the cave, in the city, on the ground," so as to better observe the particular contours that everyday politics takes. For Walzer, the task of the political theorist is to enter that fray, not to transcend it in favor of apolitical speculation about a "utopia located nowhere."[32] In *Natural Right and History*, Strauss writes that "philosophizing means to leave the cave." The quest of the political philosopher is "for the natural or best political order." One cannot join that quest except by transcending "what is actual here and now"—indeed moving "beyond all actual orders."[33] Philosophy must remove itself from the actual city, since politics can never be fully rationalized, and reason can protect itself only by retreating to higher ground. The contrast between Walzer's and Strauss's competing conceptions of why we study the history of political thought could not be more stark.

Strauss died in 1973 and did not personally engage with Rawls, but his students and successors have. In essence they see Rawls's recommendation that we "bracket" or "put aside" our substantive moral differences as but the latest version of moral relativism about values. Rawls's veil of ignorance famously kept people from knowing what their concept of a good life was. But for followers of Strauss, Rawls's veil gave new meaning to the phrase "justice is blind."

Feminism and Rawls

Shortly after *A Theory of Justice* came out, I began graduate school and had the great good luck to have Susan Moller Okin as my classmate. Susan and I went on to become colleagues and friends and indeed shared for nearly fifteen years the teaching of the very course from which this book flows. As Rawls's reputation grew, Okin joined the praise and yet pointed out to me, and to anyone else who would listen, that the book was strangely silent on questions of justice most pertinent to women— namely, those about power, property, status, and equality *within* the family. In fact, although one could assume that sex was one of the features persons in the original position did not know about themselves, Rawls did not explicitly include it on the list of attributes to be kept in the dark. He did say that persons in the original position should see themselves as "heads of households," so that they would take into consideration the interests of the next generation. But when he talked about intergenerational concerns, he typically spoke of fathers and sons; Okin thought this raised a concern as to whether Rawls was simply letting stand in the background an assumption that the household head in the original position was a man.

All this surprised me since, unlike most classical political theorists who either ignored family governance or else considered it a private domain where ties are based on love rather than justice, Rawls acknowledged that families are among the basic social institutions to which the public demands of justice apply. He emphasized that persons' life prospects were greatly affected by what happens to them in their families. And since a well-ordered society depends for its stability on members having "a strong and normally effective desire to act as the principles of justice require," Rawls knew how important it was that the family, as the place where children develop morally and learn their sense of justice, be itself just.[34]

Okin's point was that the very importance Rawls attached to the family should have led him to more critical examination of the *internal* dynamics of family life. Specifically, Okin faulted Rawls for not applying his two principles of justice to family governance. She set out to do just that, and to uncover the latent "critique of gender-structured social institutions" that Rawls's principles gesture toward, even though he stopped short of making the demands. For instance, one of the core liberties persons would choose to protect in the original position is the important liberty of "free choice of occupation." To apply *that* principle to family life would radically undermine the customary expectation that child care and household work are the obligations of the woman, not the man. Or since self-respect is "perhaps the most important primary good" that children need to develop if they are to have fair opportunities in life, Rawls's principles demand reform if the evidence is clear that gendered roles in the family undermine or at least corral the confidences of little girls from the beginning.[35] Finally, in line with Rawls's difference principle, Okin noted that inequalities of income and property between spouses have worked to the *disadvantage* of the woman; this alone called into question the fairness of traditional family arrangements, especially when it came to divorce.

It is hard to reconstruct now the heady excitement of that period when feminists began to take on Rawls and to point out the incompleteness of the liberal project when it came to issues of gender and equality. I can give personal testimony to the fact that many scholars scoffed at Okin's relentless—and it was relentless—insistence on making gender a central issue in political argument. But Rawls was not among them; instead he welcomed Okin's comments in particular as giving him hope that "a liberal account of equal justice for women is viable." Rawls acknowledged that he should have been more explicit in *A Theory of Jus-*

tice that any decent liberal state rests on "equal justice for women as well as for men."[36] But he disagreed with Okin about what a liberal theory of family life entailed. Specifically he rejected the notion that political principles of justice should apply to the *internal* life of families. The liberal state typically does not seek to govern the internal life of many associations, such as religious organizations, labor unions, or professional organizations. But this does not mean, say, that bishops can do anything they want to parishioners. Parishioners remain citizens even when they join a house of worship; and the religious group must respect the rights that members have as citizens.

The same holds true, Rawls suggests, for the relation between state and family. Since "wives are equally citizens with their husbands, they have all the same basic rights, liberties, and opportunities as their husbands." To this extent the principles of political justice do apply to families and constrain what kinds of family practices are just. But we would not—or so Rawls would have it—want to go further and politically regulate the internal lives of spouses or of parents and children. That would stifle the "free and flourishing internal life appropriate" to family life. For instance, although children have rights against abuse or neglect, and to this extent the state intervenes, we would not want politics to prescribe generally how parents should raise their children. At that point politics is out of place, and we do better "to rely on the natural affection and goodwill of the mature family members."[37]

But not too much. Rawls acknowledged that the adult members of families are "equal citizens" first and that this status trumps any independence family life otherwise enjoys. Here, acknowledging his debt to Okin and other writers who had made the case, Rawls acknowledged just how much tension exists between the woman as equal citizen and the woman as unpaid household worker:

> A long and historic injustice to women is that they have borne, and continue to bear, an unjust share of the task of raising, nurturing, and caring for children. When they are even further disadvantaged by the laws regulating divorce, this burden makes them highly vulnerable. . . . Mill held that the family in his day was a school for male despotism. . . . If so, the principles of justice enjoining a reasonable constitutional democratic society can plainly be invoked to reform the family.[38]

One concrete suggestion that both Rawls and Okin came to agree on is that, in a traditional marriage in which the wife bears the bulk of raising the children and managing the household, this unpaid work should legally entitle her to an equal share of the income her husband earns during the marriage.

Rawls died in 2002, Okin unexpectedly in 2004. I think it would have pleased them both to see how liberal ideas about family life have a way of working themselves purer over time. In an earlier era, miscegenation laws prohibiting interracial marriages were exposed for what they were: examples of rank prejudice. Today a similar transformation is taking place regarding gay and lesbian couples. Traditionally marriage has been reserved to heterosexual couples. By why should this be? Some argue that the purpose of marriage is procreation and hence that gay and lesbian couples are excluded for relevant reasons. But marriage is available to infertile heterosexual couples or even where one person is on a deathbed, so absence of procreative ability is not always a barrier to marriage. (A student once movingly related that her priest had assured her that she could be married under the sacraments of the church, despite the fact that an operation had removed her cancerous ovaries.)

Putting aside the procreation argument, opponents of same-sex marriage argue that limiting marriage (and adoption) to opposite-sex couples is in the best interests of any children they might have or adopt. But here the best response is the one Rawls made near the end of his life.[39] The question we need to ask is whether there are nonprejudicial reasons to think that gay and lesbian couples cannot love equally with heterosexual couples, or achieve orderly family life, or nurture and raise children to ensure their moral development, education, and entrance into the wider culture. Unless there are reasons to think that only the traditional arrangements can accomplish these purposes, then the principle of equal liberty prods acceptance for the justice of forms of family life beyond the customary arrangements.

It is instructive to see how actual political debates over gay rights mirror the intellectual debate between Rawls and his progressive critics. Some advocates of gay rights adopt Rawls's recommendation that we should bracket our substantive moral differences over whether gay sexuality is good or bad and simply agree to leave persons alone to express their different sexual orientations. Others argue that tolerance is not enough, that genuine change waits on public *respect* for the lives gays and lesbians lead. In this view, only by engaging directly with the underlying moral argument about sexual orientation can fundamental change come about.

I would not be so naïve as to suggest that those who make these arguments are busy studying political theory. This is not the way politics works. But it is a sign of how vital political theory is today that it captures and illumines the ongoing struggles that give politics its stunning importance.

THE PASSION FOR POLITICS

Throughout this book I have referred to the classic works of political theory as forming a "canon." By this term I mean only to point out that a tradition has been passed on for a very long time now, connecting contemporary reflection on politics with ruminations and rumblings from the past. Machiavelli was as aware as any political thinker could be of what was new in his Florentine world. Still he was better able to grasp what was changing around him by understanding that some features of politics and violence endure. Hobbes sought remedies for an England wracked by religious civil war. But he deepened his insights into the ills of his own time by making a study of how his predecessors sought peace in theirs. Rousseau was torn between admiration for the spartan lifestyle of his native Geneva and for the luxuries available in his adopted Paris. Yet he could see how the choice between ascetic Geneva and aesthetic Paris was recurrent in political history, traceable back to the choice that Greeks made between taking Sparta or Athens for their model. Rawls set out to clarify the specific, modern concept of justice in liberal democracies. But he found that our own political values come best into focus— indeed become the best they can be—when viewed as expressing the ideal of a social contract handed down from Hobbes to Locke to Rousseau to Kant.

I do not know why this particular tradition, building on Plato's study upon his own teacher, took root and survived. I do not claim that it is the only or the best tradition available to us. There are no monopolies on wisdom, and new traditions are capable of sprouting up just as old traditions sometimes should be abandoned. But I have tried to capture in this book what I have been privileged to tend in the classroom. Students already know that politics matter, in the material sense. But that politics matter in the moral sense; that politics can call out the best as well as the worst in us; that politics can make us hope as well as fear—these are issues that awaken imagination to think beyond the givens of the status quo.

A canon lives only so long as it sustains a conversation between the new and the old. There is always going to be some sense—good sense—in which to read Plato or Augustine or Machiavelli is to enter an unfamiliar world, a political world of city-states, empires, gods, Caesars, natural rights, codes of honor, and aristocratic norms. Even as we turn and return to the classical works of political theory to puzzle over enduring political dilemmas, we should resist any temptation to dismiss all that is strange, distant, and unfamiliar. Indeed it is often the very "foreignness" of the classical writers that first shakes us up by confronting prevailing wisdom with truly challenging and unsettling alternatives.

But if the canon is taught only as if it were a foreign language, then the *political* is drained from the confrontation. What remains is important and interesting—but only in the way that doing preservation work for a museum or historical site is important and interesting. About the United States Constitution, judges frequently say that it is a "living Constitution" which they are asked to interpret, even to perfect. The canon of political thought is equally a living tradition. We read the classical authors best when we argue with them, just as Aristotle argued with Plato, or Rousseau took on Hobbes, or Marx confronted Hegel. We owe the great thinkers of the past due deference for their deep insights. But we should not worship them or think that their arguments are beyond debate.

This book is based on lectures I have been giving to undergraduates for many years now. I have tried to cull from my experience those passages and examples that seemed to work best when it came to awakening first interests in political theory. But addressing as I do now a wider audience, I have attempted to combine a concern for how best to introduce young persons to political theory with attention to how to persuade those with wider political experience of the importance of reflecting once again on the great works of political philosophy.

In the classroom, written lectures do not work well; they are too rehearsed to spark the spontaneity that informal exchanges can provide. The texts remain the same each year, but politics changes in ways that suddenly make previously neglected passages rich with meaning. One year students take to Plato; other years they are Aristotelians all. After September 11, Machiavelli was their man and the problem of dirty hands was no longer a mere academic issue.

In this book I have tried to write down my thoughts on the classics while still maintaining something of an informal conversation with the reader. Politics will burst the bounds of that conversation; new examples will be needed even to make familiar points. But I hope that the passion for political argument that we learn by studying the classic texts will remain and make it imperative to bring those arguments out of the cave and into the light.

In all the years I have been teaching and writing, there has always been a war raging or imminent, a scandal brewing, corruption mounting, and just plain old mistakes and incompetences marching on. Reading the classics of philosophy, with their emphasis on ideals and the moral high ground, is difficult against the common discontent we feel with politics, whatever our partisan leanings. It used to be that I could ask students to name a politician in power who inspired them and they would have candidates. But until President Obama's election, the last person who sparked unreserved enthusiasm was Nelson Mandela. Apart from these exceptions, students, like most of us, have been quick to express disenchantment with the failures of those they once admired to deal with HIV, hunger, terrorism, poverty, global warming, discrimination, domestic violence—the list of foibles and failures is long, the list of persons who inspire us to make a political effort is small.

Given the common discontent with politics, my guess is that readers of this book will remember those passages in the texts that accentuate what goes wrong in the state: Plato's parable of the cave in particular, Hobbes's insistence that only the sword keeps people in line, Athens's decision to execute Socrates, Socrates' lament for the unbridgeable chasm separating law from justice, Machiavelli's wry note that fear is a stronger political emotion than love, Machiavelli's further acceptance of the inescapable presence of cruelty and violence in politics, Hobbes's sacrifice of liberty for security, Marx's attack on the ideological underbelly of political theory itself.

But what about political ideals, about the possibility that politics can go well? I find every year in the classroom many realists interested in learning how to get the job done, in Iraq or Afghanistan or elsewhere in the Middle East. I find a respectable number of activists who love talking about electoral strategy and what the candidate of their choice must do, or not do, to win the hearts and minds of the people. But I find precious few idealists who believe that justice actually matters. I can get students to agree with Thrasymachus easily enough, that self-interest rules politics. This does not have to make them skeptical about political life. For instance, the Thrasymachean student can get quite excited about using the leverage of money or arms to change the way great powers calculate what is in their national interests. But can ideals change the behavior of great powers? Few emerge from the study of political theory with a belief that justice has independent or even substantial influence over human affairs.

I suggest that there are two different but allied reasons why it is difficult for us to mount much enthusiasm for the study of political ideals. The first and familiar problem is that we are bound to fall short of reaching our ideals, whatever they may be. This seems to be the nature of politics—that we can never quite practice what we preach, that too much idealism renders us politically impotent. It seems much as Machiavelli said, that those who would make a profession of goodness had better not make politics their profession. Socrates said much the same thing in explanation of why he avoided political life. In his famous *Letter VII,* Plato drew a similar conclusion, that he was too idealistic ever to be a successful politician. And it is a good thing, some say, that we not try to put our ideals in practice. Many a war fought to make the "world safe for democracy" has been humbled by the messiness of facts on the ground.

This objection to the impossibility of ever fully practicing our ideals—and the danger of thinking that we can—is a strong one. It harks back to Aristotle's dissent from Plato's utopianism and his gentle reminder that politics is often the art of the possible, not the perfect. But I doubt that practical obstacles to implementing our ideals fully explain the common discontent with politics today. I suggest that there is a second difficulty, and this is that we are not clear to begin with about what our political ideals are.

One way of expressing this second difficulty is to acknowledge that political ideals are . . . political. Liberals and conservatives famously disagree about what the ideals of equality and liberty are, even if they use the same names. But there seems no end to their disagreement, no way to arbitrate it. Students introduced to political theory often come away from their readings with the attitude that "if all these great minds couldn't agree on what justice requires, then who am I to offer an opinion?"

This second difficulty is one that surprises us. After all, it should not be hard to state what our ideals are. We can certainly name them; equality, liberty, and democracy come immediately to mind. But what is the moral case as to why democracy is the best regime? What answer to give to Plato's relentless attack on the total difference between public opinion and justice? Debates over equality are even more perplexing: what to say to those who justify wide social and economic inequality in the name of rewarding talent and merit; what to do with those who condemn the same inequalities as the product of historically inherited advantages and just plain old luck? The great merit of political theory is that it confronts us with alternate visions of what our political ideals ought to be. Even before we get to the practical difficulties in implementing our ideals, we face the conceptual difficulty of knowing what our beliefs are, what vision of a just society it would be worth braving practical obstacles to realize.

I often form the impression that it is this conceptual confusion that cuts youthful idealism off at the pass. Like all of us, young people get confused as to whether there is anything more to one's ideals than one's own opinions, take them or leave them. Actual politicians are of limited help here. They reduce expressions of political ideals to the level of platitudes. Appeals to ideals are often so empty and so transparently manipulative that it is no wonder they leave us dry and disenchanted. Or maybe it is more the case that the idealistic politician first enchants us, then leaves us dry. The harder one believes politically, the farther one has to fall.

Author and reader do not meet face-to-face in the way teacher and student do. In the classroom, every once in a while—not during every lecture by any means—I see a light go on in some student's eyes. This student leans forward to hear more about Plato's noble lie, almost as if ideas have to be muscularly wrestled to the ground. That student scrunches up her face, hinting at a struggle to understand Aristotle on proper pride and whether she might be underestimating her own worth in the way Aristotle described. I have the feeling most years that many students recognize Hobbes's description of life trapped inside a rat race, as we continually chase down desires only to get somewhere else, but when we get there, we find it is not our destination but in turn only a jumping-off place to get somewhere else, and so on and so on. The arguments we inevitably have over whether religious persons convinced of the truth of their religion can tolerate religions they believe to be false—this seems to interest many and to shed light on the current world situation. How to defend the general right of individual adults to choose their own pleasures in life and yet draw limits to freedom of choice—this too seems to get intellectual motors running.

Of course there are plenty of dry and boring stretches in studying political theory; I do not mean to pretend otherwise. Almost all political philosophers offer a catalogue of regimes—monarchies, aristocracies, oligarchies, republics, democracies, and tyrannies. But it is difficult for us any longer to peruse that catalogue or go shopping for regimes; we are committed to democracy, and asking for a defense of democracy's superiority seems a bit like asking for a defense that the earth is round—an idle and silly academic exercise.

That even good students, and attentive readers, get bored with political theory neither surprises nor bothers me. Some of my colleagues say that students have gotten worse today, that they are too worried too early about their careers and making a living, that they have no patience for subjects such as political theory that promise no return on their investment. These colleagues remember some golden age of teaching that never existed, some state of nature of purely innocent students insulated from the pressures of the world.

Students and teachers come and go; the knowledge we pass on, and sometimes create, will be debated, criticized, challenged, protected, and enriched by those who come after us. I like to think, in Locke's terms, that we have left "as much and as good" to future generations of teachers and students as we received from those who preceded us. Politics will change, for better and for worse, as it always does, and the canon will have to change along with the events it seeks to illumine. But sometimes the best way to appreciate what is new is to study the old. Hegel remarked in resignation, about the tragic lateness of philosophy, that the "owl of Minerva" flies only at dusk, giving us a grasp on the politics we have been practicing only when it is about to fade from the scene. But this might not be as sad a remark as it seems. It suggests that only being alive to the new makes wisdom about the old possible in the first place. Teachers probably are not capable of that bridging wisdom, but students are, always are.

NOTES   ACKNOWLEDGMENTS   INDEX

INTRODUCTION

1. Plato, "Letter 7," in *The Collected Dialogues of Plato,* ed. Edith Hamilton and Huntington Cairns (New York: Pantheon, 1961), pp. 1574—75.

2. *Collected Dialogues,* p. 1575.

3. *Collected Dialogues,* pp. 1575—76.

4. G. W. F. Hegel, *Philosophy of Right,* trans. T. M. Knox (Oxford: Oxford University Press, 1967), sec. 138.

I. PLATO'S *REPUBLIC*

1. Plato, *The Republic,* trans. Allan Bloom (New York: Basic Books, 1968), 1.327a–328a. All citations refer to this edition.

2. 1.328a.

3. 1.328c–d.

4. 1.328c

5. 1.329d.

6. 1.329e.

7. 1.330d.

8. 1.331b.

9. 1.331c.

10. 1.331d.

11. 1.332b.

12. 1.334c.

13. 1.334d.

14. 1.335b.

15. 1.336a.

16. 1.335c.

17. 1.336b.

18. 1.337a.

19. 1.338c.

20. 1.339c–e.

21. 1.340b.

22. 1.340c.

23. 1.341c–342d.

24. 1.343a.

25. 1.343c–344c.

26. 1.346b–347a.

27. 1.342e.

28. 1.351c.

29. 1.350a–d.

30. Plato, *Gorgias,* in *The Collected Dialogues of Plato,* ed. Edith Hamilton and Huntington Cairns (New York: Pantheon, 1961), 493e.

31. The quotation actually comes from John Stuart Mill in his essay on Bentham; see Mill's *Utilitarianism, On Liberty, and Essay on Bentham,* ed. Mary Warnock (New York: New American Library, 1974), p. 123.

2. THE STUDENTS REVOLT AGAINST UTOPIA

1. *Republic* 2.357a–358d.

2. 5.474d.

3. 2.357c.

4. 2.358a.

5. 2.358e–359a.

6. 2.359a.

7. 2.359d–360d.

8. 2.360b.

9. Cf. 2.361a–d for Glaucon's sardonic argument that the "reputation" for justice is the good, not the actual doing of justice.

10. 2.362e–367e.

11. 2.369a.

12. In the *Statesman,* Plato puts the advice in the words of a "Stranger" in conversation with a young Socrates. In the *Laws,* Socrates is entirely absent.

13. *Republic* 2.372d.

14. 2.370b.

15. 2.372c.

16. 2.373a.

17. 2.373d.

18. 5.469c, 469e, 471b.

19. 2.375a.

20. 2.375b.

21. 2.375b–c.

22. 2.375b.

23. Over the years I have asked students to list some contemporary English usages of the word "spirit." Here is the list I have compiled: alcoholic spirits, school spirit, public spiritedness, spirit of a nation, spirit of the age, the *Spirit of St. Louis* (Lindbergh's airplane), esprit de corps, ghostly spirits, spirited horses, a spirited effort, lifting someone's spirits.

24. *Republic* 4.440a.

25. Benedict Carey, "The Fame Motive," *New York Times,* August 12, 2006, p. D1.

26. *Republic* 5.451d–452a.

27. 5.454c.

28. 5.455c–e.

29. Cf. Martha Minow, "Living up to the Rules: When Should Soldiers (and Others?) Disobey Orders," Harvard Law School lecture, February 22, 2006.

30. *Republic* 10.620c. I owe coming to this passage to I. F. Stone, *The Trial of Socrates* (New York: Anchor Books, 1989), p. 36.

31. *Republic* 6.501a.

32. 2.377c.

33. 3.386c.

34. 2.378a.

35. 3.388a, 391c.

36. 3.401d.

37. Allan Bloom, *The Closing of the American Mind* (New York: Simon and Schuster, 1987), pp. 68–81.

38. *Republic* 5.452b.

39. 3.391c.

40. 4.416a–417b.

41. 4.419a.

42. 4.424a.

43. 5.449c.

44. 5.460b–d.

45. 5.460d–461b.

46. 5.460c.

3. OUT OF THE CAVE AND INTO THE LIGHT—AND BACK AGAIN?

1. Plato, *Protagoras,* in *The Collected Dialogues,* ed. Edith Hamilton and Huntingdon Cairns (New York: Pantheon, 1961), 322c to 323b–c. My attention was first drawn to the importance of this passage by reading I. F. Stone, *The Trial of Socrates* (New York: Anchor Books, 1989), pp. 47–48.

2. *Republic* 4.414b.

3. 5.474c–475c.

4. 5.475a, 6.499b.

5. 5.476b.

6. 5.476d.

7. 5.478e–480a.

8. 7.514a–517a.

9. One cartoon a student gave me had three frames. In the first, two persons are trapped in a box with one saying to the other, "Did you ever think that we might be trapped inside a box?" In the second, one laughs at the insanity of the other as he literally begins to climb the walls. Meanwhile, we see in the last frame a vast Gar-

den of Eden outside the box. In the 1990s many of my students were certain that a then current movie, *The Matrix,* was inspired by Plato's cave. In this science-fiction thriller, robots have taken over the world and enslaved humans. Since the robots need to extract fluids from humans to run their batteries, they have hooked up humans to vast womblike structures that extract the necessary fluids. Only the humans do not know they are in these cocoons; the robots have programmed them into a virtual reality that gives them the illusion of being elsewhere in an active and happy life. The plot centers on how humans, who think of virtual reality as if it were *real* reality, could learn to tell the difference.

10. *Republic* 6.488a–489a.

11. *Republic* 8 and 9.

12. 8.545d.

13. 8.546b.

14. 8.547b.

15. 8.549c–550c.

16. 8.550e.

17. 8.551a–b.

18. 8.553a–e.

19. 8.551d.

20. 8.557d.

21. 8.557b.

22. 8.557a.

23. 8.558c.

24. 8.559d–561e.

25. 8.559d, 564e–565a.

26. 8.565c.

27. 8.564a.

28. 9.571a–572b.

29. 9.571c.

30. 9.572e–573a, 574d–575a.

31. 9.573b.

32. 9.579b.

33. 9.575e–576a.

34. 9.577–578.

35. 9.580c.

36. J. S. Mill, *Utilitarianism,* ed. Oskar Piest (Indianapolis: Bobbs-Merrill, 1957), p. 14.

37. *Republic* 9.582a–d.

4. BEYOND PLATO'S TRAGIC REPUBLIC

1. For a general statement of Shklar's political theory, see her essay "The Liberalism of Fear," in Judith N. Shklar, *Political Thought and Political Philosophers,* ed. Stanley Hoffman (Chicago: University of Chicago Press, 1998), pp. 3–20.

2. *Republic* 10.614b.

5. ARISTOTLE'S *ETHICS*

1. Aristotle, *Nicomachean Ethics*, trans. Terence Irwin (Indianapolis: Hackett Publishing Company, 1985), 1.1095a5–10. Hereafter cited as *Ethics*. All citations refer to this edition.

2. *Ethics* 1.1095a3–4. I should note that the old do not exactly get praised by Aristotle, either. If young people are excessively experimental, old people have "soured" on life and cannot count even on making new friends. *Ethics* 8.1158a5.

3. Aristotle, *The Politics*, trans. Ernest Barker, rev. R. F. Stalley (Oxford: Oxford University Press, 1995), 2.1264a1. All citations refer to this edition.

4. *Politics* 2.1267a2.

5. "[F]or actions expressing virtue to be done temperately or justly. . . , it does not suffice that they are themselves in the right state. Rather, the agent must also be in the right state when he does them. First, he must know [that he is doing virtuous actions]; second, he must decide on them, and decide on them for themselves; and third, he must also do them from a firm and unchanging state." *Ethics* 2.1105a30.

6. Maria Merritt, "Aristotelean Virtue and the Interpersonal Aspect of Ethical Character," *Journal of Moral Philosophy* 6, no. 1 (2009): 1–27.

7. W. F. R. Hardie, *Aristotle's Ethical Theory* (Oxford: Oxford University Press, 1968), p. 104, cited ibid., p. 7, n. 14.

8. *Ethics* 10.1179b15.

9. 2.1105a5.

10. 2.1103b22–25.

11. 1.1095b20–21.

12. 1.1096a5–7.

13. 1.1094b15–20.

14. 8.1155b5.

15. *Politics* 7.1332b12.

16. *Ethics* 2.1109a25–30.

17. 3.1115a30–35.

18. 3.1116a30.

19. 3.1116b1.

20. 3.1117b20.

21. 1.1110a3–1111b20.

22. *Ethics* 4.1119b25–1120a20.

23. 4.1120b10, 1120b10.

24. *Politics* 2.1263a40.

25. *Ethics* 4.1121b10–15.

26. 4.1121b20–25.

27. 4.1122a5–15.

28. 4.1123b3–5.

29. 4.1123b5.

30. 4.1123b10.

31. 4.1123b3.

32. Winston Churchill, *The Second World War,* vol. 1, *The Gathering Storm* (Boston: Houghton Mifflin Company, 1986), p. 601.

33. *Ethics* 3.1117b25.

34. 3.1119a15–20.

35. 3.1119a5–10.

36. *Politics* 2.1262a40.

37. *Ethics* 4.1125b30–1126a15.

38. 4.1125b30–35.

39. 8.1155a5.

40. 8.1156a15.

41. 8.1156a30–1156b5.

42. 8.1156b3.

43. 9.1165b15–20.

44. 9.1165b30–35.

45. 3.1116a20–25.

46. My attention was first drawn to the literature on the significance of Milgram's experiments for Aristotle's ethics by Maria Merritt during a seminar at the Edmond J. Safra Center for Ethics at Harvard University during our year together at the center in 2006. See, e.g., Gilbert Harman, "Moral Philosophy Meets Social Psychology: Virtue Ethics and the Fundamental Attribution Error," in *Explaining Value and Other Essays in Moral Philosophy* (Oxford: Oxford University Press, 2000), pp. 165–178.

47. *Ethics* 4.1124a15.

48. 4.1124a25.

6. ARISTOTLE'S *POLITICS*

1. *Politics* 4.1288b21.

2. Ibid.

3. 3.1274b38.

4. 1.1252a1.

5. 1.1252b2–1252b17.

6. 1.1252b27.

7. 1.1253a2.

8. 1.1252b27.

9. Ibid.

10. 1.1253a18.

11. Ibid.

12. 2.1261b32.

13. Ibid.

14. 2.1262a40.

15. 2.1263a40.

16. Ibid.

17. 2.1261a10.

18. 2.1264a1. Perhaps the best expression of such conservatism is Edmund Burke's *Reflections on the Revolution in France.* Burke argued that politics cannot

be fully rationalized without loss of the traditions and customs that tie persons to a particular place.

19. F. J. Ayala and T. Tobzharsky, *Studies in the Philosophy of Biology* (Berkeley: University of California Press, 1974), p. 225.

20. *Politics* 1.1252a24.

21. 7.1335a6–1335a28.

22. 7.1335b11.

23. Susan Moller Okin, *Women in Western Political Thought* (Princeton: Princeton University Press, 1979).

24. See Chapter 16 for an analysis of Okin's writings.

25. *Politics* 1.1253b14–1255b39.

26. 1.1253b14.

27. 1.1255a3.

28. 1.1253b23–1254a13.

29. 1.1254b27.

30. 1.1252b2.

31. 1.1255a3.

32. 1.1255a21.

33. 1.1255b4.

34. 1.1260a4.

35. 3.1280a7–1282b14.

36. See, for instance, Peter Singer, *One World* (New Haven: Yale University Press, 2002).

37. *Ethics* 5.1134b20.

38. 5.1131a10–1132b20.

39. 5.1131b25–1132a10.

40. 5.1131a10–1131b20.

41. *Politics* 3.1280a25.

42. 3.1280b6.

43. 3.1278b6–1288b2.

44. 3.1281b38.

45. 3.1281a39.

46. 3.1282a14.

47. Ibid.

48. 3.1282a41.

49. Ibid.

7. AUGUSTINE AND THE PROBLEM OF EVIL

1. Augustine, *Confessions,* trans. Henry Chadwick (Oxford: Oxford University Press, 1998), 4.7.12.

2. *Confessions* 8.7.17.

3. *The Political Writings of St. Augustine,* ed. Henry Paolucci (Chicago: Gateway, 1967), p. 147.

4. *Confessions* 3.1.1.

5. Ibid.

6. *Confessions* 2.1.1.

7. *Confessions* 2.4.9.

8. Ibid.

9. Ibid.

10. *Confessions* 2.8.16.

11. Gary Wills, *Augustine: A Penguin Life* (Harmondsworth: Penguin Books, 1999), pp. 11–13.

12. Wills, *Augustine,* pp. 14–15, quoting Augustine, *The Literal Meaning of Genesis.*

13. *Confessions* 2.5.10.

14. *Confessions* 2.9.17.

15. *Confessions* 2.3.7.

16. *Confessions* 4.4.7.

17. *Confessions* 4.6.9, 11.

18. *Confessions* 4.7.12.

19. *Confessions* 4.9.14.

20. *Confessions* 4.8.13.

21. *Confessions* 4.7.12, 14.

22. *Confessions* 4.8.13.

23. *Confessions* 2.3.5, 5.8.15.

24. *Confessions* 3.2.2.

25. *Confessions* 3.2.3.

26. Ibid.

27. Augustine, *City of God,* trans. Henry Bettenson (Harmondsworth: Penguin Books, 1972), 14.28.

28. *City of God* 1, preface.

29. *City of God* 15.1, 5.

30. *City of God* 15.5.

31. *City of God* 19.21–24, 2.21.

32. *City of God* 2.21; see also 19.21–24.

33. *City of God* 2.21.

34. Ibid.

35. *City of God* 2.19.

36. *City of God* 5.17.

37. Ibid.

38. *City of God* 4.4.

39. *City of God* 19.24.

40. *City of God* 5.12.

41. *City of God* 5.19.

42. *City of God* 18.22.

43. *City of God* 19.11.

44. *City of God* 19.12–17.

45. Paolucci, *Political Writings,* pp. 190–193, 219–220. For a general review of the shifts in Augustine's views on persecution of heretics, see Ronald Christenson, "The Political Theory of Persecution: Augustine and Hobbes," *Midwest Journal of Political Science* 12, no. 3 (1968): 419–438.

46. Paolucci, *Political Writings,* p. 224.

47. Paolucci, *Political Writings,* p. 215.

48. Paolucci, *Political Writings,* pp. 227–228.

49. Paolucci, *Political Writings,* p. 195.

50. Paolucci, *Political Writings,* pp. 242–243.

51. Paolucci, *Political Writings,* p. 228.

52. For an excellent collection of writings from medieval Islamic, Jewish, and Christian political philosophers, see Ralph Lerner and Muhsin Mahdi, eds., *Medieval Political Philosophy: A Sourcebook* (Ithaca: Cornell University Press, 1972). For work on Jewish political theory, see Michael Walzer et al., eds., *The Jewish Political Tradition,* vols. 1 and 2 (New Haven: Yale University Press, 2000–2003).

53. Lerner and Mahdi, *Medieval Political Philosophy,* p. 27.

54. Lerner and Mahdi, *Medieval Political Philosophy,* pp. 12–15.

55. One deliberately provocative statement of this thesis is offered by Samuel P. Huntington in *The Clash of Civilizations and the Remaking of World Order* (New York: Simon and Schuster, 1998), p. 70, where he argues that separation of church and state was the distinctive contribution of Christianity to Western civilization, in contrast to the state of affairs in Islamic civilizations (where "God is Caesar"), in Confucian societies ("Caesar is God"), and in Eastern Orthodoxy ("God is Caesar's junior partner").

56. Lerner and Mahdi, *Medieval Political Philosophy,* p. 165.

8. MACHIAVELLI'S DIRTY HANDS

1. *Oxford English Dictionary, s.v.* "Machiavellian."

2. *3 Henry VI,* 3.2.191–193.

3. Quoted in Max Lerner's introduction to Niccolò Machiavelli, *The Prince and the Discourses* (New York: Modern Library, 1950), p. xlii, where it is attributed to Hermann Rausching, *The Voice of Destruction: Conversations with Hitler, 1940* (New York: G. P. Putnam Son's, 1940).

4. Lerner, intro., p. xli.

5. *Prince* 15, p. 56, emphasis added. All citations are to the Modern Library edition.

6. Ibid., emphasis added.

7. Ibid., emphasis added.

8. Isaiah Berlin, "A Special Supplement: The Question of Machiavelli," *New York Review of Books* 17, no. 7 (November 4, 1971), www.nybooks.com/articles/10391 (accessed September 20, 2008).

9. *Prince* 6, p. 21.

10. *Prince* 26, p. 94.

11. *Prince* 14, p. 53.

12. *Prince* 6, p. 22.

13. Ibid.

14. *Discourses* 3.30, p. 498.

15. *Prince* 6, p. 21.

16. *Prince* 6, pp. 22–23.

17. *Prince* 13, p. 51.
18. *Prince* 7, p. 28.
19. *Discourses* 1.26, p. 184.
20. Ibid.
21. Ibid.
22. *Prince* 8, p. 34.
23. *Prince* 8, pp. 34–35.
24. *Prince* 8.
25. *Prince* 8, p. 31.
26. *Prince* 8, pp. 31–32.
27. *Prince* 8, p. 32.
28. Ibid.
29. Ibid.
30. *Prince* 8, p. 34.
31. *Prince* 18, p. 64.
32. *Prince* 18, p. 65.
33. Ibid.
34. *Prince* 18, p. 64.
35. *Prince* 7, p. 27.
36. *Prince* 18, p. 65.
37. *Prince* 18, p. 66.
38. *Discourses* 1.intro., p. 103.
39. *Discourses* 2.13, p. 319.
40. *Discourses* 1.intro., p. 103.
41. *Discourses* 1.intro., p. 104.
42. Ibid.
43. *Discourses* 1.16, p. 162.
44. *Discourses* 3.9, p. 442.
45. *Discourses* 1.16, p. 163.
46. *Discourses* 2.2, p. 287.
47. Ibid.
48. Ibid.
49. *Discourses* 1.55, p. 255.
50. *Discourses* 1.9, pp. 138–141.
51. *Discourses* 1.11, pp. 145–149.
52. *Discourses* 1.9, p. 138.
53. *Discourses* 1.9, p. 139.
54. Ibid.
55. *Discourses* 1.10, pp. 141–145.
56. *Discourses* 1.11, pp. 145–149, 3.13, pp. 318–319.
57. *Discourses* 2.2, pp. 284–285.
58. *Discourses* 2.2, p. 285.
59. Ibid.
60. Ibid.
61. *Discourses* 3.3, pp. 405–406.
62. *Discourses* 3.30, p. 498.

63. *Discourses* 3.9, p. 442.
64. *Discourses* 1.58, p. 263.
65. *Discourses* 1.58, p. 261.
66. *Discourses* 1.17, p. 166.
67. *Discourses* 1.18, pp. 170–171.

9. HOBBES AND THE KINGDOM OF MEANS

1. Thomas Hobbes, *Leviathan* (Harmondsworth: Penguin Books, 1985), author's introduction, p. 81.
2. Ibid.
3. Ibid.
4. Ibid.
5. *Leviathan* 1.5, p. 116.
6. *Leviathan* 1.6, p. 130.
7. *Leviathan*, author's introduction, p. 82.
8. *Leviathan*, author's introduction, p. 83.
9. *Leviathan* 1.6, p. 126.
10. *Leviathan* 1.6, p. 125.
11. See Elizabeth Telfer, "Hutcheson's *Reflections on Laughter*," *Journal of Aesthetics and Art Criticism* 53, no. 4 (Fall 1995): 359–369, for a review of an eighteenth-century refutation of Hobbes's views on laughter by Francis Hutcheson. Hutcheson thought that a sudden perception of one's superiority or another's inferiority was neither necessary nor sufficient to prompt laughter. As an example of humor that does not appeal to superiority feelings, Hutcheson offered burlesque or parody. As an example of feelings of superiority that do *not* elicit laughter in a person, Hutcheson offered the response of a healthy man on seeing a sick person, or a wealthy person confronting the poor (p. 359).
12. *Leviathan* 1.11, p. 160.
13. *Leviathan* 1.11, p. 161.
14. *Leviathan* 1.8, p. 139.
15. *Leviathan* 1.13, p. 183.
16. *Leviathan* 1.13, pp. 184–185.
17. *Leviathan* 1.13, pp. 185–186.
18. *Leviathan* 1.13, p. 187.
19. *Leviathan* 1.14, pp. 189–190.
20. *Leviathan* 1.14, pp. 190–192.
21. *Leviathan* 1.15, p. 201.
22. Ibid.
23. See, e.g., Howard Warrender, *The Political Philosophy of Hobbes* (Oxford: Oxford University Press, 1957); A. E. Taylor, "The Ethical Doctrine of Hobbes," in *Hobbes Studies,* ed. Keith Brown (Cambridge, Mass.: Harvard University Press, 1965), pp. 35–55.
24. Thomas Nagel, "Hobbes's Concept of Obligation," *Philosophical Review* 68, no. 1 (1959): 73–74.
25. *Leviathan* 2.21, pp. 269–270.

26. *Leviathan* 1.14, p. 199.
27. *Leviathan* 2.17, pp. 226–227.
28. *Leviathan* 2.20, p. 260.
29. Ibid.; see also *Leviathan* 2.17, p. 227.
30. *Leviathan* 2.20, p. 260.
31. *Leviathan* 1.14, p. 199.
32. *Leviathan* 2.21, pp. 268–269.
33. *Leviathan* 2.18, p. 233.
34. *Leviathan* 1.14, p. 198.
35. *Leviathan* 2.21, p. 262.
36. *Leviathan* 2.21, p. 261.
37. *Leviathan* 2.30, p. 376.
38. Ibid.
39. *Leviathan* 2.30, p. 388.
40. *Leviathan* 2.21, p. 264.

10. LOCKE, LIBERALISM, AND THE POSSESSIVE LIFE

1. For a review of these objections, see Marc Stears, "The Liberal Tradition and the Politics of Exclusion," *Annual Review of Political Science* 10 (June 2007): 85–101.

2. John Locke, *The Second Treatise of Government,* in *Two Treatises of Government,* ed. Peter Laslett (Cambridge: Cambridge University Press, 1988), sec. 222.

3. *Second Treatise* 228, 230.

4. John Locke, *A Letter Concerning Toleration,* ed. James H. Tully (Indianapolis: Hackett Publishing Company, 1983), p. 26.

5. *Second Treatise* 124.

6. *Second Treatise* 123.

7. *Second Treatise* 27.

8. *Second Treatise* 6.

9. *Letter Concerning Toleration,* pp. 26–28.

10. *Second Treatise* 7, 22.

11. *Second Treatise* 6.

12. Ibid.

13. Ibid.

14. *Second Treatise* 25.

15. *Second Treatise* 26.

16. *Second Treatise* 27.

17. Robert Nozick, *Anarchy, State, and Utopia* (New York: Basic Books, 1974), p. 175.

18. *Second Treatise* 28, 37, 40–43.

19. *Second Treatise* 33.

20. *Second Treatise* 31.

21. *Second Treatise* 34.

22. *Second Treatise* 26.

23. *Second Treatise* 27, 33.

24. For a contrary argument that Locke's natural persons are "infinitely desirous," see C. B. Macpherson, *The Political Theory of Possessive Individualism: Hobbes to Locke* (New York: Oxford University Press, 1962), pp. 263–264.

25. *Second Treatise* 37, 48.

26. *Second Treatise* 37.

27. *Second Treatise* 28.

28. *Second Treatise* 13.

29. *Second Treatise* 7–9.

30. *Second Treatise* 124–126.

31. *Second Treatise* 95.

32. Ibid.

33. Ibid.

34. *Second Treatise* 99.

35. For examples of disagreement on how to reconcile Locke on majority rule with Locke on individual rights, see Willmoore Kendall, *John Locke and the Doctrine of Majority-Rule* (Urbana: University of Illinois Press, 1959); Jacqueline Stevens, "The Reasonableness of John Locke's Majority: Property Rights, Consent, and Resistance in the *Second Treatise*," *Political Theory* 24, no. 3 (August 1996): 423–463; Jeremy Waldron, *The Right to Private Property* (Oxford: Oxford University Press, 1990), pp. 138–140; Macpherson, *The Political Theory of Possessive Individualism*, pp. 197ff.; John Dunn, *Locke* (Oxford: Oxford University Press, 1984), pp. 36–44; Nozick, *Anarchy, State, and Utopia*, pp. 174–182.

36. *Second Treatise* 97, 120, 129, 132, 140.

37. *Second Treatise* 131, 138.

38. *Second Treatise* 132.

39. *Second Treatise* 149, 221–222.

40. *Second Treatise* 90–91.

41. *Second Treatise* 136–137.

42. *Second Treatise* 221–222.

43. *Second Treatise* 211.

44. This holds true only for males; Locke does not include women directly in political life at all.

45. *Second Treatise* 95.

46. Ibid.

47. *Second Treatise* 121.

48. *Second Treatise* 116.

49. Ibid.

50. *Second Treatise* 117.

51. *Second Treatise* 116–117.

52. *Second Treatise* 116.

53. *Second Treatise* 117.

54. *Second Treatise* 122.

55. Ibid.

56. *Second Treatise* 119.

57. John Plamenatz, *Man and Society: A Critical Examination of Some Impor-

tant Social and Political Theories from Machiavelli to Marx, vol. 1 (New York: McGraw-Hill, 1963), p. 230.

58. *Second Treatise* 121.

59. *Second Treatise* 98.

60. *Second Treatise* 96.

61. *Second Treatise* 131, 138.

62. *Second Treatise* 136.

63. *Second Treatise* 137.

64. *Second Treatise* 139.

65. *Second Treatise* 131.

66. John Rawls, *A Theory of Justice* (Cambridge, Mass.: Harvard University Press, 1999), p. 29.

67. Ibid.

68. *Letter Concerning Toleration,* pp. 26–27.

69. Machiavelli, before Locke, and Rousseau after him, puts "Civil Religion" in this space Locke leaves blank, arguing that states best accomplish even civil ends by appealing to persons in religious terms.

70. Rawls, *A Theory of Justice,* pp. 189–190.

71. *Second Treatise* 135.

72. *Second Treatise* 138.

73. Ibid. See John Dunn, *The Political Thought of John Locke: An Historical Account of the "Two Treatises of Government"* (Cambridge: Cambridge University Press, 1982), pp. 53–57.

74. *Second Treatise* 138.

75. Stevens, "The Reasonableness of John Locke's Majority," pp. 423–463.

76. *Second Treatise* 243.

77. *Second Treatise* 140.

78. Nozick, *Anarchy, State, and Utopia,* pp. 169–172.

79. *Second Treatise* 223.

80. *Second Treatise* 225.

81. Ibid.

82. *Second Treatise* 208.

83. Ibid.

84. *Second Treatise* 209.

85. *Second Treatise* 211.

11. ROUSSEAU AND THE RUSTIC

1. Jean-Jacques Rousseau, *Discourse on the Origin of Inequality* (hereafter *Second Discourse*), in *"The Social Contract" and "Discourse on the Origin of Inequality,"* ed. Lester G. Crocker (New York: Simon and Schuster, 1967), pt. 2, p. 230. All citations refer to this edition.

2. *Second Discourse,* pt. 2, p. 248, note (i).

3. Jean-Jacques Rousseau, *Letter to M. D'Alembert on the Theatre,* published under the title *Politics and the Arts,* trans. Allan Bloom (Ithaca: Cornell University Press, 1977), p. 90. All citations refer to this edition.

4. *Letter to M. D'Alembert,* p. 48.

5. *Second Discourse,* pt. 1, p. 203.

6. Ibid.

7. Denis Diderot, "Supplement to Bougainville's Voyage," in *"Rameau's Nephew" and Other Writings,* trans. Jacques Barzun and Ralph H. Bowen (Indianapolis: Library of Liberal Arts, 1964), pp. 179–228.

8. *Confessions of Jean-Jacques Rousseau,* trans. J. M. Cohen (Harmondsworth: Penguin Books, 1971), bk. 2, pp. 86–89.

9. *Confessions,* bk. 2, p. 89.

10. *Confessions,* bk. 7, p. 300.

11. *Confessions,* bk. 7, p. 301.

12. *Confessions,* bk. 7, p. 311.

13. *Confessions,* bk. 7, p. 322.

14. *Second Discourse,* pt. 1, pp. 176, 200–201.

15. *Second Discourse,* pt. 1, p. 177.

16. *Second Discourse,* pt. 1, p. 179.

17. *Second Discourse,* pt. 1, p. 192.

18. *Second Discourse,* pt. 1, p. 198.

19. *Second Discourse,* pt. 1, p. 200.

20. *Second Discourse,* pt. 1, p. 185.

21. Ibid.

22. Ibid.

23. *Second Discourse,* pt. 1, p. 190.

24. *Second Discourse,* pt. 1, p. 192.

25. *Second Discourse,* pt. 1, p. 189.

26. *Second Discourse,* pt. 1, p. 200.

27. *Second Discourse,* pt. 1, p. 205.

28. *Second Discourse,* pt. 2, p. 212.

29. *Second Discourse,* pt. 1, p. 249, note (i).

30. *Second Discourse,* pt. 1, p. 256, note (o).

31. *Second Discourse,* pt. 1, p. 201.

32. Ibid.

33. *Second Discourse,* pt. 1, pp. 201–202.

34. See Benedict Carey, "Message from Mouse to Mouse: I Feel Your Pain," *New York Times,* July 4, 2006, www.nytimes.com/2006/07/04/health/04empa.html/ (accessed September 21, 2008).

35. *Second Discourse,* pt. 1, p. 203.

36. Jean Starobinski, *Jean-Jacques Rousseau: Transparency and Obstruction,* trans. Arthur Goldhammer (Chicago: University of Chicago Press, 1988).

37. *Second Discourse,* pt. 1, p. 190.

38. *Second Discourse,* pt. 1, p. 188.

39. *Second Discourse,* pt. 2, p. 216.

40. *Second Discourse,* pt. 2, p. 220.

41. *Second Discourse,* pt. 2, p. 218.

42. *Second Discourse,* pt. 2, p. 245.

43. *Second Discourse,* pt. 2, p. 224.

44. *Second Discourse,* pt. 2, p. 240–241.

45. *Second Discourse,* pt. 2, p. 241.

46. *Second Discourse,* pt. 2, p. 212.

47. *Second Discourse,* pt. 2, p. 220.

48. *Second Discourse,* pt. 2, p. 223.

49. *Second Discourse,* pt. 2, p. 221.

50. *Second Discourse,* pt. 2, p. 220.

51. *Second Discourse,* pt. 2, p. 225.

52. *Second Discourse,* pt. 2, p. 227.

53. Jean-Jacques Rousseau, *The Social Contract,* in Crocker, *"The Social Contract" and "Discourse on the Origin of Inequality,"* bk. 1, p. 7.

54. Marx is no crude materialist, however, and I will argue in Chapter 15 that he placed great emphasis on human consciousness as working to transform the environment.

12. ROUSSEAU AND THE POLITICAL

1. *Second Discourse,* pt. 2, pp. 253–254, note (i).

2. Jean-Jacques Rousseau, *Émile, or On Education,* trans. Barbara Foxley (London: Everyman's Library, 1961), bk. 1, p. 3.

3. *Social Contract,* 1.10, p. 26.

4. For an account of Rousseau's views on liberating authority, see Claudia Schaler, "Liberating Authority and Rousseau's Politics," unpublished manuscript on file with author.

5. *Social Contract* 1.6, p. 18.

6. Ibid.

7. *Social Contract* 2.3, pp. 30–32.

8. *Social Contract* 2.3, p. 31.

9. *Social Contract* 1.8, p. 22.

10. *Social Contract* 4.2, p. 111.

11. *Social Contract* 4.2, p. 113.

12. *Émile,* bk. 1, p. 5.

13. *Social Contract* 3.16, pp. 98–99.

14. Jean-Jacques Rousseau, *The Government of Poland,* trans. Willmoore Kendall (Indianapolis: Library of Liberal Arts, 1972), p. 12.

15. *Government of Poland,* p. 7.

16. *Government of Poland,* pp. 6–7.

17. *Letter to M. D'Alembert,* pp. 16–17.

18. "You should prohibit . . . gambling, the theater, comedies, operas—everything that makes men unmanly, or distracts them, or isolates them, or causes them to forget their fatherland and their duties, or disposes them to feel content anywhere so long as they are being amused." *Government of Poland,* p. 14.

19. *Letter to M. D'Alembert,* p. 125.

20. *Letter to M. D'Alembert,* p. 135.

21. *Letter to M. D'Alembert,* p. 127.

22. *Government of Poland,* p. 87.

23. Ibid.

24. *Social Contract* 2.7, p. 43.

13. KANT'S CROOKED TIMBER

1. Immanuel Kant, *Groundwork of the Metaphysic of Morals,* trans. H. J. Patton (New York: Harper and Row, 1969), preface, 390.ix.

2. *Groundwork* 1.397.9.

3. *Groundwork,* preface, 389.vii.

4. *Groundwork* 2.426.61.

5. *Groundwork* 2.441.89–95.

6. *Groundwork* 1.395.6.

7. *Groundwork* 1.402.17–403.20.

8. *Groundwork* 1.421.52.

9. *Groundwork* 2.422.54–55.

10. *Groundwork* 2.427.64–430.69.

11. *Groundwork* 2.429.67, emphasis omitted.

12. *Groundwork* 2.431.70–433.74.

13. *Groundwork* 2.419.49.

14. *Groundwork* 2.432.73.

15. *Groundwork* 2.433.75.

16. *Groundwork* 2.438.84.

17. Immanuel Kant, *Metaphysical Elements of Justice,* trans. John Ladd (New York: Macmillan, 1985), intro., sec. C.231. This translation is of the first part of Kant's *Metaphysics of Morals.*

18. Immanuel Kant, *Perpetual Peace,* trans. Lewis White Beck (New York: Library of Liberal Arts, 1957), app. 1, p. 46.

19. *Perpetual Peace,* app. 1, p. 37.

20. Ibid.

21. *Perpetual Peace,* app. 1, p. 39.

22. *Perpetual Peace* 1.6, p. 8. Here Kant gives the example of each state's duty to restore freedom to other states but notes that duty "allows a delay to prevent precipitation which might injure the goal striven for."

23. Immanuel Kant, "On the Common Saying: 'This May Be True in Theory, but It Does Not Apply in Practice,'" (hereafter "Theory and Practice"), in *Kant: Political Writings,* ed. Hans Reiss, 2d ed. (Cambridge: Cambridge University Press, 1991), p. 61.

24. *Perpetual Peace,* app. 1, p. 37.

25. *Metaphysical Elements of Justice,* intro., sec. E.232.

26. *Metaphysical Elements of Justice,* pt. 2, sec. 43.311.

27. *Metaphysical Elements of Justice,* pt. 2, sec. 45.313.

28. "Theory and Practice," p. 79; *Metaphysical Elements of Justice,* pt. 2, sec. 45.313.

29. "Theory and Practice," p. 79.

30. Ibid.

31. "Theory and Practice," p. 85.

32. The distinction between decent societies and ideally just societies is one John Rawls makes in *The Law of Peoples* (Cambridge, Mass.: Harvard University Press, 1999). I take up this issue in Chapter 16.

33. *Metaphysical Elements of Justice,* pt. 2, sec. 49.

34. *Metaphysical Elements of Justice,* pt. 2, sec. 49.320.

35. "Theory and Practice," p. 81. See also *Metaphysical Elements of Justice,* pt. 2, sec. 49.

36. Immanuel Kant, "A Renewed Attempt to Answer the Question: Is the Human Race Continually Improving," in *Political Writings,* p. 182.

37. "Theory and Practice," p. 79n.

38. *Groundwork* 2.433.75–434.76.

39. *Metaphysical Elements of Justice,* pt. 2, sec. 47.316.

40. "Theory and Practice," p. 74.

41. "Theory and Practice," p. 80.

42. "Theory and Practice," pp. 74–77.

43. "Theory and Practice," p. 76.

44. Ibid.; *Metaphysical Elements of Justice,* pt. 2, sec. 46.314.

45. "Theory and Practice," p. 75.

46. "Theory and Practice," pp. 77–79.

47. "Theory and Practice," p. 78.

48. "Theory and Practice," p. 78n.

49. *Perpetual Peace,* sec. 2, First Definitive Article, p. 11.

50. *Perpetual Peace,* sec. 2, First Definitive Article, p. 14.

51. Ibid.

52. *Metaphysical Elements of Justice,* pt. 2, sec. 52.

53. *Perpetual Peace,* sec. 2, First Definitive Article, pp. 14–15.

54. Immanuel Kant, "Idea for a Universal History with a Cosmopolitan Purpose," in *Political Writings,* p. 51 (8th proposition).

55. *Perpetual Peace,* sec. 2, Second Definitive Article, p. 19.

56. *Perpetual Peace,* First Supplement, p. 31.

57. *Perpetual Peace,* sec. 2, First Definitive Article, pp. 12–13.

58. *Perpetual Peace,* sec. 2, Second Definitive Article, p. 16.

59. *Perpetual Peace,* First Supplement, p. 32.

60. *Perpetual Peace,* sec. 2, Second Definitive Article, p. 16.

61. *Perpetual Peace,* sec. 2, Third Definitive Article, p. 20.

62. *Perpetual Peace,* sec. 2, Third Definitive Article, pp. 21–22.

63. *Perpetual Peace,* sec. 2, Third Definitive Article, p. 21.

64. *Perpetual Peace,* app. 1, p. 44.

65. G. W. F. Hegel, *The Philosophy of Right,* trans. T. M. Knox (Oxford: Oxford University Press, 1967), sec. 130.

66. Immanuel Kant, "On a Supposed Right to Tell Lies from Benevolent Motives," in *The Critique of Practical Reason,* ed. Mary J. Gregor (Cambridge: Cambridge University Press, 1997), appendix.

67. *Metaphysical Elements of Justice,* pt. 2, sec. 49.E.1.

68. Hegel, *Philosophy of Right,* secs. 135, 138.

14. JOHN STUART MILL AND THE DEMANDS OF INDIVIDUALITY

1. *Autobiography of John Stuart Mill* (New York: Signet Classics, 1964), chap. 5, pp. 107–108.

2. John Stuart Mill, "Bentham," in *Utilitarianism, On Liberty, and Essay on Bentham,* ed. Mary Warnock (New York: New American Library, 1974), p. 123, referring to Jeremy Bentham, *The Rationale of Reward,* bk. 3, chap. 1.

3. John Stuart Mill, *On Liberty* (Indianapolis: Hackett Publishing Co., 1978), chap. 3, pp. 55–56.

4. John Stuart Mill, *On Utilitarianism* (Indianapolis: Library of Liberal Arts, 1957), chap. 2, p. 14.

5. Mill is a self-described utilitarian, since he continues to rely on the *consequences* for their happiness of leaving persons free. But Mill's self-understanding does not wholly capture those arguments in *On Liberty* already foreshadowed in a remark such as "It is better to be Socrates dissatisfied than a fool satisfied." Here freedom emerges as having ethical value independent of its utility to what satisfies a person in the usual utilitarian calculations.

6. *On Liberty,* chap. 1, p. 9.

7. Ibid.

8. *On Liberty,* chap. 1, p. 12.

9. See "Limiting the State's Police Power: Judicial Reaction to John Stuart Mill," *University of Chicago Law Review* 37 (1970): 605–627, for one older review of court decisions citing *On Liberty.*

10. *On Liberty,* chap. 4, p. 83.

11. The number of states requiring motorcyclists and their passengers to wear helmets appears to be declining. A recent review found only twenty states with laws requiring helmets. Marian Moser Jones and Ronald Bayer, "Paternalism and Its Discontents: Motorcycle Helmet Cases, Libertarian Values, and Public Health," *American Journal of Public Health* 97, no. 2 (February 2007): 208–217.

12. *On Liberty,* chap. 1, p. 12.

13. *On Liberty,* chap. 4, p. 78.

14. *On Liberty,* chap. 1, p. 11.

15. *On Liberty,* chap. 3 generally.

16. *On Liberty,* chap. 5, p. 95.

17. *On Liberty,* chap. 5, p. 101.

18. In fact, to deal with obvious problems in singling out the *hijab,* the French legislation as finally passed extends the ban to prohibit any large or obtrusive religious clothing or symbols in classrooms, such as presumably a Jewish skullcap or Roman Catholic cross. But the debate remained centrally about proper ways to integrate Muslims into French society.

19. *On Liberty,* chap. 1, p. 9.

20. *On Liberty,* chap. 5, pp. 103–106.

21. *On Liberty,* chap. 5, p. 104.

22. *On Liberty,* chap. 5, p. 95.

23. Ibid.

24. The Nozick example is referred to by Gerald Dworkin in his "Paternalism," *The Monist* 56 (1972): 64, 83–84.

25. *On Liberty,* chap. 4, p. 95.

26. *On Liberty,* chap. 4, p. 89.

27. Ibid.

15. HEGEL, MARX, AND THE OWL OF MINERVA

1. G. W. F. Hegel, *Philosophy of Right* (hereafter *PR*), trans. T. M. Knox (Oxford: Oxford University Press, 1967), preface, p. 11.

2. Ibid.

3. *PR,* preface, p. 10.

4. *PR,* preface, p. 12.

5. *PR,* preface, p. 13.

6. Karl Marx, *Theses on Feuerbach,* no. 11, in *The Marx-Engels Reader,* ed. Robert C. Tucker (New York: Norton, 1978), p. 145.

7. *PR,* preface, p. 10.

8. *PR,* preface, p. 11.

9. *PR,* translator's note 33, p. 303.

10. *Macbeth* 5.5.31–33.

11. *PR* 199.

12. *PR* 258, addition.

13. *PR* 258.

14. Karl Marx, *Contribution to the Critique of Hegel's Philosophy of Right,* in Tucker, *Marx-Engels Reader,* p. 18.

15. Karl Marx, *On the Jewish Question,* in Tucker, *Marx-Engels Reader,* p. 34.

16. Karl Marx, "Afterword to the Second German Edition" of *Capital* (1873), in Tucker, *Marx-Engels Reader,* p. 302.

17. *Contribution to the Critique of Hegel's Philosophy of Right,* p. 18.

18. The phrase is from *On the Jewish Question,* p. 33.

19. Marx, "Afterword to the Second German Edition," p. 302.

20. *PR* 279.

21. Quoted in Shlomo Avineri, *The Social and Political Thought of Karl Marx* (Cambridge: Cambridge University Press, 1972), p. 15.

22. *PR* 313.

23. Barrington Moore Jr., *Social Origins of Dictatorship and Democracy: Lord and Peasant in the Making of the Modern World* (Boston: Beacon Press, 1993), pp. 34–38.

24. Avineri, *Social and Political Thought of Karl Marx,* p. 31.

25. *On the Jewish Question,* p. 35.

26. *On the Jewish Question,* p. 31.

27. *On the Jewish Question,* p. 34.

28. *On the Jewish Question,* p. 49.

29. *On the Jewish Question,* pp. 49, 50, 52.

30. Karl Marx, *The German Ideology,* in Tucker, *Marx-Engels Reader,* p. 170.

31. *German Ideology,* pp. 170–171.

32. *German Ideology,* p. 156.

33. *German Ideology,* p. 149.

34. Avineri, *Social and Political Thought of Karl Marx,* p. 76.

35. Karl Marx, *Theses on Feuerbach,* no. 3, p. 144.

36. *German Ideology,* p. 155.

37. *German Ideology,* p. 154.

38. Ibid.

39. Karl Marx, *For a Ruthless Criticism of Everything Existing,* in Tucker, *Marx-Engels Reader,* p. 14.

40. Karl Marx, *The Poverty of Philosophy,* in Tucker, *Marx-Engels Reader,* p. 219.

41. Karl Marx, *The Communist Manifesto,* in Tucker, *Marx-Engels Reader,* p. 490.

42. *Communist Manifesto,* p. 475.

43. Karl Marx, *Critique of the Gotha Program,* in Tucker, *Marx-Engels Reader,* p. 537.

44. Richard Adamiak, "The 'Withering Away' of the State: A Reconsideration," *Journal of Politics* 32, no. 1 (February 1978): 7–8.

45. Friedrich Engels, *Anti-Dühring,* quoted in Adamiak, "The 'Withering Away' of the State," p. 15.

46. Karl Marx, *Economic and Philosophic Manuscripts of 1844,* in Tucker, *Marx-Engels Reader,* p. 83.

47. *Critique of the Gotha Program,* p. 538.

48. *Communist Manifesto,* p. 490.

49. Karl Marx, "After the Revolution: Marx Debates Bakunin," in Tucker, *Marx-Engels Reader,* p. 543.

50. *Communist Manifesto,* p. 482.

51. Karl Marx, *The Grundrisse,* in Tucker, *Marx-Engels Reader,* p. 291; Marx, *The Holy Family,* in Tucker, *Marx-Engels Reader,* p. 134.

52. *Poverty of Philosophy,* p. 218. See also *Contribution to the Critique of Hegel's Philosophy of Right,* p. 64: "A class must be formed which has *radical chains,* a class in civil society which is not a class of civil society, a class which is the dissolution of all classes, a sphere of society which has a universal character because its sufferings are universal, and which does not claim a *particular redress* because the wrong which is done to it is not a *particular wrong* but *wrong in general.* There must be formed a sphere of society which claims no *traditional* status but only a human status. . . . This . . . is the *proletariat.*"

53. *The Holy Family,* p. 134.

54. *Poverty of Philosophy,* pp. 218–219.

55. *Critique of the Gotha Program,* p. 531.

56. *Economic and Philosophic Manuscripts,* p. 84.

57. *Economic and Philosophic Manuscripts,* pp. 70–75.

58. *Critique of the Gotha Program,* p. 531.

59. *German Ideology,* p. 160.

60. *For a Ruthless Criticism of Everything Existing,* p. 15.

61. Ibid.

62. *Communist Manifesto,* p. 481.

63. Karl Marx, "Notebooks on Epicurean Philosophy," quoted in Tucker, *Marx-Engels Reader,* p. 10.

64. "We have to register a definite protest against this endless, nebulous and unclear ratiocination of those German liberals who think they honor liberty by relegating it to the starry heaven of imagination instead of basing it on the firm foundation of reality. It is to these masters of imaginary ratiocination, to these masters of sentimental enthusiasm, who are afraid lest their ideal be desecrated by its coming in touch with profane reality—it is to them, then, that we Germans owe our situation in which liberty is still a matter of imagination and sentimentality. Out of too much reverence for the ideas they are not being realised." Quoted in Avineri, *Social and Political Thought of Karl Marx,* p. 137.

65. The *Holy Family,* quoted in Avineri, *Social and Political Thought of Karl Marx,* p. 142.

16. THE REVIVAL OF POLITICAL THEORY

1. *German Ideology,* p. 165.

2. John Rawls, *A Theory of Justice,* rev. ed (Cambridge, Mass.: Harvard University Press, 1999), sec. 14, p. 75.

3. *Theory of Justice,* sec. 3, pp. 10–11; sec. 4, pp. 15–19; sec. 11, p. 56.

4. *Theory of Justice,* sec. 12, pp. 63–64; sec. 17, p. 89.

5. *Theory of Justice,* sec. 11, p. 56; sec. 22, p. 111.

6. *Theory of Justice,* sec. 11, p. 53; sec. 39, p. 220; sec. 46, p. 266.

7. *Theory of Justice,* sec. 11, p. 53.

8. John Rawls, *Political Liberalism* (New York: Columbia University Press, 1993).

9. *Theory of Justice,* sec. 46, p. 266.

10. *Theory of Justice,* sec. 11, p. 53; sec. 46, p. 266.

11. *Theory of Justice,* sec. 11, p. 56.

12. Ibid.

13. *Theory of Justice,* sec. 12, p. 63.

14. *Theory of Justice,* sec. 42, p. 242; sec. 43, p. 248.

15. *Theory of Justice,* sec. 12, pp. 62–64.

16. *Theory of Justice,* sec. 13, p. 65. Rawls should not, however, be interpreted as requiring a just society to correct for every way in which a person's talents are affected by luck. He acknowledges that a child's motivations to learn, to make the effort required to develop natural talents, are influenced by what family the child happens to be born into; in this sense, fair equality of opportunity is never perfect. But in general Rawls's theory of justice "only requires equal life prospects in all sectors of society for those similarly endowed and motivated." *Theory of Justice,* sec. 46, p. 265.

17. See, e.g., Frank I. Michelman, "In Pursuit of Constitutional Welfare Rights: One View of Rawls' *Theory of Justice," University of Pennsylvania Law Review* 121 (1973): 962.

18. *Theory of Justice,* pp. xiv–xv. On this point, see William E. Forbath, "Not So Simple Justice: Frank Michelman on Social Rights, 1969–Present," *Tulsa Law Review* 39 (2004): 597.

19. Robert Nozick, *Anarchy, State, and Utopia* (New York: Basic Books, 1974), p. 161.

20. It should be noted that Rawls rejected the notion that his theory rested on any particular conception of the self, Kantian or otherwise. He described his theory of justice as resting on political rather than philosophical considerations—specifically the practical interest citizens in modern constitutional democracies have in dealing with the fact that they disagree on their ultimate moral values. See John Rawls, "Justice as Fairness: Political Not Metaphysical," *Philosophy and Public Affairs* 14 (1985): 223–252. For Sandel's defense of his views, see Michael J. Sandel, *Democracy's Discontent: America in Search of a Public Philosophy* (Cambridge, Mass.: Harvard University Press, 1996), pp. 17–20.

21. *Theory of Justice,* sec. 84, p. 491; Sandel, *Democracy's Discontent,* p. 12.

22. Sandel, *Democracy's Discontent,* pp. 14–15; see also Michael J. Sandel, *Liberalism and the Limits of Justice* (Cambridge: Cambridge University Press, 1982), pp. 179–183.

23. Sandel, *Democracy's Discontent,* pp. 20–21.

24. Michael Walzer, *Spheres of Justice: A Defense of Pluralism and Equality* (New York: Basic Books, 1983), p. xiv.

25. Ibid.

26. Walzer, *Spheres of Justice,* pp. 313–314.

27. Allan Bloom, *Giants and Dwarfs: Essays, 1960–1990* (New York: Simon and Schuster, 1990), p. 316.

28. John Rawls, *The Law of Peoples* (Cambridge, Mass.: Harvard University Press, 1999); see also Rawls, "The Law of Peoples," in *Collected Papers,* ed. Samuel Freeman (Cambridge, Mass.: Harvard University Press, 1999), p. 558.

29. "Law of Peoples," p. 530.

30. Leo Strauss, *Natural Right and History* (Chicago: University of Chicago Press, 1970), pp. 5, 9.

31. Strauss, *Natural Right,* p. 4.

32. Walzer, *Spheres of Justice,* p. xiv.

33. Strauss, *Natural Right,* pp. 12, 15.

34. *Theory of Justice,* sec. 69, p. 398; sec. 70, p. 405.

35. *Theory of Justice,* sec. 43, p. 243; sec. 67, p. 386; Susan Moller Okin, *Justice, Gender, and the Family* (New York: Basic Books, 1989), pp. 101–109.

36. John Rawls, "The Idea of Public Reason Revisited," in *Collected Papers,* p. 595, n. 58.

37. "Idea of Public Reason," pp. 597–598.

38. "Idea of Public Reason," p. 598.

39. "Idea of Public Reason," p. 596, n. 60.

ACKNOWLEDGMENTS
_____

I owe an archaeology of acknowledgments, in layers dating back to my first teachers. Sadly, some are no longer here to read my thanks. These include William Kennick, my first—and first pipe-smoking—philosophy professor; Dita Shklar, my Ph.D. adviser and most intimate critic; and Susan Moller Okin, my colleague and loyal friend. Happily, I can hope that George Kateb and Michael Walzer will recognize in these pages tidbits from their great lectures on political theory that have stayed with me over the years. Thanks as always to Michael Sandel and Nancy Rosenblum, this time for encouraging me to publish my lectures on political theory in book form.

Dennis Aftergut, Kiku Adatto, Russell Muirhead, Tamara Metz, and Maria Merritt read all or parts of this book, giving me valuable suggestions about how persons interested in politics, but not necessarily academic philosophy, might be wooed into reading the classics of political theory. Thanks also to my graduate students Carly Baruh, Rebekka Friedman, Tzvetomira Kaltcheva, Anja Karnein, Jinmin Lee, Timothy McCarty, and Claudia Schaler for reading earlier drafts, checking citations, and permitting me to try out ideas in class. Peggy Brundage, Rosanne Colocouris, and Claire Cincotta provided much-needed administrative support.

My two favorite students, who happen to be my daughters Anna and Sarah, encouraged me to think that young persons especially might be interested in a fresh approach to the teaching of political theory. This book would not exist but for their faith and frankness. My parents remain my most loyal readers, and the memory of their poring over this manuscript and so continuing their education will always be with me. Special thanks to my editor at Harvard University Press, Michael Aronson, for believing in this project from the beginning, and for encouraging me to write the book I wanted to write. My copyeditor, Amanda Heller, saved me from many an error.

Much of the actual writing of this book took place over consecutive summers on the Outer Cape (Cod), seated next to my wife, the historian Jacqueline Jones, writing away on her own book on Savannah during the Civil War. She would stop and read me a particularly eloquent passage she had just written about Savannah at a crossroads, how the city and the country faced a moment of choice when justice was stake. I would then go back to work on ancient Athens, or Renaissance

Florence, but convinced more than ever that some political arguments are eternal and that studying political theory is at its best when the *political* stakes are acknowledged.

For many years I have had the privilege of teaching the history of political thought to college undergraduates. Perhaps as many as 1,500 students have sat through the lectures from which this book has grown. It is entirely their fault that it has taken me so long to finish; there was always a new question, a fresh observation, a quizzical look that made me see something new in old texts. I hope that this book will find its way into the hands of some of those students and that they will smile in recognition at an example they gave me, a question unanswered still.